The Trouble with Men

Masculinities in European and Hollywood Cinema

The Trouble with Men

Masculinities in European and Hollywood Cinema

Edited by Phil Powrie, Ann Davies and Bruce Babington

WALLFLOWER PRESS LONDON & NEW YORK

First published in Great Britain in 2004 by
Wallflower Press
4th Floor, 26 Shacklewell Lane, London E8 2EZ
www.wallflowerpress.co.uk

A catalogue for this book is available from the British Library

ISBN 1-904764-08-8 pbk
ISBN 1-904764-09-6 hbk

Book design by Elsa Mathern

Printed by Antony Rowe Ltd., Chippenham, Wiltshire

CONTENTS

SECTION 4: BODIES

ACKNOWLEDGEMENTS

A version of chapter 7 was published as 'The Queer Jew: From Yidl to Yentl and Back Again', *Jewish History and Culture*, 3/1 (Summer 2000), 23–44.

Sections from chapter 13 were published in 'New Jersey Childhood: *Happiness*', in Emma Wilson (2003) *Cinema's Missing Children*. London: Wallflower Press, 41–53.

A short version of chapter 17 was published as 'The W/hole and the abject', *Paragraph*, 26/1&2 (March/July 2003), 232–44.

A longer version of chapter 18 was published as 'Last Laughs: *Batman*, Masculinity and the Technology of Abjection', *Men and Masculinities*, 2/1 (July 1999), 26–48.

We are grateful to the publishers concerned for their permission to use material previously published.

Our thanks also go to the delegates of the 'Exploring Masculinities and Film' conference organised by the Centre for Research into Film and Media at the University of Newcastle upon Tyne in July 2001 for the stimulating debates which have informed many of the pieces in this volume; and to our colleague Chris Perriam for his constant support and valuable advice. And finally to Yoram Allon of Wallflower Press for his enthusiasm and commitment to cinema studies.

Michele Aaron lectures on Film at Brunel University. She is editor of *The Body's Perilous Pleasures: Dangerous Desires and Contemporary Culture* (Edinburgh University Press, 1999) and *New Queer Cinema: A Critical Reader* (Edinburgh University Press, 2004), and author of *Spectatorship: The Power of Looking On*, forthcoming from Wallflower Press.

Bruce Babington is Professor of Film in the School of English Literature, Language and Linguistics at the University of Newcastle upon Tyne, where he teaches Hollywood, British and New Zealand cinema. With Peter William Evans he wrote three studies of Hollywood genres; *Blue Skies and Silver Linings: Aspects of the Hollywood Musical* (Manchester University Press, 1985), *Affairs to Remember: The Hollywood Comedy of the Sexes* (Manchester University Press, 1989) and *Biblical Epics* (Manchester University Press, 1993). He has more recently edited *British Stars and Stardom* (Manchester University Press, 2001) and written *Launder and Gilliat* (Manchester University Press, 2002). He is currently co-authoring a volume on film adaptations of *Carmen* and writing a book on New Zealand cinema.

Pamela Church Gibson is Senior Lecturer in Media and Cultural Studies at the London College of Fashion. She has published work on film, fashion, fandom, heritage and history; she is the co-editor of three collections of essays: *Dirty Looks: Women, Pornography, Power* (British Film Institute, 1993), *The Oxford Guide to Film Studies* (Oxford University Press, 1998) and *Fashion Cultures: Theories, Explorations, Analysis* (Routledge, 2000). She is currently working on a monograph which examines the relationship between cinema and consumption in the post-war era.

Steven Cohan is Professor of English at Syracuse University, where he teaches courses in film, gender and cultural studies. His books include *Telling Stories: A Theoretical Analysis of Narrative Fiction* (with Linda M. Shires, Routledge, 1988), *Screening the Male: Exploring Masculinities in Hollywood Cinema* (co-edited with Ina Rae Hark, Routledge, 1992), *The Road Movie Book* (co-edited with Ina Rae Hark, Routledge, 1997), *Masked Men: Masculinity and the Movies in the Fifties* (Indiana University Press, 1997) and *Hollywood Musicals: The Film Reader* (Routledge, 2002). The essay in this volume is drawn from his forthcoming book, *Incongruous Entertainment: Camp, Cultural Value, and the MGM Musical*.

Timothy Connelly is a doctoral student in the English department at Syracuse University. His dissertation uses female stardom as a site for investigating the cultural significance of working women in the US during the Great Depression.

Ann Davies is Lecturer in Spanish at the University of Newcastle upon Tyne. She formerly worked as Research Associate for the Carmen Project at the Centre for Research into Film and Media, University of Newcastle, and is co-authoring a volume on film adaptations of the Carmen story and co-editing, with Chris Perriam, an anthology of essays on the same subject. She has also written various articles on Spanish film, and a book on gender relations in don Juan plays (forthcoming, Edwin Mellen Press).

Graeme Hayes is Principal Lecturer in French and European Studies at Nottingham Trent University. He has written several articles on masculinity and French film, and is developing a long-term project on the French crime genre. He also researches public policy and social protest, and is the author of *Environmental Protest and the State in France* (Palgrave, 2002).

John Hill is Professor of Media Studies at the University of Ulster. He is the author of *Sex, Class and Realism: British Cinema 1956–63* (British Film Institute, 1986) and *British Cinema in the 1980s* (Oxford University Press, 1999), and co-editor of *The Oxford Guide to Film Studies* (Oxford University Press, 1998).

James Leggott has recently completed a PhD thesis at the University of Newcastle upon Tyne on the handling of space in the British social realist film from the New Wave to the present.

Peter Lehman is Director of the Interdisciplinary Humanities Program at Arizona State University. He is author of *Running Scared: Masculinity and the Representation of the Male Body* (Temple University Press, 1993), *Roy Orbison: The Invention of an Alternative Rock Masculinity* (Temple University Press, 2003) and editor of *Masculinity: Bodies, Movies, Culture* (Routledge, 2000).

Rikki Morgan-Tamosunas is Professor of Hispanic Studies and Head of the School of Social Sciences, Humanities and Languages at the University of Westminster. She has published widely on Spanish cinema and culture, particularly in relation to historical representation and gender and sexuality. She is the co-author of *Spanish Contemporary Cinema* (Manchester University Press, 1998) and co-editor of *Contemporary Spanish Cultural Studies* (with Barry Jordan, Arnold, 2000) and *Inside Out: Images of Self and Other in Postcolonial European Cinema* (with Guido Rings, Winter, 2003).

Phil Powrie is Professor of French Cultural Studies and Director of the Centre for Research into Film and Media at the University of Newcastle upon Tyne. He has published widely on French cinema, notably *French Cinema in the 1980s: Nostalgia and the Crisis of Masculinity* (Clarendon Press, 1997), *Jean-Jacques Beineix* (Manchester University Press, 2001) and, with Keith Reader, *French Cinema: A Student's Guide* (Arnold, 2002), also, as editor, *Contemporary French Cinema: Continuity and Difference* (Oxford University Press, 1999). He is the general co-editor of the journal *Studies in French Cinema*. He is co-authoring a volume, with Ann Davies, on film adaptations of the Carmen story, preparing an edited volume, *The Cinema of France* (Wallflower Press), and a co-edited volume on the films of Luc Besson (with Susan Hayward, Manchester University Press).

Robert Shail is a lecturer in film studies at the University of Wales, Lampeter. He has published work on both British and American stars and on masculinity in film. He is currently working on a study of Tony Richardson for Manchester University Press.

Andrew Spicer is Reader in Visual Culture at the Faculty of Art, Media and Design, University of the West of England and Programme Leader of the MA Film Studies and

European Cinema. He has published widely on British cinema, including *Typical Men: The Representation of Masculinity in Popular British Cinema* (I. B. Tauris, 2001) and is the author of *Film Noir* (Longman, 2002). He is currently editing a collection of essays on European Film Noir and completing a study of Sydney Box, both to be published by Manchester University Press.

Paul Sutton lectures in Film and Television Studies at the University of Surrey, Roehampton. He has published articles on cinematic spectatorship and deferred action, as well as articles on French cinema. He is currently working on a project entitled *Afterwardness and Film*.

Carrie Tarr is a Research Fellow in the European Studies Research Centre, Kingston University, and Visiting Research Fellow at the University of Leeds. She has published widely on gender and ethnicity in French cinema. Recent publications include *Diane Kurys* (Manchester University Press, 1999), *Women, Immigration and Identities in France* (co-edited with Jane Freedman, Berg, 2000) and *Cinema and the Second Sex: Women's Filmmaking in France in the 1980s and 1990s* (with Brigitte Rollet, Continuum, 2001). She is currently preparing a book on Beur and *banlieue* cinema in France.

Calvin Thomas is Associate Professor of English at Georgia State University in Atlanta. He is the author of *Male Matters: Masculinity, Anxiety and the Male Body on the Line* (University of Illinois Press, 1996) and the editor of *Straight with a Twist: Queer Theory and the Subject of Heterosexuality* (University of Illinois Press, 2000).

Emma Wilson is a Reader in French at Cambridge University and Fellow of Corpus Christi College. She is author of *Sexuality and the Reading Encounter* (Clarendon Press, 1996), *French Cinema since 1950* (Duckworth, 1999), *Memory and Survival: The French Cinema of Krzysztof Kieslowski* (Legenda, 2000) and *Cinema's Missing Children* (Wallflower Press, 2003). She is currently working on a study of the films of Alain Resnais.

Mary Wood is Reader in European Cinema, and Course Director of the Continuing Education Media Studies programme, Birkbeck College, University of London. Her publications include 'Woman of Rome: Anna Magnani', in *Heroines Without Heroes: Female Identities in Post-War European Cinema 1945–1951* (edited by Ulrike Sieglohr, Cassell, 2000). Her current projects include chapters on Italian film noir for *European Film Noir* (Manchester University Press, forthcoming), a book on Contemporary European Cinema (Arnold), and a book on Italian cinema.

introduction

TURNING THE MALE INSIDE OUT
Phil Powrie, Bruce Babington and Ann Davies

The study of men in film has assumed increasing importance since the 1990s. This volume is intended as a contribution to the debates. It collects a number of essays, many of which were originally papers at the conference 'Exploring Masculinities and Film', organised by the Centre for Research into Film and Media at the University of Newcastle upon Tyne in July 2001. These have been supplemented by commissioned papers from scholars working in the field. In this introduction, we shall sketch out a brief history of scholarship in this area, focusing in particular on some key collections of essays on masculinities and film, so as to situate our own project within the debate.

A brief history of the study of film masculinities

The study of the representation of men in films has always been widespread in Film Studies; after all, it is hardly possible to write about a number of film genres – the western, the war film, the gangster film, romantic comedy, the biblical epic, film noir all spring immediately to mind – without touching on masculinities. However, what concerns us in this volume – the systematic exploration of masculinities anchored in the gender paradigm, and which we shall call 'Masculinities in Film Studies' for short – developed as an afterthought of the feminist-inspired spectatorship paradigm of the period 1975–85. Although it was marked out by Pam Cook and Steve Neale with key articles in *Screen* in the early 1980s (Cook 1982; Neale 1983), it was never constituted as a discipline in the same way as feminist film analysis. There are several reasons for this, which are related to the internal dynamics of Film Studies and to the way in which academic disciplines were organised in this period. The combination of these two factors arguably prevented Film Studies from interacting with other disciplines working on masculinities.

First, theoretical work in Film Studies in the 1980s was heavily focused on a few key issues in spectatorship theory. Work in this area questioned the simplistic male/active, female/passive paradigms of 1970s screen theory, leading to fruitful complexities. These established the pleasure of multiple spectator identifications and their connections with masquerade and performativity. In this work, the position of the woman as screen-object as well as spectator was the key issue, leading to a very necessary refocusing of the 1970s concept of the 'male gaze', as discussed by Laura Mulvey (1975). The emphasis on male representation was, to put it bluntly, unnecessary for this refocusing to take place.

Second, there was the rather more specific work in Gay and Queer Studies, which engaged differently but no less acutely with representations of men in films. Crucially, though, this occurred only as part of a much wider frame of reference; its object of study was not so much representational 'norms', as deviance from those 'norms', thus side-stepping the investigation of heterosexual masculine structures.

A third reason which prevented a strong focus on masculinities developing can be found in the at least initially unproductive relationship between Film Studies and the renewed emphasis on masculinity in the social sciences, partly in response to feminism and feminist theory. Here the work was, in general, very detailed: historical or ethnographic explorations of different social organisations or of norms in Western social structures. The empirical detail of such work was often far removed from the more abstract theorising of Film Studies, and seemingly did not have much to offer it. For example, 1980s case histories such as Christine Heward's study of English public schools, or Michael Herzfeld's study of masculine performance and sheep-stealing in a Cretan village seemed unlikely to help explore the representation of men in feature films. Both of these are mentioned by Robert Connell in his overview of the study of masculinities. Connell points out that such detailed work is necessary, but that it should be placed within a wider perspective. However, that wider perspective raises the opposite problem for the study of screen masculinities. He situates the four-hundred-year history of masculinity within 'the unprecedented growth of European and North American power, the creation of global empires and a global capitalist economy' (Connell 1995: 186). Whereas in the ethnographic case histories the approach was too detailed to help the analysis of screen masculinities, in this *longue durée* approach, the detailed specificities of textual work in Film Studies would have been overshadowed by global historical shifts extending well beyond the short history of film.

For these three reasons then – the emphasis on representations of women, the development of Gay and Queer Studies, and the inappropriateness of sociological paradigms for screen masculinities – little concentrated theoretical work was done in this area until the 1990s. By the 1990s the Althusser and Lacan-inspired paradigms of the 1970s had worked through to what theorists accepted were impasses. The final position of feminist-inspired theorising led to the concept of the masquerade (Doane 1982), and interest shifted to related issues of performance, using Judith Butler's work. Partly because the 'problem' of the female spectator was no longer resolvable and had shifted sideways into new and productive areas (related to masquerade, such as costume; see Cook 1996 and Bruzzi 1997), and partly because the shift into 'performance' was clearly an issue for men as well as for women, work on screen masculinities, after its false start in the early 1980s as an addendum to feminist work, began to assume more importance.

This was helped by developments in the film industry, and the appearance or reappearance of specific genres. It is hardly coincidental that Frank Krutnik's 1991 volume on *film noir* came in the wake of a resurgence of the genre, the neo-noir films of the 1970s and 1980s. Similar points could be made about the resurgence of the western during the late 1980s and 1990s with films such as *Silverado* (Lawrence Kasdan, 1985), *Dances with Wolves* (Kevin Costner, 1990), *Unforgiven* (Clint Eastwood, 1992) and so forth. These postmodern westerns were followed by renewed academic interest in the genre (Cameron and Pye 1996, Buscombe 1998, Saunders 2001, Holmlund 2002a). The rise of the action movie during the 1980s also led to a concentration of academic work in this area (Tasker 1993b, Jeffords 1994). In the UK the renewal of the British film industry occurred partly as a result of the 'lad' films and social-realist films of the early 1990s; this, too, led to an interest in representations of masculinity in UK cinema (Spicer 2001, Monk 2000a; 2000b).

The bulk of the work in this area since the 1990s has been on American cinema, however. The major general work in this respect is Steven Cohan and Ira Rae Hark's 1993 anthology.[1] *Screening the Male* is predicated on two basic theses. First, masculinity is not monolithic, as the feminist work of the 1970s had understandably but too easily assumed (hence the subtitle 'masculinities in Hollywood cinema'); second, following Neale's 1983 *Screen* article (which serves as the first chapter of the volume), men on screen are no less a spectacle than women: 'instead of the unperturbed monolithic masculinity produced by a de-contextualised psychoanalysis, this volume portrays filmed men and male film characters overtly performing their gender, in neurotic (and even psychotic) relationships to it, or seeking alternatives to masculinity as their culture defines it' (Cohan and Hark 1993: 3). Thus, whereas Dennis Bingham (1994) focused on James Stewart, Jack Nicholson and Clint Eastwood, Cohan and Hark's first section, 'Star turns', contains essays on male dancers, the clearest example of the performing male (Valentino, Astaire *et al.*).[2] A second section, 'Men in women's places', explores role reversals, such as Eastwood assuming the role of victim in a slasher-stalker narrative, or men as monsters in the horror film. The third section, 'Man to man' explores homosociality and homoeroticism, and includes work on black masculinity. The final section, 'Muscular masculinities' focuses on the action movie genre, and the stars Sylvester Stallone, Arnold Schwarzenegger and Bruce Willis.

Screening the Male was rapidly followed by two anthologies edited by Pat Kirkham and Janet Thumim (1993 and 1995a), which had broadly the same underlying theses as *Screening the Male*: the plurality of the masculine, and its spectacularity. The first volume collected essays by male academics on screen masculinities, the idea being that 'it is important for men themselves to write about the construction and representation of the masculine in relation to their experience' (Kirkham and Thumim 1993: 11). The majority of the fourteen essays focused on American cinema, either actors (Rock Hudson, Clark Gable, Robin Williams, Robert De Niro), or well-established American genres (historical epic, Tarzan adventures, Vietnam War film, sci-fi, sports film). Only one essay, on the horror film, considered the genre trans-nationally and generically (Hutchings 1993), and there were only four essays on non-American films: on *The Spanish Gardner* (Philip Leacock, 1956) with Dirk Bogarde (Medhurst 1993); a film which explores London's Greek-Cypriot community from an ethnographic perspective (Panayi 1993); the various versions of *The Thirty-nine Steps* (Ryall 1993); and an essay on the Bollywood star Amitabh Bachchan (Sharma 1993). The essays by Andy Medhurst and Tom Ryall are particularly interesting in that they focus on, as Medhurst puts it, 'what it means to be male in a particular culture at a particular time' (Medhurst 1993: 96), thus teasing out specifically *English* masculinities.

This volume was followed two years later by an anthology of seventeen essays, all by women (Kirkham and Thumim 1995a). As the editors point out, there were some differences between the academic men and the academic women's approaches. One of these was the types of films focused on. Whereas the men tended to focus on 'action and spectacular display of the male body, and the epic, war, horror and science fiction genres', the women tended to go for 'thrillers, westerns and melodramas', there being no essays at all on science fiction, the epic, or the musical (Kirkham and Thumim 1995b: 12). It is the emphasis on melodrama which prompts the editors to suggest a genderised refocusing, the association of the genre with the woman's film perhaps allowing them 'to gain access to the "problematic" of masculinity' (ibid.). A second difference was the rather more acute emphasis by the women academics on the fragility of masculinity, and a closer look at the fragilised male body, perhaps, the editors suggested, because women, being already disempowered, are less likely to feel threatened by the examination of elements which undermine masculinity. However, like the first volume, the bulk of the essays focus on American cinema with only five on European cinema, covering stars (Albert Finney and Jean Gabin; see Geraghty 1995 and Vincendeau 1995 respectively), and individual films from Italy (Caldwell 1995), Great Britain (Young 1995) and Spain (Morgan 1995).

There have been few volumes specifically on European cinema. Kaja Silverman's 1992 volume, although it contains illuminating work on Fassbinder and masculinity, is more a work of theory, and does not confine itself to film. Where more tightly-focused volumes are concerned there is Phil Powrie's volume (1997) on French cinema and masculinity. Ginette Vincendeau made a major contribution to masculinities in French cinema with her work on Jean Gabin (Vincendeau and Gauteur 1993), part of which appeared in Kirkham and Thumim's 1995 volume (Vincendeau 1995), and later with her collection of essays on French stars more generally (Vincendeau 2000b), which includes work on Max Linder, Louis de Funès, Jean-Paul Belmondo and Gérard Depardieu. In British cinema studies, there are two recent volumes dealing with stars and masculinity respectively (Babington 2001; Spicer 2001). And in Spanish cinema studies Chris Perriam (2003) has focused on contemporary Spanish male stars.

This volume forms part of this recent development in the study of European masculinities and film. Fourteen of the nineteen chapters have a European focus. It might be argued that our conception of 'Europe' is somewhat limited since we cover the national cinemas of only five European countries: France, Great Britain, Germany/Yiddish, Italy and Spain. On the other hand, like the editors of previous anthologies, we are constrained by what our academic colleagues choose to work on.

There are several essays on masculinities in American cinema, however, even if the balance between European and American cinema has been reversed. A double focus nevertheless appears to us necessary. While it seems important to us to reverse the balance obtaining in previous collections on masculinities and film, it would have been perverse to pretend that European cinema operates in a vacuum; indeed, a European focus might have had the effect of enforcing the ghettoisation of European cinema as a kind of 'special case', wholly different from a Hollywood configured as a the 'norm'. The same can be said about scholarship in film studies: scholars such as Steven Cohan, Peter Lehmann and Calvin Thomas are working in ways which illuminate the field more generally. The inclusion of essays by them provides a necessary continuity, as well as a development of theorisations of screen masculinities.

The volume is divided into four sections, reflecting areas of interest within masculinities and film: stars, class and race, fathers and bodies. There are clear overlaps with previous volumes. This is partly because some of the contributors are pursuing work which was already evident in earlier volumes. This is the case for Cohan who has returned to the stars of the musical which he had begun to explore in 1993, but felt he did not have the space for in his volume on masculinity in the films of the 1950s (Cohan 1997); similarly, Peter Lehman returns to what he terms the 'melodramatic penis' (Lehman 2001b). The overlap is also partly due to the fact that some star issues remain constant, such as the emphasis on working-class stars: Albert Finney in 1995 (Geraghty 1995), Michael Caine here. Some stars seem to function iconically for the study of screen masculinities; this is the case for Clint Eastwood (see Knee 1993, Smith 1993, Bingham 1994, Thumim 1995, Holmlund 2002b), and for Clark Gable whose study in this volume refers back to an essay in Kirkham and Thumim's 1993 volume (Fisher 1993). Some broadly generic issues remain constant as well, such as the emphasis on the male body. Significantly, however, the male bodies explored here exemplify a shift of scholarly interest since the mid-1990s. Gone is the hard body of the action film, or the scarred body of the lone hero. Here, we explore self-criticism, fatherhood, trauma, abjection, the limp penis. The screen male would appear even more fragile, more 'damaged', more ruined than a decade ago. We shall return to this issue after we have outlined the chapters in this volume.

Stars

Six of the chapters are on male stars. Stars are indubitably central to the filmic representation of sex and gender, as the literally embodied site where masculinity and femininity take on their most idealised, powerful and immediate forms, those impressions of lived authenticity which star study attempts to deconstruct and analyse. The six stars written on here, Clark Gable, Gene Kelly, Michael Caine, Hugh Grant, Alain Delon and Paco Rabal, spread across four cinemas – Hollywood, British, French and Spanish – and a timespan from the early 1930s to the present. Part of this book's specificity is its concentration on European as well as Hollywood masculinities, and this is reflected in the writers' choice of star subjects. They form an interesting group, which, without slighting the vitality of the recent work done on 'hard' and 'spectacular' bodies, might be thought to provoke in their more clothed variedness opportunities for more necessarily nuanced approaches to masculinity than the action film gives rise to. The six stars also cross numerous genres, some of which – the musical (Kelly), the woman's film (Gable), comedy (Grant, to some degree Caine) – tend to be left on the margins of debates about masculinity, suggesting critical difficulties in dealing with texts (both films and stars) that exhibit self-consciousness about their representations.

Timothy Connelly's essay on Clark Gable, though on one of the most apparently uncomplicatedly masculine of American stars – an essay by Joe Fisher in the earlier Kirkham and Thumim anthology bears the iconic (part) title 'Clark Gable's Balls' – takes a surprising route. Analysing early films often associated with a rather crude, even violent assertiveness, Connelly uncovers a more complicated involvement not just with major screen actresses associated with the 'woman's film', Greta Garbo, Norma Shearer, Joan Crawford, but with the genre itself and its feminisations. In these films, as the chapter analyses it, Gable pursues a trajectory parallel to the heroine's involving similar sacrifices and sufferings, rather than a typical male hero's trajectory. This essay implicitly poses the question of whether any remnants of this feminisation carry over into the consolidated, apparently unfissured, later image of 'the King's' masculinity.

Steven Cohan's chapter on Gene Kelly, as befits a star in the musical genre, pursues questions of the erotic objectification of the male body. The denial of that objectification constitutes one of the implausibilities in early influential theories of the gaze, restricting the look to the male, while the female is the object of the gaze. Cohan's essay concentrates on the musicals which precede *Singin' in the Rain* (Stanley Donen and Gene Kelly, 1952) These, he argues, represent a phase of ambivalence in Kelly's image which tends to be forgotten in later 'normative' assessments, tributes and memoirs (with their parallel to the above-cited article on Gable in their invocation of Kelly's 'balls'). Alongside close reading of the star's films and his performances in them, Cohan brings to bear recent gay historiography to argue that Kelly's performances as male dancer, a culturally ambivalent role to start with, are marked by features that call into being both the heterosexual and homosexual gaze.

The scarcity of writing about comic versions of masculinity makes Andrew Spicer's chapter on Hugh Grant especially welcome. Though noting Grant's appeal to American (and Japanese) audiences, Spicer's main concern is with Grant as an English star operating most successfully in the recent revival of British romantic comedy. Spicer places Grant both within the larger framework of more or less enduring English male comic stereotypes and within the more recent one of those much commented on antithetical recent shifts in mass definitions of masculinity, shorthanded at least in English film and cultural studies as 'laddism' and the 'new man'. All this is further complicated by the recurring role played by the star in these films (and to some degree off screen) of the cautious lover riven by the difficulties of 'commitment' in the self-conscious world of modern romance.

Grant's very English middle-class figures contrast with those equally English but very differently lower-class (at least in origin) characters of Michael Caine whose early career, especially in films such as *The Ipcress File* (Sidney J. Furie, 1965) and *Alfie* (Lewis Gilbert, 1966) is examined by Robert Shail. Caine's originating image, still referred to more or less overtly thirty years later in the older international star's gallery of parts, embodies a masculinity clearly responding to social change, 'a working-class hero' in metamorphosis from constricting social beginnings in a context where a perceived proletarian energy in the popular arts was displacing a previous middle-class hegemony. The cocky disruptiveness which Shail analyses, though it has its dark sides, suggests, like aspects of the masculinities of all the stars under discussion, that Kirkham and Thumin were only half right when they wrote, as quoted by Shail, of masculinities: 'Marked, time and again, as delicate, fragile, provisional: it is under threat, in danger of collapse: it is an impossible ideal – most of all it seems to be an impediment to the desirable human experience of pleasure-in-being' (Kirkham and Thumim 1995b: 11).

Graeme Hayes' examination of Alain Delon, 'a significant figure for the construction of French national and masculine identities', focuses on the star's roles in the ubiquitous *policier* film, where relations with two other icons of French masculinity, Jean Gabin and Jean-Paul Belmondo, are struck, reminding us that stars and their meanings do not stand alone but in relation to both closely related and antithetical individual-types. Noting that the *policier* is often called the French *film noir*, Hayes makes the point that the world of the French genre is overwhelmingly masculine, built around male solidarity and cameraderie, with no real equivalent to American *film noir*'s *femme fatale*. Pursuing arguments outside the restrictions of the early definitions of the spectacle of the male body on screen as having to be marked by de-eroticising elements such as suffering, he shows that, though there are instances of the latter, Delon is often presented erotically without them, something which it is argued can only be recuperated by a highly defined heterosexuality in the narrative, the presence of which causes a rupture in the male world of the *policier*, marking Delon as betrayer and manipulator.

Finally, Rikki Morgan-Tamosunas' authoritative essay on the long-enduring Spanish star Paco Rabal guides the reader through multiple Hispanic versions of the forces that tend to traverse filmic constructions of maleness irrespective of nationality and genre: class, sexuality, the aura of 'authenticity'. In Rabal's case, there are more precise affiliations with artistic movements than is common with anglophone stars, and the kind of transitions that can take place over a long career as the actor passes from young to older man, from representations of youthful forms of masculinity to ones of patriarchal wisdom and life experience, remind us that the older male as sage and chieftain has an important role in the cinema; again, as ever, contradictory, constructed and performed, but enacting pleasures that we should not underestimate, and should seek to place within their very specific contexts.

The masculinities displayed and analysed in these chapters are indeed revealed as 'delicate, fragile, provisional', but we should not necessarily assume that masculinity is 'an impediment to the desirable human experience of pleasure-in-being' (Kirkham and Thumim 1995b: 11), which presumes a separation of pleasure-in-being from pleasure in being male (or female). Each of the stars dealt with here exhibits the latter as part of their meaning – from Delon's animal grace, to Rabal's earthiness, to Caine's insubordinate charm – though the question is, at what expense to self and others in the specific worlds of the films.

Class and race

The contributors who deal with the clashes of identity between class, race and masculine gender in men who are not white and middle class, indicate how different forms of masculine identity are frequently reconciled through the exclusion of women from the supposedly masculine sphere, though the results of this exclusion can vary.

Michele Aaron's chapter tackles the way in which cross-dressing and male impersonation simultaneously challenges and reinforces the notorious anti-Semitic figuring of the Jew as effeminate and thus inferior. Anti-Semitism thus served to displace a crisis in masculinity onto the Jew, implying another reason for the eradication of Jewishness, that of ensuring a stable patriarchy and masculine identity. But, as Aaron elucidates in her discussion of the film *Yidl Mitn Fidl* (Joseph Green, 1936), this crisis of Jewish masculinity posed by anti-Semitic thought is in turn displaced on to the woman impersonating the man. The comedy literally engendered by the woman's attempt to be a man offers the opportunity for the effeminate stereotype of the Jewish male to be exposed, ridiculed and undermined, but this more positive evaluation of the Jewish man is achieved at the expense of the Jewish woman, who must ultimately be returned to her proper place. Nonetheless, this ultimately patriarchal move can be and is challenged in Barbra Streisand's more recent *Yentl* (Barbra Streisand, 1983), which reclaims the cross-dressing Jewish woman for a more positive queering of Jewish identities.

John Hill explores representations of British working-class men, specifically miners. In earlier films such as *The Proud Valley* (Pen Tennyson, 1940) and *Kes* (Ken Loach, 1969) and, to some extent, later with *Billy Elliot* (Stephen Daldry, 2000), we find that male manual labour is in decline as working practices become increasingly feminised. Again, we find that a positive identification with working-class masculinity requires an insistence on traditional gender roles, so that when these disappear such identification is eroded. This may not necessarily be a bad thing for the central characters concerned: *Kes* indicates that manual labour both alienates and stifles creativity, a notion heightened in *Billy Elliot*, where Billy's ability to express himself through dance only emerges as male working-class structures crumble. The attempt to reassert working-class male values through the miners' strike in particular becomes oppressive, thwarting Billy's ambitions to go to dancing college for lack of money. This critique of traditional masculine identities does not, however, offer much that is positive to replace them. Apart from the displacement of the crisis of masculinity onto Michael, Billy's cross-dressing friend (in a move reminiscent of *Yidl Mitn Fidl*), and onto ballet as an art form that is barely sketched in the film, we have no real sense that male identities are being reconfigured in the light of new understandings of gender relations. Women are still excluded from the male working-class sphere, through death, madness or different class values. The British working-class male identity turns out to be little more than a historical curio that leaves contemporary working-class men in limbo, while the very real contribution of women to British working-class struggle is erased completely. British class conflict has been historicised and thus put at a safe distance.

With Carrie Tarr's discussion of marginalised young men in urban France we confront both class and race as potentially determining factors in establishing male identities. The films she surveys appear to offer at first glance a positive integration of different ethnic identities, equated through the marginalisation of youth. This cross-race integration is nevertheless purchased at a price: on the one hand an almost clichéd escalation of violence and on the other a virtually total lack of communication between men and women. The stereotype of violent youth is softened to some extent by the inclusion of white central characters, thus undermining an all too automatic connection of ethnic youth and violence: it also opens up opportunities for comedy, though only if the action is displaced away from the urban sphere (to Biarritz, in this case). As Tarr demonstrates, the recourse to violence, when it does occur, is ultimately emasculating, achieving the opposite of what it intended. But the characters of these French films never seem to realise this. There is the danger, perhaps, of implying that better communication with women would improve the situation – dangerous because it presumes an inherent nurturing and peaceful side to women that has rightly become highly debateable. Dangerous, too, because it seems to lock marginalised male youth into the position of permanent victim, with a possible retrograde hint that women carry some of the blame for these men's inability to find peaceful solutions to their problems. The male as victim becomes ultimately a pleasurable spectacle which absolves the characters of any responsibility to work towards positive change.

Fathers

One of the key masculine roles in all societies is that of the father; as a role, this has perhaps changed most radically in the last thirty years or so, although this has not been addressed in Film Studies to any great extent. Fathers on film are many and various, even if generally there are not many shades of grey between the controlling patriarch on the one hand and the weak and often ridiculed father on the other. With the advent of the New Man in the 1980s there came an academic emphasis on fathering, primarily, like so many other issues in masculinities, in work in the social sciences, and to some extent in cultural studies (for example Seidler 1996 (originally published 1988)), but not in Film Studies. There is nothing along these lines for example in the three key collections mentioned above (Cohan and Hark 1993, Kirkham and Thumim 1993; 1995a). During the 1990s, interest in men as fathers began to be shown in Film Studies, something this section tries to reflect (see, for example, Reeder 1995, Blackwell 2002, Sjödin 2002). The 'fathers' explored here include characters who are fathers within the film diegesis, as well as symbolic fathers, or indeed a combination of both. The disparate conception of what a 'father' might be in this section reflects the fragmentation of the father's role in many contemporary European societies, and the questioning of that role. The one thing the chapters all have in common in this section, however, is the father/son relationship.

Bruce Babington explores symbolic father/son homosocial bonding in a late silent film by Ernst Lubitsch – one of the many versions of The Student Prince (*The Student Prince of Old Heidelberg*, 1927, starring Ramon Novarro) – showing how a certain type of masculinist ideology rooted in nationalism and militarism is critiqued through that bonding. The film's twin love stories – Karl Heinrich's doomed romance with Käthi, and his homosocial romance with the members of the Corps Saxonia, one of the aristocratic all-male student societies – take place against subtly realised racial and historical realities, constantly invoking different modes of masculinity and fatherhood, and the losses entailed by the repression of femininity in an ultra-patriarchal society. The complexly feminised masculinity of Karl Heinrich/Novarro is placed between two father figures: his uncle, the stern, militaristically unbending King, and his tutor. The tutor functions as a kind of father-cum-lost-mother figure for an oppressively patriarchal society. Unlike Novarro, he is masculinised in appearance, but he is also feminised and clearly Jewish, thus bringing together in one person the father, the mother, the central but marginalised Jew of Wilhelmine culture, and a humane intellectuality doomed to redundancy in a nationalist military state.

The intersection between national identity and fatherhood is also explored in Mary Wood's study of two generations of Italian stars, older actors who had established their careers during the fascist period, and younger actors who obtained public recognition in the immediate post-war period. Focusing on two representative stars, Wood shows how the persona of the older Amedeo Nazzari is connected with the stability of patriarchal values at a time of political and social upheaval, while the younger Vittorio Gassman, who played as many young villains as heroes, rehearses a range of masculine behaviour and the attractions and difficulties of each. In both cases the very fleshiness of their objects of desire suggests the attraction of post-war prosperity which required the working out of new ways of being a father, as well as a son, lover and worker in a changed world.

We stay with Italian cinema in Paul Sutton's chapter on the contemporary director, Nanni Moretti. Sutton shows how Moretti's films – *Caro Diario/Dear Diary* (1993), *Aprile/April* (1998) and *La Stanza del Figlio/The Son's Room* (2001) – combine the search for a new kind of cinema with the search for a new kind of masculine identity, one that is associated explicitly with fatherhood and issues of what it is to be 'authentic' in an inauthentic society, a project intimately bound up with self-inscription in Moretti's pseudo-autobiographical films. In *Aprile*, as was the case for the generational shift explored by Wood, this takes place against the backdrop of cultural change. The film records a period of almost three years that charts the right-wing Berlusconi election victory in March 1994 to the left-wing triumph in April 1996, an event that coincides with the birth of Moretti's son Pietro. The film contrasts Berlusconi with Moretti, the private/good/fragmented father and the public/bad/fascist father, while at the same time examining personal and political responsibility, and locating these oppositions in a further opposition between 'deceitful' television and 'authentic' autobiographical cinema.

The final two chapters in this section focus less on the father than on the son. French film of the 1990s has frequently represented male adolescence as a period of dispossession, disenfranchisement and loss, most obviously in *La Haine/Hate* (Mathieu Kassovitz, 1995), amongst other *banlieue* films (some of which are discussed in Carrie Tarr's chapter in this volume). Emma Wilson's chapter focuses on *Olivier, Olivier* (Agnieszka Holland, 1991) and *La Classe de neige/Class Trip* (Claude Miller, 1997), which offer a prehistory of this dispossession, exploring traumatic transitions between childhood and adolescence. Both films use the theme of the missing child and sexual abuse to dramatise more widespread questions of masculine individuation and identification. The son in each of these films is compelled to imagine and make sense of a primal scene which challenges the possibility of boy/father identification. The films refuse catharsis, judgement or solution, working instead to open out new, historically contingent representations of the young male subject amongst the ruins of fatherhood.

Filiation is a key issue in the British social-realist films of the 1990s, where father/son relationships abound; although here the role of the son is less to contemplate the ruins than to give succour. James Leggott shows how the figure of the angelic boychild rises up from the ruins of fatherhood to 'save' the fallen father. Fathers in these films, aware that their paternal role is ruined beyond repair, attempt to give the performance of virility a new lease of life by literal performance, stripping in *The Full Monty* (Peter Cattaneo, 1997) or playing music in *Brassed Off* (Mark Herman, 1996). These performances lead nowhere, and it is the parallel but very different performance of the dancing or flying angelic boy which literally 'rejuvenates' the obsolete paternal role; albeit, as Leggott ruefully admits, skirting around the troublesome issue of responsibility, and the messy business of life in the real world, where bodies are not as clean as Peter Pan's.

Bodies

The final section of the volume focuses increasingly on the troubled male body, first as object of the gaze in chapters by Pamela Church Gibson and Ann Davies, then as abjected protrusion in the form of the limp penis of often dead characters 'troubling' the 'phallicised' field of vision. Finally, the last two chapters go behind, almost literally, the spectacularised male body, and behind the detumescent penis, to the anus, to show how the hard body is not so much feminised as liquefied, 'shittified'. In a gesture of pre-Oedipal anality the male body seeks phantasied rebirth in a spectacularly scatontologised version of the ideal ego, to borrow a term coined by Calvin Thomas, and used by both Thomas and Phil Powrie in the two final chapters.

First, Church Gibson pursues the debate on masculinity begun in Jonathan Rutherford and Rosalind Chapman's 1988 collection, *Male Order: Unwrapping Masculinity* (re-edited in 1996), arguing that the current cinematic configurations of masculinity, and their reception, can only be properly understood in the context of debates around the male consumer, and increasingly through fashion. Drawing on Frank Mort's (1996) work on masculinity and consumption, she explores how the male-on-male looking which began within the 'style magazines' of the 1980s has filtered through into film. Taking as her examples two films targeted at young men – *Face/Off* (John Woo, 1997) and *Fight Club* (David Fincher, 1999) – and whose emotional epicentre is a relationship between men, she locates the same-sex appeal of their stars in a broad 'lad culture'.

Ann Davies takes us away from the homosocial contexts of consumption into the heterosexual dynamics of women gazing at males within films. The Carmen narrative, created by Prosper Mérimée and made famous in Bizet's opera, has formed the basis of some eighty films over the course of cinema history. Although the Carmen character is usually positioned as the object of a male gaze, cinema Carmens often gaze back, questioning the male body and its visibility as an object of desire. Davies looks in detail at one of the more familiar versions of the Carmen story, Carlos Saura's flamenco *Carmen* (1983), which functions as a commentary on the supposedly newly-liberated Spanish woman and the effect of her liberation on men. Carmen, a rebellious Galatea, challenges her mentor Antonio, and in the process makes of his body not just an object of her desire, but exposes it as a site of inadequacy. The tension over the male body ends in the time-honoured way with Carmen's death: the female gaze and the female body must be destroyed in order that the male body can survive. Saura's film thus provides an overt example of a male fear of being looked at, and demonstrates how the cinematic Carmen narrative illustrates the weakness of masculine hegemony even as threatened masculinity reasserts itself in the crudest way possible, through murder.

We have gone from the impact of fashion culture to female screen characters gazing at men. Peter Lehman takes us to what usually is under wraps and hidden from all gazes, whether male or female, the penis, his concern being the appearance in so many films of the late twentieth century – by men and women, and across many national cinemas – not of the erect member of pornography, but a limp appendage associated with dead or dying screen characters. This dead penis seems to signal the detumescence of masculinity as a whole. He links the dead penis to what he calls the melodramatic penis (that is, the penis tied to excessively melodramatic events; see Lehman 2001b), arguing that it signals the disintegration of the phallic economy.

The two closing chapters bring together American action cinema and French art cinema to show how two apparently radically different forms of cinema work around the same kernel of fascination: the male body abjected, either implicitly in *Batman* (Tim Burton, 1989) or explicitly in two films by Gaspar Noé; the hard body of the 1980s is exploded, regressed, in enigmatic deliquescence, decomposed and decomposing, much as the hardly recognisable body parts or objects in Dalí's paintings of the 1920s. Noé's two films *Carne* (1990) and *Seul contre tous/I Stand Alone* (1998) recount the biography of a lonely butcher who rants fascistically against the world in an abusive inner monologue, made all the more unsettling by novel and disruptive cinematographic procedures. The butcher reappears briefly at the start of Noé's acutely observed, formally fascinating and much-criticised *Irréversible/Irreversible* (2002). Phil Powrie's chapter focuses on the first two films, exploring how their narratives can be understood as an example of the Kristevan abject, and how the narrative of the second film is structured on an exploration of the most obvious intertextual references, taken from Martin Scorsese's *Taxi Driver* (1976). With reference to Calvin Thomas' work, Powrie shows how rigidity and fluidity, vaginal and anal economies interact to create what Thomas calls scatontological anxiety, whose resolution is gestured at in an appeal to a fantasied representation of semen.

Scatontological anxiety is at the heart of Thomas' own chapter on *Batman*. Because it deals with a male 'superhero', *Batman* inevitably thematises certain issues concerning masculinity. Specifically, Burton's film foregrounds an anxious relation between 'armoured' masculine subjectivity, the male body, and the mechanisms of photographic and cinematic representation. Thomas' close reading of *Batman* argues that the film articulates a specifically masculinist anxiety about the very medium of cinema, a constitutive unease about a mass cultural 'technology of abjection' that both threatens and enforces the boundaries of normative, heterosexual masculinity. By thematising its own material engulfment in the 'feminising' mass culture it attempts to transcend, *Batman* complicates the very terms of masculinity on which it insists.

Conclusion

We pointed out above that the screen male appears to be even more damaged than ten years ago, according to the work of many of the contributors to this volume. There are two poles of spectacular masculinity represented in this collection. At one extreme, we have the man feminised by spectacle and display, whether the dancer or the ephebic youth of the fashion pages, or the angelic boy of 1990s British social-realist films; at the other, we have the damaged man, whether Antonio the dancer who crumbles under Carmen's gaze, or Claude Miller's dysfunctional father, or Gasper Noé's Ordinary Joe whose inwardly-turned fascism causes him to explode and implode at the same moment. There has been a difference in the damaged man in comparison with earlier periods of film. The damaged man is more often than not damaged *from the start*, either in the way in which he is presented by our contributors, and/or from the start of the film in which he appears (and one cannot help thinking that the films chosen by our contributors have been chosen because they exemplify what the contributors see as ontological damage). The damage is not just a climax, a moment of spectacular display, as might be the case, thinking back to Steve Neale's 1983 article, for the shoot-out of the western, the war film, or the action movie. How can we theorise this shift?

The two poles can be mapped on to Rosalind Chapman's theorisation of the fragmentation of the 'flawed whole' of the 1980s New Man into the 'uneasy mixture' of the nurturer and the narcissist, represented for her by two rather different types of magazine, *Cosmopolitan* and *Arena* respectively (Chapman 1996: 230), the former for the 'listening' man, the latter for the pleasure-seeking hedonist with a disposable income. As she argued in 1988, using Barbara Ehrenreich's work (1983), these varieties of masculinity, though separate social types, had one thing in common: the revolt against the 1950s 'breadwinner ethic' and the 'hardline masculinity' which accompanied it (Chapman 1996: 234), and thus might be seen to represent a new 'feminised' man. However, it is equally possible to argue, she suggested, following Ehrenreich, that this merely represents a repositioning or realignment within patriarchal power structures, 'producing a hybrid masculinity which is better able and more suited to retain control' (Chapman 1996: 235). What then of the rather more damaged man of the 1990s?

One of the examples Chapman adduces to expose continuing gender inequality is the way in which there are more images of naked or semi-naked men than there used to be, as Church Gibson points out in this volume in relation to *Fight Club*; but the penis remains hidden, or at least used to, until, as Lehman points out, also in this volume, the prevalence of the penis associated with death. Similar to Chapman's argument that the uneasy mixture of nurturer and narcissist is symptomatic of a realignment of power structures, we could argue that the damaged man is a melodramatic *mise-en-scène*; it is male hysteria as a kind of smokescreen for that realignment: 'look how I suffer, look how I am feminised through that suffering (but don't look at the way in which I consolidate my power over you)'.

Ten years on, can we theorise the shift more positively than this? Two contributors to Kirkham and Thumim's 1995 anthology pointed out that the damage done to men on screen made those men more accessible to female spectators. For Christine Gledhill, Deckard in *Blade Runner* (Ridley Scott, 1982) is 'a man wounded by patriarchy but redeemable through his capacity to identify with the female character. For the female viewer such a figure may offer the gratifying spectacle of masculinity crossing the gender divide, revealing a vulnerability beneath the tough exterior' (Gledhill 1995: 87). And, in a discussion of Frank Borzage's films, Pat Kirkham similarly argues for the redemptive function of damage: 'The ideal man is one who is partly de-masculinised in order to be partly feminised; who is *deconstructed* to be *reconstructed* ... Wounding makes men more accessible to women's imagination' (Kirkham 1995: 107; her emphasis). Commenting on the first of these two passages in their introduction, the editors caution us against facile optimism, using the same argument as Chapman which we outlined above: 'the masculine crossing of the gender divide is an adventure largely conducted in the interests of the male subject' (Kirkham and Thumin 1995b: 31). It is striking that the point next made in that introduction refers directly to the less threatening, possibly less 'culpable', more redemptive, and somehow less damaged youth: 'The male youth can be considered as feminised because he is not yet fully mature and he presents an ambivalent figure, a figure which invites the dangerous contradiction for masculinity implicit in the homo-erotic spectacle' (ibid.). It is therefore no surprise that in our own volume, ranging from early Lubitsch through Noé's incestuous father, to the recent films by Moretti, there are many instances of a related nexus of issues: fathers and sons, filiation or counter-filiation, continuity or discontinuity. But these issues, we would suggest, are as connected to the central issue of damaged masculinity as the others discussed above, they are not a displacement into some kind of less-tainted masculinity.

Further, there is no reason to assume that the kind of redemptive function ascribed to the damaged male on screen cannot operate as much for male as for female spectators. True, on one level, as we argued above, this could be complacent male hysteria, the 'look at how good I am at suffering' argument. But it can equally well be argued that this hyper-damage has a positively destabilising function within cultural forms, and that it is not just a reaction to socialisation, as the psychologist Roger Horrocks suggests when he writes that male fascination with damage and with death are 'the result of masculinisation itself, the process of becoming a man under patriarchy, which is deeply damaging' (Horrocks 1995: 173).

This view of redemptive or perhaps more properly *reconstructive* damage is related to the debates surrounding masochism and spectatorship in the early 1990s, whereby the pre-oedipal masochistic position was explored as an alternative theoretical construct to the 1970s' oedipalised male gaze. The damaged male, we might argue, forces male and female viewers to reconstruct a theoretical space which precedes patriarchal law. By identifying with damaged males on screen, both men and women are obliged to reconstruct the space of a return (or multiple returns), to reconstruct the space of the maternal (or multiple maternals), to reconstruct the space of the material rather than what Lacan calls the Symbolic, the structure of laws and language. It is our hope, then, that these texts, and our readings of them, may help make a difference within the larger arena of social change. As Robert Connell points out, the operation we are talking about here – the location of texts which degender (as he calls it), and their collocation to suggest how such degendering may be reflected in social change more widely – is an essential move:

A *degendering* strategy, an attempt to dismantle hegemonic masculinity, is unavoidable; a *degendered* rights-based politics of social justice cannot proceed without it … The degendering strategy applies not only at the level of culture and institutions, but also at the level of the body – the ground chosen by defenders of patriarchy, where the fear of men being turned into women is most poignant. It is hardly a coincidence that a surgical procedure for doing just that was created at the same historical moment as the most radical challenge to the gender order. The striking consequence is that surgery provides the popular figure of gender change, a procedure performed by authoritative, affluent men on anaesthetised bodies.

A politics of social justice needs to change body-reflexive practice, not by losing agency but by extending it, working through the agency of the body – exactly what is negated by the anaesthetist. Rather than disembodiment involved in role reform, this requires *re-embodiment* for men, a search for different ways of using, feeling and showing male bodies. (Connell 1995: 233; his emphasis)

The patient chronicling of images of men on screen for what they can tell us about social and historical shifts – whether based in class, ethnicity or gender, or a mixture of all of these – can only help destabilise patriarchal hegemony by showing us that masculinities are various, shifting and comprised of 'flows', in the Deleuzian sense.

We hope to have shown that the study of masculinities is not just an issue of relocating the feminine in the masculine, of 'feminising' men. Men are not somehow 'better' because they seem more like women, particularly not, one might argue, when 'being like a woman' involves passivity, masochism, disempowerment. Such reductiveness merely reinforces the binary oppositions upon which patriarchy and capitalism thrive. What we hope to have done in this volume as a whole is to locate *moments of becoming*, the interstitial moments which undermine fixed ontologies, as cinema attempts to come to terms with change.

Notes

1   We are discounting Trice 2001, whose discussion of the 75 most popular films 1921–99 is too open a field, and Bingham 1994, whose focus on three stars is, on the contrary, too closed. In Lehman 2001a, where 15 out of 17 chapters are film-specific, the emphasis is also on Hollywood cinema.

2   The essay on Valentino (Studlar 1993), forms part of a wider study by Studlar on screen masculinities in the 1920s (Studlar 1996), which also includes work on Douglas Fairbanks, John Barrymore and Lon Chaney.

SECTION 1 STARS

SECTION 2 CLASS & RACE

SECTION 3 FATHERS

SECTION 4 BODIES

chapter 1

DANCING WITH BALLS IN THE 1940s: SISSIES, SAILORS AND THE CAMP MASCULINITY OF GENE KELLY

Steven Cohan

In 'Why Am I So Gone About that Gal?' from *Les Girls* (1958), Gene Kelly performs a show number which takes off Marlon Brando's biker figure in *The Wild One* (1953). *Les Girls* was the last musical Kelly starred in for MGM as a contract player, and this number, the final one in the film, is a fitting coda to his tenure as a leading man at the studio. Jack Cole is credited with the choreography of *Les Girls* but the ideas behind 'Why Am I So Gone About that Gal?' – the playful impersonation of Brando, the recuperation of a confident heterosexual masculinity through dance, the homosocial bonds reinforcing that masculinity – are in keeping with Kelly's athletic, sexually aggressive dancing style and the virile star image it reinforced.

After all, it was Kelly himself who once declared that he was 'the Marlon Brando of dancers' as compared to Fred Astaire's Cary Grant. Kelly made this comparison to describe their singular approaches as 'two highly individual dancers', ranging from their dissimilar styles to their different signature costumes (Hirschhorn 1984: 116). However, by invoking Grant and Brando as his touchstones, Kelly's comparison also acknowledges how his star image drew upon recognisable gender tropes to make his dancing appear legible as an authentic masculine activity. 'He was not a very good dancer at all', commented Jack Cole, 'but he was interesting as a phenomenon. It's a cultural thing that he happened to succeed – which is always the way with popular art. There is always the establishment attitude about dancing and men dancing in the right way' (quoted in Delamater 1981: 197).

Obviously not a fan, Cole criticised Kelly for using dance to project a reassuring image of 'men dancing in the right way' – dancing, that is to say, in full conformity with the cultural norms regulating masculinity during the heyday of the MGM musical. What this 'right way' required of Kelly was vividly recalled by his collaborator, Stanley Donen:

And I remember being impressed by Gene as soon as I saw him on the stage. He had a cockiness, a confidence in himself, and a ruthlessness in the way he went about things that, to someone as young and green as myself, was astonishing. I also found him cold, egotistical and very rough. And, of course, wildly talented. He was the only song-and-dance man to come out of that period who had balls. There were good dancers around, like Don Loper, Jack Cole, Gower Champion, Charles Walters, Dan Dailey – even Van Johnson. But they somehow weren't as dynamic as Gene. No one was. That's why he was such an explosion on the scene. It was the athlete in him that gave him his uniqueness. (quoted in Hirschhorn 1984: 74)

Donen's comment that Kelly stood out as 'the only song-and-dance man to come out of that period who had balls' assumes that a male dancer cannot prove his manliness unless, as in Kelly's case, he makes a spectacle of attributes that testify to his inherent masculinity: confidence, athleticism, egotism, ruthlessness, in short, 'cockiness' in all senses of the word. After Kelly's death in 1996 the obituaries evoked the same virile image. Choreographer Twyla Tharp noted in a *Los Angeles Times* memorial that 'Gene Kelly is rightly credited with bringing a massive and much needed dose of vitality, masculinity and athleticism to American dance' (Tharp 1996). That colleagues and admirers still remember Kelly in these terms is not surprising. The normative star image was featured prominently in the extra-filmic commentary about him throughout his career, and it was reiterated by his MGM screen persona. On the face of it, insistence upon the dancer's normality wherever one looks seems unrelenting enough to deserve John McCullough's critique that the Kelly image was 'simplistically dogmatic and not complex enough to embody the inherent contradictions and conflicts of the period', except symptomatically as 'an image of hysteria and anxiety' about patriarchal masculinity (McCullough 1989: 44, 46).

Historically, however, what Kelly signified as a male dancer during his tenure at MGM was more complicated, less stable and coherent, than McCullough recognises or retrospective accounts such as Cole's and Donen's recall. Far from being fixed early on and all of a piece, the Kelly image embodied a provocative disjunction of gendered and sexualised understandings of masculinity, which in turn produced an indecipherable picture of what it meant to dance 'in the right way'. The extra-filmic commentary about Kelly at that time defined the particularities of his star image by focusing on the way his dancing troubled rather than secured masculine norms. Kelly was perceived through the worry that he might really be a 'sissy dancer' but what his possible effeminacy connoted was indeterminate because the category itself was still a variable one at mid-century. Kelly's musicals display this same indeterminacy, most notably in what some critics have observed but not pursued far enough: in the films' crafting of a homosocial persona for Kelly through the prominence given to his comparative pairing with a male co-star such as Frank Sinatra and in the exhibitionist solo numbers that focus attention squarely on the dancer's body. The musicals and extra-filmic commentary work together to foreground how Kelly embodied what amounted to a cultural oxymoron, namely, the erotic spectacle of a male dancer, which problematised binary formations of masculinity and heterosexuality. In doing so, this star image established the ground for viewing Kelly's dancing from a camp perspective.

Who's a sissy dancer?

Throughout his career, the extra-filmic commentary approached Gene Kelly's dancing as a problem by raising the question of whether or not his profession undermined his outwardly virile physical appearance. For instance, a short magazine piece about Kelly, published after his great popular and artistic success in *Anchors Aweigh* (1945), recounted the following 'off-screen' incident:

> It was lunchtime, and he was hungry, so he ducked into one of the thousands of hamburger joints that dot New York's sidestreets, slid onto a stool at the counter, and ordered one medium rare, please – and don't spare the onions. 'Coming up', said the waitress briskly, 'right away, sir – *oooooooh!*' and down went the burger on the floor and up went a pair of large, believe-it-or-not looking eyes. '*Pardon me*', she breathed, 'but aren't you Gene Kelly?' The sailor glared, and shoved his cap further over his bright brown eyes, very tough-like. 'What?' snorted Gene. 'Me, a sissy dancer? I should say not! *I'm* a sailor!' 'Well, I'm sorry', the waitress muttered', I didn't think *he'd* eat *here*, anyway!' Which goes to show how wrong a girl can be.[1]

Referring to Kelly's leave of absence from Hollywood when he joined the navy toward the end of World War Two, this anecdote has the ostensible purpose of showing that he is not 'a sissy dancer', and it gives the star himself the opportunity of voicing the disclaimer. This end is achieved, though, by having Kelly undertake a rather self-conscious imitation of virility, when he glares and lowers his cap 'very tough-like', so the story layers one mask upon another. Which is the pose and which is not, sissy dancer or tough sailor? It is not easy to tell. The disbelieving waitress loses her bearings as soon as she recognises the star – becoming breathless, dropping the food, fixing her eyes upon him, clearly responding to his 'charisma' – and she does not perceive his ordinariness as just another sailor until he denies he is Gene Kelly, 'sissy dancer'. For this reason, while the anecdote 'show[s] how wrong a girl can be', the cause of her error is ambiguous. The waitress mistakenly agrees with Kelly that dancers cannot be sailors and that movie stars are too pretentious to eat at lunch-counters like everyone else, but she also errs when she no longer sees 'Gene Kelly' seated in front of her, and may even be most 'wrong' when she no longer sees him as 'a sissy dancer'. The anecdote follows a strategy of defining the sailor as the manly opposite of the dancer, yet its comedy of misrecognition depends upon knowledge that Kelly is both, a dancer in a sailor suit and a sailor who dances.

The lunch-counter anecdote typifies how extra-filmic commentary about Kelly placed 'effeminacy' and 'manliness' in opposition to reinforce the impression of his virility, but the ambiguity in the piece is also symptomatic of how his star image compromised the opposition structuring it. Because he was a virile movie star who danced, the dualism had the ultimate effect of representing him as manly *and* effeminate simultaneously. In another example, this time from a point later in Kelly's career following his departure from MGM, the same antithesis determined how Richard Griffith phrased his introductory comments in the programme published for the Museum of Modern Art's 1962 tribute. 'Gene,' Griffith wrote, 'a superb specimen of manly beauty, doomed, you'd say, to matinee idolatry, has neatly escaped from the trap of dancing and miming in such a way that you would never mistake him for anybody but an ordinary Joe' (Griffith 1962: 3).

The economy with which Griffith offers this appraisal compacts rival cultural frameworks for evaluating Kelly's masculinity in relation to dance, placing him at their intersection. The critic concedes that Kelly's 'dancing and miming' put his 'manly beauty' on display, allowing his body to be appreciated as 'a superb specimen'. The remark that the dancer could, as a consequence, have been 'doomed … to matinee idolatry' refers to a long-standing journalistic tradition of dismissing as unmanly male stage stars who were valued primarily for their looks. The matinee idol was perceived negatively as a 'woman-made' man, that is, a strikingly handsome star whose appeal to female fans undermined his manhood because it focused so much attention on his body (Studlar 1996: 111). With his dancing raising comparable suspicion, for Kelly this negative connotation translated into his potential for being viewed as the 'sissy dancer' of the lunch-counter incident. Alluding to this doubt, Griffith insists that Kelly avoids the matinee idol's 'trap' of emasculation, because this dancer is 'unmistakable' as just another guy, an 'ordinary Joe' who fully conforms to the status quo. By calling Kelly an 'ordinary Joe', Griffith links the star with another instantly recognisable cultural stereotype while casting this normalising epithet in direct opposition to the more pejorative 'matinee idol'.

Framing the time span of his career at MGM, these two accounts protest too much, raising suspicion that Kelly is 'a sissy dancer' even while rigorously asserting the contrary. Such defensiveness characterises the extrafilmic commentary about Kelly as a whole, not only in fan magazine articles and career tributes, but also in interviews and television appearances.[2] Nearly two decades after leaving MGM, the goal of normalising Kelly's dancing still set the agenda of Clive Hirschhorn's authorised biography, originally published the same year as the first instalment of *That's Entertainment!* (1974). In describing the star's impact as a dancer on screen, Hirschhorn emphasises Kelly's great success in *On the Town* (1949), remarking that 'the big test' of the dream ballet in this film

> was whether Gene, personally, would be able to make the transition from wise-cracking sailor to ballet-dancer without jarring the audience … His problem in *On the Town* was to retain his sailor-boy characterisation in the ballet and convince audiences that what they were watching rang true and was in no way incongruous. (Hirschhorn 1984: 155)

According to Hirschhorn, this 'test' proved easy enough to pass because of Kelly's athleticism, which countered any inference of his being a sissy dancer in a sailor suit:

> And instead of alienating his male audiences, which he feared he might do, he made them identify with him and won them over by the virility of his dancing. There was nothing sissy or effeminate about him, and they relaxed completely in his presence. Gene was 'safe'. 'Like a guy in their bowling team – only classier', as Bob Fosse put it. Women found his smile and the cockiness of his personality most attractive and responded to his sex appeal. (Hirschhorn 1984: 157)

Hirschhorn goes out of his way to insist that, as a male dancer, Kelly is *not* 'effeminate' or a 'sissy', but 'safe'. The biographer's remarks nonetheless indicate what could have made

Kelly's dancing seem dangerous enough to test his masculine mettle: not the transition from sailor to ballet dancer, but the fact that men as well as women watched him dance, and they did so with pleasure. After admitting that audiences of both sexes found Kelly appealing to look at, which is presumably why men would have trouble relaxing in his presence, Hirschhorn then explicitly heterosexualises the dualism structuring his account. The biographer concedes that women 'responded to his sex appeal', seeing the erotised matinee idol in the dancer, but declares that men identified with 'the virility of Kelly's dancing', recognising the normative masculinity they shared with this ordinary Joe. That Kelly's dancing does not easily accommodate Hirschhorn's neat gender categorisation, however, is signalled by the odd phrasing of the Bob Fosse quotation, included to authenticate the star's normality by comparing it to working-class masculinity. Fosse notes that the dancer's style makes him 'like a guy on a bowling team', but then immediately throws the affiliation awry by adding, 'only classier'. Kelly is just like them, yet he's not, and this uncertainty makes his dancing a troubling spectacle. Virile *and* sexy, his dancing has an erotic potential that disturbs the manly/effeminate antithesis imposed upon it.

In an interview in *Dance* magazine promoting *That's Entertainment, Part II* (1976), as Kelly looked back on his career, he reiterated the problematic ground of his dancing when he explained the purpose of his signature costume, the sailor suit worn in *On the Town* and before that, *Anchors Aweigh*, the same outfit that also provided the premise of the lunch-counter anecdote. For audiences in the 1940s, the timely connotations of the sailor suit instantly linked his dancer persona with normative masculinity, identifying him as an ordinary Joe, but that is not Kelly's point here.[3] 'A sailor costume ... is the *best* ... for a man to dance in if he's playing a role', he observed. 'It is one way to avoid the balletic convention of the tights' (quoted in Stoop 1976: 71). He then went on to joke:

> The greatest contribution Gene Kelly made to American dance ... is that he's finally shown the male dancer how to dress! You can't play a *part* and come out in ballet slippers, and you can't come out in regular shoes, so I sort of invented the wearing of moccasins (which bend like ballet shoes) and white socks, and made sure that the pants were very tight and rolled up a bit, and wore a shirt or a sweatshirt or something that would show the figure. Like I said, a sailor suit was ideal because you outline the body, practically like a pair of tights, except for the flare at the bottom; so you could get by and still be real. (quoted in Stoop 1976: 73)

To defend the 'realism' of his dancing, Kelly claims that his sailor costume worked against the outright objectification of his body. Wearing tights, the costume associated with the female chorus as well as the *corps de ballet*, would have diminished his masculine presence, so his great contribution was his re-masculinisation of male dancers, even though, in another gender reversal, that amounted to his showing them 'how to dress!' The sailor suit served Kelly as more than a manly compromise with 'the balletic convention of the tights' because the costume did not obscure his spectacular value. On the contrary, as he points out, the costume was close-fitting enough to 'outline the body', so when he struts, flexes, leaps, even wiggles his buttocks while dancing in the sailor suit– all common moves of his on screen – he might just as well have been wearing tights. Indeed, even when performing in casual dress, Kelly notes, his pants were 'very tight', his shirt chosen to 'show the figure'. Associated closely enough with his dancing to continue serving as a metonymy of it in the 1970s, the sailor suit epitomised the gender incoherence of Kelly's virile star image. A cultural symbol, the suit condensed the effeminate/manly dualism that made his virility legible; but in serving as a theatrical costume as well, it gave him an erotic significance when he danced on screen that exceeded those binary terms.

In contrast with the way that Jack Cole remembers, then, extrafilmic accounts of Kelly continued to be mediated by uncertainty as to whether or not he was 'dancing in the right way'. The rhetorical strategy of making him appear 'safe', as Hirschhorn puts it, by measuring Kelly's virility against the suspicious effeminacy of the 'sissy dancer', constructed his star image in response to the presumption that a man dancing immediately troubles normative masculinity, even if he does it in a sailor suit. No doubt as far as Kelly himself was concerned, defensiveness about being a sissy because he danced had an autobiographical source; as his interviews stated, with dancing shoes in hand, he gave taunting kids a black eye to prove he could give better than he got (see, for instance, Proctor 1943: 37; Skolsky 1954), and he often declared, as reported at his 1985 AFI tribute, that what he had really wanted to do was play professional baseball, not dance for a living.

For Kelly's star image, though, the ambiguity about what to see when he danced was more ideologically loaded. As Ramsay Burt explains in his book on masculinity and ballet, the prejudicial dismissal of a male dancer for being a sissy not only assumes that dancing is an emasculating activity, but it perceives it as such through the secondary postulate that '"effeminate" is a code word for homosexual' (Burt 1995: 12). In Kelly's case, the extrafilmic commentary refers to that assumption by being obliged to declare, in one way or another, that he is *not* a sissy dancer. But much more important, the cultural coding of the 'sissy dancer' as both effeminate and homosexual had a more specific historical meaning for Kelly's virile star image during his movie career. 'Effeminacy' was an indeterminate category; when invoked as a means of establishing his normality by describing just what he was *not*, the term made Kelly's image much less stable than is now readily apparent.

The indeterminate sissy

According to Burt, the prejudice against men dancing theatrically did not exist until the early twentieth century, when professional dance began to give prominence to men. This prejudicial view 'did not … arise because of any actual belief that male dancers were homosexual', but from a cultural need to 'police any infringement of heterosexual norms' occurring through the visual objectification of the male dancer (Burt 1995: 28). The prejudicial stereotype of the sissy dancer as effeminate and homosexual worked to safeguard heteronormality by equating gender and sexuality: male dancers were perceived as homosexual because they were seen as effeminate, and they appeared this way because they were presumed to be homosexual. Based in this circular reasoning, the stereotype obscured how gender and sexuality were ideological categories with unequal cultural histories. As Alan Sinfield points out,

Effeminacy preceded the category of the homosexual, overlapped with and influenced the period of its development, and has continued in potent interaction with it. To run the two together prematurely is to miss the specificity of their relation, both in historical sequence and as they overlap. (Sinfield 1994: 78)

Sinfield analyses the history of the effeminate homosexual – the dandy – in British culture prior to and following the publicised trial of Oscar Wilde, but his cautionary observation has relevance for a parallel development in the US, where the equivalence of 'effeminacy' and 'homosexuality', now culturally axiomatic, had a comparable uneven history. In his documentation of gay social life in New York City during the first four decades of the twentieth century, George Chauncey records how the ideological weight of sexuality and gender as mutually informing categories of identity varied according to class location. The category of 'gender' did not correspond to or determine sexual practices for urban working-class culture, as was already the case for the middle class (Chauncey 1994: 48). Effeminacy or manliness, not homosexual or heterosexual activity, served to make visible differences among working men, dividing them according to who were 'fairies' and who were 'normal'. By contrast, pre-war middle-class culture equated 'manliness' with 'exclusive heterosexuality', privileging object choice over demeanour (Chauncey 1994: 116–17).

The instability of 'effeminacy' and 'manliness' as cultural categories was powerfully evident at mid-century in the contradictory reasoning of official military policy regarding the exclusion of homosexuals during World War Two. A ground-breaking 1942 regulation instructed examiners at induction centres to look for outward signs of 'gender deviance' (Bérubé 1990: 19). This policy, concerned with a man's ability to fight in combat, was 'based on exaggerated stereotypes of both the combat soldier and the sissy "queer"' (Bérubé 1990: 176). The 'sissy queer', set in opposition to the 'combat soldier', provided the index through which the army screened out homosexuals under the assumption that they were visibly different because of their gender demeanour, so it seemed to follow that a 'dancer' – like 'interior decorator' and 'window dresser' – was an effeminate profession, instantly signalling men who had 'difficulty with their "acceptance of the male pattern"' (Bérubé 1990: 20). Soon after the 1942 regulation was issued, the military incorporated into its screening methods the medical establishment's psychological view that 'effeminacy' was a 'personality trait' identifying homosexuals absolutely (and pathologically) as 'pseudo men who did not fit the profile of the masculine, aggressive soldier', because they were 'womanly in their bodies, mannerisms, makeup, and interests' (Bérubé 1990: 157, 156).

Predictably, the screening process produced contradictory results. The policy governing it conformed to middle-class ideology in theory, treating gender and sexuality as equivalent identity categories, but the procedure itself followed working-class ideology in practice, determining who was fit and who was not according to whether they appeared manly or effeminate. The screening process could therefore target 'sissy' men who happened to be heterosexual while passing over 'masculine, aggressive' homosexuals whose physical appearance belied the psycho-sexual profile and who went on to function for the military as perfectly capable soldiers.

In fact, according to veterans that Charles Kasier interviewed for his history of modern gay culture, many homosexual men enlisted just to prove their 'manhood' in the face of the prevailing belief that 'all homosexuals are effeminate'. When these men enlisted, 'despite the elaborate new regulations developed to discriminate against gays in the army, the only obstacle many of them encountered at induction centres was the

"Do you like girls?" question' (Kasier 1997: 32). Certainly, the need to maintain sizeable armed forces during the war accounted for the willingness of officials to simplify the screening process, turning 'a blind eye to almost anyone who was willing to put up the right front for the three minutes or less that the standard interview took' (Loughery 1998: 137). But while filling quotas may have been the motive, the lack of a uniform cultural agreement about 'effeminacy' and 'manliness' made each an indeterminate sign, capable of blurring rather than equating the categories of gender and sexuality, which enabled the military's scrutinising if hypocritical eye to be so easily blinded.

Within the same-sex environment of military life, furthermore, the effeminate/manly dualism that structured wartime masculine culture enabled just as much as it regulated gender and sexual irregularities. The military had to depend upon many of the same professions that, considered effeminate at the time of induction, supposedly signalled a homosexual personality for the screening process. Routine duties such as 'male secretary, typist, or stenographer' labelled 'a man as gay' but were nevertheless crucial to the bureaucratic infrastructure, so the men who performed these jobs were tolerated, even valued for their work, despite the sissy identification (Bérubé 1990: 61). This tolerance also extended to civilian professions like a dancer. One inducted gay stage performer, C. Tyler Carpenter, remembers that the proportion of show-business personnel drafted into the army 'far exceeded all other professions' (Carpenter and Yeatts 1996: 45). Whatever the veracity of his claim, it reflects the importance given to all-male army shows organised by local talent like Carpenter, which encouraged a visible drag subculture, often attracting 'heterosexual men who loved to entertain' even when that meant impersonating Gypsy Rose Lee (Carpenter and Yeatts 1996: 46).

On the other side of the coin, the proper gender demeanour was no surer an index of a GI's sexual behaviour. Despite occasional purges (the numbers increased in severity after the war), it was recognised that military life fostered 'deprivation' or 'situational' homosexuality (Costello 1985: 106; Loughery 1998: 141). In this setting thousands of men confronted their homosexuality and found a sense of community they had not imagined. But, as importantly, some men had sex with each other without necessarily thinking of themselves as homosexual afterward. Carpenter, for instance, recalls several trysts with a married lieutenant who 'preferred to cheat with men instead of women. There were many GIs like Buck – married soldiers who sought sex with other soldiers rather than the available whores' (Carpenter and Yeatts 1996: 131). Another way in which military culture gave primacy to same-sex bonds was the 'buddy system', which 'formally organised men into pairs' (Bérubé 1990: 188). This official practice encouraged close male friendships that, in their emotional intensity as well as official status, could rival with as well as substitute for heterosexual activity, even when physical intimacy was not a by-product.

The contradictions circumscribing military life as an unstable gendered institution and equally unstable sexualised environment were extreme, perhaps, a product of wartime; but these contradictions were not exceptional insofar as they manifested the lack of cultural consensus about perceptions of male normality more generally at mid-century. Kelly's star image, itself linked to the military through film roles that cast him as a sailor, soldier or veteran, registered comparable uneven overlapping of a gendered understanding of 'manliness' and 'effeminacy' and a sexualised one of 'heterosexuality' and 'homosexuality', and the sissy dancer encoded this indeterminacy in the extra-filmic commentary.

The lunch-counter incident from 1946 is again exemplary and for this reason worth a second look. The anecdote demonstrates that the real Kelly is more proletarian sailor than elitist movie star, authenticating his masculine identity in terms of gender. When the star claims he cannot be 'Gene Kelly' because he is obviously not a sissy dancer, he means that he has a manly demeanour like that of any other enlisted man and he proves it through his cocky performance, not his heterosexual orientation, which is taken for granted. But as already stated, because the waitress only perceives his ordinariness when she fails to see the actual star standing before her, the anecdote does not liberate 'dancer' from its pairing with 'sissy'. On the contrary, it leaves the loaded phrase 'sissy dancer' in place and attached to Kelly, whose appearance in the sailor suit remains juxtaposed to his professional identity as a movie star. In the story being recounted, Kelly and the waitress 'meet cute' around the same kind of misunderstanding that was a convention of musicals, his included. The story's premise, moreover, is that Kelly is already well known enough for him to be recognised as a star of musicals, so it calls upon awareness of the athletic, muscular body which those films feature in his dance numbers. On screen the star does not have an effeminate-looking body, so why should the question of his being a sissy dancer even arise? Unlike Kelly the sailor, Kelly the star troubles the gendered logic by which the waitress becomes convinced of his authenticity, raising suspicion that deviation from sexual norms may be the real issue. The anecdote does not automatically intimate homosexuality when it invokes the sissy dancer as the antithesis of 'Gene Kelly', but neither does it *not* do so. The anecdote can allow for either reading because 'sissy dancer' was not yet fixed to a single referent in the culture's thinking.

The wolf and his mouse

The gender-sexuality slippage condensed in the spectre of the 'sissy dancer' historically shaped the cultural valence of Gene Kelly's onscreen masculinity in his 1940s musicals. An early scene involving Kelly and co-star Frank Sinatra in *Anchors Aweigh*, in fact, displays much the same indeterminacy as the lunch-counter incident. *Anchors Aweigh* follows other Kelly musicals in teaming him with 'a meek and mild guy', as Donen described Sinatra's portrayal of this sidekick role (quoted in Hillier 1977: 27). The musical opens with Kelly's Joe Brady and Sinatra's Clarence Dolittle departing from their ship on a three-day pass. Although Joe intends to make a date with a former fling, Lola, once he reaches shore, Clarence continues to follow his friend after they arrive in Hollywood; each time Joe turns around to catch sight of Clarence tailing him, the latter smiles self-consciously and shyly waves. Joe finally confronts Clarence to ask about this shadowing act. It appears that Clarence, unlike his pal, is still a virgin – 'even in Brooklyn', he confesses, 'things can go wrong' – so he implores Joe, 'the best wolf in the navy', to help him out by 'getting him started'.

After much persuasion, Joe finally agrees and on the street poses as a 'dame' in order to sample Clarence's technique there and then. With one hand on his hip, the other limp-wristed and poised in midair, and broadly wiggling his body as he walks, Joe overacts the woman's part.[4] He looks like a swishy fairy picking up a sailor for trade, which is just what a passer-by thinks, causing the two friends to make a hasty retreat. 'Listen, Brooklyn', Joe advises after they have eluded the gaze of the passer-by, 'when you're going hunting it's how you feel that counts. You'll be looking for cheese and that's what you'll get. But if you feel like a wolf, nothing can go wrong.' While Joe gives mousey Clarence a lesson in how to perform as a wolfish male – 'you gotta feel manly' – it turns out that Joe himself is only passing as a wolf. He never does meet up with Lola, and instead spends the entire evening with Clarence when they tend to young Donald (Guy Stockwell), a runaway boy who wants to be a sailor, which leads them to meet his aunt and guardian, Susie (Kathryn Grayson). The next morning, when the sailors perform 'I Begged Her' to an audience of impressed servicemen, both are bragging about heterosexual conquests the night before that did *not* take place.

The scene on the street in *Anchors Aweigh* clearly means to establish a hierarchical ordering of Kelly's virile character and Sinatra's more effeminate one. As the 'mouse' to the other's 'wolf', Clarence enacts how the sissy functioned with respect to his manlier opposite. This 'pickup' scene stages the same kind of situation that Allan Bérubé describes when he reports how effeminate GIs frequently modelled their behaviour, as one veteran put it, on 'the roughest, toughest guy[s]', copying everything they did in order not to be labelled a 'sissy' or a 'fruit' (Bérubé 1990: 54). Here, Clarence is the one seeking instruction on how to meet a woman, which, in Joe's view, amounts to teaching the virgin how to appear manly. When that passer-by observes the two sailors on the street, though, his glance calls attention to the sexual disturbance which the buddies pose as a couple despite their gendered difference as wolf and mouse, since all the stranger sees is sexual sameness. As mediated by the perspective of this onlooker, the scene alludes to homosexual gossip about sailors, how they have long been part of a 'sexual folklore about men in uniform … because they were out at sea without women for long stretches of time, they were younger than men in the other branches and their tight uniforms looked boyish, revealing, and sexy' (Bérubé 1990: 110–11). If the passer-by sees the gender role-playing of the two sailors as a homosexual pickup, the scene raises the possibility that even Joe's wolfish virility may be more a matter of his only appearing to be straight – in fact, as far as the observer is concerned, Joe is the sissy sailor soliciting Clarence.

The scene consequently alludes to an ambiguous cultural context for representing the virility of Kelly's character in contrast with that of Sinatra's. It depicts the teaming of wolf and mouse in such a way as to intimate a confusion of gender (with sissy behaviour characterising a meek and mild effeminate guy who illuminates the wolf's virility) and sexuality (with the same sissy behaviour implying homoerotic desire that implicates the wolf, despite his virility). This confusion makes the sailors' close friendship, well, hard to read exactly because it can be viewed in sexualised or gendered terms. Whereas Joe himself stages the pickup as a lesson for Clarence in proper manly behaviour, the passer-by sees their encounter as a budding sexual transgression. More to the point, the film's spectator has to perceive the gap between the sailor's intention and the observer's interpretation in order to get the gag that ends the scene. Although the scene seems to be making a joke at the sissy's expense, its variable logic exceeds the manly/effeminate duality ostensibly characterising the two sailors, and the slippage in reference invites a camp perspective of Kelly's wolfish character and Sinatra's mousy one together.

Camping in the right way

Traditionally, a camp appreciation of the Hollywood musical has been equated almost exclusively with a gay subculture's longstanding fascination with the genre's great female stars – Judy Garland, Carmen Miranda, Esther Williams – and the excessive representation of femininity in their musical numbers. But camp is more than attraction to excessive artifice or veneration of star divas. Historically speaking, camp was the code of the closet, a rhetoric of passing – of queer men posing as straight by passing between the cultural categories of 'gender' and 'sexuality' and exploiting their slippage. Articulating a stance from which to reread mainstream culture from its margins, pre-Stonewall camp appropriated the terms of straight representation and deployed them for different ends (camaraderie, cruising, consuming), so it required of gay men a knowing, usually ironic awareness of the multiple codes regulating heteronormality. As Jack Babuscio puts it, 'camp resides largely in the eye of the beholder', which is to say that it 'is never a thing or person *per se*, but, rather, a relationship between activities, individuals, situations, *and* gayness' (Babuscio 1984: 40–1). As a cultural rhetoric of passing which depended upon the double meaning, camp is most recognisable as a style or aesthetic taste, slyly manifesting itself in the witty *effect*; but camp is, more subtly, also the production of a specific form of *affect*, a queer pleasure derived from causing or perceiving category dissonance in representations of gender and sexuality.

In the case of Kelly's musicals, for all his own disavowals of camp intent and declarations of heteronormality, gay men worked with him as artisans, choreographers, directors, writers, composers and co-stars.[5] As Matthew Tinkcom argues about the Freed Unit at MGM, a camp style of visual excess, closely associated with the studio's product as one of its key selling points, enabled Kelly's closeted co-workers to mark their labour as 'gay' and to make it more evident to audiences 'in the know', so to speak. This camp style produced what Tinkcom describes as the MGM musical's 'multivalence, in that it can be consumed by queer and non consumers alike for retaining camp features or not' (Tinkcom 2002: 46). But even putting aside questions of intentionality, the camp affect orchestrated by that multivalent style of MGM musicals was also brought to the films by the manly/effeminate dualism structuring Kelly's star image and condensed in the question of his being a sissy dancer, which historically determined how his dancing could be legible as a camp performance of manliness crossing the categories of gender and sexuality.

The Pirate (1948), critics now agree, most successfully realises the camp implication of Kelly's star image in relation to his dancing. In particular, 'The Pirate Ballet', as Richard Dyer notes, simultaneously functions as a 'turn-on', in the eroticisation of Kelly's body, costumed in black vest and cut-offs, and photographed primarily in full or three-quarter shots, and a 'send-up', in the equally obvious parody of heterosexual machismo which the choreography stages (Dyer 1986: 185). Kelly's display of hypermasculinity is so exciting yet parodic in this number that, judging from the close-up of Judy Garland which re-establishes her point of view after the ballet concludes, it appears to intoxicate her – or to give her a headache, one is never entirely sure from the expression on Garland's face.

Commenting on *The Pirate*, Jane Feuer agrees that Kelly's Serafin is 'highly eroticised' in this number, but goes on to mention that he is 'also coded as effeminate' (Feuer 1993: 143). In explanation, she states that he fails to be the 'fully phallic male', which the pirate represents in the fantasy of Garland's character, Manuela, and that he is simultaneously made the sexual object of her desire in the ballet. Serafin's masquerade as the notorious pirate, Macoco, Feuer goes on to say, results in a feminine reformulation of heterosexual masculinity, which has the residual effect of allowing Serafin to be readable as 'a gay icon'

Gene Kelly as Seraphin in *The Pirate* (Vincente Minnelli, 1948)

(ibid.). This does not make him a sissy dancer, however. Whether impersonating Macoco, performing as an actor, or wooing Manuela, Serafin does not exaggerate feminine characteristics, and neither does Kelly's dancing in achieving its hetero- and homoerotic impact. Feuer can nonetheless see in Kelly's Serafin an eroticised, effeminate male, even a gay icon, just as Dyer can view Kelly's dancing as half turn-on, half send-up, because, in both characterisation and performance, the figure's references to gender and sexuality do not fall into alignment, resulting in the ambiguity that the two critics describe. Male yet not entirely manly, heterosexual yet not fully heterosexualised, eroticised yet parodic, Serafin's own 'flaming trail of masculinity', to borrow from Manula's song about Macoco, cannot be fixed to a determinate meaning one way or the other.

Kelly's first solo number, 'Niña', makes perfectly clear that Serafin's masculinity can, in camp parlance, be 'flaming' without ceasing to represent him as male. The number begins with Serafin's celebration of his voyeurism in song. 'When I arrive in any town', he boasts, 'I look the ladies up and down.' The virtuoso dance that follows choreographs his heterosexual arrogance as an act of male exhibitionism. He climbs up a balcony to serenade one woman, turns away when he catches the eye of another, stretches his body backward, one leg in the air, as he makes love to this one, and continues in this same manner from woman to woman, throwing his body around the town square with great bravado, and much wiggling of hips and buttocks. At one point Kelly even takes a cigarette from a woman, rolls it inside his mouth before kissing her, and then exhales afterward! The female dancers, in turn, far from serving as objects of his desire, as the Cole Porter lyrics seem to avow, are instruments of the dance, directing his movement from one to the other, in effect appropriating his gaze.

As a result, Brett Farmer observes, Serafin 'assumes a "feminine" position of erotic objectification', so a 'position of desire for any one gender is thoroughly undermined'. But if the shifting specular dynamic of the choreography 'unleashes a wild eruption of communal desire', as Farmer describes it, that is because Kelly's dancing in 'Niña' visually draws the men of the village into its orbit as well as the women with whom he partners (Farmer 2000: 108). The number thus inescapably registers what Tinkcom calls the camp homoeroticism staged by 'the pleasure of Serafin with the spectacle of his own movement' (Tinkcom 2002: 67). Serafin, in fact, initially addresses the number to the men as his means of explaining why every female is the same to him, justifying his calling them all 'Niña', the generic 'girl'. Throughout the number, when Kelly uses his eyes, face, arms or torso to draw the other dancers toward him through mime, his movement continually directs the attention of everyone watching – men and women, on screen and off – to his body as a source of ambiguous sexuality: is Serafin performing more for the women, the men or himself? The answer is all of the above, since 'Niña' characterises Serafin as an arrogant, insincere, narcissistic seducer more interested in the game (and the gaze) than its outcome.

At the number's conclusion, however, Serafin poses before a banner advertising his troupe, so the dance can immediately be re-read as self-conscious enactment of male posturing, a form of advertising meant to promote the actor himself as the spectacle worth watching. Serafin's objective in the number from the start may simply have been to solicit an audience of men and women for that evening's performance of his show. Watching 'Niña' as a camp exhibition of ambiguous eroticism embedded in a gender masquerade of machismo – each put in quote marks, so to speak, by the number's purpose as advertising for the theatrical troupe – is in perfect accord with *The Pirate*'s plot, which never relieves Serafin from the need to perform his masculinity in some outrageous fashion.

The exhilarating flamboyance of Kelly's performance in *The Pirate* is not limited to this musical but can be seen in his other films of the 1940s too. In *Anchors Aweigh*, for instance, the dancer's big solo numbers deploy choreographic conceits similar to those in *The Pirate*, and Kelly's dancing in these numbers challenge Joe's outwardly 'safe' position as the virile 'wolf' contrasting with Clarence's sissified 'mouse'. Once Kathryn Grayson's character, Susie, triangulates the buddy relation, *Anchors Aweigh* goes on to differentiate the two male stars in musical terms. Whereas formerly they sang and danced together in three numbers, Sinatra now starts to sing solos and Kelly to dance them; but whereas Sinatra, the idol of 1940s bobbysoxers, croons of romance to turn into the film's straight man, Kelly now dances to express the childishness, vulnerability and dreaminess previously exhibited by Sinatra's character, turning into the film's not-so-straight man.

In the most famous of these, 'The Worry Song', Jerry the Mouse succeeds Sinatra as Kelly's dance partner. Young Donald asks his idol Joe for an account of his Silver Medal and the sailor gives a fanciful version, telling Donald and the latter's classmates to close their eyes and imagine what he narrates. A dissolve on the boy's face marks the transition to the number's animated setting, where Joe discovers he is not allowed to sing or dance because, a squirrel informs him, 'there's a law, there's a law, there's a law!' 'I'll sing and dance where 'ere I will/No law on Earth can keep me still', the sailor defiantly exclaims in verse. Since King Jerry has banned music from his kingdom because he himself cannot sing or dance, much as he does with Clarence on the street, Joe helps the mouse by getting him started.

With its mixing of cartoon and live action, 'The Worry Song' redefines what dancing means for Kelly's wolf in *Anchors Aweigh*. This number eroticises Kelly as none of the previous duets with Sinatra have done. Forsaking the black sailor uniform he sports at other times in the film, Kelly wears a brightly coloured striped T-shirt that displays his muscular build and white sailor pants that stretch tightly across his crotch, thighs and buttocks. The choreography then features Kelly's eroticised body as the object of spectacle dominating the animation. He performs a number of gymnastic steps that push him forward and backward in space; he bounces Jerry from bicep to bicep, slides the mouse down his leg, swings him in the air, under his legs, dances over him.

The camp affect of the choreography derives from its eroticisation of Kelly, which exceeds the number's narrative purpose and diegetic address as a child's fantasy of what the sailor narrates. For although 'The Worry Song' means to visualise how Kelly's dancing liberates him from gravity and other earthly constraints much as pen and ink do for a cartoon mouse, the number's eroticisation of the dancer's body is not necessarily heterosexualised in its aim or energy; after all, he *is* dancing with a male mouse and the number *is* being imagined by a boy. Far from making Kelly seem effeminate when turned into a spectacular object, 'The Worry Song' celebrates his virility and directs appreciation of it to viewers of any gender since this number's use of space and camera angles is not in any way reflective of or bound to the heterosexualised gaze of a diegetic female spectator.

Numbers such as 'The Worry Song' and 'Niña' are typical of how Kelly appears in his musicals of the 1940s: not as a sissy dancer but a very sexy one who can as easily lose as perform his heterosexuality when dancing and yet still signify maleness. To be sure, the athleticism of Kelly's dancing, like the aggression in his screen persona, is a means of compensating for the spectatorial attention to his body which his solo numbers require and actively solicit by making his body the main focus of attention. As if to go out of his way to prove he is not a sissy dancer, Kelly's choreography often overemphasises his gendered demeanour in accordance with what Stephan Prock analyses as the dancer's 'developing "masculine" aesthetic' (Prock 2000: 315). Hence the costumes that accentuate Kelly's well-built torso, the mixture of formal dance moves (tap, ballroom, ballet) with athletic stunt work or ordinary physical movement in order to give the precision of dance weightier connotations of muscularity and strength, the medley of contrasting orchestral arrangements of the music to keep redirecting the rhythm of his motion and establish his body as an expressive tool, and the exaggeration of gestures that calls as much attention to his arms and face as his feet. But while Kelly's solos display such conventional tropes of manliness in film after film, so that Donen's retrospective description of his collaborator as a dancer with balls seems quite apt, the numbers also take their choreographic conceits from self-conscious underlining of those tropes, redefining their value for camp affect through the eroticisation of Kelly's body. Donen's description then seems all the more fitting, though with a very different implication. Indeed, that Prock sees Kelly's dancing 'rigorously *resisting* objectification' (Prock 2000: 315, my emphasis) while I see the dancing *performing* it well catches the camp dynamic of gender/sexual 'passing' which informs the choreography.

Whether Kelly is miming seduction with a prop, mugging before children, or leaping and climbing tall ladders and high buildings almost as readily as he taps and spins, the solos in his 1940s musicals engage him in gender hyperbole, while investing his body with equally pronounced erotic value for a viewer. In acknowledging his spectacular value as camp for its contrast with his 'ordinary Joe' persona, furthermore, many of Kelly's 1940s films find a correlative for the affect of his dancing in the tradition of swashbuckling action stars such as Douglas Fairbanks, whom Kelly reportedly took as his inspiration for *The Pirate*: Kelly plays a former circus trapeze artist in *Thousands Cheer* (1943), Black Arrow, a Zorro type, in the long fantasy segment of *DuBarry Was a Lady* (1943), another Zorro-styled bandit in a solo dance in *Anchors Aweigh*, and finally, D'Artagnan in the non-musical remake of Fairbanks' *Three Musketeers* (1948). Although *The Pirate* contributed most to Kelly's 'reputation as the Douglas Fairbanks of dance' (Harris 1996), these other films similarly presume that Kelly was perceived as a 1940s-styled 'matinee idol' because of his dancing, and that he could be read straight or as camp.

Singin' in the Rain, in which Kelly plays a silent-movie star, Don Lockwood, also modelled after Fairbanks, shares this presumption. An actual scene from Kelly's *Three Musketeers* is even included to represent Lockwood's own silent epic, *The Royal Rascal*. However, when *Singin' in the Rain* quotes from its star's career and links this past to Lockwood's, the film disavows the ambiguous eroticism of Kelly's 1940s image in what has to be seen as a conscious effort to efface its camp inflection as played out by the star's earlier musicals. Inserted in *Singin' in the Rain* to epitomise Lockwood's hammy overacting through his body, the footage of Kelly's D'Artagnan is recontextualised and underlined as a pseudo-camp quotation in order to devalue the fictional star for being a 'matinee idol' – the very trap that, a decade after the release of *Singin' in the Rain*, Richard Griffith said Kelly himself could have fallen into if he were not an ordinary Joe. *Singin' in the Rain* reinvents Lockwood as an ordinary Joe by transforming him into a song-and-dance man just like Gene Kelly, or more precisely, the film uses Lockwood to revise Kelly's camp masculinity according to the alignment of gender and sexuality that, as I have argued elsewhere, became hegemonic in the 1950s (Cohan 1997).

That Kelly is now primarily remembered as an unproblematic representation of normative masculinity is in no small part due to the impact of *Singin' in the Rain*. This film's fame has further detached its leading man and director from the gender-sexual ambiguity of his 1940s star image and the camp affect of his dancing. 'More than any star, I think,' Fred Astaire states in *That's Entertainment*, 'Gene Kelly became the symbol of the MGM musical of the 1950s.' The symbolic association of Kelly and MGM through *Singin' in the Rain* is still entrenched in the popular imagination. Until his death, interviews in print and television, newspaper and magazine articles, and documentary programmes confirmed Kelly's role as elder statesman of the MGM musical; this role also became increasingly more prominent with each issue of the *That's Entertainment* franchise, and it was further validated by the critical canonisation of *Singin' in the Rain* and Kelly's status as its *auteur*. A shot of Kelly dancing in the rain now instantly stands for 'MGM musical' when inserted in a compilation of clips or used to promote Turner Classic Movies on cable as much as it represents his own stardom. Decades before he became the poster boy of the studio's Golden Age, however, Kelly's star image raised an entirely different set of meanings for his dancing.

Notes

1   Untitled magazine clipping, October–November 1946, no source; Gene Kelly clipping file, Margaret Herrick Library of the Academy of Motion Pictures Arts and Sciences. The anecdote appears as a lengthy caption to a signed photo of Kelly and is probably from a Sunday newspaper supplement such as *Parade*. It goes on to recount a second sort of self-effacing imposture, mentioning 'how he even fooled his [future] wife once', when, trying out for a job at Billy Rose's Diamond Horseshoe supper club, Betsy Blair mistook him for 'that janitor – or stagehand', not the revue's dance director.

2   Most notably, in 1958 Kelly hosted an episode of NBC's *Omnibus* entitled 'Dancing – A Man's Game', which was designed to support the star's oft-repeated assertion that 'any man who looks sissy while dancing … is just a lousy dancer' (Hirschhorn 1984: 225). See Gerstner 2002 for a thoughtful examination of the programme's aesthetic and cultural politics, which resulted in a highly problematic realisation of Kelly's aim to depict 'the creative process *as a process of masculinisation* that stressed the male-as-artist was not an effeminate creature' (Gerstner 2002: 59).

3   On the sailor used as a distinctive American type in Kelly's choreography as well as Jerome Robbins', see Genné 2001.

4   There are similar moments of Kelly doing this type of broad impersonation of a fairy in *Cover Girl* (1943) and *On the Town* but not to the extent of this scene in *Anchors Aweigh*.

5   On the history of queer labour at MGM, specifically in the Arthur Freed unit where Kelly did much of his work, see Ehrenstein 1998: 181–3; Mann 2001: 170–82; and Tinkcom 2002: 35–71.

chapter 2

HE IS AS HE IS – AND ALWAYS WILL BE: CLARK GABLE AND THE REASSERTION OF HEGEMONIC MASCULINITY

Timothy Connelly

The onset of the Great Depression caused a crisis at all levels of American culture. While emerging as an economic crisis, the subsequent job losses set in motion a range of events that suggested the demise of the American way of life. Declining marriage and birth rates seemed to herald the end of the family.[1] Massive job loss and the occurrence of a number of highly publicised strikes and riots signalled the end of working life as it had existed.[2] And the lengthening breadlines and regular sight of men out of work and on the street pointed to the demise of something less tangible: American masculinity.

This image of the out-of-work man walking the breadline or standing, waiting for work, coalesces many of the tensions and anxieties about the depression. As a site where both the social and economic impact of the depression come together; the image of the jobless man points to where the problem of the depression was seen the most – on the male body – and seemed to weigh the most – on masculinity. Traditional forms of masculinity, those defined through the workplace and the home as well as the enjoyment of a consumer culture, were increasingly seen as insufficient or even destructive in the face of the upheaval both through the inability of men to find or hold jobs as well as through the perception of a causal relationship between lifestyles of the 1920s and the economic crisis.

It is in this general context of a crisis of masculinity in the depression that Clark Gable becomes popular, and important. As his title later in the decade comes to mark, Gable was indeed 'The King' and, as such, the masculinity he represented was seen by many as the exemplar of Depression-era manhood. Premised on his virility and aggressiveness, it is generally held that Gable's popularity in the 1930s was due to the way in which this virility and aggressiveness presented him as one who could represent the common man against the forces of the depression. As Joe Fisher notes in his discussion of Gable's role in *It Happened One Night* (Frank Capra, 1934):

This quality is found, essentially, in the nature of Gable's/Peter's masculinity: in an 'integrity' which cannot be easily overcome because it represents an independent and incorruptible manhood, big and strong enough to take on corporate America and win: at least in the terms of the parable presented here. (Fisher 1993: 41)

This description of the power of Gable is rather typical in the way that it understands him in the context of the Depression. Generally focusing on *It Happened One Night* and *Gone With the Wind* (Victor Fleming, 1939), while mentioning other films, these readings present Gable as the virile everyman who gets on in spite of everything else. While this is at its base a valid interpretation of the power of Gable and his masculinity, such renderings ignore other contexts of his stardom, in particular the status of his work in the woman's film from 1931 to 1934. Furthermore, in the period from 1931–34, the fan press works to stabilise and masculinise Gable's persona so that he can emerge, with *It Happened One Night* and after, as the iconic representative of Depression-era manhood. By presenting Gable simply as the everyman hero, however, renditions of Gable's masculinity and popularity that ignore his work prior to 1934 fail to account for the

Clark Gable (Rodney) and Greta Garbo (Susan Lenox) in *Susan Lenox: Her Fall and Rise* (Robert Z. Leonard, 1931)

more complex negotiations being performed in his star text, particularly in its early stages, between positions of class and gender. Motivated by the woman's films' own negotiations of the same positions, the masculinity of Clark Gable does come to represent a position of working-class masculine authority, but does not simply nor easily occupy it.

1931 marked Gable's debut with MGM in over twelve films, most notably opposite Greta Garbo in *Susan Lenox: Her Fall and Rise* (Robert Z. Leonard), Norma Shearer in *A Free Soul* (Clarence Brown) and Joan Crawford in both *Laughing Sinners* (Harry Beaumont) and *Possessed* (Clarence Brown). These films, his most popular of that year, situate Gable as *the* male romantic lead for MGM in the early 1930s.[3] His work in the woman's film continues in 1932 with *Red Dust* (Victor Fleming) opposite Jean Harlow, and *Strange Interlude* (Robert Z. Leonard) with Norma Shearer. In 1933 he repeats what will become a common pairing with Joan Crawford in *Dancing Lady* (Robert Z. Leonard), a pairing followed up in 1934 with two other films opposite Crawford: *Chained* (Clarence Brown) and *Forsaking All Others* (W. S. VanDyke).

In the context of his work to this date, then, *It Happened One Night* stands as something of an aberration among Gable's film, an aberration generated through his being loaned out to Columbia. So, while the film may indeed solidify or codify some of the elements of the Gable persona, in particular his status as the working-class hero of the New Deal, to focus solely on *It Happened One Night* without consideration of Gable's work in the previous three years misses the development of Gable's masculine persona as it is classed within the context of the woman's film in conjunction with his role as a leading romantic figure.

The woman's film, films featuring narratives which revolve around a female protagonist and are designed to appeal to a mostly female audience, generally involve a conflict in which interpersonal relationships present the heroine with a dilemma whose resolution usually entails loss.[4] These films have often been read as either reinforcing or criticising the cultural double-bind of relationships that require the female partner to suffer the loss. Lea Jacobs shows how variants of the 'fallen woman' film, a subset of the woman's film that many of the early Gable films belong to, developed out of their literary antecedents and through the 1920s to emerge, in the 1930s, with 'a new emphasis on social mobility, and hence female aggressivity' (Jacobs 1991: 15). Additionally, she shows how 'the downward trajectory of the fall' of the female protagonist so common in earlier versions of the fallen woman narrative is 'replaced by a rise in class' in the fallen woman films (Jacobs 1991: 11). The fallen woman films of the 1930s thus negotiate questions of both class and female sexuality as they interrelate with one another through the figure of the female protagonist, often conflating one with the other.[5]

Within these films, men often work narratively to cause the female protagonist's fall and they do so regardless of whether they are the romantic partner of the woman or the 'villain' of the film. Gable's position in the woman's film of the early 1930s is, however, distinct from those of other male co-stars or secondary players in that he often occupies a position similar to the female protagonist's. Unlike other woman's films where the object of romantic desire remains either oblivious to, unconcerned by, or completely above the social restraints that control the sexual desire of the female protagonist, Gable repeatedly shares in her displays of desire, frustration and inability to choose or act. In his films, Gable remains devoted to the woman he loves regardless of the suffering it may cause him; and his suffering is often displayed on screen for the audience to see.

In *Susan Lenox: Her Fall and Rise*, for example, Susan (Garbo) runs away from home when her arranged husband attempts to rape her. She then meets and falls in love with Rodney (Gable), an engineer. While he is away presenting designs for a bridge, Susan's father locates her, causing her to run away again. With nowhere else to go, she joins the circus as a model. While there, she is forced to sleep with the owner in exchange for him not giving information about her to her father. Rodney finally catches up with her, but, finding that she has slept with another man, he walks out on her condemning her for her 'gold-digging' life and loose ways. She decides to live up to his condemnation of her life and proceeds to sleep her way, quite literally, to the penthouse.

Up to this point, and even with the ensuing fall of Susan from her glamorous life, the film retains the narrative structure of a typical fallen woman film. After the point at which he walks out on her, however – that is, for the final third of the film – there is also an emphasis on Rodney's suffering as the jilted lover. He loses one job working on a construction site when a bridge he designed collapses as a result of his neglect due to alcoholism, and he is unemployed when Susan plans to humiliate him in front of her friends. She arranges to have him invited to a dinner party without him knowing that she is the hostess. During the dinner, she chastises Rodney – via a story about 'a friend' – for walking out on her and not thinking that she could still be in love with him. He, however, is able to turn the joke around on her with the revelation of his suffering as a result of their separation. He divulges his feelings about her and their relationship and leaves the party, leaving her to walk out on her patron and follow him, eventually, to South America where he is still running from her and their love.

In this film, then, we have Gable as a romantic hero who does not just walk out on his lover when she is unfaithful, never to return. Nor does his life go on as usual while he waits for her to realise the extent of their relationship. Rather, the film narrativises the fall of Rodney, from wealthy engineer to poor South American miner, as well as Susan's. In this way the film presents a dual trajectory of decline in which the masculine hero falls as hard and as far as the female protagonist.

Possessed offers a similar depiction of the Gable character though it does so by presenting itself somewhat backhandedly as a parody of the woman's film. The film suggests that it is doing something different with the genre, specifically with the female protagonist. I would also contend that it is, similarly to *Susan Lenox*, doing something different with Clark Gable's male lead.

With its opening, the film presents itself as fully aware of the conventions of its genre as a fallen woman film. Early in the film, Marian (Joan Crawford), a factory girl, stops to watch a train go by on her way home from work. In the windows of the train she sees passing before her images of an 'upper class' life: servants preparing dinner, a couple dining together, and another dancing in eveningwear. Finally she meets a wealthy New Yorker riding at the end of the train who begins a discussion with her.

The trajectory of their discussion makes the viewer aware that the film knows its genres. Wally (Skeets Gallagher) offers Marian champagne, joking, 'Can city slicker tempt smalltown girl with liquor?' When she claims to want to move to the city in order to have a better life, in other words to marry a millionaire, he feigns surprise, 'You mean to tell me that you don't have a sick mother at home who needs you?' While Marian eventually does go to New York City, where she meets and becomes the mistress of politician Mark Whitney (Gable), this interchange reveals the way in which the film is aware of its own narrative trajectory – or at least what that trajectory should be – as the film then shifts the terms of Marian's fall in the city. And in shifting the terms of Marian's fall, the film presents us with a masculine figure in Gable's Whitney that is again distinct from the romantic partner in similar films.

Most significantly, the narrative of the film turns on Whitney's resistance to marrying Marian, but not because he is a typical 'big bad city slicker'. Rather, Whitney refuses to marry out of pride. He has been married before and his first wife humiliated him publicly, and also clearly caused him emotional pain, by having an affair with their chauffeur. Thus, while the narrative result is the same as in other fallen woman films – the man refuses to marry the protagonist – this film evokes some sympathy for Whitney and his reasons for not getting married. The lengths to which this 'humiliation' is discussed in the film, coupled with the fact that he clearly loves Marian, lends more sympathy to the character than he might otherwise warrant as a 'sugar daddy'.

Furthermore, when Whitney's colleagues approach him about running for the governorship of New York State, they do so with the recommendation that he leave Marian before he announces his candidacy so as to avoid a scandal over their relationship. He refuses their offer, willing to sacrifice his career and standing for their relationship. Marian, however, finds out about his sacrifice and pretends not to love him anymore. In this way she can leave him, allowing him to run for governor. He does run and in the course of the campaign they are reunited when the scandal over their relationship is revealed but defused by Marian.

What is most interesting about the final third of the film, though, is that the focus from the moment of Whitney's decision not to run until the end of the film is as much on him and his suffering as a result of their decisions as it is on her. The burden of their relationship, and the social contradictions it imposes, are seen to be equally shared by the partners as the film moves towards its resolution.

In these ways we see how Gable's characters often occupy a position resembling more closely that of the traditional female protagonist of the woman's film than is usual with other male leads. In addition to providing the romantic partner, Gable repeatedly offers a version of masculinity that recognises and shares in the suffering caused by sexual desire in the modern age, a sexual desire that cannot, because of the rules of society, express itself freely or fully. The woman's film turns around the frustrated expression of female sexual desire and Gable is able to emerge in the genre as romantic hero who suffers alongside and for his lover.

It is the woman's film then that links these questions of sexual desire with those of class mobility and status. As mentioned, Jacobs notes how the films of the 1930s turn questions of sexual prowess into those of class mobility, and so it is no surprise that his prominence in these films is part of what imparts upon Gable the classing of his persona. While in most if not all of his films Gable plays characters who are anything but working-class, he does emerge from them with a decidedly working-class inflection. And while this comes from the work in fan magazines and other outlets to present him in such a way, it is also his placement within the genre of the woman's film that affects this reading of his masculinity.

The suffering that Gable accrues through his place in these films further reinforces the working-class nature of his masculinity through its resonance with the status of suffering in the depression as a whole. Just as the films in which Gable stars in the early part of the 1930s are melodramatically concerned with the morality of suffering, so the culture as a whole in the depression gave suffering an equally melodramatic and moral reading, especially in relation to the working classes. And it is in the fan press from 1931 to 1934 that we can see the transition in the Gable persona from suffering and devoted romantic hero to virile working-class man most clearly.

Two articles from *Photoplay* in 1932, both by regular columnist Ruth Biery, demonstrate this shift. In an article entitled 'I'm Not So Sure' from January of that year, only shortly after *Possessed* had been released and while it was probably still playing in some theatres, Biery begins thus: 'The bare facts of Clark Gable's life have been written before. But what was happening inside the lad's head and his heart has never been told' (Biery 1932a: 69). The article then describes Gable as a suffering man with 'the heart of a poet, the physique of a Dempsey' and claims that all of the struggles he has endured in his life result from this dual nature: 'his great sensitivity to art and beauty was always warring with the two-fisted training of his father' (ibid.). Mobilising the tropes of the woman's film, this article casts him as the internally suffering romantic hero he was playing at the time trapped in the body of a boxer. These two sides are reconciled, however, in the fan press by shifting the focus there away from the romantic hero inside and onto the body outside.

Thus, in the later article entitled 'Will Clark Gable Last?', from August 1932, when it is clear Gable is becoming a big star, Biery defends him from accusations he is nothing more than a 'personality boy' with neither real acting talent nor range. She does so by establishing that Gable, in fact, cannot play a range of characters. Rather, 'he is as he is – and always will be. Versatility is the ability to change with each characterisation a screen story demands – to feel as if one were a hundred different people. Of that Clark Gable is almost incapable' (Biery 1932b: 67). Gable cannot and will not change. No matter the circumstances, what you see is what you get.

And what you get is the physically attractive and sexually desiring and desirable Clark Gable. Biery goes on to describe Gable as 'the epitome of the ruthless, handsome, knock-'em-down, treat-'em-rough, virile, modern cave man. And not only the women in Keokuk and Medicine Hat went crazy about Clark, but the actresses in Hollywood as well' (ibid.). Suggesting that lust for Gable is not just a product of the screen but something affecting even the greatest of Hollywood actresses, the article situates Gable as the natural embodiment of desirable manhood. Thus this second article suggests continuity between the interior and exterior of the man by reframing and masking the interior of the persona. Suffering and devotion here are turned into lust and sex through a focus on the desirable and constant body of Clark Gable.

This focus on the natural virility of Gable then comes to dominate discussion of him in the pages of *Photoplay* magazine. In addition to describing the background of Gable as that of a hard-working travelling man, articles come to emphasise both the sexual prowess of Gable as well as his 'down-to-earth' nature and status as a 'man's man'. Some examples of this type of fan article include one from 1933 on 'How 12 Stars Make Love'. The entry for Gable makes it clear: 'His technique is brusque, direct, almost savage at times. The elemental male who recognises his physical and spiritual hungers and goes out spontaneously to satisfy them.' And later, 'He "treats 'em rough" because it is his instinct to do so – the instinct of the vigorous, self-assertive, conquering male' (Lynn 1933b: 104).

This discussion of the sexual power of Gable is echoed in another article from March of the same year, 1933. 'Which Movie Star Dominates You?' begins by making the distinction that 'there are two normal classifications into which most normal women will fall: Those who want to be dominated by their men. Those who want to do the dominating. Women who want to be possessed. Or women who want to possess' (Lynn 1933a: 102). The article then types actors for their ability to dominate women and Gable leads the first grouping:

Type I: The masterful, dominating male: assured, self-assertive, highly-satisfactory lover. (a) The rough, tough, two-fisted, direct he-man lover. He knows what he wants and goes after it in somewhat primitive fashion. Examples: Clark Gable, Jimmy Cagney, Johnny Weismuller, Chester Morris. (ibid.)

While this shows again the way in which Gable's virility and masculinity are figured as both dominating and natural, it also suggests that he was not alone in presenting a masculinity as such, though the types of films Gable had been making up until this point are decidedly different from those of the other actors. While he had played some gangsters, he was not known as one, nor did his roles overtly suggest a savagery like those of Weismuller. These other actors were in many ways either threatening or inaccessible to the women around them: Gable was not.

The continued reference to the 'natural' virility and stability of the Gable persona worked to imbue Gable with a 'commonness' that distanced him from the glamour of other stars at MGM and we can see that by 1935, the year after *It Happened One Night*, descriptions of Gable in *Photoplay* are fully developing the working-class persona he will emerge with after the film. For example one article describes Gable thus: 'Gable has had his ears well beaten down by short-lived one-night-stand fames, wetted down by disappointments. He had considered himself set once on Broadway and found himself shagging the sidewalks the next month hunting a job' (Greene 1935: 24). Later, the article refers to Gable's past as a factory worker, oil driller and mountain engineer. The continual reference to his hard-working, travelling the country history (other articles note his work as a timekeeper, a lumberjack, an oil-field labourer) further strengthens his position as a working-class hero, drawing him as the hobo who has come in off the rails to make a life in the movies.

This naturalness and stability of person and persona then anchor the working-class masculinity Gable performs and hold it in concert with the more traditional virility and aggressive power of masculinity. This stability is further reinforced through his consistent pairings with the 'great actresses' of MGM, in particular Joan Crawford. Seen already by the early 1930s as a changing and reinventing persona, their constant pairing, with her roles changing yet his remaining very similar, serves to heighten the perception of Gable as a stable and constant source of authoritative masculinity.

The stability seems to have won out. Gable is indeed the icon of 1930s masculinity, but an icon forged through the careful reinforcement of his natural, primitive status as 'man' and articulated in film through a context of the woman's film with its emphasis on classed, suffering subjectivities. Out of these contexts, Gable, paradoxically, is able to emerge as the virile, aggressive, man's man: 'as he is – and always will be'.

Notes

1   See Mintz and Kellogg 1988, especially chapter 7, and Kessler-Harris 1982, especially chapter 9, for more information about the problems of the American family in the Depression.

2   By 1933 the unemployment rate had reached 25 per cent (McElvaine 1984: 75).

3   While all did well at the box office, *A Free Soul* can be considered Gable's 'break-out' role and was later touted as such by MGM.

4   For definitions of the woman's film in the 1930s see Haskell 1974; Jacobs 1991; and Basinger 1993.

5   One can think of the famous series of images from *Baby Face* (Alfred E. Green, 1934) of the protagonist's 'sleeping her way to the top' being represented through a series of shots moving up the outside of the bank where she works, to see how this occurs. Her sexual encounters and class rise are brought together in the shots so that one implies and motivates the other.

chapter 3

FRAMING THE WOLF: THE SPECTACULAR MASCULINITY OF ALAIN DELON

Graeme Hayes

Recently, a growing number of academic studies have begun to focus on the role and importance of stars in French cinema (Gauteur and Vincendeau 1993; Maillot 1996; Vincendeau 2000b; Austin 2003), with one of the most interesting examples being the identity and significance of Alain Delon. The major discussions of the meaning of his screen persona primarily place his emergence in the late 1950s along with Jean-Paul Belmondo (whose career has developed in tandem with Delon's and with whom he is frequently contrasted) in the context of changes in the French social structure, revolving around a fascination with American culture and the development of a modernising, consumerist society (for example, Forbes 1992). In Pierre Maillot's rather pessimistic analysis, in fact, there is a sense of social and geographical dislocation contained within the Delon character which, as with Belmondo, is symptomatic not only of the advent of consumer society but also of a betrayal of French values (Maillot 1996: 170–1). For Ginette Vincendeau, in contrast, Delon is less an agent of change than of continuity. She argues that Delon, and indeed Belmondo also, should be seen within the context of a national-cultural paradigm of 'ambiguous masculinity' dating back to Jean Gabin,

> incorporating 'feminine' vulnerability in macho and essentially misogynist figures and, when they reached middle age, by fitting into the father/daughter pattern, whereby they acted as sexual and paternal partners to young women. (Vincendeau 2000: 185)

The argument that will be developed here agrees that Delon is a significant figure for the construction of French national and masculine identities, but takes a different tack, focusing on his importance within the framework set by the French *film policier,* or crime film, the most prolific of genres in post-war France. Of French actors, Delon is the most closely associated with the genre; Olivier Philippe calculates that as many as 922 French *films policier* were produced between 1957 and 1990, with Delon starring in 29 of them – five more than Belmondo – both as a gangster and, after 1972, also as a cop (Philippe 1996: 36). Delon's association with Gabin and Belmondo is, of course, evident in the films they have made together, and his career trajectory shadows Belmondo's to the point that Belmondo is an ironic presence even when absent (as in Delon's second picture as director, *Pour la peau d'un flic/For the Death of a Cop,* 1981). However, such comparative analysis implicitly plays down the specificity of the Delon persona, and in particular the significance of the rupture represented by his early screen performances. It is this rupture which forms the basis of the present study.

As is implicitly recognised by the frequent characterisation of Delon as an 'homme fatal' (Maillot 1996: 149–50; Vincendeau 2000b: 175–7), where the explicitness of his sexuality is central to an allure based on the urgent pursuit of sex and money – in Chris Straayer's analysis, Delon's Ripley is 'handsome, wanting, duplicitous, enticing, unknowable, and fatal' (Straayer 2001: 118) – this rupture operates primarily within and in opposition to nationally-established genre conventions, and is grounded within dominant tropes concerning the construction and representation of masculinity. As we shall see, this is principally played out in terms of the relationship between the individual and the collective: the values and narrative motivation with which Delon is associated operate in contrast to the dominant discourse of collectively negotiated masculinity of the French crime film from the mid-1950s to the mid-1960s. Spanning his career as a whole but concentrating on the emergence of Delon before his departure in 1964 for the first of two short-lived stays in Hollywood, this chapter therefore argues that his screen identity presented a paradigm of masculinity sharply contrasting with dominant national discourses and representations, and that this new paradigm had a significant influence on the subsequent development of the crime film in France. Divided into two main sections, it will first briefly examine the generic context set by 1950s French crime cinema before discussing the relevant elements of the Delon screen persona.

The French crime film

Observers have tended to cast the development of the French crime film in post-war France in terms of its relationship to Hollywood, highlighting what Emma Wilson refers to as the 'internalisation and re-invention' of American *film noir* (Wilson 1999: 68). Indeed, critics and academics alike have consistently used *film noir* to characterise French crime cinema, to the extent that the term is frequently used as a synonym for *film policier* (see, for example, Jousse and Toubiana 1996: 63; Philippe 1996: 15). There are clear advantages to the use of this terminology, not least because it provides a framework which stresses the continuity of French post-war cinema with the *noir* mood of late 1930s poetic realism (see in particular O'Brien 1996) and its sources in the pulp fiction of the *série noire* imprint launched by Gallimard in 1946, whilst underlining the importance of the French critical reception of American *film noir* to the emergence of a domestic generic canon from the mid-1950s onwards. Whilst Raymond Borde and Etienne Chaumeton's landmark 1955 study of American *film noir* generally reserved only scathing contempt for the then state of French crime cinema, it also detected the first serious attempts at the construction of a 'French school of *film noir*' with the release of Jules Dassin's *Du Rififi chez les hommes/Rififi* in 1955 (Borde and Chaumeton 1955: 173), a film which François Truffaut also famously referred to as the best *film noir* he had ever seen.

Above and beyond the debates over the precise nature of American *noir* (movement, genre or film style) and the problematic mapping of an American mode of cultural production onto a very different French economic, ideological and industrial context, the definition of French crime films as *noirs* raises a series of concerns centring on specific socio-cultural contexts, in particular representations of gender and the social response to World War Two. Discussions of the meanings of American *film noir* are widespread, but it is worth recalling here that a central feature of *noir* is its construction of destabilising discourses of masculine anxiety in the face of the new social and economic power of women in the wartime and immediate post-war periods. The social and sexual power of the *femme fatale*, the central iconic figure of American *noir*, is necessarily demonstrated so that she and it may be punished and destroyed; American *noir* displays an overtly misogynistic worldview. It is nonetheless important to underline that the hostility directed against women in these pictures also serves to reinforce the problematising nature of their discourse on masculinity; as Frank Krutnik argues, the dominant position of the *femme fatale* points to an 'erosion of confidence in the structuring mechanisms of masculine identity and the masculine role' (Krutnik 1991: 64). Similarly, for Richard Dyer, the central problematic of *film noir* is 'a certain anxiety over the existence and definition of masculinity and normality' (Dyer 1998: 115).

If the American cultural context lent itself to oppressive, paranoid narratives of female sexual power and the destabilisation of masculine authority, the French context was very different, however. As Noël Burch and Geneviève Sellier point out, the 1950s saw the re-appearance of narratives structured around the demonstration of masculine camaraderie and 'virile friendships', re-asserting the values common to late 1930s narratives whilst repressing the possible expression of anxieties produced by the humiliation of the Occupation (Burch and Sellier 1996: 250–3). Such narratives were subsequently at their most marked in the crime genre. On the heels of Jacques Becker's *Touchez pas au grisbi/ Grisbi* (1954), films such as Dassin's *Du Rififi chez les hommes*, Becker's later *Le Trou/The Hole* (1960), Jean-Pierre Melville's *Bob le flambeur/Bob the Gambler* (1956), *Le Doulos/ The Finger Man* (1963) and *Le Deuxième souffle/Second Breath* (1966), Henri Decoin's *Razzia sur la chnouf/Chnouf* (1955) and Pierre Chenal's *Rafles sur la ville/Trap for a Killer* (1958) established a narrative structure based on a functional homosocial economy of masculine action, the marginalisation of women and an ethic of collective solidarity. The codification of these films was so significant that Armand-Jean Cauliez, writing about the first of them in 1956, argued that they presented a new departure within the crime genre, and should be seen as 'third degree crime films'. Offering a 'metaphysical poetics of criminality', these films revealed the systems of regulation and desire structuring a contractualised criminal action which was already and inevitably programmed to a final defeat whose terms were 'not so much *moral* as *normal*' (Cauliez 1956: 66).

The demonstration of collective masculine action articulated by these films does not serve simply to repress potential anxieties relating back to the Occupation, but also – in the classic structure of Freudian disavowal – re-enacts them through consistent narrative and iconographic evocation of the war. This is present in the importance of the generic structure of the settling of scores between rival clandestine gangs, the use of hand-grenades and sub-machine guns, and the privileging of the interrogation as a key site for the construction of national and masculine identities. The invitation to connect the clandestine, armed, highly organised worlds of the criminal *milieu* (underworld) and the internal Resistance is made clear in the escape by Gu Minda (Lino Ventura) from prison in Lyon at the start of *Le Deuxième souffle*, which directly (and celebratedly) cites Robert Bresson's 1956 Resistance drama *Un condamné à mort s'est échappé/A Man Escaped*, and is equally present in the advance of police vehicles across a field in the dénouement of *Razzia sur la chnouf*, and the interrogation of Fifi (Daniel Cauchy) in *Touchez pas au grisbi*.

Though such films shared an at least implicit emphasis on pre-determination with American *film noir*, they also therefore introduced the gangster as a specifically *French* phenomenon, grounded in national cultural practice; according to François Guérif, they construct the *milieu* as a place of mythification, with its own codes and values (Guérif 1986: 105–8), The focus is placed explicitly on the criminal environment, and specifically on the organisation of crime. It is interesting therefore that many of these films are heist films (*Bob le flambeur*, *Du Rififi chez les hommes*) or post-heist films (*Touchez pas au grisbi*, *Le Doulos*), whose narratives foreground a dramatic emphasis on planning, rigour, self-control, technical sophistication and the importance of hierarchies (see Lacourbe 1969), values and abilities which are represented as exclusive to male collective organisation. Though these films share the misogyny of American *noir*, the form and specificity of the misogyny they offer is very different, more explicit, and less open to counter-readings of female control. Indeed, to the extent that female characters retain narrative importance in the French crime films of the mid-1950s to mid-1960s, they are subordinated to secondary and subservient roles, categorised as nurturing mother figures or fetishised commodities (*Du Rififi chez les hommes, Touchez pas au grisbi*), prostitutes, molls or passive and submissive child-women (*Bob le flambeur, Razzia sur la chnouf, Le Doulos*). Occupying neither the destabilising nor the redemptive roles of women in American *noir*, their narrative function is reduced to a source of betrayal, primarily because they are external to (and by essence unable to maintain) the code of silence central to the clandestine, masculine homosocial community. Crucially therefore, this betrayal does not threaten masculine identity and authority, but reinforces it.

In American *noir*, the objectification of the female body is to some extent countered by the narrative significance of female agency and control. In the French crime films discussed here, no such equation is possible. Indeed, in films such as *Du Rififi chez les hommes* and *Le Doulos*, there is an explicit connection between the formation of male group identity on the one hand and the seduction of and perpetration of violence upon women on the other. In *Du Rififi chez les hommes*, Toni le Stéphanois (Jean Servais) only feels able to assent to and organise the heist once he has bidden his former, apparently faithless, girlfriend Mado (Marie Sabouret) to strip off her jewels and clothes, and then whipped her naked body with his belt. Coyly, the camera cuts to a photograph of the previously happy couple. In *Le Doulos*, Silien (Belmondo) is only able to rescue Maurice (Serge Reggiani) from the police by extracting information on his whereabouts from Maurice's girlfriend Thérèse (Monique Henessy); the scene is shot as a seduction, before Silien brutally punches Thérèse to the ground, ties her to a radiator by a belt round her neck, and hits her until she speaks. The film cuts to the heist being carried out by

Maurice through an edit which contrasts a yapping poodle with Thérèse's eroticised and bleeding body.

The argument here is not here that the Alain Delon persona developed the genre by making it less misogynistic. The significance of the Delon identity functions rather at the level of the archetypal representation of masculinity within the crime film, and particularly at the set of values it embodies and propagates. The next section will therefore go on to discuss a series of oppositions created by the Delon films, centring on the relationship between subjectivity and objectification, the individual and the collective, and class and space, before finally arguing that these oppositions have been worked into a new generic framework of masculinity particularly prevalent in the 1970s and 1980s.

The Delon screen identity

In 1996 the Cinémathèque française staged a season of films celebrating Alain Delon's career. In the programme for the retrospective, Jack Lang – François Mitterrand's flamboyant minister of culture from 1981 to 1986, and again from 1988 to 1993 – summed up Delon's appeal thus: 'Young wolf, feline, thoroughbred ... At barely twenty, Delon burst onto the screen untamed, with neither stage nor screen training, only his amazing actor's instinct, which from the very first take ushered him into his natural environment' (Cinémathèque française 1996: 77). Lang's homage reproduces a number of well-established elements of the Delon persona, including the actress Edwige Feuillère's often-quoted remark of the young Delon that 'one doesn't stop a thoroughbred at full gallop'. Indeed, Lang's description is notable for the way it articulates the principal features of the Delon myth, notably the emphasis on the natural and the untameable; whether as an actor or a character, Delon is frequently described in terms which underline the unmediated and instinctive (see, for example, Benayoun 1964; Buache 1987: 63). Delon's movement and acting style are frequently likened to an untrained naturalism based on intuition, animal grace and power; in an enthusiastic biography, for example, Henri Rode refers to the Delon of 1964 as a 'young animal, capable of breaking the bars of any cage, even a gilded one' (Rode 1974: 11).

Such metaphors are problematic in gender terms, and – often used in conjunction with each other – encapsulate the fundamental ambivalence of the masculine archetype presented by Delon. On the one hand, the wolf, closely associated with a threatening hypermasculinity through the European folktale tradition, is frequently mobilised to represent Delon-as-animal: he is a 'lone wolf' signifying ambition and appetite. Such references are explicitly integrated into diegetic explanations of his character in René Clément's 1964 film Les Félins/The Love Cage (and later in Melville's Le Samouraï/The Godson (1967)) and are central to the narrative trajectory of Alain Cavalier's L'Insoumis/The Unvanquished (1964), whose original working title, La Mort du loup ('The Death of the Wolf'), refers to the capacity of wounded wolves to travel long distances back to their dens to die (see Cavalier in Quinson 1964). On the other, a direct association with cats – in for example Les Félins and Le Choc/The Shock (Robin Davis, 1982) – in both diegetic and paratextual commentaries emphasises the feline, 'feminine' qualities of Delon's character and performance. As Robin Wood points out, the explicit inscription of assertive female sexuality as cat-like is an archetype of the classical Hollywood cinema, transcending individual genres, from screwball to horror, melodrama and psychological thriller (Wood 1986: 62).

All this is somewhat confusing, particularly given that Delon is further associated with birds, the caged bullfinch owned by Delon's professional killer Jef Costello in *Le Samouraï* operating as an intertextual play on 'the bird-killer' evoked by Delon's Thomas in *L'Insoumis*. Apart from Brigitte Bardot, no French actor has been so often and so directly associated with an animal menagerie as Delon has been. This dialectic of feminisation and predatory masculinity is reinforced by the way that the camera tracks, pans and frames Delon; Vincendeau highlights the representation of his body as a process of commodification, where the narcissistic spectacle of erotic male display is integral to his screen persona (Vincendeau 2000: 173–7). Indeed, in all three of the 'Riviera crime films' he completed from 1959 to 1964 – Clément's *Plein soleil/Purple Noon* (1960) and *Les Félins*, and Henri Verneuil's *Mélodie en sous-sol/Any Number Can Win* (1963) – Delon is consistently framed in and reflected by a play of light, water and mirrors, from what Straayer identifies as Ripley's 'homo-narcissistic' doubling in front of the wardrobe in *Plein soleil* (Straayer 2001: 120), to the literal and metaphorical game of mirrors in *Les Félins*.

Discussing the relationship between narcissism and identification in the display of the male body, Steve Neale argues that the infliction of pain and suffering is a necessary precondition for its display, motivating the look in terms of narrative rather than spectacle:

> in a heterosexual and patriarchal society the male body cannot be marked explicitly as the erotic object of another male look: that look must be motivated in some other way, its erotic component repressed. (Neale 1983: 8)

Indeed, the importance of physical suffering to the display of Delon's body is fully integrated into the narrative trajectories of *Plein soleil* (sunburn), *L'Insoumis* (ultimately fatal bullet wound to the stomach) and *Les Félins*; as Jean-Marc Bory describes it, the opening sequence gives us 'Delon battered, Delon beaten, Delon bruised, bleeding, hunted, safe at last? Ouf – better looking than ever' (Bory 1964: n.p.).

Yet it is also the case that throughout his career, the Delon body is presented directly as a site of erotic spectacle without the disqualifying intermediation of physical suffering. The importance of physical objectification to Delon's star image is evident in both his contemporaneous promotion (such as the publicity poster for *Plein soleil*, and even the name of his own short-lived production company *La Delbeau*), and the critical reception of his performance; Bory also writes in his review of *Les Félins* that Delon is 'not an actor, but an object. A marvellous cinematic object, whose physique, with its astonishing "presence", serves as talent' (ibid.). In the much later crime film *Le Choc*, an only barely-motivated shower scene directly displays the by-now 47-year-old Delon body for lengthy spectatorial contemplation; in *Mélodie en sous-sol*, the young Delon body is even more lengthily displayed, emphasised by excessive framing devices, especially at the initial poolside scene. Crucially, however, where similar objectifying techniques operate to deny female subjectivity, they are here deployed to underline and enhance Delon's agency. In the poolside scene in *Mélodie en sous-sol*, his character, Francis, also functions as a relay point for the spectatorial look, doubled by a narrativised objectification of the female bodies on display, an exaggerated emphasis on heterosexuality, and the demonstration of Francis' economic and generic power (excessive tipping, drinking whiskey).

ROBERT et RAYMOND HAKIM
présenté

ALAIN DELON
MARIE LAFORET
MAURICE RONET

PLEIN SOLEIL

D'APRÈS LE ROMAN "M* RIPLEY" DE PATRICIA HIGHSMITH
GRAND PRIX DE LA LITTÉRATURE POLICIÈRE
ADAPTATION ET DIALOGUE DE
RENÉ CLÉMENT et PAUL GEGAUFF
AVEC
ERNO CRISA • FRANK LATIMORE • BILL KEARNS • AVE NINCHI
AVEC LE CONCOURS DE
ELVIRE POPESCO
IMAGES DE HENRI DECAE • MUSIQUE DE NINO ROTTA • CHEF DÉCORATEUR PAUL BERTRAND
EASTMANCOLOR   ROBERT ET RAYMOND HAKIM

Jean Mascii's original publicity poster for *Plein soleil* (copyright ADAGP, Paris, 2001; by kind permission)

It is particularly significant therefore that the instabilities created by such objectification can only be resolved narratively through an excessive emphasis on heterosexuality. It is here that the rupture presented by the Delon character in generic terms is most sharply focused. As we have seen, the dominant trope in the French crime film at the point of Delon's emergence subordinates (hetero)sexual conquest to the construction of male communities whose virility is expressed through collective organisation and action. The

Delon persona functions in opposition to this structure. Delon narratives subordinate collective action to an individualism which both emphasises star status and ultimately operates as a destructive force for the criminal enterprise. Again, therefore, the Delon screen identity internalises the function previously assigned to female characters. This is, however, counterbalanced by a subordination of the homosocial order in favour of a narrative trajectory predicated upon overt heterosexual quest. Three examples demonstrate this.

Mélodie en sous-sol is the first crime film to unite Delon with Gabin, in the tale of Charles (Gabin), an aging ex-con embarking on one last job before retirement and emigration, and his disaffected protégé Francis (Delon), whom he enlists to rob the bank vault of the Palm Beach Hotel, Nice. That the operation goes wrong despite Charles's leadership and planning is explained in terms of the two central elements of the Delon persona: Francis's main goal is not the careful planning of the robbery but the seduction of a Swedish dancer in the troupe performing in the hotel's ballroom; and the photograph on the front page of *Nice Matin* the morning after the robbery blows Francis's cover, as a chance shot of the ballroom displays Delon framed in close-up, once again the inescapable object of the camera's gaze.

Released the following year, *L'Insoumis* tells the fictional story of Thomas (Delon), a legionnaire who deserts the army during the final stages of the Franco-Algerian war to join the OAS fascist insurrectionary group, and participates in the kidnap of Mᵉ Dominique Servais (Léa Massari), a left-wing lawyer come to Algiers to defend two Muslim separatist suspects;[1] he is instructed by his commanding officer to guard the lawyer pending further orders. Though not ostensibly a crime film, *L'Insoumis* adopts the iconography and narrative structure of the genre, particularly during the sections set on the French mainland, and its key sequence directly evokes Silien's interrogation of Thérèse in *Le Doulos*. In what is literally and metaphorically a keyhole moment for the Delon character, Thomas's fate turns on his view through the door of the exhausted, suffering Dominique handcuffed to a radiator. Here, the film fetishises female suffering, presenting the body of the distressed lawyer as a site of erotic spectacle. But rather than subordinating this to a reinforcement of male collective identity, the image is instrumentalised as the impetus for the break with group solidarity, as it arouses Thomas' desire; caught giving the lawyer a drink through a straw, he kills his fellow OAS gaoler, is shot and seriously wounded in the process, and imprisons his commanding officer. His sexual pursuit of the lawyer on his return to France is mirrored by their subsequent flight from the OAS and then the police; his stomach wound untreated, Thomas expires on reaching his farm in Luxembourg, echoing Sterling Hayden's Dix Handley in *The Asphalt Jungle* (John Huston, 1950), and Silien again in *Le Doulos*.

His first film as producer, *L'Insoumis* represents the fulfilment of the emergent Delon myth: the structured, ordered masculine communities of gang and army are unable to contain Thomas, whose narrative trajectory rejects the collective, articulating instead discourses of instinct, intuition and primitiveness. By the time of *Le Clan des Siciliens/The Sicilian Clan* (1969), Verneuil's second crime film bringing together Delon and Gabin (and also, this time, Ventura), the generic difference of the Delon screen identity is so firmly established that the contrasting star narratives can be played out to within an ace of caricature. Whilst Ventura is the honest, resourceful and persistent detective, and Gabin the bourgeois patriarch at the head of the Manalese clan, Delon (Roger Sartet) is an outsider whose sexual potency – memorably demonstrated when he kills an eel with his bare hands, before making love to the wife of one of the gang members on the beach – ultimately tears apart the gang, following the success of the audacious international jewellery robbery. The Manalese family's need for retribution to salvage its lost honour leads inevitably to double-cross and the killing of Sartet, and the capture of the rest of the gang.

Here as in each of the Riviera films and most explicitly in *L'Insoumis*, Delon's character breaks the fundamental code of the 1950s crime film, as he follows a course of action predicated upon the manipulation or betrayal of those closest to him. It is thus interesting that many of Delon's early films, like those discussed in the first section of this chapter, are also heist films. In his early piece on the sub-genre, Roland Lacourbe identifies the emergence of the heist within the French crime film as the dramatisation of the revenge of the 'downtrodden man' on the institutional symbols of a corrupt and exploitative capitalist society, be they banks, casinos, jewellers or bookmakers (Lacourbe 1969: 58–9).

On one level, of course, we can even read *Plein soleil* as a kind of heist movie, with its emphasis on organisation, overcoming apparently failsafe security mechanisms, and a narrative dénouement where the Delon character is the flawed agent of his own demise, entrapped – as is typical of the sub-genre, and is often the case in Delon's early films – by the workings of chance, the sudden significance of a seemingly unforeseeable oversight. The attempt of the financially and socially disadvantaged individual to acquire the means central to his ambitions is, in *Plein soleil* as in the sub-genre, inevitably doomed to failure; as Lacourbe points out, in the heist film stolen goods are always returned to their original owner. The heist movie thus also articulates class fixity, setting the boundaries to mutability in the emergent consumer society. *Plein soleil*, like *Les Félins* and *Mélodie en sous-sol*, therefore advances contradictory discourses on social mobility, and does so through its representation of masculinity. Relocating the crime film from its sociological-realist, working-class urban spaces, such films purport to show the attainability of consumer lifestyles made possible by social transformation; yet this goal is always ultimately unattainable. To articulate this contradictory discourse, class must be narratively subordinated in favour of the male body, which must itself become a locus of consumption, display and spectacle.

In a persuasive comparison of the treatment of class and (homo)sexuality in *Plein soleil* and Patricia Highsmith's original novel *The Talented Mr Ripley*, Straayer argues that Delon's Ripley, unlike Highsmith's, is locked into a socially- and sexually-fixed identity which denies his capacity to adopt the upper-class heterosexual identity of Philippe Greenleaf (Dickie in the novel). In this reading, where in the novel Ripley enjoys a 'total lack of allegiance to any former identity', in Clément's film he is locked into a working-class identity, as Philippe (Maurice Ronet) infantilises Tom by pointing out his inability to eat properly. For Straayer, Ripley's desire for Philippe is reduced to homo-narcissistic display, whilst his inability to adopt correct table manners is both key to his murderous intent and a signifier of the film's 'essentialist discourse on class' (Straayer 2001: 117–18). Significantly, despite the importance of Philippe's social superiority to Ripley's motivation, the lengthy introductory sequences establishing the social context of Ripley's relationship with Dickie, present in both Highsmith's novel and Anthony Minghella's recent adaptation (*The Talented Mr Ripley*, 1999), are absent from the Clément film, in which male bodily display is consistently privileged over psychological enquiry. For Delon's Ripley, the killings of Philippe and Freddie Miles (Bill Kearns) have no psychological, moral or social consequences. The fish market sequence fetishises the face and body of Delon as he wanders between stalls in Naples, inextricably linking his cool amorality to his physicality, offered up once more as a site of spectatorial pleasure.

The 'freedom from determination and fixity' of class and sexuality in Highsmith's novel is underpinned by the resonance of the Mediterranean location, which – from a 1950s American perspective – evokes cultural difference as class distinction and freedom from a sexually repressive national context (Straayer 2001: 129 n.2). Within the rather different socio-cultural context of the *film*'s production, however, the location opens up a number of different readings, inscribing transformations in the French social structure on the masculinity-as-spectacle of the Delon identity. The Riviera, both attainable holiday resort and aspirational symbol of class mobility, is also symbolic of changes in the French social structure at the end of the 1950s. The social transformations of the 1950s and 1960s created by France's post-war industrialisation and motorisation, articulated mobility, in Kristin Ross's phrase, as 'the categorical imperative of the economic order, the mark of a rupture with the past' (Ross 1995: 22). The subsequent explosion of car ownership in particular broke down established temporal and spatial barriers and enabled the institutionalisation of the national holiday. It is in this context that *Mélodie en sous-sol* depends on an explicit dramatisation of the alienating and castrating effects of urbanisation, technological development and the availability of travel and leisure time to the masses as narrative motivation, both for Charles and Francis, for whom the heist offers the possibility of escape from an oppressive (working-)class identity.

In generic terms, the Mediterranean location produces a series of geographic and iconographic ruptures, and depends on a new topography of gender codification. Whilst the Mediterranean backdrop provides a suitable frame for the *mise-en-scène* of Delon's physical beauty, it also decontextualises the conventions of the crime thriller: the Riviera films eschew the iconic spaces and display little of the expressionism or iconography of confinement of the *série noire*. Instead of Paris, so central to the genre, the action takes places in Nice, Cannes, Italy. Absent are the generic claustrophobic masculine spaces; entrapment and isolation are represented, in the case of *Les Félins*, within feminised and vaguely supernatural spaces.

In the French crime film, space is therefore mapped within a gendered economy of exclusion. This is most apparent in iconic spaces such as the bar and night-club, where space is encoded according to a masculine-feminine division between spectatorship and display, consumption and production. In *Mélodie en sous-sol* in particular the spaces inhabited by the central male characters signal an erasure of such boundaries. Three spaces are of particular importance: the baths where Charles goes to discuss the heist plan with Mario (Henri Virlogeux), who must drop out through ill health, enabling the generational conflict at the heart of the masculine couple to be constituted; the *Olympique Billard Club* where Charles engages his former cell-mate Francis in the scheme; and the hotel swimming pool, where Charles directs Francis to hand over the money after the original plan is compromised. The first two spaces are rigorously coded to define masculine activity, as complicity is enacted through sporting display and the concomitant marginalisation or exclusion of women.

Nonetheless, the representation of Gabin and Delon in these spaces works not simply to establish the generational opposition between them, but also the contrasting operation of their masculine identities. When Charles meets Mario at the Paris bathhouse, he is defined in opposition to male bodily display, both through his dress and his movement, as he clearly skirts the bathing area in order to fulfil his rendezvous. Similarly, during the final ill-fated handover of the money at the swimming pool, Charles occupies a space peripheral to the action, and is only present at the pool area where it is safely masculinised, through its exclusive occupation by male characters engaged in productive work (in this case, detection). In contrast, Francis occupies both peripheral and central areas of the pool area, and is feminised not only through the framing discussed earlier, but also through his enjoyment of leisure time through sunbathing (his pose at the water's edge, repeated in the final scene). In contrast to the rigid delineation of masculine topographies articulated by Gabin therefore, Delon's movement and spatial occupation breaks down the barriers between masculine and feminine spaces and the attendant differentiation between subject and object of the cinematic gaze.

As we have seen, dominant discourses in the French crime film at the time of Delon's initial appearance in film were structured around masculine complicity, homosocial affiliation and the marginalisation of women. By contrast, Delon narratives – though they similarly instrumentalise women – are structured around individual heterosexual quest, breaking with the generic value system. Betrayal remains central to the ultimate downfall of the criminal enterprise; yet in Delon films, its dynamic is quite different from generic expectations; for whilst the underlying structure of betrayal can still be traced back to the disruptive influence of women, it is now Delon himself who is the agent of treachery, sometimes consciously, sometimes inadvertently. Despite his evident muscularity, the Delon masculinity is emphatically not a hypermasculine performativity; his characters are ultimately the passive victims of their own misfortune or mistakes. It is significant that in both *Plein soleil* and *L'Insoumis*, in fact, the killings carried out by the Delon character are dramatised as a loss rather than an assertion of control.

From the mid-1960s onwards, and particularly after *Le Samouraï*, the Delon persona demonstrates an increasing internalisation of conflict, allied to an increasingly impassive acting style based on restraint, suppression and the exaggeration of physical characteristics, 'a glacial perfection in which the merest twitch of eyebrow or mouth is significant' (Forbes 1992: 56). Yet the figure of the individual operating either outside or in opposition to the collective, familiar from Delon's later films, is a development established by Delon's initial breakthrough into French genre films. As François Guérif and Pascal Mérigeau note, Delon's screen identity was pivotal to the departure from traditional French representations of crime in the 1970s, particularly the internalisation of the American tradition of the private detective operating outside the law, opposed to both organised crime and the institutional police (Guérif and Mérigeau 1982: 72–3).

It is important to stress that, within the framework of the French crime film, Delon presents a point of rupture: the 'lone wolf' is a genre archetype established through Delon's screen persona. Frequently shorn of a social context and remarkable for his lack of moral principles, the Delon character's motivation is founded not on a shared, negotiated set of values but rather on a masculinity presented as a site of narcissism and spectacle. As Clément says of his Ripley, 'My character is asocial: he cuts himself off from society, makes himself an enemy of it, is not troubled by it. And in this role, Alain Delon is marvellous' (quoted in Moulin 1960).

Delon's screen persona is marked by his refusal to be contained by a group identity or hierarchical stratification. Though repeatedly a criminal in crime films, Delon rarely plays a gangster as such, and his star identity is reinforced through his narrative and spatial dissociation from the membership of a community, notably through framing and camera movement. Delon's early French films therefore construct a quite different filmic identity from the breakthrough Italian films which forged his reputation, particularly Luchino Visconti's *Rocco e i suoi fratelli/Rocco and His Brothers* (1960) and *Il Gattopardo/The Leopard* (1963), where Delon is integrated into and motivated by familial and social relations. By contrast, in *Les Félins*, Delon's character is constructed in opposition to an organised gang who pursue him not because of any criminal activity on his part, but because of his sexual power; in *Plein soleil*, Ripley has neither friends nor allies; in *Mélodie en sous-sol*, Delon is characterised by a lack of discipline and refusal to submit to patriarchal hierarchy. This very specific screen identity of (disruptive) individualism informs much of Alain Delon's best later work – notably *Le Samouraï* and Joseph Losey's *Mr Klein* (1976) – and in the generic context of French crime cinema sets a template for the subsequent construction of a performative, virile, individualistic masculinity.

Note

1   On release, the film was withdrawn from cinemas after a week due to a legal challenge from Mc Mireille Glaymann, who argued that the film was based on and seriously misrepresented the events she experienced in January 1962.

chapter 4

DECONSTRUCTING PACO RABAL: MASCULINITY, MYTH AND MEANING
Rikki Morgan-Tamosunas

Announcing the sudden death of veteran Spanish actor Francisco Rabal, on 30 August 2001, Spain's leading national newspaper, *El País*, declared that 'The death of Paco Rabal has deprived Spanish cinema of one of its greatest myths' (Fernández Santos 2001).[1] Stardom and myth are both 'modes of signification' that 'transform meaning into form' (Barthes 1973: 117). Although 'myths' essentially recount stories about supernatural beings, like stars, their significance and impact lies in the ways in which they articulate cultural values and beliefs. Both modes have been noted for their characteristic ability not only to embody, but also, seemingly, to resolve conflicting values and forces in the society within which they emerge (Lévi-Strauss 1972: 224; Dyer 1979: 59–81). Rabal's consecration as a 'myth' reflects his charismatic appeal and powerful screen presence, and the extent of his cultural resonance in Spain. However, the other-worldly connotations of this 'mythical' status combine, almost paradoxically, with his popular image as a roughly-hewn, earthy 'man of the people' (Torres 2001). Peter Evans has referred to Rabal's off-screen image as that of 'a darker, Spanish Richard Burton', the 'powerful, sensitive, thoughtful proletarian, hard-living and hard-drinking, and eroticised' male (Evans 1995: 93). It is a heavily class- and gender-coded image, firmly rooted in his working-class Murcian origins, his very public adherence to communism, his well-known lust for life and its pleasures, and a 'warts-and-all' kind of sincerity. Indeed that 'ordinariness' is often presented as a defining characteristic of his '*extra*ordinariness', a duality reflecting the essential ambiguity of both stardom and myth, and captured in Maruja Torres's obituary description of him as 'a colossus of the people' (Torres 2001).

Rabal's long career, with almost two hundred films as well as stage and television performances to his credit, spans more than fifty years, starting and ending in two very different socio-cultural and political periods. His early image as a leading '*galán*' (Aguilar and Genover 1996: 504)[2] was established in a Spanish cinema constrained by the strict censorship and funding structures of the Franco dictatorship which channelled film production of the 1940s and 1950s into a narrow range of genres dominated by historical epics of heroism, religious dramas and folkloricism. His discovery for *Nazarín* (Luis Buñuel, 1959) launched his career abroad, consolidated by further work with the Aragonese director (*Viridiana*, 1961; *Belle de Jour*, 1966) and with such prestigious international filmmakers as Antonioni, Chabrol, Visconti, Saura and Torre-Nilsson. However, a low point in his career, including some disastrous roles (such as in *Cabezas cortadas/Severed Heads*, Glauber Rocha, 1970, and *N.P. Il segretto/N.P. The Secret*, Silvano Agosti, 1970) which seriously damaged his artistic credibility, led to Rabal's virtual disappearance from Spanish screens in the 1970s.[3] His resurgence in the early 1980s coincides very specifically with the end of Spain's transition from dictatorship to democracy and the election of the first Socialist (PSOE) government in 1982 which was to give a new lease of life to Spanish cinema.

Focusing on this latter stage of his career in particular, this chapter explores Paco Rabal's embodiment of a particular and evolving articulation of working-class masculinity. It examines some of the ambiguities and tensions inscribed within key class-, gender- and sexually-related elements of the composite image, and focuses particularly on its construction through discourses of authenticity and nostalgia which work to resolve or erase these tensions, and secure his broadly-based critical and popular appeal. These characteristics are mapped against the cultural context of socio-political change in Spain in the 1980s and 1990s.

Authenticity, masculinity, ambiguity

Paco Rabal's abiding image is a classic example of Richard Dyer's notion of the 'structured polysemy' of stardom: a multi-faceted collection of meanings, gradually 'structured' by promotional media, publicity, the film roles themselves and critical commentary (Dyer 1979: 3). However, the emphasis on authenticity which characterises star discourse tends to mask this process of construction, purporting to reveal hidden layers of reality about the star, 'constantly ... reconfirm[ing] our understanding ... of the "truth" behind the image' (Tasker 1993a: 233). In articles, interviews and biographies, Rabal's career is typically presented as a 'drama of recognition' (Gledhill 1991: 212) in which his persona is selectively re-constructed, in retrospect, as a story of obstacles and setbacks overcome – his working-class origins, his first job as an electrician with a burning ambition to be an actor at the Chamartín Film Studios, the political constraints of the Franco years, the 'lightweight' profile of his early career, two serious car accidents, and the major slump in his career in the 1970s – but all culminating in his triumphant *renacimiento* (renaissance) in the 1980s. The discourse of authenticity structuring these accounts is particularly dominant because of the class- and gender-coding of the Rabal image itself.

Pierre Bourdieu's work on the socio-cultural distinctions of class provides a range of insights to which I shall refer throughout this chapter, and which can help to understand the centrality of 'ordinariness' and authenticity to the kind of working-class masculinity Rabal embodies:

> [Working-class m]en especially are forbidden every sort of 'pretension' in matters of culture, language or clothing ... not only because ... aesthetic refinement ... is

reserved for women by a representation, more strict than in any other class, of the sexual division of labour and sexual morality; or because it is more or less clearly associated with dispositions and manners seen as characteristic of the bourgeoisie … It is also because a surrender to demands perceived as simultaneously feminine and bourgeois appears as an index of a dual repudiation of virility, a twofold submission which ordinary language, naturally conceiving all domination in the logic and lexicon of sexual domination, is predisposed to express. (Bourdieu 1986: 382–3)

From the start, Rabal's strong physique, proletarian looks, rasping voice and the strong accent of his native Murcia (south-eastern Spain) marked him as working class, securing him class-coded roles at home and abroad, as, for example, a miner in *La Guerra de Dios/ God's War*, Rafael Gil, 1953), a mariner in *Amanecer en Puerta Oscura/Dawn in Puerta Oscura* (José María Forqué, 1957), a bullfighter in *Los Clarines del miedo/Bugles of Fear* (Antonio Román, 1958) and *Currito de la Cruz* (Rafael Gil, 1965), and on the margins as a gangster in *Belle de Jour*, and a bandit in *Il Morte di un bandito/Death of a Bandit* (Giuseppe Amato, 1961) and *Llanto por un bandido/Lament for a Bandit* (Carlos Saura, 1963). In films such as *La Guerra de Dios*, physical strength as a sign of masculinity, consistent with Bourdieu's observation of the 'practical philosophy of the male body as a sort of power, big and strong' (Bourdieu 1986: 192), is foregrounded. The muscular physique of Rabal's character, Juan, a militant miners' leader, is emphasised by framing and lighting, particularly in sequences where his body is exposed at work underground. 'Muscularity', as Richard Dyer observes, 'is the sign of power – natural, achieved, phallic' (1992: 273–4), paradoxically combining essentialist notions of 'naturalness' with the achievement orientation of the socially-constructed masculine ideal. However, as Leon Hunt notes, the frequent eroticisation of the male body through 'the evidence of suffering and endurance marked on the surface of the body in such signs as bulging muscles and sweat', introduces 'troublesome' dimensions into this kind of display of masculinity, since 'sweat, representative of bodily fluids, may allude to *both* vulnerability *and* power' (cited in Kirkham and Thumim 1993: 12–13). This dichotomy may provide one of the keys to understanding Rabal's inscription of an appealingly humanising (male) authenticity. Indeed, as the 'prototype of the young man facing all manner of difficulties' (Pérez Perucha 1992: 76), the early Rabal regularly re-enacts 'the drama of power and powerlessness intrinsic to the anxiety of masculine identity and authority embedded in the figure of the struggling hero' (Tasker 1993a: 243) in his early screen roles and, retrospectively, in the narrative of his public life and profile.

A further element of ambiguity lies in the erotic appeal of Rabal's combination of rough, tough, proletarian physicality with the latent sexuality of the characteristically 'husky voice and ardent look' for female audiences (Hidalgo 1985: 140). Barbara Creed points out that 'putting men on display for the female gaze tends to violate conventional codes of looking which have built up around the socially sanctioned practice whereby men look and women are looked at' (Creed 1992: 262). In roles such as the aforementioned Juan, as the ambitious radio-presenter in *Historias de la radio/Radio Stories* (José Luis Sáenz de Heredia, 1955), or the dashing Marqués de Bradomín in *Sonatas* (Juan Antonio Bardem, 1959), he is clearly displayed for a female – or, indeed, homoerotic – gaze in one of the few contexts in which female desire could be recognised in 1940s and 1950s

Spain, albeit tacitly, and safely restricted to the confines of fantasy and the cinema screen. Notwithstanding the ambiguous power relations between the bearer and the object of the gaze, Rabal's sexual magnetism is firmly established in these films, and his eroticised image is an important influence on potential readings of subsequent, very different, roles. As the abstemious priest Padre Nazario, for example, whose religious fervour arouses sexual desire in his less chaste companions in Buñuel's *Nazarín*, the casting of Rabal strengthens the director's habitual use of irony.

Rabal's biographer, Miguel Hidalgo, sees the visible credentials of the early *galán* years as a mask concealing a true potential only realised in maturity when Rabal becomes 'himself' (Hidalgo 1985: 140). This biographical discourse of increasing authenticity is more comically paralleled in references by various friends to his eventual abandonment in the 1970s of the 'ridiculous' wig (used to disguise the early onset of baldness) as a symbol of self-acceptance; from then onwards, as poet Rafael Alberti declared, 'he appears with all the splendour of his great actor's pate' (quoted in Gabriel Martín 1992: 138). The ageing process and the scars of the two accidents resulted in the familiar 'gnarled face' (Borau 1998: 728), and increasing corpulence which, in contrast with his more youthful denial of hair loss, Rabal accepts with sanguine equanimity in his late sixties (in interview with Boyero 1992a: 28–9). The physical wear-and-tear, and his facial characteristics in particular, become increasingly cited as the index of 'a life lived to the full' (Hidalgo 1985: 140), a signifier of experience and wisdom, emphasised in the greater use of the close-up, that 'window on soul' as Bela Balázs called it (Balázs 1974), and through Rabal's more effective engagement with the camera in maturity (Heredero 1992: 100). The mature Rabal thus becomes 'an accumulation of experiences … an actor full of wisdom' (Beltrán 1992: 60), his status is one of 'solidity, wisdom, human emotion' (Gabriel Martín 1992: 138).

These qualities also characterise the roles he plays in the 1980s and 1990s: characters connecting with natural, mystical or more visceral 'truths', and embodying earthiness and worldly wisdom. This is most visible in his 'rural sage' performances, especially in *El Disputado voto del Sr Cayo/Mr Cayo's Disputed Vote* (Antonio Giménez Rico, 1986) and *Los Santos inocentes/Holy Innocents* (Mario Camus, 1984). The nonchalant and self-sufficient folklore and understanding of the laws and cycles of nature demonstrated by the elderly peasant subsistence farmer, Sr Cayo, by turns infuriates, baffles and humbles the self-important political campaigners from the city, and the simple 'innocence' of Azarías (*Los Santos inocentes*) is morally and ethically overshadowed by his harmonious relationship with the natural world and the sense of natural justice he embodies. A parade of other characters, superficially limited in their understanding or analytical capacities, display similarly disconcerting insights: the intuitive blind beggar of *Lázaro de Tormes* (Fernando Fernán Gómez and José Luis García Sánchez, 2000), the 'wise madman' reincarnated as the muddled grandfather of *Pajarico* (Carlos Saura, 1998), the drunken friend dispensing home truths to Fernando Fernán Gómez in *Los Zancos/The Stilts* (Carlos Saura, 1984), or the troubled visions of the ageing artist in *Goya en Burdeos/Goya in Bordeaux* (Carlos Saura, 1999).

These characters' articulation of a kind of Foucaultian 'subjugated knowledge' is also paralleled in the witty insights of Rabal's more humorous creations, such as the petty thief and seasoned jailbird, Ginés, in *Truhanes/Truants* (Miguel Hermoso, 1984). Ginés strikes a deal to protect a smooth-talking con-man in prison for the first time, in exchange for a reciprocal helping hand once they are released. Both inside, and more strikingly later in the more sophisticated outside world, Ginés amusingly (for the audience) and embarrassingly (for his companion) crudely articulates the sordid home truths the more refined trickster is less willing to recognise. As for the homespun sayings generated by Rabal's retired bullfighter Juncal (of Jaime de Armiñán's 1988 television serial of the same name), they became a something of a sociological phenomenon in the 1980s, quoted endlessly by Spanish audiences.

Even when marginalised or superficially diminished by their social standing or physical or mental incapacities, these characters still generate a palpable sense of authority. Their experiential gravitas and screen presence is emphasised spatially in lighting, framing, camerawork and other elements of narrative and *mise-en-scène*. In *Truhanes*, Ginés is imaged to stress the charisma and dominance he enjoys within his own sphere of authority in the prison where he is respected for his native wit, streetwise experience, his ability to organise a *juerga* (wild party), and his judicious choice of friends (who tend to be large and loyal). He is repeatedly framed at the centre of groups in the prison cell or the exercise yard, and the respect and admiration of his fellow inmates is visually confirmed through the structure of looks which Rabal orchestrates gesturally and with his own dominant look. In *El Disputado voto del Sr Cayo*, the spatial dynamics of the group, together with framing and camera angles, emphasise the elderly farmer's authority within the natural environment, seemingly controlling the trajectory of the tracking camera within the familiar territory of his own rural context. Azarías (*Los Santos inocentes*) is often imaged in slightly low-angle shots suggestive of his moral stature, sometimes strikingly static at the magnetic centre of his natural world, as in the sequence where he stands motionless and quietly commands his pet rook – his '*milana bonita*' – to fly to him. In *El Hombre que perdió su sombre/The Man Who Lost His Shadow* (Alain Tanner, 1991) Rabal, playing a returned communist exile with a chequered past, is also located spatially and experientially as the centre to which the younger protagonists gravitate for guidance in their moment of personal and professional crisis. In *Goya en Burdeos* tight-framing of Rabal's corpulent artist persistently underlines his reflective authority.

In a word, Rabal's mature characters have 'presence'. They are founts of popular and natural wisdom, and the roles seemingly endow the star image with similar qualities, illustrating Christine Gledhill's point that both 'generic roles and star personae are produced through similar processes of repetition, differentiation, sedimentation and interchange' (Gledhill 1991: 215); 'each successive appearance in the genre further solidifies the actor's screen persona until he no longer *plays* a role but *assimilates* it to the collective entity made up of his own body and personality in past screen roles' (Colin McArthur quoted in Gledhill 1991: 215; my italics). The sense of lived experience associated with both the characters and the public persona of the actor is an important element in the establishment of the nostalgia discourse to which I shall return later.

Performance signs [4]

Clearly Paco Rabal's 'immediately recognisable' performance style (Boyero 1992b: 48) and screen presence bring crucial elements to these films and roles through the confident, self-sufficiency of his acting style. Commentators again cast the development of that style within the discourse of authenticity, as a transition from the 'declamatory, uncertain and forced' style of his youth, to the more fluid, easy screen dominance of, for example, his Juncal or Goya (ibid.). Although his acting apprenticeship was in the theatre in the 1940s and 1950s when the Method and the Actor's Studio were in vogue, Rabal claims that 'life has been the best school', perhaps making a virtue of necessity, but again stressing the 'naturalness' of his development and style (Boyero 1992a: 36). Indeed, he has assimilated elements of a range of styles to draw on as appropriate. This is demonstrated in the contrast between, for example, the contemplative 'inside-out' Method-like feel of the Goya characterisation in *Goya en Burdeos* (1999), compared with the studied 'outside-in' composition of Azarías (*Los Santos inocentes*), or Muecas in *Tiempo del silencio/Time of Silence* (Vicente Aranda, 1986), a low-life shanty-town dweller scratching a living from scrap, who ends up responsible for his daughter's death by performing a botched illegal abortion to cover up his own incestuous impregnation of her.[5]

The alignment between star image and character is critical; Dyer identifies three different kinds of 'fit': 'perfect', 'selective' (where certain aspects of the star image may be drawn on and others ignored) and 'problematic' (Dyer 1979: 142–9). In most of Rabal's later films the 'fit' is selectively close, although powerful performances where the fit is more 'problematic', such as his portrayals of Azarías (for which he received Cannes' Best Actor award), and Muecas (*Tiempo de silencio*), may more emphatically evidence his acting ability. In promotional material and critical commentaries the idea of the close fit is again articulated through the authenticity discourse: 'Rabal *is* Juncal', the video sleeve announces; 'what you have before you is for real' declares Carlos Boyero (1992b: 49). This image/character relationship, not least because of its apparent guarantee of audience satisfaction, prompts analogies with psychoanalytical interpretations of the pleasures and satisfactions derived from the identification processes involved in film spectatorship.[6] Parallels with Lacanian explanations of the constitution of the subject, and especially with the misrecognition of the self and the super-ego in the mirror phase, convey the seductive pleasures – the sense of 'wholeness' – in the elision or 'fit' between role and star image, and of the performance style itself. Further parallels of this kind can be drawn with what I shall be suggesting are the nostalgic dimensions of the Rabal image and their similar promise of an – albeit illusory – sense of plenitude.

Carlos Heredero refers to a 'symbiosis' between Rabal and his 'fictional beings' (1992: 100). However, he points out that Rabal's acting style is no De Niro- or Brando-style 'chameleonic model'; rather, he maintains a shifting balance between 'absorption' and 'surrender', whereby his performances simultaneously accommodate the actor *and* the character in different degrees of 'contiguity' (Heredero 1992: 104). This relationship retains a critical separation between actor and character, which ensures the integrity and autonomy of each. Sartrian theories of the nature of human consciousness offer a useful conceptual analogy for understanding the significance of this relationship within the broader context of Rabal's class- and gender-coded image. The resistance to total absorption by the character parallels Sartre's conceptualisation of the power struggle between Self and Other in the process of self-definition and assertion of 'Being-for-Itself', the conscious self-awareness separating humans from other living creatures (Sartre 1969). Competing subjectivities are locked in a struggle to assert dominance over, and avoid surrender to, the Other. In as far as this notion also reflects the power relations of dominance and subordination which are at play within the social relations of class and gender, Rabal's resistance as an actor to absorption by the character can be clearly related to his particular image of masculinity. In this respect we might recall Bourdieu's comments on the working-class male conception of all domination 'in the logic and lexicon of sexual domination' cited above (Bourdieu 1986: 383).

However, in the Sartrian model, the ego is also, ironically, dependent on the Other for recognition and confirmation of dominance, a double bind which could only be resolved through the impossible fusion of Self and Other (Sartre 1969: 51). This concept of unattainable fusion may provide a means of understanding the distinct, but linked, stature achieved by both the actor *and* the character through the performance, and the satisfying illusion of 'wholeness' it conveys to the spectator. Interestingly, the director of *Truhanes*, Miguel Hermoso, characterises the relationship Rabal's acting style establishes between the spectator and the role in similar terms: rather than *identifying* with the character, the spectator is '*bound*' to him (Hidalgo 1985: 127).

Sartre's conundrum, and the troubling paradox embodied in Rabal's acting style is visually articulated in the actor's guest appearance in a fascinating sequence from Carlos Saura's *Los Zancos* (1984). In a drunken heart-to-heart Manuel (Rabal) consoles and advises his friend Ángel (Fernando Fernán Gómez), hopelessly infatuated with his much younger, married lover, on the rebound from his wife's recent death. Accusing Ángel of having '*perdido los papeles*' (a play on the double meaning embodied in this idiomatic expression to suggest that he has both gone out of his mind, but also lost sight of the fact that his casting of himself as the 'ridiculous-old-man-hopelessly-besotted-by-younger-woman' is merely a role he has chosen to adopt), Rabal/Manuel contrasts this with his own separation of role and essence, and the philosophy and practice of the detached, light-hearted philanderer. In their inebriated state the friends record and observe their own images on a TV screen. Whereas Fernán Gómez/Ángel looks directly to camera, bemoaning his wretched failure, Rabal/Manuel refuses the direct look, thereby figuratively resisting surrender to the controlling look of his own Other, more interested in the analysis of their respective self-images projected on the screen. The close-fit reflection of the real-life friendship of the two actors, together with the verisimilitude of the drunkenness, and the raw quality of the images relayed through the TV screen, invites reflection on the relationship between actor and character, thereby also rehearsing director Saura's perennial concern with performance and role-play.

Nostalgia, politics and masculinity

Many of the films consolidating Rabal's mature profile reflect the dominant aesthetic and cultural priorities of the Socialist (PSOE) government of the post-transition period. The influential Miró Law (1983) ushered in new film policy and legislation designed to reflect and promote a new socio-cultural agenda: 'a Europeanisation of the Spanish cinema, which would simultaneously reaffirm Spanish cultural identity and promote a combination of high-quality films with commercial potential' (Jordan and Morgan-Tamosunas 1998: 32). This strategy generated a large number of heritage films: literary adaptations, historical and costume drama, and the predominance of what critic Esteve Riambau disparagingly termed '*polivalencia*' (multi-purpose cinema), a formulaic combination of '*auteur* cinema + genre + literary adaptation + star system + formal look' (quoted in Gubern *et al.* 1994: 421). Rabal's filmography of the 1980s includes many examples of this formula, such as *La Colmena/ The Hive* (Mario Camus 1982), *Tiempo de silencio*, *Los Paraísos perdidos/Lost*

Paradise (Basilio Martín Patino 1985), *Luces de Bohemia/Bohemian Lights* (Miguel Ángel Díez, 1985), *Divinas palabras/Divine Words* (José Luis García Sánchez, 1987) and, of course, the paradigmatic *Los santos inocentes*. This latter film united the adaptation of a Miguel Delibes novel of social realism with direction by Mario Camus, and starred Rabal alongside veteran comedy actor Alfredo Landa.[7]

Many of the 'heritage' films of the 1980s and 1990s are criticised for a perceived homogenisation of Spanish cinema, brought about by their emphasis on style and surface qualities and their middlebrow liberalism. Their frequently domestic and personalised narratives are charged with exercising a nostalgic depoliticisation of historical memory, reflecting and promoting the consensus politics of 1980s Spain (Monterde 1989: 56).[8] However, the casting of Rabal in such films (and indeed Landa, in *Los Santos inocentes*) has an important re-politicising function, reinforcing and reactivating their usually social realist discourse through the combined effects of characterisation, performance and persona. Rabal's association with a heavily class- and gender-coded 'authenticity' also counterbalances any 'simultaneously feminine and bourgeois evidence of "pretension" in matters of culture' (Bourdieu 1986: 382–3) implied in the critique of the heritage film. Indeed the 'authenticity' of Rabal's characters is frequently characterised by a 'vulgarity' which is distinctly masculinist in character.

Interestingly, like these 'heritage' films, the phenomenon of stardom is similarly associated with personalisation and the bourgeois ideology of individualism, and also criticised for its perceived depoliticising effect on the grounds that 'stars serve to mask people's awareness of themselves as class members' so that 'collective experience is individualised and loses its collective significance' (Dyer 1979: 31). Rabal's public image, however, is very clearly class-coded, and many of his roles are overtly politicised, such as the Cuban revolutionary leader in *El Che Guevara* (Paolo Heusch, 1968), or the politicised outlaws of *Morte di un bandito* (Giuseppe Amato, 1961) or *Llanto por un bandido* (Carlos Saura, 1963), the anarchist Hippolyte of Luis Buñuel's *Belle de Jour*, or, his embodiment (twice) of the anti-totalitarian, pro-Enlightenment painter, Francisco de Goya (Nino Quevedo, 1970; Carlos Saura, 1999).[9] Rabal's own ideological commitment is legendary; a member of the Spanish Communist Party since the 1960s, he is saluted, in his obituaries, as 'the committed actor', 'the face of the left' (Martín-Lunas 2001). His outspoken views on political matters – 'I don't mince my words', he proudly claims to a Cuban interviewer (Rivero 1987: 71) – also reflect the 'plain speaking' Bourdieu has associated with working-class 'virility', defined through its opposition to 'bourgeois restraint, rules, manners' (Bourdieu 1986: 194, 196).

However, this politicised image has an undoubtedly nostalgic quality. Even though, born in 1926, Rabal's only direct experience of the pre-Civil War period was as a child, his political image evokes the populist left-wing utopianism of Spanish Republicanism in the 1930s. The actor himself has described his political commitment as a 'romantic communism', a 'communism of ideas', and his 'activism' has always been at the level of protests and petitions associated with the artistic and intellectual Left (Hidalgo 1985: 140; 66).[10] The appeal of Rabal's particular brand of nostalgic socialist idealism relates very clearly to the *desencanto* (disillusionment) of the late 1980s and early 1990s in Spain. This period of disillusionment was particularly associated with PSOE's evident abandonment of the more radical socialism of its clandestine years, its movement to the centre of party politics, and the government's increasing discredit in the light of political and financial scandal. Rabal's more idealist socialism, seemingly more genuine than the PSOE antics of the late 1980s, adds a further dimension to the discourse of authenticity his image inscribes. These nostalgic qualities, consistent with a more generalised nostalgia frequently attributed to the de-centred nature of contemporary society, also link him to the notion of a more 'authentic' past, 'a past that was unified and comprehensible, unlike the incoherent, divided present' (Case and Shaw 1989: 29).

Rabal's particularly ostentatious parading of his political persuasions, however, tend to make them more of an affect, rather than a force for change since, as Barry King argues, even stars with an overtly political identity unavoidably 'obscure the political issues they embody simply by demonstrating the lifestyle of their politics and displaying those beliefs as part of their personality' (cited in Dyer 1979: 31). As Bourdieu again notes, 'political choices … involve the more or less explicit and systematic representation an agent has of the social world, of his position within it and of the position he "ought" to occupy' (Bourdieu 1986: 454), thereby signalling a self-defining agency which, within the context of the patriarchal order, is continually associated with power and masculinity (Kirkham and Thumim 1993: 18). The very public assertion of political commitment is thus a further defining characteristic of Rabal's composite masculine identity.

Another key element of Rabal's image of masculinity relates to his off-screen reputation as something of a rake (linked to the sexually-charged image of his youthful roles as the seductive *galán*) (Hidalgo 1985: 94). Undoubtedly some of his 'closest fitting' mature performances draw heavily on this reputation, which has been variously demonised and indulgently condoned at different stages in his career. Less generous interpretations of the legendary *juerguismo* (wild revelling) – reaching a climax in adverse press reports linking his first car accident to a reputation for excessive drinking and philandering at one of the lowest points in his professional career – are posited as an explanation of the perceived distancing from Rabal by the New Spanish Cinema of the 1960s and early 1970s, and by the new generation emerging in the transition period (Hidalgo 1985: 113–14). In recent years, this reputation is recast as a kind of 'picaresque innocence' (Villán 2002), simultaneously distanced and condoned as 'childlike mischief' (Marinero 1992: 56). This treatment is extended to his characters too: Ginés and his crass vulgarity are endearingly presented as 'picaresque', as is Juncal (a role involving considerable improvisation and Rabal's collaboration on the script), for whom the diminutive 'don Joselín' has similar connotations. Performances such as these stress a 'conviviality' which, according to Bourdieu, characterises the working-class *bon vivant*, in opposition to middle-class bourgeois 'restraint and reticence' (Bourdieu 1986: 179). This opposition is visibly illustrated in the contrast between Rabal's convivial Ginés and the more restrained 'up-market' con-man, Gonzalo (Arturo Fernández) in *Truhanes*.

Sexual mores are very clearly implicated within this class-coded opposition between conviviality and restraint in the construction of Rabal's popular image, as demonstrated in his book of shared memoirs jointly published with Carmen Sevilla, a major star of the Spanish cinema's golden age of the 1930s and 1940s folkloric musicals (Rabal and Sevilla, 1999). The memoirs present contrasting recollections and interpretations of that period, dynamically structured along parallel lines of class, gender and political difference, and with a strong emphasis on the differing attitudes to sexual behaviour: Sevilla representing the privileged world of the Spanish bourgeoisie with its 'apoliticism' and somewhat hypocritical code of sexual restraint; Rabal representing the under-privileged, politicised working-class with a 'liberal' (in every sense of the word) and self-indulgent behavioural code. Despite Rabal's persistent focus on the harsh realities of working-class life, the period as a whole is presented in an unmistakably nostalgic mode.

It is the operation of this discourse of nostalgia which seemingly reconciles – or ignores – the contradiction in the Rabal persona between the convivial philanderer on the one hand and, on the other, the family man firmly rooted in his 'clan', with a very public family life, partly due to the stage and film careers of his wife and children (Boyero 1992a: 24).[11] Rabal's working-class identity also functions as a curious apologia for a sexual predatoriness which might otherwise grate against more contemporary values and expectations. This is illustrated in director Carlos Saura's 'discretely sepia-coloured' association of Rabal's image with the

> look of a hungry wolf for whom a woman is the prey it must hunt down … That kind of man was common in those days, hungry for a woman, for sex, pure and simple. Some of them had little mustaches, some were fascists with American cigarettes and an unpleasant air, who frequented the Pasapoga and the Villa Romana. Paco was one of the others, one of those who make up for the hunger of the past by devouring everything. (quoted in Hidalgo 1985: 94)

Pascual Vera Nicolás points out that in many of his later roles Rabal is actually cast as 'probably the purest *antigalán* cinema has ever known' (1992: 110), seemingly emphasising the ambiguities less overtly inscribed within the masculine identity of his more youthful roles. The mature roles often feature characters whose masculinity and capacity for dominance is in some way physically or mentally undermined or circumscribed, the veneer of confident male superiority apparently slipping to reveal the underlying vulnerability and anxiety of masculine identity and authority: Máximo Espejo in *Átame/Tie Me Up! Tie Me Down!* (Pedro Almodóvar, 1989) is wheelchair-bound, Goya is deaf and losing his sanity, Azarías is mentally retarded, and so on. However, the discourses of authenticity and nostalgia ensure that the loss of one form of power and authority is substituted with another. The dominance associated with physical strength and sexual magnetism in the younger Rabal is displaced onto other forms of authority discussed earlier, such as experience and worldly wisdom. However, the magnetic sexuality of the early years, and the continuing reputation for concupiscence, remain as a tacit force behind these later roles, underpinning them with a latent desire which can surface occasionally in quite disturbingly powerful ways, as in the voyeurism of Máximo Espejo, or when the elderly Goya reaches out to touch his daughter's breast (*Goya en Burdeos*). Reminders of a similarly ever-present male aggression can erupt in sudden, emotional surges of anger, as when Goya snaps out of his senile hallucinations to shout at strangers who annoy him, or throwing a teacup across the room when he loses patience with his daughter, or, indeed, in Azarías's more calculated execution of the *señorito* who humiliated and exploited his family, and shot his pet bird for amusement. The powerful presence of these characters is thus clearly underwritten by what we might term the 'nostalgic masculinity' of the Rabal persona which either reinforces their strength and authoritative status, or increases their poignancy by tacitly counter-pointing their vulnerability.

From the 1980s onwards, Rabal is often presented as an emblem of national identity, a 'genuine product of this country' (Boyero 1992b: 48–50). His 'mythical' status was acquired at a critical moment of change, when the institutional cultural agenda of the 1980s was seeking to dissolve the profound political divisions of the Spanish Civil War and dictatorship, and economic, industrial and legislative change was having a major impact on the arch-conservative, and hypocritical, patriarchal structures and role models of the Franco era. Although these developments represented a predominantly positive and progressive change for the better, the dismantling of the anachronisms of the past also generated a sense of uncertainty, a magnified version of what is frequently described as the fragmented and de-centred cultural experience of the late twentieth century. The 'destabilisation' of the concept of the nation state, challenged very specifically in Spain by the creation of the regional autonomies and integration into the European Community, within the wider context of increasingly global economic activity and communications systems, focused attention on questions of national and other forms of cultural identity.

Given the very prominent concern with questions of identity in this period, and the very culture-specific characteristics of Rabal's public image, it is perhaps inevitable that he began to be constructed in terms of an emblematic Spanishness which is in itself ambiguous: he is 'a bit of a Quixote ... and a bit of a Sancho' (Vera Nicolás 1992: 112). As noted above, his heavily gendered and politicised image embodies the nostalgic myth of a past in which identities seemed more clearly defined, however problematically, and despite their intrinsic ambiguities. He offers a light-hearted response to contemporary Western society's crisis in masculinity, and is presented as the 'quintessence' of a nostalgically 'picaresque Spain' (ibid.). However, whilst capturing the significance of Rabal's popular appeal, such representations, and specifically the complicit indulgence of his 'nostalgic masculinity', actually constitute a remystification of the anachronistic gender role model he represents. This irony is captured, presumably unintentionally, in the San Sebastián Film Festival press release announcing the posthumous award of the Premio Donostia for a lifetime's work to Paco Rabal in September 2001. He had been, it declared, 'A great actor. Every inch a man.'

Notes

1   All translations of quotations from the Spanish original are mine.

2   The theatrical use of the word *galán* in Spanish, meaning 'hero' or 'leading man', also carries specific connotations of the seductive lover or 'ladies' man'.

3   These two films, with their experimental directorial techniques, pushed Rabal to extremes of physical and mental toleration and humiliation which resulted, according to some accounts, in the actor's near breakdown (Hidalgo 1985: 103–8).

4   See Richard Dyer's discussion of 'performance signs' (Dyer 1979: 151).

5   Miguel Hidalgo gives an account of Rabal's detailed preparation for the role of Azarías which involved extensive research in Extremadura, having a mouthpiece made to affect the voice, and the purchase of authentic clothing (Hidalgo 1985: 133–4).

6   See, for example, Graeme Turner's overview on the film spectator and psychoanalysis (Turner 1988: 127–40).

7   The film not only achieved the Cannes Best Actor award for Landa and Rabal jointly, but also became the highest grossing film in Spanish film history at that point.

8   As I have argued elsewhere, such blanket dismissal fails to recognise that the location of narratives within the private sphere corresponds to the way historical reality is experienced by individuals and in popular cultural memory, especially in Spain under Francoism where opposition was excluded from the public

sphere (Jordan and Morgan-Tamosunas 1998: 39–42; Morgan-Tamosunas 2000: 115–16). In this sense, the personal is, indeed, always political.

9   Even overtly right-wing films of the early years are susceptible to subversive readings prompted by Rabal's own politicised image. The powerful resistance embodied in his representation of Juan, militant leader of the exploited miners in *La Guerra de Dios* (Rafael Gil, 1958), for example, arguably exceeds the containment of the narrative resolution which imposes a depoliticising reconciliation of class conflict through the drama of an 'act-of-God' tragedy and the intervention of the village priest.

10 This is particularly reflected in his work with directors such as Luis Buñuel, Carlos Saura, Michelangelo Antonioni and Luchino Visconti, his stage career, and his literary association with the poets of the Spanish Generation of '27, whose work is the subject of various sound recordings and documentaries made by Rabal. These (predominantly lyrical) poets were particularly concerned with the valorisation of popular culture, and generally associated with the Left, either through their political affiliations, as in the case of the Communist Rafael Alberti, or because of their appropriation by oppositional and marginalised groups, as in the case of Federico García Lorca. Dámaso Alonso, a member of the group and neighbour to the Rabal family in Madrid, was instrumental in helping to initiate Rabal's career in the theatre. In later life Rabal becomes something of a 'poet of the people' in his own right, writing his own popular verses and *coplas*, often alluding to contemporary issues, and paradoxically printed on a regular basis in Spain's right-wing daily *ABC*. Frequently photographed in his iconographic cap or *boina* (beret), he even displays an uncanny (and surely not unintentional) resemblance to the '27 poet Rafael Alberti!

11 Rabal was married to the well-known stage actor, Asunción Balaguer, in the 1950s; their daughter, Teresa Rabal, is a well-established actor, and their son, Benito Rabal, a film director.

chapter 5

MASCULINITY AND CLASS: MICHAEL CAINE AS 'WORKING-CLASS HERO'
Robert Shail

This chapter concerns itself with the concept of masculinity as a historically defined construct, with the specific case of Michael Caine, and in particular with his persona in 1960s British cinema, used as an exemplar of how cinematic representations play their part in this process. Underlying its approach is an acknowledgement of the arguments proposed by Judith Butler in her study *Gender Trouble*. Butler suggests that all gender definitions are culturally conditioned constructs which bear only a superficial relationship with biologically defined sex. However, rather than seeing gender as a construct which is imposed from outside by a repressive system, namely patriarchy, Butler argues that it is taken on internally by the individual through a process of social identification and role-play affirmation. In a patriarchal system, traditional notions of maleness are the formative 'norm' towards which identification is focused (Butler 1990: 8–13). At the same time, this process of identification is dependent upon dominant notions of gender identity which are specific to a given historical moment as, for Butler, gender is always historically placed and necessarily reflects the specific wider cultural conditions within which it functions. These functions vary according to the exact nature of that context. Gender, like any other social phenomenon, can therefore be examined as being symptomatic of wider historical processes. This concept of gender construction is particularly helpful in relating representations of gender in the cinema back to the changing cultural and social context in which they were produced.

Butler also acknowledges that culture and society are in a constant state of flux and change, so that the construction of a gendered identity is always reliant upon identification with representations which are unstable and fluid:

As historically specific organisations of language, discourses present themselves in the plural, coexisting within temporal frames, and instituting unpredictable and inadvertent convergences from which specific modalities of discursive possibilities are engendered. (Butler 1990: 145)

Butler describes patriarchy as a system which has to operate within historical specifics to which it reacts and constantly adapts. Although its value system remains relatively constant, its continuation depends upon an essential cultural and social elasticity. Butler sees this interpretative model as being positive in its consequences in that this openness in the functioning of patriarchy allows for its possible subversion and adaptation by the individual within given historical parameters. She contrasts this with more traditional, deterministic forms of feminist thought which she describes as being based on 'foundationalism'. She argues that 'the internal paradox of this foundationalism is that it presumes, fixes and constrains the very "subjects" that it hopes to represent and liberate' (Butler 1990: 148). By proposing a model of patriarchy which is both flexible and subject to historical conditions, she also allows for a recognition of the complex forms this system might take, as well as acknowledging the wide variety of possible reactions and responses to it that might be possible.

If the functioning of patriarchy itself is less monolithic and deterministic this could be seen to imply that the filmic construction of masculinity is open to fluidity and variety in its representations. This relation between cinema and the dominant ideology has been addressed by Pat Kirkham and Janet Thumim in the introductory essay to their collection of essays on masculinity written by women, *Me Jane*. They argue that images of masculinity are always caught up with issues of control and the underlying structures of social power which support patriarchy (Kirkham and Thumim 1995b: 18). The images of masculinity created by cinema necessarily play on values and attitudes drawn from wider social and cultural conditions. However, this relationship is not simply one which reinforces a set of dominant assumptions in a deterministic manner. It is capable of playing out contradictions, anxieties and dysfunctions which exist within such power structures. Kirkham and Thumim see this as being particularly appropriate for contemporary notions of masculinity, when masculinity is 'marked, time and again, as delicate, fragile, provisional: it is under threat, in danger of collapse: it is an impossible ideal – most of all it seems to be an impediment to the desirable human experience of pleasure-in-being' (Kirkham and Thumim 1995b: 11).

This is a particularly useful analysis when looking at a period such as the 1960s in Britain, when Michael Caine rose to prominence, which tends to be characterised by social and cultural change of a quite dramatic nature. The deconstruction and reconstruction of masculinity then becomes symptomatic of a wider process of change affecting various forms of power structure.

Kirkham and Thumim suggest that such is the nature of gender construction that it can be used in an almost arbitrary way to carry any number of ideological attributes and play these out in a form of moral conflict (Kirkham and Thumim 1995b: 28–9). This could incorporate a variety of issues other than gender, including ethnicity and class, but is always related to the exercising of power relations. They also propose that the particular character of traditional representations of masculinity facilitates an examination of key areas of the power structure from which they are derived. One such area would be the depiction of class (Kirkham and Thumim 1995b: 19–21). This again has particular relevance to the nature of British cinema and society in the 1960s, where the fracturing and restatement of masculine identity is frequently tied in with a disintegration of normal class boundaries and the desire to rebel against the constrictions which those boundaries construct. The case of Michael Caine is particularly appropriate here in that, as I will demonstrate, Caine's representation of masculinity is so intrinsically caught up with notions of class identity.

The appropriation of class as a means of defining the construction of masculine identity in the Britain of the 1960s has been thoroughly analysed by John Hill in his study *Sex, Class and Realism* and is easily documented through its centrality to the personas established by many of the new male stars of the period; Albert Finney, Tom Courtenay and Richard Harris are all typical of the phenomenon. Similarly, Caine's persona played heavily on his working-class credentials, although the specifics of his established image differed in one or two key areas. In place of a masculinity forged in the harsh industrial landscapes of the north of England, Caine offers us a southern masculinity rooted in the cultural landscape of working-class London. The tough, aggressive, sometimes violent, maleness of Finney and Harris is replaced by a more playful, humorous, although equally self-confident, identity. This tends to give him a particular affinity with his fellow Londoner Terence Stamp. What they all share is a notion of masculinity in which rebellion against the constraints of more traditional versions of British male identity is articulated both through gender representation and through the mobilisation of a certain definition of class identity. Although Caine's later persona often continued to play on elements of this construction of working-class maleness (*Mona Lisa*, Neil Jordan, 1986; *Dirty Rotten Scoundrels*, Frank Oz, 1988; *Little Voice*, Mark Herman, 1998), or has also developed his position as an international character actor (*Educating Rita*, Lewis Gilbert, 1983; *The Cider House Rules*, Lasse Hallström, 1999), it is during the 1960s in Britain that it has most cultural resonance. Caine is distinctive in that he is one of only four British stars to have achieved real star status within Hollywood (the others being Sean Connery, Richard Burton and Anthony Hopkins) whilst, unlike Burton, Connery or Hopkins, never having made any attempt to disguise his origins as the son of a porter at Billingsgate fish market, a working-class Londoner who had come up the hard way. In fact, he has created a screen persona which deliberately plays upon the qualities associated with his background. The acceptance, and indeed success, of so defiantly proletarian a star indicates the kind of social changes which had taken place in Britain during the 1960s. This chapter will analyse the image of proletarian ascendancy which Caine projected in four films of the period: *The Ipcress File* (Sidney J. Furie, 1965), *Alfie* (Lewis Gilbert, 1966), *The Italian Job* (Peter Collinson, 1969) and *Get Carter* (Mike Hodges, 1971).

One of the dominant perceptions of the 1960s remains the idea that British culture shifted decisively away from its traditionally middle-class basis (constructed through the prevalence of the highbrow arts, conventional morality and political consensus) and moved towards a working-class-dominated culture (built around the popular media, a more liberal morality and political radicalism). Arthur Marwick, whilst at pains to dispel the myth of classlessness in the 1960s and emphasise that the British remained acutely aware of class difference, suggests that the working classes increasingly perceived themselves to be at the centre of most aspects of British life (Marwick 1996: 123–4, 134–44). Much of this change of emphasis grew from a recognition that 'a liveliness and a spirit of innovation not seen in British society for generations' was reaching the public consciousness through pop music, photography, fashion and the cinema, and that this new energy had its source primarily in the young working classes (Marwick 1996: 140). This cultural development was mirrored by social and economic improvements for the working classes brought about by the relative scarcity of skilled labour and the gradual extension of unionisation in the work place. Greater financial security added a level of class confidence previously unavailable. This affluence and confidence, as well as the rebellion against middle-class conformity, found an available expression initially in representation of the working-class rebel hero in the New Wave films, but was subsequently reflected in the screen persona developed by Michael Caine.

The British cinema was quick to identify the shift that had taken place within its own indigenous market. Between 1955 and 1963 over two-thirds of the audience and over half of the cinemas in Britain had disappeared (Perilli 1983). The audience that remained was predominantly young, male and working class, a fact which was soon exploited by producers once they had identified which films were more successful with this new audience (Laing 1986: 109–11). Such an environment had facilitated the success of actors like Finney, Courtenay and Harris, and Caine himself was able to utilise the opportunity that changed circumstances offered to him, along with the other working-class Londoner he shared lodgings with, Terence Stamp. American audiences similarly responded to the novelty of British actors who did not conform to the established stereotypes made familiar to them for generations by the likes of Ronald Coleman, David Niven and Laurence Olivier. For an industry whose senior personnel were still drawn largely from the ranks of the upper classes, such a radical sea-change was inevitably something that took time to properly assimilate, particularly as Caine's brand of southern proletarianism represented a set of qualities rather different from those of the northern working-class heroes. Caine's particular form of metropolitan, working-class assertiveness may have seemed rather too close for comfort for the executives of London-based production companies and somewhat less manageable than the more distant new breed represented by the northern stars.

If Finney, Courtenay and Harris were angry, tough and intense, then Caine, in David Shipman's words, was 'recognisably the fellow who served you on the barrow, or stood next to you downing a pint, friendly, glib and myopic' (Shipman 1989: 89). John Caughie describes his persona as being that of 'the crafty Cockney Lothario … never a romantic hero, marked indelibly as basically an "ordinary bloke" by his accent' (Caughie and Rockett 1996: 41). Caine's public image, from the mid-1960s onwards, was carefully constructed through the media and built around his identification with the values of the newly ascendant, young, urban working classes. An article in the *Daily Express* in 1965 noted that, along with Terence Stamp, Lionel Bart and David Bailey, Caine's was 'one of those names lending a stamp of approval on where to eat, where to dance, where to take your "birds", what after-shave and shirts to wear' and Caine himself is quoted as acknowledging that 'the world of models, photographers and actors is the New Aristocracy' (Leslie 1965). This new elite was predominantly young, working-class, male and, with the exception of the Northern pop stars, from London. Caine's ability to tap into a deep seam of comfortable recognition in the new British cinema audience is confirmed by his rapid ascent to the top of the British star popularity polls by 1966 (Shipman 1989: 90). His combination of an astute sense of urban style and a streetwise canniness made him an immediate icon of the fashionable male proletarian ascendancy. Even his 'National

Health specs' became part of the downbeat image. Caine's persona brought together a sense of ordinariness, which made it easy for audiences to identify with him, with a feeling that his rough-edged, quick-wittedness was the essential ingredient in his success, a quality that any working-class lad might equally possess. The success of this persona needs to be seen in specific relation to the cultural climate in which it was created. He was seen as having risen to success in the newly meritocratic Britain of the Wilson government, but still carried with him the native intelligence and self-assurance bred of hardship.[1] If he now had the trappings of material affluence and a flat in Grovesnor Square, his audience could vicariously share in the achievements of man who was ordinary and everyday, just like them. Caine's particular construction of masculine identity reflected both a notion of rebellion against the drab conformity of the 1950s which was articulated in class terms and an embodiment of the new myth of classlessness represented by the breakthrough into the public arena of a generation of distinctively working-class icons.

Caine's earlier career had been spent largely in minor supporting roles, with his only notable success coming when cast against type as the effete Lieutenant Bromhead in *Zulu* (Cy Endfield, 1964). His recognisable public image was really first introduced in *The Ipcress File*. His performance as the spy Harry Palmer established the characteristic Caine persona for cinema audiences. Palmer/Caine is clearly working class, with his strong South London accent, and his appearance is defiantly ordinary, with those horn-rimmed glasses and his shabby raincoat. At the same time we see that there is an unexpected level of sophistication and evident self-education in Palmer: he is a fine cook, with a taste for good wines and whiskey, and he enjoys classical music. In a seminal sequence, he is found by his boss in what was, at the time, a newly fashionable supermarket, buying champignon mushrooms. His superior is clearly a product of the old British class system, university educated, an officer and middle class. Yet here, in this emergent Britain, he is the one who is socially adrift; confused and outsmarted in every department by his one-time inferior. An element of rebelliousness is intrinsic to the character and to Caine's performance: we are informed early on that he has been recruited from an army prison where he had been sent for striking an officer. Critics were quick to recognise the freshness of the role and its social relevance. Alexander Walker, in the London *Evening*

Michael Caine as Harry Palmer in *The Ipcress File* (Sidney J. Furie, 1965)

Standard, referred to the way Palmer 'cultivates those tiny acts of insolence – like leaving doors open behind him – that annoy his chiefs' (Walker 1965). The film deliberately set out to establish Caine's Harry Palmer persona in opposition to the suave, playboy image of the British spy already made internationally popular by Sean Connery in the Bond films. Palmer operates in a world of drab offices and grubby, congested London streets, photographed in appropriately muted colours by Otto Heller. The tedium and routine involved in his job is emphasised, with its dull surveillance assignments and its endless form filling. He is far from the infallible, jet-setting figure audiences were beginning to associate with British spy films of the period. The poster campaign for the film played on this, with images of the bespectacled Caine in his grubby 'Mac' and references to 'the thinking man's *Goldfinger*'. However, this created a mythic image of its own. If Bond was a projection of classless, consumerist fantasies, then Palmer was definitely 'one of us'; a working spy, doing his rather unpleasant job for Queen and country, but using his native, working-class guile to get the best deal out of it that he can. Even if he could not match the longevity of Bond, Palmer was still to reappear in two 1960s sequels, *Funeral in Berlin* (Guy Hamilton, 1966) and *Billion Dollar Brain* (Ken Russell, 1968), and has been revived again more recently, albeit rather unsuccessfully (stripped of his 1960s context he made a much less resonant figure).

The role of the 1960s working-class hero was taken to new levels by Caine in *Alfie*, where his swaggering womaniser works his way through a succession of 'birds' before realising the essential emptiness at the heart of his swinging lifestyle. Such was the impact of his performance in the title role that he became synonymous with the part. This personal affinity between Caine and the character he played was central to the way the film was promoted. Its promotional posters proclaimed that 'Michael Caine *is* Alfie, *is* Wicked, *is* Crafty, *is* Irresistible'. This level of identification between star and role has become a fairly routine advertising device, but the effect of it in 1966 is confirmed by Alexander Walker who records the impact it had on an audience who were unused to such an approach (Walker 1986: 306). Caine/Alfie is presented as the embodiment of the new, Swinging London meritocracy. When he declares 'I've been doing things all my life that I'm not supposed to', the audience is invited to cheer on his rebellion, even if this is achieved through a single-minded pursuance of his own personal pleasure at almost any cost. In her review in the *Spectator*, Isobel Quigley astutely observed that the Caine/Alfie persona, once 'Thought totally un-English, is now being fished out of the proletarian pond where Englishness of the traditional kind never flourished. Like the new bright clothes on the new bright boys, he suggests a subterranean national character rising to surprise even the locals' (Quigley 1966).

With the accompaniment of Sonny Rollins' jazz score, the careful use of London locations and street scenes, and the array of attractive actresses who find his charms impossible to resist, Caine's Alfie exudes the kind of joyful male hedonism which increasingly characterised the ethos of the mid-1960s. The key to Caine's achievement in drawing the audience's sympathy was the decision to have him speak directly to the camera. He was clearly aware of the example already set by Albert Finney in *Tom Jones* (Tony Richardson, 1963), but chose to adopt a more intimate, personable tone, so that the audience are invited to feel that Alfie is one of them. With his slow delivery, sleepy eyes and the occasional knowing grin, it becomes almost impossible not to be won over by his charm, no matter how disparaging he is of the women he so frequently seduces.

However, despite the exuberant glee with which the film depicts the conquest of his innumerable 'birds', including the girl in the dry cleaners where he can satisfy himself and get his suit pressed at the same time, the film shifts mood strikingly in its final third. Here Alfie meets his comeuppance after witnessing the grim reality of a backstreet abortion and being rejected for a younger man by the even more predatory Shelley Winters. Director Lewis Gilbert acknowledged the film's double-edged quality: 'Alfie was an infinitely sad character. He was a charming rogue. He was immoral, but the damage he inflicted was on himself. That comes out at the end of the film' (Gilbert 2001). Existing critical analysis reflects a certain confusion over this sudden change of moral emphasis. Robert Murphy sympathetically assesses Alfie as a genuinely muddled 1960s male, whose 'attitude to women is less misogyny than a failure to communicate on anything but the most basic level' (Murphy 1992: 144). By contrast, Alexander Walker finds the film's final shift to a traditionally moralistic tone hypocritical and unconvincing:

> His clear-eyed amorality ('I don't want a bird's respect, wouldn't know what to do with it'), so unflinchingly conveyed by Caine's voice-over narration, is far more convincing than the cautionary moral he extracts from his experiences at the end of the film ('I ain't got my peace of mind and if you ain't got that, you got nothing'). (Walker 1986: 307–8)

Certainly, the message of the final sequences, which suggest that Alfie must pay for his excesses, is rather contradicted by the sheer pleasure which the audience is invited to share in during his whole-hearted pursuit of personal gratification in the first half of the film, although the roots of this internal conflict in the film can be traced to the 1950s moral context reflected in its original source.[2]

This tendency to hold back from fully embracing the kind of sexual and cultural freedoms which the 1960s was introducing is characteristic of many of the Swinging London films (Murphy 1992; see chapter 7). In *Alfie*'s obvious precursor *Tom Jones* the hero finally settles for the safety of marriage to his true love and in *The Knack* (Richard Lester, 1965) it is Michael Crawford's conventional Colin who wins out over the more typical 1960s hedonist Tolen (Ray Brooks). The version of masculinity offered by *Alfie* reflects many of the confusions apparent in mid-1960s notions of male identity. There is the celebration of a liberated, hedonistic working-class male who is characterised through his self-confidence and dynamism. This is then tempered by a concern for the possible negative moral consequences of his selfishness and shallowness, with the alternative of a more conventional social role still held up as an exemplar. At the same time, the model of rampant male heterosexist arrogance represented by Caine's Alfie is an obvious precursor to more contemporary versions of 'laddishness' where the character's misogyny has been recycled to provide a reassuring endorsement of conventional male attitudes. The re-emergence of such a persona at a time of a perceived crisis in masculinity is not dissimilar to the function of *Alfie* in the mid-1960s, where the possibilities of radical changes in male identity produce a sense of social unease and a consequent reaction by the forces of conformity.

A more convincingly exuberant, if simplistic, endorsement of the kind of changes taking place at the time in male identity can be found in *The Italian Job*. If the film remains a fairly inconsequential caper movie, this does not detract from the fact that it contains a revealing exposition of the kind of male class transgressions which had already become accepted during the decade. Caine's character, Crocker, is deliberately juxtaposed with the master criminal Mr Bridger, played with monarchical dignity by Noel Coward. Here the 'new aristocracy' is contrasted with the old. Coward, who carries with him all the associations of a long career of establishment snobbery, is unmercifully parodied. Resplendent in his cell decorated with pictures of the royal family, his criminal plans are motivated by a patriotic desire to boost the British economy (by stealing from the Fiat car plant in Turin). His final triumph is greeted by the ironic sight of the whole prison population gathering to applaud him. In contrast, Caine is the epitome of the new male working-class elite. Our first image of him is of his mocking face grinning into the camera. We follow him as he leaves prison, is collected by his glamorous girlfriend, picks up his Aston Martin and gets his new suit from the tailors. Whilst the upper-class Coward languishes in a false sham of authority in prison, his underling has stolen all the trappings and symbols that were his. It is Caine who masterminds the robbery and who directs the services of his proficient, and mainly working-class, team. The only middle-class participants in the robbery, Chris, Tony and Dominic, are known as the 'chinless wonders'. With a confidence bordering on arrogance, the film assumes a complete acceptance by its audience of a class structure which has been turned on its head. The reconstruction of male identity here is dependent upon a self-confidence which, if limited in its aspirations, has its roots in a representation of a proletarian superiority. Working-class masculinity becomes a means to achieve the overthrow of the accepted power structure of British male society.

It is useful at this point to refer back to Richard Dyer's model for the analysis of subversive or alternative star types (Dyer 1998: 52–9). Dyer describes a star type which contradicts the prevalent signifying system of stardom by failing to conform to dominant cultural values. Such 'rebel' types embody instead a notion of 'anomie' which refers to a person who is estranged from mainstream society because they do not 'fit in with prevailing norms and/or because they see the latter's pointlessness' (Dyer 1998: 52). This might suggest itself as an appropriate analytical framework within which to understand the function performed by a star like Michael Caine. However, I would suggest that it is actually more useful to identify Caine's persona as operating in a manner which resembles Dyer's definition of the 'hero'. Dyer argues that 'most stars discussed as social types are seen as representing dominant values in society, by affirming what those values are in the "hero" types' (ibid.). Caine's persona can be seen as conforming to this definition, the startling difference being the fact that the dominant values in operation have clearly altered. Rather than supporting bourgeois ideology, Caine's heroes reflect an ideological system in the process of being inverted. The oppositional ideology of the working-class 'rebel' has actually become normative. Caine becomes a 'hero' for an alternative system of dominant values. This reversal is analogous to the kind of restructuring of gender identification which Steve Neale has previously pointed to (Neale 1983). Whilst in conventional terms of gender politics, Caine's persona remains rooted in a fairly traditional discourse of masculinity, it operates in a much more radical respect in its depiction of class. In Neale's terms, Caine does not act so much as to fetishise masculine identity, as he does to fetishise a specific masculine *class* identity.

Nowhere is this clearer than in *Get Carter*. Here Caine pushes his personification of normative/subversive working-class 'heroism' to the absolute extreme. Caine acknowledged that part of his motivation for taking on the role of the defiantly unpleasant, but charismatic, gangster Jack Carter was to show the reality of the violence involved in such a way of life (Caine 1992: 272–4). To this end, acting as his own producer, he employed Mike Hodges as writer and director on the strength of his background in gritty television documentaries (Hodges worked throughout the 1960s for Granada's groundbreaking investigative programme *World in Action*). Nonetheless, the film adopts a style which mythologises and fetishises the conduct of its central character. This is apparent from the promotional material for the film which centred almost entirely on images of the aggressive violence and mythic strength of Carter. The promotional photographs used frequently show Caine as the confident predator, either in purely sexual terms with the women he seduces or in dispensing with the men who get in his way. The poster campaign showed an iconographic figure of the gangster in his black trench coat, wielding a crudely phallic double-barrel shotgun, under the banner heading 'Caine *is* Carter *is* a Killer'. The violence contained in the film, although superficially justified by a sociologically intentioned authenticity, is also clearly designed to shock. Reactions like that of Felix Barker in the London *Evening Standard* show just how well the film succeeded in this: 'What is that strange smell in my nostrils? What is the garbage clinging round my ankles? It is a film called *Get Carter*. At any time this would be a revolting, bestial, horribly violent piece of cinema' (Barker 1971). The power of the film rests greatly on exactly its ability to combine realist tropes with a carefully formulated process of stylisation. The mythic aspect is established from the outset by the overt references to Raymond Chandler (Carter reads *Farewell My Lovely* on his train back to the North). The utilisation of realist devices, which were currently re-emerging in contemporary television drama, such as location shooting, natural lighting and the use of non-professional actors, has been noted by critics like George Perry (1985: 270) who recognised what appeared to be a resurgence in the naturalistic British crime film; Richard Burton appeared at roughly the same time in *Villain* (Michael Tuchner, 1971). *Get Carter* makes elaborate use of its Newcastle locations, with key sequences at the racetrack and along a devastatingly ugly stretch of industrial shoreline. Zoom lenses are used to allow Caine to walk into a superbly smoky pub and order his pint of bitter 'in a thin glass' amongst the men genuinely using the bar. The director of photography, Wolfgang Suschitzky, had been trained in 'fly on the wall' documentaries and made particularly adept use of long shots with deep focal length, producing a voyeuristic sensation in the spectator. At the same time the dialogue is minimalistically terse, so that exchanges like that with the king of the slot-machines, Brumby, have become part of the mythology surrounding the film: 'You're a big man, but you're out of shape. With me it's a full-time job. Now behave yourself.' The level of formalism which dominates the film is typified by the sequence in which Carter is pounced upon by his enemies whilst in bed with his landlady. His rivals are rapidly pursued from the house at the point of a shotgun by a naked Caine, who is then seen in long shot across a street, with a passing marching band in the foreground. Such scenes combine a sense of documentary authenticity with stylised visual motifs drawn from the generic vocabulary of the tough gangster film.

The characteristic vision of Britain as depicted in *Get Carter* is one of a culture that is homogeneously working-class in basis. The film portrays no character or social situation which is outside of this proletarian sphere. This does not mean that the film is confined to the traditional arenas of male working-class drama; the pub, the football match or the workplace. Here, the typical settings of the dominant middle classes have been appropriated, so that the master criminal, played with a suitable irony by John Osborne, has become a kind of decadent lord of the manor living in his country house with all of his lower-class friends, playing at being the aristocracy. This is an almost hermetically sealed new world, where the familiar codes of class conduct inherited from the 1950s have entirely vanished. In this setting there are only *good* working-class characters or *bad* working-class characters; no one else exists. In this context, Carter's search for justice, portrayed in an exaggerated, formalist manner, is raised almost to the stuff of Jacobean revenge drama or Elizabethan tragedy, as he is propelled towards his inevitable fate against the backdrop of grimy back-to-backs and boarding houses, leaving the scene strewn with the obligatory corpses. In his essay on the film, Robert Murphy compares Carter to Flamineo in Webster's *The White Devil* (Murphy 1999: 132). This is Shakespeare for its time, communicating to a popular audience whilst aiming at an almost mythic level of aesthetic and moral iconography. The depiction of working-class male identity remains richly layered, with Carter representing both a stylised embodiment of its virtues (strength, dynamism and certainty) and of the limitations (misogyny, brutishness, arrogance) which seem to seal its, and his, inevitable fate.

The development of Caine's persona, from Alfie to Carter, tends to indicate a hardening of his proletarian version of masculinity. The essentially good-natured rebelliousness of Harry Palmer rapidly becomes the belligerent and defensive cynicism of Jack Carter. This change tends to reflect the historic shift from the exuberance which marked the working-class emancipation of the early 1960s, to the besieged mentality which was to become a characteristic of the strikebound 1970s. The promised classless society of the 1960s had patently failed to materialise for the vast majority of British people and there was a consequent hardening of politicised class positions in the new decade.[3] Whilst acknowledging that Caine's success in the 1960s had a tendency to perpetuate certain rather archaic myths about what constitutes the nature of working-class life, he did, nonetheless, manage to achieve a level of audience response rivalled by only a few stars in the history of British cinema. This was in part due to his ability to convey the sense that material success had not altered his ability to remain true to the values and characteristics of his proletarian background. If he made bad films just for the money, then it was to pay for a nice house for his mother, a testament in itself to his familial and class loyalty. If he exalted in his wealth, then there was the pleasure for audiences of seeing an East End boy getting his own back on the British class system. As a result he remains an iconographic figure of the period, embodying both the strengths and limitations of a historic moment when the credentials required to be the all-conquering hero were essentially to be male, young and working-class.

Notes

1 Caine was able to win audience and media approval simply by emphasising his origins; an interview with Graham Fisher in the *Sunday Express* (21 May 1967) was screamingly headlined 'My father was on the dole but food was cheap then'.

2 *Alfie* was first conceived by its author, Bill Naughton, as a radio play called *Alfie Elkins and his Little Life* in 1962. Crucially, both this version and the stage adaptation starring Terence Stamp which followed it were set in the 1950s. As Robert Murphy observes, 'Alfie Elkins belongs to the semi-criminal world of spivs and wide-boys which dated from the war years rather than the Swinging 1960s' (Murphy 1992: 143).

Although Caine largely succeeds in establishing Alfie as a working-class hero for the new, liberated decade, the film exhibits attitudes which are rooted in a view of British life which comes from the 1950s. For further discussion of the changing social and cultural climate of the period see Marwick 1998, Green 1999 and MacDonald 1995.

3   For further discussion of the changing social and cultural climate of the period see Marwick 1998, Green 1999 and MacDonald 1995 (the introduction).

chapter 6

THE RELUCTANCE TO COMMIT: HUGH GRANT AND THE NEW BRITISH ROMANTIC COMEDY

Andrew Spicer

Erm, I am, as ever, in, er, bewildered awe of anyone who makes the kind of commitment Angus and Laura have made today. I know I couldn't do it, and, er, I think it's wonderful they can.
– Charles/Hugh Grant in *Four Weddings and a Funeral*

Hugh Grant is arguably the most successful current British star, famous throughout the world, able to sell a film on the strength of his name alone and commanding a US$6 million fee per picture. Grant's popularity is intertwined with a revival of British romantic comedy, a genre that has always relied on the charismatic presence of its leading actors, stars who can play comedy but who are not comedians. Like all popular genres, romantic comedy uses recognisable cultural types and Grant's performances are, respectively, the flustered twit in *Four Weddings and a Funeral* (Mike Newell, 1994), the boy-next-door in *Notting Hill* (Roger Michell, 1999), the Byronic cad in *Bridget Jones's Diary* (Sharon McGuire, 2001) and the Man About Town in *About a Boy* (Chris and Paul Weitz, 2002).[1] All these figures share a central characteristic: the reluctance to commit, and yet the need to find love meaningful and central to well-being and happiness. Grant's popularity, I shall argue, is bound up with the comedic exploration of this dilemma. Despite the scale of his popularity, Grant has received virtually no academic attention.[2] Because the sporadic critical comments that have surfaced show that he is often derided as a product of a debased popular taste, it is particularly important to subject his persona to disinterested investigation and analysis, as this will afford significant clues about contemporary masculinity.

Romantic comedy: characteristics and contemporary currency

In *Affairs to Remember*, Bruce Babington and Peter Evans define romantic comedy as a genre that 'centres on the couple, celebrating the passionate but hopefully companionate love that brings them together, and typically ending at the moment of passage into the responsibilities of marriage' (Babington and Evans 1989: 234). By making marriage the culmination of the narrative, romantic comedy effaces the basic contradiction between love as an intense, all-consuming short-lived passion, and its social function as the cornerstone of stable, lifelong monogamy (Wexman 1993: 8). As a fantasy genre with a tolerant and optimistic view of life, romantic comedy has close affinities with the fairytale, which allows a magical resolution of conflicts or dilemmas, confusions and misunderstandings and provides a 'generous space' for reconciliations and forgiveness. The romance is also a process of self-discovery through which both parties come to understand their own identities.

As Steve Neale has noted, romantic comedy's periods of greatest success have coincided with crises in the institution of marriage (Neale 1992: 285). In a post-AIDS, post-feminist era of accelerating divorce rates, where there is a general scepticism about marriage and commitment, romantic comedy provides a licensed space for the confident embrace of an idealised romantic union and, following a conspicuous American revival in the late 1980s and 1990s, is now more popular than ever in its history, a popularity that shows no sign of waning (Rubinfeld 2001: xiii–xiv). This revival seeks 'to reconcile old-fashioned romance with the erotic openness that is a legacy of the 1960s' (Krutnik 2002: 138). In Britain the revival inaugurated by *Four Weddings* has produced, in addition to the Grant films, over twenty examples, including *Sliding Doors* (Peter Howitt, 1997), *Fanny and Elvis* (Kay Mellor, 1998), *If Only* (Maria Ripoll, 1998), *This Year's Love* (David Kane, 1999), *Born Romantic* (David Kane, 2000), *Maybe Baby* (Ben Elton, 2000) and *Crush* (John McKay, 2001). However, as Frank Krutnik has argued so persuasively, contemporary romantic comedy's idealisation of love has a characteristically postmodern playfulness, a knowing mockery of genre conventions. Drawing on Umberto Eco, Krutnik contends that, in 'an age of lost innocence', writers and filmmakers are able to speak the language of love through foregrounding, even flaunting, generic conventions *as conventions* which allow their message to be articulated in the context of a self-protective irony. Audiences are invited to recognise the fabrication, but also to emotionally endorse the sentiment, to 'love the lie' (Krutnik 1998: 15–36).

I shall argue that Grant's films and his persona are layered with such self-protective irony, but also that his performances are geared to reveal the ambiguities and insecurities of contemporary masculinity, an ambiguity that has replaced the traditional enigma of femininity as the central issue of romantic comedy (Babington and Evans 1989: 280). It is this insecurity and lack of confidence, with the partial exception of *Bridget Jones*, that are the defining characteristics of Grant's characters, who are social and career failures, reluctant to commit themselves to the potentially powerful hazards of romantic union. This insecurity is generic, generational (the particular province of thirtysomethings) and specifically English. As Grant has acknowledged, his role is to explore a particular type of English inhibition and reserve, 'how embarrassing and funny it is to be English' (Grant in Chaudhuri 1994: 22).

Four Weddings and a Funeral: the diffident twit

In the first British romantic comedy for a generation, Hugh Grant's Charles in *Four Weddings* drew upon a familiar cultural type: the well-bred but hopelessly repressed, tongue-tied, awkward and self-deprecating Englishman, what Alexander Walker called the 'emotionally arrested sort of Brit twit we all know well, frequently love and laugh at immoderately' (Walker 1994: 32). Charles exists on the fringes of English high society: 'a slightly scatty middle-class boy who does not go to all the right Sloane parties' (Kenworthy 1994: 15). Charles's floppy-haired gaucheness and his stammerings, together with the ability to be surprised by almost everything, recalled P. G. Wodehouse's Bertie Wooster. However, his good looks and charm – the disingenuous lopsided grin – are those of a leading man, not the caricatured Silly Ass, the role played by his friend Tom (James Fleet), the seventh richest man in England. Charles's repeated humiliations as he blunders from one disaster to another evoked the strong burlesque tradition in British romantic comedy, notably the interwar films of Jack Buchanan such as *This'll Make You Whistle* (Herbert Wilcox, 1937) and the postwar films of Ian Carmichael including *Happy is the Bride* (Roy Boulting, 1958), where sentiment is always leavened by mockery. Although Grant's character was frequently derided, his comic timing was much admired. His performance was admirably summed up by one, unusually sympathetic, reviewer as a 'small marvel of acute observation, a credible amalgamation of flustered *faux pas*, timid lust, embarrassed ineptitude and confused emotional awakenings' (Andrew 1994: 65).

These 'emotional awakenings' could only be credible if Grant's character had some depth. Richard Curtis, who wrote the original screenplay, thought Grant's greatest strength, aside from his good looks, was the ability to speak his lines with an 'exuberant naturalism', that made a plausible and three-dimensional character from the exaggeration and caricature that is the staple mode of Curtis' comedy (Curtis 1994; also Bradbury and McGrath 1998: 103). Director Mike Newell also admired Grant's 'ability to speak [the dialogue] precisely and at the same time be believable', and saw his performance as the key to transforming a funny but directionless script into a coherent exploration of the problems of commitment (Newell in Kagan 2002: 19, 48). As Charles acknowledges, he is a 'serial monogamist', going the rounds of others' weddings which are characterised by embarrassment and desperation, admiring the couples' ability to commit themselves, but unable to do the same. At the funeral of Gareth (Simon Callow) – only the gay couple seem capable of commitment and true happiness – set in an industrial area on a miserable, rainy day in striking contrast with the first, sunlit weddings amidst leafy, verdant Home Counties pastoralism, Charles confides to Tom his fears about the difficulties, perhaps impossibility, of meeting a 'soul mate', and of impending disillusioned middle age.

Such fears have been sharpened because Charles believes he has seen his soul mate, the beautiful but enigmatic American Carrie (Andie MacDowell). Having been told that Carrie 'used to work at *Vogue*, quite out of your league', Charles is amazed when she skilfully contrives to sleep with him, only to disappear immediately afterwards. Her capricious appearances and reappearances unnerve Charles, who endures his deepest humiliation when she asks him to choose her wedding dress as she prepares, unaccountably, to marry an older man. Characteristically, of both his emotional repression and *Four Weddings*' intertextual postmodern irony, Charles can only declare his love hesitantly and parenthetically: 'In the immortal words of David Cassidy, when he was still with the Partridge family, "I think I love you".' Carrie's next reappearance at Charles's own wedding throws him into renewed confusion and indecision, finally jilting 'Duck Face' who floors him with a right cross, as his brother urges him to be true to his own feelings. This prepares for the final romantic union with Carrie, which, as Geoff King notes, takes the form of a disavowal of marriage (King 2002: 57). Even so, after preview audiences had judged that scene was too serious, a further scene was added whose conspectus of subsequent weddings lightly mocks generic conventions (Gitten 1995: 21). It was this comic deflation that perhaps allowed audiences to 'love the lie' of Charles and Carrie's union complete with child.

The new romantic idol

A modestly budgeted first attempt at reviving the genre, *Four Weddings* was hugely successful, earning £27.7 million in the UK and becoming, at this point, the highest-grossing British film ever (Roddick 1995). It opened in the States where adroit marketing allowed it to build an audience (Lukk 1997: 1–20). Already a hit, *Four Weddings* was aggressively marketed in Britain, though the British campaign, unlike the American, emphasised comedy more than romance (Blundy 1994: 16). Examination of the film's audience profiles reveals that it appealed predominantly to the ABC1 band (69 per cent) and to older cinemagoers with over 40 per cent of the audience aged over 35.[3] If British audiences enjoyed Grant's flustered foppishness and inept bunglings, for American women he represented the quintessence of diffident, old world charm. Unlike the stars of American romantic comedy, Grant was slightly fey without being gay, his sexuality built upon wit and irony not homespun sincerity, which made his seduction by an uninhibited American woman all the more satisfying (Muir 1994: 24). Sheila Johnston judged his success the triumph of 'wimp power', a backlash against the stone-faced action hero that had been the dominant male type (Johnston 1994: 26).

Grant was already a star in Japan, the heartthrob of teenage girls who saw him as the incarnation of the unworldly English aesthete after the release of *Maurice* (James Ivory, 1987), but *Four Weddings* made him a truly international star whose image was endlessly promoted in 'subsidiary circulation', in tabloid newspapers articles, television chat shows and magazine profiles, especially in mass circulation women's magazines (Tressider 1996: 139–47). Grant was careful to play up to the image of the affable and self-deprecating English gent. His interviewers commented frequently on his romantic attractiveness, a modern matinée idol, blue-eyed, very good-looking in a classically English way, with his floppy hair and charming smile, his impeccable manners leavened by the occasional expletive. Grant also exuded glamour, especially through his high-profile relationship with model and actress Elizabeth Hurley; the pair were one of *the* celebrity couples of the 1990s. His popularity survived the apparent disaster of his encounter with the prostitute Divine Brown in Los Angeles in June 1995: the revelation of his 'dark side' has served to give his persona extra depth. It has also been enhanced by his much-publicised break-up with Hurley in May 2000. The public's sense that he still carries a torch for Hurley, acting as a caring friend throughout her pregnancy in contradistinction to the churlish behaviour of the father, Steve Bing, has given his image pathos and old-fashioned chivalry.

Hurley and Grant formed a production company – Simian Films – in October 1994, which has survived their separation. It has allowed Grant considerable control over his choice of parts and enabled him to market himself as a particular, and highly desirable, commodity that could guarantee an audience. Simian Films is underwritten by Ted Turner's Castle Rock Entertainment, which provides development funds and the major finance for any approved project: 'The deal is that I try to find something I like and a writer to develop it and, in return, they get first refusal of what results' (Grant in Malcolm 1995: 8). However, Grant's career faltered in the mid-1990s. Two British films, *An Awfully Big Adventure* (Mike Newell, 1995) and *The Englishman Who Went Up a Hill But Came Down a Mountain* (Christopher Monger, 1995), misfired. The first cast Grant in an unsympathetic role; the second was too whimsically Ealingesque. *Nine Months* (Chris Columbus, 1995) and *Extreme Measures* (Michael Apted, 1996) were Simian's attempts to break into the American market. *Nine Months* was a limp romantic comedy lacking in any irony and wit. *Extreme Measures* was a medical thriller with Grant as a conventional hero thereby losing all his distinctiveness. These failures showed how important it was for Grant to have a good script to work with and his career was revived by the writer who truly understands his *métier*, Richard Curtis, in the long awaited 'sequel' to *Four Weddings*, *Notting Hill*, released in May 1999. Working Title, an independent company backed by the financial resources, distributional and promotional power of a major studio, marketed and exhibited the film like an American blockbuster.[4] The same strategy was used for *Bridget Jones* and *About a Boy*.

Notting Hill: the triumph of ordinariness

The widespread expectation that *Notting Hill* was a sequel prompted Curtis, producer Duncan Kenworthy and director Roger Michell to stress the film's autonomy and, in particular, the differences in Grant's role (Curtis 1997: 35; Kenworthy 1999: 4; Michell in Paxton 1999: 12). Whereas *Four Weddings* caricatured the debonair gentleman amidst an archaic Home Counties England, Grant's William Thacker, as the film's trailer insisted, is an 'ordinary bloke', a humdrum middle-class divorcee who leads 'a strange half-life', as he puts it in the opening voice-over, a narrative device that creates a strong identification between character and audience, especially as William is wittily self-deprecating about his problems. Whereas Charles gradually emerges as a figure of some depth rather than being merely amusing, William is at once offered as a sympathetic Everyman, the quintessentially decent boy-next-door (Spicer 2001: 80–101, 186–8). William is dressed in deliberately everyday clothing, nondescript shirts and trousers and, though clearly middle-class, speaks without eccentricity, his quotidian normality underscored by the exaggerated comic excess of his flatmate, slovenly Spike (Rhys Ifans) and the hopelessly gauche shop assistant Martin (James Dreyfus). As Grant commented, 'William is much more mature, married and divorced and able to speak about his emotions and doesn't have a speech defect' (Grant in Cavendish 1999: 18).

Notting Hill also displays a greater confidence in its handling of genre conventions. Eschewing the complicated contrivances of *Four Weddings*, *Notting Hill* relies quite unashamedly on chance and coincidence to propel the central relationship. Curtis observed that: 'The film is a concealed fairytale – the Princess and the Woodcutter as it were – but we tried to make it seem as though this sort of thing might actually happen

– realistic direction, pretty realistic performances, not too slushy music' (Curtis 1999: 13). Of course, as a modern fairytale, its Princess is a Hollywood movie star – with Julia Roberts playing 'herself' as Anna Scott, the most successful American female star of the 1990s – and its woodcutter an unsuccessful travel bookshop manager enjoying a form of genteel poverty in a very contemporary, fashionably chic Notting Hill. Like the idyllic New York of *You've Got Mail* (Nora Ephron, 1998), *Notting Hill* creates an enchanted, faux-carnival London, an urban village of little shops, street markets, tasteful but ailing restaurants and secluded gardens, a magical setting where unlikely romances can blossom.[5]

In many ways Grant gives a more accomplished comic performance in *Notting Hill*. His facial expressions and body language are more nuanced, his comic timing even better, delivering Curtis' script in a diffident banter that works by taking a line and letting its second half tail off into a succession of tics and shrugs. This is best exemplified in the beautifully constructed scene when William, expecting to catch Anna alone, finds himself part of a media circus, having to extemporise by pretending to be the film correspondent for *Horse and Hound*. That scene is largely comic but, as William is a man of acute sensitivity, his embarrassments and humiliations are often painful, especially when they result from the capricious Anna's concern for her status and career. In, for instance, the scene when the media scrum that is pursuing Anna has gathered outside his door, William acts with an old-fashioned chivalry that makes him a more sympathetic character than the often-egotistical Charles. Moments of pathos and reflection in *Notting Hill* are more frequent, the sense of loss and fear at never finding happiness stronger, including the scene where William moves disconsolately through the street market whilst the seasons change to the strains of Bill Withers' plangent 'Ain't No Sunshine When She's Gone' on the soundtrack. In a more pronounced gender reversal than in *Four Weddings*, Anna is the competitive high achiever whilst the underachieving William plays the woman's traditional role as the one who waits and suffers (see Barthes 1979: 14).

However, in the film's utopian fantasy, William represents a quotidian England that is much more attractive and civilised than the philistine and tawdry America that we never see but glimpse through the boorish behaviour of Anna's boyfriend Jeff (Alec Baldwin), or the inanities of the script for her new film. It is this muted, lacklustre England that the film embraces when Anna returns to William's bookshop to confess that 'the fame thing isn't really real', presenting herself as 'just a girl, standing in front of a boy, asking him to love her'. The film avoids mawkishness by having William hesitate, still reluctant to commit, only able to articulate his true feelings in the context of that most public and pre-packaged media event, the press conference. This self-protective irony was an attempt to prepare an audience for an overtly sentimental ending in which the camera circles round the happy and fertile couple in their idyllic English garden.

Notting Hill was even more successful than its predecessor, grossing £30.7 million in the UK and $116 million in the US (Dyja 2001: 39, 43). Although audiences occasionally demurred at the ending – 'a bit gooey' – they enjoyed the film and Grant's performance. He was, as one woman put it, 'so marvellous as that rather bumbling but attractive type. Isn't it great to come out of the cinema with a smile on your face?' (Pam Haybittle in McKimm 1999: 7). He had become the most celebrated screen embodiment of that powerful construction of masculinity, the 'New Man' who represented a tolerant and caring alternative to the macho tough guy. The New Man's sensitivity, desiring a committed, companionate relationship with the opposite sex above career ambitions, allows him to embrace positively feminine roles and qualities, and thus embody values that were central to the feminist critique of traditional competitive masculinity and to aspects of the men's movement (Chapman 1988: 225–48). Andrew Rutherford argues that Grant's persona allayed the insecurities and confusions about manliness felt by contemporary middle-class Englishmen in an era of casualisation and instability in the professions where work ceases to confer status and self-esteem. He represents a liberal and tolerant response to the rising aspirations and assertiveness of women, in the certainty that being nice, fundamentally decent, easy-going and sensitive, will win the day (Rutherford 1997: 139–42).

Bridget Jones's Diary: the Byronic cad

Notting Hill probably pushed Grant's embodiment of bumbling ordinariness as far as was possible to go, requiring a change of image. In the pre-publicity for his next film, *Bridget Jones's Diary*, Grant was fanfared in the tabloids as 'No More Mr Nice Guy', and photographed in women's magazines bare-chested in tight leather trousers to reveal his new leaner and more muscular body, no longer the chicly scruffy 'Hughie' of old (see Hiscock 2001: 22–3; Millea 2001: 12–18). In *Bridget Jones* it is the heroine (Renee Zellwegger) who plays the self-deprecating underachiever while Grant plays her predatory boss at the publishing house, Daniel Cleaver, a sophisticated, sexy professional with long, flowing dark locks and a rakish air. Cleaver is another familiar archetype, the Byronic anti-hero. The essence of the type is its fascinating eroticism, the product of contradictory qualities, combining an amoral ruthlessness with vulnerability and a refined nature (Thorslev 1962). Cleaver is contrasted with Mark Darcy (Colin Firth), playing the repressed Englishman, an uptight human rights lawyer. It was a second piece of adroit counter-casting: Firth had made his name playing a Byronic Darcy in the highly successful television adaptation of *Pride and Prejudice* (Simon Langton, 1996).

If Cleaver is fickle and capricious, seducing Bridget while at the same time renewing an affair with a New York publisher, he is also cultured, witty and fun to be with. Curtis, who co-wrote the screenplay, paid tribute to Grant's ability to embellish his dialogue, particularly in the scene where he first seduces Bridget:

> The scene where he is undressing Bridget and he says, 'Silly little boots, silly little dress and these fuck me absolutely enormous pants. Don't apologise, I like them. Hello Mummy!' That's all him. I'd have written 'What the fuck are those knickers?' or something similar. He fooled around a lot on *Bridget* because it was in line with his own style of naughtiness. (Curtis in Raphael 2002a: 13)

Yet underneath this suave sexual assurance, Cleaver is also uncertain, recognising Bridget as a kindred spirit, another thirtysomething who is unable to forge a lasting relationship: 'The truth is we're the same, you and me. We're two people of a certain age looking for the moment to commit and finding it really hard.' In Cleaver's eyes they should accept each other as the best that can be realistically hoped for. In the utopian discourse of romantic comedy this compromise solution is rejected and Bridget unites with Darcy, who is capable of transformation and therefore a 'fitting' hero. Cleaver, unable to change, remains outside this magical world. To counterbalance the idealised union of Bridget and Darcy, the film concludes with a satirical glimpse of Cleaver's post-Bridget 'conquests', an ending suggested by Curtis.

Bridget Jones was another huge hit, grossing over £42 million at the UK box office (see Dyja 2002: 42). Although its success was partly based on the interest in Helen Fielding's international bestselling novel, and Zellwegger's incarnation of its eponymous heroine, Grant's performance was also singled out: 'Playing a creep with no morals he excels. As Bridget's caddishly concupiscent boss and later boyfriend, Grant's Wodehousian twittishness is enhanced with a womanising leer and curdled suavity. No woman could resist him' (Andrews 2001: 13). Some judged that he, like many Byronic males, was more attractive than tedious virtue: 'Daniel is mad, bad, dangerous and extremely funny to know. He's much more interesting than dull old Darcy' (Bradshaw 2001: 14). Grant's charismatic presence thus complicates the moral of the fable and has ensured that his character will be retained in the projected sequel.

About a Boy: tribulations of the man about town

Grant's next film was another significant change of role. *About a Boy* is adapted from Nick Hornby's 1998 bestseller, a writer whose *Weltanschauung* is more downbeat and less sanguine than that of Curtis. Hornby has emerged as one of the most significant English novelists of the 1990s and *About a Boy* was the third Hornby novel to be screened. *Fever Pitch* (David Evans, 1996) starring Colin Firth, by common consent, missed the particular tone of Hornby's writing, while *High Fidelity* (Stephen Frears, 2000) transposed North London to Chicago to accommodate its American star John Cusack. Although *About a Boy* has American directors – Chris and Paul Weitz, who also co-wrote the screenplay – the action takes place in Hornby's patch of London, even if the rather more upmarket and photogenic Clerkenwell and Finsbury Park are preferred to the novel's Holloway.

Hornby's distinction has been to create a particular version of the modern male – 'Homo Hornbiensis' – who occupies that fraught and uncertain space between the two dominant constructions of contemporary masculinity: New Man and New Lad. His middle-class anti-heroes have an awareness of feminism and a self-reflexivity about their masculinity, are sensitive, in touch with their emotions and introspective, almost neurotic. But they also cling stubbornly to old modes of masculine behaviour, exhibiting laddish traits of self-centredness, the obsessive pursuit of 'hobbies' and an often-chauvinist view of women.[6] Grant's image was transformed for his role as Will Freeman, his hair short and spiky and sporting a range of designer T-shirts and jackets, his accent noticeably demoticised, as he comments with acerbic wit on his own situation. Will is the contemporary Man About Town, another archetype, sophisticated, witty, unencumbered and urbane, a man with the leisure – his income derives from the royalties of his father's novelty Christmas hit song – to cultivate his own favoured pursuits.[7] Will lacks the exuberance and gregariousness of earlier versions of the type. Instead, his pleasures are often solitary, egotistical and rather defensive. In his trendy flat,

Will avidly reads male style magazines, the 1990s phenomenon that has partly created him, absorbed in a self-enclosed world where he luxuriates in the meticulous pleasures of the discriminating modern consumer: amassing carefully chosen collections of CDs and videos/DVDs, or watching cult programmes on his widescreen television, which fills up several 'units' of time in his meticulously planned day, dedicated to the varied pleasures of being 'cool'.

As a man who prides himself on having reached his late thirties without entering into any long-term commitment, Will has intuited that single mothers offer the best prospects for romance: 'passionate sex, a great ego massage and an easy, guilt-free parting'. However, as he creates sympathetic interest from this group by pretending to have a son, that subterfuge becomes sharply real as he finds himself becoming a surrogate father to the twelve-year-old Marcus (Nicholas Hoult). Initially Will is quite comfortable as the decidedly 'uncool' Marcus's style adviser, but as their relationship develops, Will undergoes a classic moral awakening from selfishness to caring responsibility, experiencing that 'warm, fuzzy feeling' that comes from emotions not based on calculation. But in the process he becomes acutely conscious of his own emptiness: 'I'm nobody. Who do you think I am? What do you want from me, Marcus? I can't help you with anything that means anything.' Will's fears and self-doubt are far deeper than Grant's previous characters, an existentialist terror at his own lack of identity: 'I'm blank. I'm really nothing.'

His redemption comes through an emotional commitment to Marcus. In a brilliant dénouemnt, Will is prepared to be utterly uncool, to humiliate himself by singing 'Killing Me Softly' along with Marcus at the school rock concert. It is this action that prepares the ground for a settled relationship between Will and the single mum he has fallen for, Rachel (Rachel Weisz), in a reaffirmation of traditional values: love, commitment, responsible parenthood, caring for others. However, although the final scene is very different from the more ambiguous, downbeat and messy ending of the novel, it does not centre on marriage and the nuclear couple.[8] Will is no longer an island, spending his Christmas in a free-wheeling group that includes Marcus and his mother Fiona, Rachel and her son Ali, Tom, an acquaintance from Will's time on the Amnesty helpline and Marcus's girl friend from school, Ellie. Although not exactly sexually radical, this ending represents a future that is not simply the happy marriage of an idealised couple. As reviewers recognised, *About a Boy* is a generic hybrid – 'semi-confessional romantic comedy', 'romantic-comedy-with-an-edge' – an indication that it was stretching the bounds of the genre to accommodate a range of relationships.[9]

Reviewers, without exception, praised Grant's performance, detecting great subtlety and a new maturity. They judged that he had made an essentially shallow and selfish character interesting and appealing: 'blokes finally have their own icon to cheer for' (White 2002: 92). His impeccable timing, precise delivery of lines and command of facial expression were used to create a complex portrait of self-centredness and uncertainty, acerbic wit coupled with blankness and doubt. In interview, Grant seemed to play up to this image, witty and charming as ever, but expressing his own fears about turning forty and still being single, of becoming 'the oldest swinger in town'.[10] *About a Boy* performed well in the UK with a gross of £16.5 million, but lacking the presence of a Hollywood star and the resonantly upbeat ending that American audiences prefer, its US box-office has been modest at only $32.5 million.[11]

A contested icon

Although a popular icon of middle-class Englishness, Hugh Grant's success has been accompanied by a marked critical animus. This is partly through his association with romantic comedy, which is often seen as an essentially conservative genre, reaffirming monogamous heterosexual love as the social norm and family life as the ultimate fulfilment (Preston 2000: 232, 242). Both *Four Weddings* and *Notting Hill* have been attacked as nostalgic and disingenuous, avoiding the realities of contemporary Britain in favour of a fey, middle-class never-never land. Philip Kemp described *Four Weddings* as 'an innocuous romantic comedy set among the idle rich, tricked out with heritage-British locations and dripping with self-deprecating charm' (Kemp 1999: 64); while Nick James thought *Notting Hill* kept 'the inhabitants of these islands half in love with their now distant past' (James 1999: 22). Grant's persona has been condemned as insular and reactionary, part of 'an attempt to recover one nation Toryism', refusing to acknowledge its homosexual desires and assenting to the insidious (because ostensibly liberal) triumph of patriarchal values (Rutherford 1997: 141–2).

Much of this is redolent of a political correctness that is embarrassed by popular sentiment and optimistic fantasy, especially if they seem to be complicit with Hollywood's cultural hegemony. Academic criticism of British cinema has generally been much more comfortable with films about the alienated and the oppressed, with sombre social realism or with 'subversive' genres (horror and crime) that support transgressive images of masculinity. However, as Judith Williamson has acknowledged, although these romantic comedies might be intellectually embarrassing – films that are 'uncool to like' – they provide for a broad public the framework through which strong emotions may be dealt with: 'failure and insecurity and hesitation: about the pain of emotionally screwing up' (Williamson 2001: 1). As I have argued, Grant's characters' discovery of 'true love' allows audiences to feel comfortable about a difficult area of modern living: the problem of commitment. They provide, with the enjoyable exception of *Bridget Jones*, a way for underachieving and insecure males to feel good about themselves and for women to entertain dreams of a sensitive, caring soul-mate. Hugh Grant's star image, which has changed and developed more than is generally recognised, has made therefore an important contribution to the construction of contemporary masculinity, reanimating popular archetypes in a renewed bid for the cultural hegemony of the middle class.

Notes

1   For a discussion of the function of cultural types see Spicer 2001: 1–5.

2   The one discussion I have located is Gael Sweeney 2001: 57–67; but her take on Grant's persona is how American audiences perceive him.

3   Cinema Advertising Association/Cinema and Video Audience Research (CAA/CAVIAR) survey 14 (1994). The audience profiles for *Notting Hill* and *Bridget Jones* were very similar: see CAA/CAVIAR 17 (1999) and CAA/CAVIAR 19 (2001). I am grateful to Samantha Newsom, Senior Research Executive, CAA/Carlton Screen Advertising, for supplying this information. The proportion of ABC1 cinemagoers increased significantly during the 1990s, while the over-40 audience increased tenfold (Dyja 2002: 38).

4   For useful overviews see Finney 1996: 85–90; Baillieu and Goodchild 2002: 133–4; Kuhn 2002: 57–68.

5   See Murphy 2001: 292–300; *Notting Hill* was frequently attacked for avoiding the realities of multicultural Notting Hill, a view that misunderstands the idealistic basis of romantic comedy.

6   I am indebted here to Whannel 2002: 77; see also Johnston 2002. For a discussion of 'laddism' see Edwards 1997: 81–3.

7   For the origins of the Man About Town see Breward 1999 and Donald 1999.

8   Hornby commented that 'The end I wrote as mine was bathetic, and bathos doesn't work in movies, so I completely understood why they did it' (Davies 2002).

9   For these descriptions see Johnston 2002 and Walker 2002. Tim Robey observed that *About a Boy* 'isn't quite a romantic comedy' (Robey 2002).

10   See the interviews in Kursk 2002; Raphael 2002b; and an earlier one, Picardie 1999.

11   The UK figure, as at August 2002, is given in Dyja 2002: 52; the US figure as at June 2002 is given in *Guardian G2*, 28 June 2002, 7.

SECTION 1 STARS

SECTION 2 CLASS & RACE

SECTION 3 FATHERS

SECTION 4 BODIES

chapter 7

CINEMA'S QUEER JEWS: JEWISHNESS AND MASCULINITY IN YIDDISH CINEMA
Michele Aaron

The aim of this essay is to explore the construction of masculinity in a key Yiddish film, *Yidl Mitn Fidl*, Joseph Green's 1936 cross-dressing musical comedy. More specifically, I am concerned with the film's relationship to the idea of the 'Jew as Woman', an anti-Semitic notion of the time that encapsulated the 'popular' belief in the Jew's, that is the male Jew's, effeminacy and inferiority. As such, the discussion of masculinity will prove to be irrevocably bound to the discussion of femininity. But it is not just the Jewish question that binds them, but the formal properties and social implications of the cross-dressing film. I will say more on this later. On one hand, then, this essay joins a growing body of work within Jewish cultural studies which similarly forges the discussion of Jewishness and gender through the historical context of early twentieth-century Europe, and in particular through this period's developing discourse of sexual and racial difference (see Gilman 1991 and 1993). On the other, it offers a useful meditation upon the co-dependency of race and gender within early cinema, and, as I will come to suggest, one that persists, in this case in terms of the enduring link between queerness and Jewishness within more recent cross-dressing films.

Immediately the notion of the queer Jew summons the cultural legacy of the anti-Jewish demonisation and feminisation of the Jewish man, how he has been perceived and portrayed historically: the Jew as passive, perverse or 'anti-gentleman' has been seen to punctuate gentile depictions and anti-Semitic discourse (Hoberman 1995b: 147; see also Gilman 1991 and Erdman 1997). But this depiction also haunts Jewish self-representations and, thus, the derogatory nature of queerness is complicated by the self-perpetuation of stereotypes. The slur of queerness is also undone through the term's evolution and elevation in the late twentieth century to a critical status, as an 'oppositional stance' (Meyer 1994: 3). Queerness, as the confronting and undermining of the conventions, or categories, of gender and sexuality, becomes a politicised attribution of counter-hegemonic value, and in 'illuminating' Jewishness through it, the representation of Jewishness might gain this defiant edge.

Hugely popular, *Yidl Mitn Fidl* 'launched ... the "golden age"' of Yiddish cinema and the 'Polish phase of its sound films' (Pevner 1999: 50–1), and 'was the first Yiddish feature to play the major theatre chains – Loew's, York, and United Artists' and to be seen all over the world (Goldberg 1983: 107). The film was a star vehicle for the irrepressible Molly Picon, Yiddish Cinema's 'darling, comic genius' (Cohen 1999: 23) who, during the 1920s, was 'the highest-paid Yiddish stage performer in the world' (Hoberman 1995a: 69). Set in the Eastern European Jewish community early in the twentieth century, Picon plays a young Jewish woman who disguises herself as a boy (Yidl) to ease her passage as a travelling musician alongside her father, Arie. Having joined musical forces with another two men (Isaac and Froim), Yidl falls in love with one of them, Froim. Performing at a wedding, the group rescues the bride, Taybele, from the arranged marriage. She joins the musicians, and Yidl fears Froim's interest in Taybele. Taybele is 'signed' by a music theatre, but flees with her fiancé before the wedding, just before she is due on stage. Yidl takes up her costume and goes on in her place. Yidl reveals herself as a woman to Froim and to the audience who applaud her comic performance. Following her success Froim fears he is disrupting her career and takes his leave. The two are reunited as 'Yidl' sails to the US on a singing tour.

Yidl Mitn Fidl provides the perfect case study for an investigation of the intersection of Jewishness and masculinity for several reasons. It epitomised Yiddish cinema's location amidst a flourishing European anti-Semitism and the lure of the New World. In telling the story of a Jewish girl pretending to be a boy, it can be seen as being in explicit dialogue with the feminisation of the Jewish man and, more precisely, with the anti-Semitic notion of the 'Jew as woman'. As a cross-dressing film (and love story to boot), it is, inevitably, preoccupied with queer subjects as our female/male protagonist is implicated in a range of romantic scenarios and in the blurring of gender identity. Yet, the cross-dressing genre is known for its conservatism; as Annette Kuhn has noted, such films 'problematise gender identity and sexual difference ... only to confirm the absoluteness of both' (Kuhn 1985: 57). Typically, cross-dressing films or musical comedies, like *Some Like It Hot* (Billy Wilder, 1959), *Victor/Victoria* (Blake Edwards, 1982) and *Mrs Doubtfire* (Chris Columbus, 1993), follow conventional narrative patterns, highly dependent on happy endings that restore order predominantly through heterosexual union (see Kuhn 1985: 48–73; Straayer 1996: 42–78; Aaron 2001: 92–6). A further question, then, that this essay addresses, is what happens when racial difference intervenes in the genre's 'soft-play' upon sexual difference.

The film's construction of Jewishness will be found to be haunted not only by anti-Semitism but by the misogynistic and homophobic imperatives which accompany Jewish effeminacy and the ultimate orthodoxy of this popular genre. The conflation of Jewishness with the Jewish male experience punctuates this essay; after all, as Ann Pellegrini asks, 'what room does the intense, anti-Semitic identification of male Jews with "woman" leave for Jewish women? In the collapse of Jewish masculinity into an abject femininity, the Jewish female seems to disappear' (Pellegrini 1997: 109). Nowhere is this obfuscation of the woman rendered so visible (or so risible) than in the cross-dressing film with its Jewish female star.

The (little) Jew as woman

In the early twentieth century enduring and burgeoning notions of Jewish inferiority coalesced in Otto Weininger's 1906 book *Sex and Character*, the thesis of which identified women as physically and mentally deficient to the (Germanic/gentile) male, and identified Jews as like women. As Sander Gilman notes, 'the appeal of Weininger's work was not innovation but summation' (Gilman 1991: 133), and his scientific study can be seen as reifying long-standing myths concerning the feminisation of the Jewish male, from medieval accounts of peculiarly Jewish afflictions which rendered male Jews womanly in their 'actual' menstruation or in their 'copious haemorrhages and haemorrhoids (all involving loss of blood)' (Trachtenberg 1983: 50), to the late nineteenth-century's intensifying differentiation of gentile and Jew on the plane of masculinity. *Sex and Character* 'became an immediate best-seller and established [Weininger] as a serious contributor to the discourse about the relationship between race and gender at the beginning of the century' (Gilman 1991: 133).

Beyond its impressive scholarship, social and psychological insights, and moral and scientific inadequacies (Gilman 1993: 78–9), the book's popularity can be attributed to several causes. In addition to the fact that he was born Jewish, Weininger 'sensationalised [the] urgency' (Hyams and Harrowitz 1995: 3) of his thesis by taking his life shortly after its publication and, what is more, in so doing he 'proved', despite (or rather through) his conversion to Protestantism the year before, that the pathology of Jewishness was inescapable. *Sex and Character* also appears as the ultimate expression of what John Hoberman has called the 'Jewish male predicament' of the late nineteenth/ early twentieth century, the Jewish man's anxious struggle 'to achieve a viable male identity in the face of anti-Semitic folklore and discriminatory practices' which were rooted in his inferiority as a man (Hoberman 1995b: 142). Indeed, 'the feminisation of the Jewish male body was so frequent a theme in this period that Jewishness – more precisely, the Jewishness of Jewish *men* – became as much a category of gender as of race' (Pellegrini 1997: 108). Weininger's equation of the Jew with the weak woman encapsulates the unviability of Jewish male identity (and his suicide expresses it). But the book is 'a symptom of the *Zeitgeist*' in more general terms (Hoberman 1995b: 153). Weininger's resounding conjunction of misogyny and anti-Semitism works as a response to the activation of both in Europe during this time: the proliferating discourse of anti-Semitism and the developing first wave of feminism. Along with 'the openly homosexual subcultures that were starting to appear', these events arouse the more general 'non-Jewish (and Jewish) Western, heterosexual, male crisis of masculinity' (Breines 1990: 37).

Weininger's tract makes this crisis of masculinity a Jewish condition. Most importantly, it indicates how anti-Semitism at this time is not simply wedded to misogyny, but becomes a part of, or a displaced, misogyny. Anti-Semitism provides a ready site for the expression of this male crisis, and of the hatred of women. In a similar vein, Andrea Freud Loewenstein asserts of literary depictions that 'the Jewish character, in particular the male Jew, offered the male gentile author a less complicated and less conflictual web of signs and referents upon which to inscribe his fear and loathing of the female. Historical and cultural circumstances placed the Jew in an ideal situation for this purpose' (Loewenstein 1996: 146). The 'Jew as woman' is the apotheosis of his suitability and this displacement. Anti-Semitism, then, which is about the male Jew, is always bound up with the (Jewish) female predicament.

In *Yidl Mitn Fidl* the central Jewish 'man' is a woman or rather, this woman is representative of the 'little Jew' (the translation of *yidl* from Yiddish). Yidl is constructed as an effeminate Jewish man. Of course Yidl is not really a man, a truism which is fundamental to the film's various dramatic, generic and emotive intents. However, the ease with which 'she' is able to assume the identity of a Jewish man, and sustain a blurring of gender roles even when 'herself', ensures that a queerness of Jewishness remains.

Yidl Mitn Fidl

Yidl Mitn Fidl is explicit in its engagement with the notion of the (little) Jew as woman. The viewer is constantly reminded that Yidl is a woman in disguise: quite unlike later cross-dressers, Yidl keeps confessing her true identity. In fact, the film enacts her de-masking in ever more public ways: to her father, to Isaac, to Froim and a theatre audience, and then, it is implied, to an ever-broader audience as her success continues and she goes on tour (this broadens endlessly with the international audience that *Yidl Mitn Fidl* received).

Yidl Mitn Fidl, I would suggest, is implicitly involved in undoing the myth of the 'Jew as woman'. Beyond the narrative drive towards de-masking, towards the assertion of essential identities, this politicised intent takes place primarily through the sharp contrast between Yidl and the male hero of the film, Froim. As Eve Sicular has pointed out, Yidl, as the 'high-strung, loquacious, neurotic, weak and apparently effeminate young man' (Sicular 1999: 252), exists in opposition to the muscular, capable, 'straight' man, Froim. Yidl's frailty and preciousness is distinguished from Froim's competence. Yidl polishes shoes, where Froim builds tables: Yidl almost drowns; Froim saves 'him'. But while Yidl is, thus, 'a perfect foil in the then-current debate over Jewish "fitness" versus so-called degeneracy' (ibid.), these are not the random attributes of gender differentiation but a direct response to anti-Semitism's idealised masculinity.

The late nineteenth-/early twentieth-century rhetoric of ideal masculinity drew upon specific deficiencies of the Jew that can be seen as answered in *Yidl Mitn Fidl*. The notion of the Jew as anti-gentleman, a 'Germanic critique … [which] focused on his lack of personal dignity in terms of his appearance, his demeanour' (Hoberman 1995b: 147), translates into the poise, manners and refinedness of Froim. Despite his homelessness as a travelling musician, Froim, in comparison to the scruffier members of the troupe, is clean-shaven, well-dressed and handsome. While Weininger asserted that 'what is meant by the word "gentleman" does not exist among the Jews' (Weininger 1910: 308), Froim, in his kindness and protectiveness to both Yidl and Taybele, is deliberately constructed as gentlemanly. According to John Hoberman, the Jew's 'estrangement from alcohol … an anti-Semitic theme that appears throughout the nineteenth and twentieth centuries' (Hoberman 1995b: 153), underlies Weininger's claim that the Jew 'has no transcendental quality' (Weininger 1910: 320). In this way, the Jewish man was deemed incapable of participating in the social and metaphysical liberties afforded by drink. In *Yidl Mitn Fidl*, however, the four musicians celebrate their earnings with an evening of drinking. Following a rowdy song, a veritable tribute to intoxication, 'Drink, Fellows, Drink', a sturdy but smiling Froim puts the *shika* (drunken) Yidl to bed. Unlike the (other) men, Yidl passes out. Yidl is distinguished from them, just as they are all distinguished from the pathologically sober stereotype. Notions 'about the inability of the Jews to … swim' (Hoberman 1995b: 145) are also addressed by *Yidl Mitn Fidl*, where in another pivotal scene encapsulating Yidl's feminisation and Froim's manliness, Froim dives in to rescue Yidl who, hungover, has stumbled into a lake.

A recurring discussion of the Jew during this period distanced him from the land, 'from the world of agriculture and its cultural symbolism: rootedness in the soil, the timeless rhythm of the seasons, the sheer vitality of nature, the endless struggles against wind and weather' (Hoberman 1995b: 145). Yet *Yidl Mitn Fidl* is firmly placed in a pastoral location. As a prototypical folk musical, it is marked by this rural setting, but also by the 'abundance' and 'energy', in other words, the 'sheer vitality' which characterises the genre and its stars, as embodied by Picon (see Dyer 1986: 180–1). The scene of Froim's carpentry establishes him as the practical, 'handy' craftsman, but specifically places him with sleeves rolled up, hammer in hand, so that these qualities are framed by the rural location. This is the most contrived scene of the film serving no narrative function other than the assertion of Froim's manly attributes in contrast to Yidl and his failings. When Yidl tries to help, she gets hurt and Froim's work is interrupted by Yidl's injury and continuing complaints.

This alignment with a masculinisation of the great outdoors works to distinguish Froim as model Jew and model man. It is also attached to this Yiddish film in more general terms in order to recover Jewish masculinity from the feminising intent of anti-Semitic discourse and, in particular, its distancing of the Jew from the land. Yidl and her father climb aboard a hay-wagon at the start of their travels. It is here that the main song occurs. 'Yidl Mitn Fidl', the showpiece for the film, Picon and Yiddish music, invokes the joys of freedom and of the country. It begins with the lines: 'Over fields and roads on a wagon full of hay, with mud and rain, two musicians make their way.' Rather than being 'exclu[ded] from a European ideology of adventure' (Hoberman 1995b: 145), through this distance from the land, *Yidl Mitn Fidl* recounts the spirited adventures of four Jews on the road. The middle section of the film, when the four are staying in a barn, contains many long shots and long takes of the rural landscape: a field of haystacks and long shadows; lilies on water and a flowing stream; a lightning-splintered sky. Without clear narrative purpose, these establishing shots and cinematic flourishes are precisely about appropriating the cultural symbolism of nature to serve in the inscription of Jewishness. The combination of social and aesthetic agendas was, however, Green's purpose. He aimed to 'avoid the *goles Yid* [the negative stereotype of the Diaspora Jew] … artistically without heavy-handed propaganda' (quoted in Hoberman 1995a: 239). What I am demonstrating, however, is how this stereotype is not avoided but exploited, the 'Jew as woman' does not simply haunt the text but determines it.

The film contains a further example of Green *using* the negative stereotype, for how does this image of a free-spirited and free-footed Yidl square with the figure of the wandering Jew? The film's involvement with the land is inevitably framed by the men as travellers. Rather than confirming the statelessness, or the wandering, of the Jews, *Yidl Mitn Fidl* charts the various characters' move away from a nomadic lifestyle: Isaac decides to settle down with his girlfriend in Warsaw, Taybele recovers her fiancé and will get married, Yidl and her father do not have to go back on the road following her success. Wandering is asserted as a temporary state, a financial necessity, or a profession, as in Yidl's US tour. The stereotype is, again, indulged so that it can be undone.

As another formulation of the wandering Jew, Weininger expounded on his statelessness as a further characteristic of Jewish deficiency: 'Citizenship is an un-Jewish thing' (Weininger 1910: 307). Yet, I would suggest, Yiddish cinema itself defies this anti-Semitic notion, for, as James Hoberman points out, 'Yiddish cinema … was not just a national cinema without a nation-state, but a national cinema that, with every presentation, created its own ephemeral nation-state' (Hoberman 1995a: 5). Yiddish cinema, inevitably, invoked yet countered the statelessness of the Jews. It was an American-Jewish cinema targetted (primarily) at the new citizens yet dependent on their émigré status (marked by Yiddish). It was immediately locked into conversation with the dispersal of the Jewish community, and yet united it. *Yidl Mitn Fidl* is typical of this conversation, with its incorporation of Old and New World values, the traditional and the secular, and its good dose of the promise of America. Such a 'conversation' characterised Froim as 'new Jew' and Yidl as unconventional Jewish woman (as new woman). It was also embodied by Picon in her 'Old World credentials … [and] New World energy and insouciance' (Hoberman 1995a: 66).

I have so far argued that *Yidl Mitn Fidl* is directly engaged with countering anti-Semitic notions, specifically with 'unqueering' the Jewish man. By enacting the myth of the 'Jew as woman', the worst of the character of Yidl differentiates the ideal qualities of Froim. *Yidl Mitn Fidl* distances the negative stereotypes of the Jew through two interrelated means: the establishment of the new Jew as an ideal man, and the denigration of effeminacy and of womanliness. *Yidl Mitn Fidl*'s redemption of the Jewish man is achieved through the ridiculing of the Jewish woman and homosexuality.

As the little Jew, Yidl becomes a parody of the anti-Semitic notion of the 'Jew as woman'. 'He' represents all the weaknesses attached to the little Jew and then 'comes out' as female. In this way, these weaknesses are transferred back to the woman, their natural home. Yidl's effeminacy is made explicit throughout the film. 'He' is frequently shown and said to be girlish, as Froim says: 'He's worse than a girl.' Yidl hurts 'his' finger, moans, cries, nearly drowns, is weak and constantly mocked. Girlishness becomes the sum of these negative qualities. Female characteristics are condensed into the stereotypical and damning definitions of a woman. In other words, the denigration of femininity is used to rescue Jewish masculinity. Homosexuality is used in a similar way, as Sicular notes of the film: 'The issue of men casting off unmanly ways is portrayed here with … many an oblique reference to homosexuality as its supposed opposite' (Sicular 1999: 252). Homosexuality is rejected in the film: just as the theatrical manager at the side of the theatre stage casts off his colleague's arm, which has fallen upon his shoulder, with a glare and a grimace, so Froim drops Yidl when 'he' swoons in his arms and then tries to kiss him.

The notion of the 'Jew as woman' is rendered ridiculous in the film, through making femininity and homosexuality a joke. This happens chiefly in Yidl's climactic theatre performance towards the end of the film, which trades on the absurdity of womanliness and of homosexuality, conveyed through the collective derision of the audience. Yidl recounts her story centre-stage, appealing to the audience for sympathy. They greet her screwball story with uproarious laughter: 'What are you laughing at?' she cries. The collectiveness or universal weight of this reaction is achieved in various ways. Firstly, through the shots and soundtrack of the laughing audience which construct the audience as a community of like-minded people sharing a joke. This emphasis upon them as a cohesive group (albeit an ephemeral group) is reiterated by the collective quality of laughter and of comedy itself. Yidl's performance also acts as a kind of epilogue to the previous theatricalities, like the self-reflexive spiel ending a Shakespeare play: Yidl recounts her tale, appealing to the audience in her direct address. That we are constructed as part of that audience – by aligning us with Arie, Isaac and his girlfriend in the balcony, and frequently filming from the back of the audience – this collective response (the rejection of the 'Jew as woman') is all the more persuasive and pervasive.

Where anti-Semitism can be seen to integrate misogyny, here misogyny (and homophobia) works to dislodge anti-Semitism. Such tactics of countering anti-Semitism have been identified elsewhere. Freud's theories, for example, have been seen to scapegoat women (and homosexuals) to recover Jews, that in rooting neuroses in the feminine condition and in homosexuality, the spotlight of deficiency moves away from the Jew (see Gilman 1993). Zionism has also been seen as transferring some of the idealisation of the gentile to the new Tough Jew (see Breines 1990). *Yidl Mitn Fidl* employs both these tactics to counter anti-Semitism. Where the nineteenth-century texts revered the Aryan male through contrast to the Jewish male, *Yidl Mitn Fidl* shifts the axis of worth to between the Jew as woman (Yidl) and Jew as ideal man (Froim). Froim is counterposed to effeminacy, and the Jew is severed from the slur of queerness. While this is a persuasive interpretation of the film, I would like to suggest that queerness is not, cannot be, rejected altogether, for the film maintains a blurring of gender even as it promotes the essentialness of identity. The ease with which Yidl becomes a Jewish man, not only depends upon the (myth of the) effeminacy of the Jewish man, but upon the masculinisation of the Jewish woman. This is a further, although less pervasive, aspect of the slur of queerness; as Pellegrini notes 'the anti-Semitic imagination often paired the "womanly" male Jew off with a "manly Jewess"' (Pellegrini 1997: 119). Yet we do not receive a pairing of these types in the film but a combination of them in the figure of Yidl. As a boy, Yidl expresses the weakness of woman; as a woman she is masculinised. When we first meet her she is playing her fiddle for money in the village market. She is immediately positioned as different to other girls, or rather to the housewives around her. When a man wants to pay her for a dance, that is, wants her to behave in a far more conventionally feminine way, she agrees but her dance (in which she leads an abbreviated boisterous jig) is not what he had in mind. When the man refuses to pay, another man steps in to argue. The Picon character stands beside her defender, echoing his words and actions. In her assertiveness and aggression, she is masculinised from the moment we meet her; she is also clearly attracted to the male role. When her father despairs over the difficulties of his daughter travelling, it is with a gleam in her eye that she adopts the male garb. That we later encounter a female character who experiences no trouble in travelling – Taybele – Yidl's choice seems that much more gratuitous.

While the plot of *Yidl Mitn Fidl* has been seen as arbitrary, that Green injected Picon into a story by 'chang[ing] one of the musicians to a girl who, in order to travel with her father, would disguise herself as a boy' (Goldberg 1983: 105), I have argued that the use of cross-dressing is far from casual. Despite the film's ('disguised') preoccupation with anti-Semitism, and its split ending, the figure of Yidl does sustain a challenge to the conventions of gender expression, a challenge which the character delights in and Picon was famous for. However, anti-Semitism remains *Yidl Mitn Fidl*'s governing but unspoken theme, determining its construction of masculinity through the characterisation of both its hero and heroine.

Yentl: a queerer Yidl

Barbra Streisand's 1983 film *Yentl* (in which she is both director and star) is strikingly similar to *Yidl*; structurally, thematically and, most importantly, in terms of its interconnection of Jewishness and gender through the 'apparent' masculinity of the central character. Both films are 'yiddishe' musical comedies that share the same basic plot. Set in the East European *shtetl*, a woman whose mother has died looks after her aging father. She loses her home (in *Yidl Mitn Fidl* she is evicted with her father; in *Yentl* the father dies). She disguises herself as a boy in order to gain a necessary freedom, and pursue her 'career' (as travelling musician in *Yidl Mitn Fidl* or as the scholar Anshel in *Yentl*). She falls in love with a man she 'works' beside (Froim in *Yidl Mitn Fidl*, Avigdor in *Yentl*) which leads to the revelation of her disguise. Such elements – the need to take on a disguise, the ready heterosexuality – are typical of the cross-dressing narrative, but there are many other conspicuous commonalities that firmly connect these two films. Both start in the *shtetl* market and end on a ship bound for the US. As in *Yidl Mitn Fidl*, Streisand's film opens with the young woman in the village market, and relies upon cross-cutting to construct the crowds and activity of the location and to emphasise the gossiping women and our heroine's difference from them. The similarities between the two opening scenes is underlined by the fact that both women buy fish for their fathers at the market. The gamine Yidl and Anshel in their black jackets, trousers and caps look (perhaps inevitably) alike, but Streisand also reconstructs various scenes of the earlier film. Both Yidl and Anshel try and fail to catch a lift on a hay-wagon when they are first leaving town. In both films, our protagonist settles down awkwardly to sleep next to a man. Both have (un)orthodox wedding scenes: traditional ceremonies mark the marriage of two women in *Yentl* (Anshel and Hadass, Avigdor's love interest), and of a wife who will subsequently flee in *Yidl Mitn Fidl*.

These commonalities are not coincidental. Indeed, they mark *Yentl*'s departure from Isaac Bashevis Singer's 1967 short story, upon which it is based, and in doing so they highlight Streisand's determined repetition of the earlier film. Norman Jewison has acknowledged the inspiration he gained from *Yidl Mitn Fidl* for *Fiddler on the Roof* (1971), the only other major film representation of the *shtetl*, and it has been well-recorded that Streisand immersed herself in modern Jewish history in preparation for *Yentl* (see Edwards 1996: 401 and Riese 1995: 455). *Yentl*, however, is far less concerned with defying Jewish stereotypes than with defying gendered stereotypes. While it cannot help but be haunted by anti-Semitism, in reviving *Yidl Mitn Fidl*, *Yentl*'s construction of Jewish masculinity has an alternative agenda.

Anshel, with his fragile frame, timid nature, and soft voice, his beardless face and bookish demeanour, epitomises the effeminate Jewish man. We are shown him tumbling under the weight of books, and picked on by brawnier men. Like *Yidl Mitn Fidl*, *Yentl* moves away from the anti-Semitic myth of the 'Jew as woman'. Anshel certainly contrasts sharply to Avigdor's height and hirsuteness, but this is never contrived to idealise Avigdor as a model Jew, nor is it at the woman's expense. Indeed, Anshel and Avigdor are equal contenders for the role of ideal man, which in this film is measured by the ability to answer the Rabbi's questions, or the suitability to partner Hadass. Anshel even exceeds Avigdor's merits: correcting Avigdor's reply to the rabbi, replacing Avigdor as groom when he is deemed unfit through the taint of his brother's suicide. Like *Yidl Mitn Fidl*,

Yentl contains a scene of drinking, only this time it is a sturdy smiling Anshel who puts an intoxicated Hadass to bed. Similarly, in another scene, all the yeshiva students, except for the slight Shimmele and the protesting Anshel, enjoy a swim. Drinking and swimming, as well as other 'markers of deficiency', now have nothing to do with Jewishness but everything to do with Anshel's exceptional circumstances.

Marjorie Garber writes that *Yentl* 'allegorises this subtext of the Jew as always-already a woman in a spirit diametrically opposed to the vituperative claims of anti-Semitism' (Garber 1992: 227). While I agree with Garber's sentiment, this 'diametric' opposition is a more fitting description of *Yidl Mitn Fidl*; *Yentl* meanwhile is, as I argue elsewhere, reconjuring the queer Jew for its own effects and feminist ends (and those of its director-star), that are never immediately about anti-Semitism (see Aaron 2000: 125–31). Where *Yidl Mitn Fidl* derides homoeroticism, *Yentl* indulges it. The scenes depicting Hadass's growing interest in our cross-dresser are humourous in her 'mistake', yet they are eroticised beyond the call of comedy. For example, during the song 'No Wonder he Loves her', in which Anshel 'gets' Hadass's appeal, a flustered Anshel (and audience) are confronted with Hadass's chest centre frame. The film's eroticism is often dismissed by viewers, and is certainly made safe (disavowed) by the text: reminders that Anshel is a woman precede 'heated' scenes lest we forget that this is all fakery. What has been deemed the more controversial homoeroticism (presumably because it is based on an admission rather than a suppression of same-sex desire) is Avigdor's long and loaded looks at Anshel, his 'always grabbing' the younger man.

The film will neatly correct its characters' queerness by the end. Anshel leaves the marriage, removes the disguise and confesses 'her' love to Avigdor. Avigdor's homosexuality is recovered as the most essential form of heterosexuality: 'I thought there was something wrong with me.' But what of Hadass? Hadass it seems is merely gullible, succumbing to Anshel's kindness and gentleness (and later falling back in love with Avigdor). While this might seem a powerful statement on the performativity of gender – Anshel is a man because to Hadass she looks and acts like a man – this is too generous a reading, for instead the film implies that Hadass was blind to the female essence of Anshel where Avigdor was wise to it, however unconsciously. It is this rather suspicious fable which underwrites a final dequeering of the film, yet what remains undeniable is the way in which the film incorporates and opens up not only a homoerotic economy but a queer potential, and implicates Anshel within it. Norman Jewison described *Yidl Mitn Fidl* as 'fifty years ahead of its time' (Picon and Grillo 1980: 68); *Yentl*, I would suggest, is that future, queerer, incarnation, some 47 years later.

This study sits within my broader interest in the cultural inevitability of the queer Jew – that there is something about Western cinema's figuring of Jewishness that requires expression not just through gender but through queerness. In seemingly unrelated films a queerness of the Jew has surfaced time and time again, whether as a deviant or defiant gender identity, the masculinisation of the Jewish mother or JAP ('Jewish American Princess'), or the feminisation of the *shlemeil* (the fool) or *sheeny* (the villain), or as a growing number of independent gay Jewish films, such as *Chicks in White Satin* (Elaine Holliman, 1993), *Next Year in Jerusalem* (David Nahmod, 1997) and *Trembling Before G-d* (Sandi DuBowski, 2001). However, nowhere is Jewishness more queer, or queerness more Jewish (or my argument so always-already) than in Jean-Jacques Zilbermann's *L'Homme est une femme comme les autres/Man is a Woman* (1997), which opens with a man walking through a gay sauna cruising to the strains of klezmer. And nowhere is the significance of *Yidl Mitn Fidl* (and *Yentl*) within the discussion of the queer Jew (or of the Jewish 'man as a woman') more evident. *L'Homme est une femme comme les autres* is the next link in the chain of the Jewish cross-dressing comedy, for in it, this time, an economically desperate musician (Simon) 'disguises himself' as straight in order to restore his finances. The *shtetl* is present in the form of his wife's (Rosalie's) Hasidic family, another bogus but orthodox wedding takes place, and musical numbers are provided by Simon's and Rosalie's various performances. But the film also references its predecessors. It incorporates a scene right out of *Yentl* – when the rabbi tells Simon how to treat a woman during lovemaking, just as Avigdor advises Anshel – and, later, Rosalie sings 'Yidl Mitn Fidl', the film's main song, as part of her repertoire. *Yidl Mitn Fidl* and *Yentl* are, thus, consecrated as the seminal if not canonical texts for cinema's queer Jews and, despite their diverse contexts, reflect a continuum of critical issues framing the filmic articulation of Jewishness and masculinity.

chapter 8

A WORKING-CLASS HERO IS SOMETHING TO BE? CHANGING REPRESENTATIONS OF CLASS AND MASCULINITY IN BRITISH CINEMA
John Hill

In November 2000, following the collapse of the UN summit on climate change, the UK Deputy Prime Minister John Prescott was denounced as an 'inveterate macho' by Dominique Voynet, the French Environment Minister and Green Party member, whom he had accused in a radio interview of being too 'tired' to understand the detail of a proposed agreement to cut carbon emissions. Subsequently, in the House of Commons, Prescott made light of the accusation, jokingly commenting: 'As to whether I am accused of being a macho man – moi?' (Waugh and Lichfield 2000). However, it later emerged that Prescott had in fact been stung by the macho tag and wanted to be seen as more caring and sensitive. In support of his claim, it was reported that he had been to see the film *Billy Elliot* no less than four times (Routledge 2000: 12).

This is, in fact, a telling antidote. As is well known, Prescott has performed an important symbolic function for 'New Labour'. The son of a railwayman, a former merchant seaman and National Union of Seamen official, he has retained an air of 'Old Labour' class politics and, in becoming Tony Blair's deputy in 1994, he played a crucial role in welding traditional labour constituencies to Blair's 'modernising' project. In a sense, the macho label attached to Prescott derived much of its plausibility from his association with a working-class background and an earlier era of labour activism. However, *Billy Elliot* (Stephen Daldry, 2000) is itself a film about an earlier era of working-class militancy and it clearly says something that it became, in public discourse, some kind of touchstone for male sensitivity. What I want to do, therefore, is look at how the film articulates its themes of class and gender and consider in what ways, and with what effects, it mobilises its anti-macho sentiments. In order to do so, I want to place it in a context of previous mainstream representations of the working class, particularly those involving – as in the case of *Billy Elliot* – the miners. In doing so, I will focus on two films

– *The Proud Valley* (Pen Tennyson, 1940) and *Kes* (Ken Loach, 1969) – as emblematic films which help to identify the changes in representation involved.

The Proud Valley

Writing in the context of her revisiting of Orwell's journey to Wigan Pier, Beatrix Campbell exclaims that 'the socialist movement in Britain has been swept off its feet by the magic of masculinity, muscle and machinery. And in its star system, the accolades go to the miners – they've been through hell, fire, earth and water to become hardened into heroes. It is masculinity at its most macho that seems to fascinate men' (Campbell 1983: 97). In miners, she goes on, there is an equation between 'elemental work and elemental masculinity' which carries over into 'working-class politics' in which the 'miners are the Clark Gables ... of class struggle' (1983: 98). Although Campbell invokes cinematic metaphors to account for what she sees as the fascination of socialism with the miners, mainstream British cinema itself has shown only intermittent interest in them, as, indeed, it has more generally in the lives of the working class. However, because of what Campbell characterises as the miners' battle with the elements, the mining disaster has provided the dramatic ingredients for a number of movies. I want to begin by looking at one of these, *The Proud Valley*, because, although its politics are now generally seen to have been subdued, it still remains one of the most outspoken of its period. In many respects, it was a left-wing film in conception. The original story was written by Herbert Marshall, a member of the Communist party, and it was directed by Pen Tennyson, an active trade-unionist who advocated the nationalisation of the film industry (Berry 1994: 166–72). It also starred Paul Robeson, an active supporter of a number of left-wing causes, including the Republicans during the Spanish Civil War.

In the original script, miners take over a colliery after it has been closed by the owners following an underground explosion. In the actual film, this ending is altered: the miners march to London and persuade the owners to co-operate in re-opening the pit in the interests of the war effort. Although this is often taken to involve a political compromise, a shift from conflict to consensus, it is also interesting how, at the same time, the mining community is re-imagined as the emblem of the national community. Thus, as Charles Barr indicates (1977: 20–1), the men's march to London involves a displacement of hostility towards the bosses on to Germany and, when the men get to London, their case is made in terms of an appeal of coal's importance to 'national defence' (echoing a line in Alberto Cavalcanti's 1936 documentary *Coal Face* in which the narrator claims that 'coal mining is the basic industry of Britain'). In this way, the politics of class conflict are not straightforwardly suppressed insofar as it is the standard-bearers of the working class who resurface as the heroes – even, perhaps, the Clark Gables – of the nation as a whole.

However, it is, of course, a vision of community that relies upon strictly divided relations of gender. The community is predominantly shaped by the male universe of work – in which men work down the pit 'like our fathers did before us' – and also of leisure – represented by the Blaendy male choir and its hopes for success at the Eisteddfod. Campbell suggests how celebration of the miner is also bound up, as in Orwell, with an admiration of the male body and the film's scenes down the pit reveal a regard for the miner's physical strength and physique during the attempt to re-open the mine (although, in this film, as a result of the presence of Robeson, it also entails a certain displacement of fascination onto the *black* male body; see Dyer 1986). In relation to the film's narrative of patriarchal lineage whereby the son (Simon Lack) follows in the footsteps of his father Dick Parry (Edward Chapman), the women characters occupy the familiar roles of (potential) wives and mothers (especially 'our mam', the long-suffering Mrs Parry played by Rachel Thomas).

Despite its political timidity, *The Proud Valley* remains a testament to a certain kind of longing for a new society based on the principles of decency, mutual support and honest labour which the film locates within the industrial working class. However, if this film is future-oriented, charting the possible birth of new forms of filiation, the kind of community it celebrates is already seen to be in decline by the end of the 1950s in the films of the British 'new wave'. While none of these are explicitly about mining communities (although Frank Machin in Lindsay Anderson's *This Sporting Life* (1963) has abandoned mining for rugby league, both of which – the film implies – involve a commodification and exploitation of his physical strength), they are generally about the decline of the kinds of traditional, working-class communities found in mining villages. The threat to these communities is not, as in *The Proud Valley*, natural disaster or exploitative relations of production but rather the onset of 'affluence', consumerism and mass culture. This threat is also configured in terms of a perceived 'feminisation' of the working class, whereby traditional working-class masculinity, grounded in hard physical labour and tough political activism, is seen to be succumbing to economic acquiescence and political passivity. As a result, a degree of sympathy is extended towards the young virile, working-class male – such as Arthur in *Saturday Night and Sunday Morning* (Karel Reisz, 1960) – who seeks to resist the embourgeoisement and social conformity (and, by implication, the 'feminisation') that is overtaking the 'new' working class (Hill 1986).

A key trope, in this regard, is that of individual escape. It is significant, for example, that Emlyn, Dick Parry's son, in *The Proud Valley* has been attending night classes in order to make a fitting husband for his fiancée and to take on a management role. However, there is no sense of his wanting to move out of the community or of the desirability that he should do so. Indeed, the most unsympathetic character in the film is his future mother-in-law, the local shopkeeper and post mistress, whose petty-bourgeois sense of superiority to the community is revealed as snobbish and selfish. Moreover, when the move beyond the community is made – in the form of the men's march to London – it is as a collectivity rather than as individuals pursuing solitary goals. In the 'new wave' films, we find the beginnings of a different sensibility which pits the individual's aspirations (usually male) against those of the community which is seen to be at odds with their full expression. It is, of course, this paradigm which is adopted by *Billy Elliot* but with further twists that are partly supplied by *Kes*.

Kes

In the case of the 'new wave' films, the decline of the working-class community is linked to economic well-being and social improvement and there is little sense of the poverty and hardship faced by the jobless miners in *The Proud Valley*. In Ken Loach's post-new wave film *Kes*, however, there is a much stronger sense of how the life of the 'affluent worker' remains one of material, as well as emotional, disadvantage. The film is focused on the young boy Billy (David Bradley) for whom life seems to hold few prospects.

Unlike *The Proud Valley*, in which the son happily follows in his father's footsteps, Billy is determined not to go down the mines, a job for which he appears to be both physically and temperamentally unsuited. On the other hand, the society around him is itself ill-equipped to offer him a satisfactory outlet for his talent and imagination and, even if he avoids the mines, his destiny is likely to remain that of dead-end manual labour. His 'escape', albeit temporary, is through his passion for the kestrel which he teaches himself to train and whose flight becomes an emblem of Billy's own desire for excitement and transcendence.

While Ken Loach's films are commonly criticised for a supposed romantic attachment to the working class, Loach's Marxist-based hostility to capitalism, and its consequences, leads in fact to a portrait of the working class that lays bare the ways in which lives are wasted, and even brutalised, by the economic inequalities of the society in which they live. Hence, there is little heroisation of manual labour (or celebration of the male working-class body) in the film's treatment of Billy's miner-brother Jud (Freddie Fletcher), who has neither the nobility of the miners in *The Proud Valley* nor the charismatic swagger of an Arthur in *Saturday Night and Sunday Morning* for all that he may be the 'cock o' t'estate' (as he is described by Billy in both film and novel). Jud is presented as mean, small-minded and violent, responsible for bullying Billy and ultimately killing his kestrel in a malicious and uncaring act of spite at the film's end. However, while the film extends little sympathy to him, Jud is not straightforwardly viewed as a villain. In Loach's work characters are the products of their economic and social circumstances, so that while Jud may be a victimiser he is himself a victim of alienated labour and cultural disadvantage. In an astute review at the time of the film's release, Paul Barker drew attention to how the film uses images of imprisonment to suggest how the two brothers are, in their different ways, 'caged' (Barker 1969: 823). Thus, in contrast to the national allegorising of *The Proud Valley*, Jud's status as 'cock o' t'estate', built upon his physical strength and sexual prowess, is revealed as little more than a dubious compensation for his real lack of economic and social power (his actual position at 'the bottom o' the world' as he himself describes his work to a fellow miner).

It is, of course, *Kes* that many have identified as the main precursor of, and influence upon, *Billy Elliot*. It too is set in a mining community and focuses on a young boy's desire for escape from it. The relationship of Billy to his brother Tony (with whom he shares a room) also closely parallels that between Billy and Jud and a number of incidents (such as the stealing of a book) occur in both films. However, while there are undoubted lines of continuity there are also significant differences. One of the most obvious of these is the ending. Whereas the materialist logic of *Kes* pushes towards a melancholic, downbeat conclusion, *Billy Elliot* follows *Brassed Off* (Mark Herman, 1996) and *The Full Monty* (Peter Cattaneo, 1997) in attempting to resolve social tensions through affirmative endings. There is, however, more than the calculation of audience response at stake here. The producer of *Kes*, Tony Garnett, recalls how, in raising finance for the film, he encountered pressures to make the film's end more positive, such as Billy – with the help of his teacher – getting a job in a zoo. However, as Garnett observes, that would have been to betray the film's point of view which is concerned to raise questions about 'the system' rather than individuals (Garnett 1970). In this respect, the film sets itself explicitly against the conventional drama of individual escape found in earlier 'new wave' films in order to emphasise the *systemic* aspects of economic and social disadvantage.

This attempt to undermine the individualising logic of the escape narrative also links to the Loach/Garnett view of working-class agency. Unlike *The Proud Valley* (or *Coal Face*) there is little emphasis upon the nobility or rewards of manual labour in itself which is generally seen as unpleasant and the site of exploitation and alienation. Thus, in *Kes*, Billy does not expect any satisfactions from work but he will at least get 'paid for not liking it'. If there is heroisation in Loach's portrayal of the working class, it is not to be found in actual work but, rather, in organised industrial protest, as in *The Big Flame* (1969), the television drama that preceded *Kes*, which deals with a workers' take-over of the Liverpool docks (albeit that even this results in failure).

Hence, while *Billy Elliot* does share with *Kes* a plot structure in which a young boy is pitted against a family and community which is unsympathetic to his talents, there are also clear differences. The family and community which, in *Kes*, is identified as oppressive as a result of its disadvantaged economic and social position is now located as a 'primary' rather than 'secondary' source of oppression. Moreover, what in the Loach/Garnett films is identified as resistance to the inequities of the social system – industrial militancy – is itself identified as a problem rather than any kind of solution. The key to understanding this shift lies in the film's attitude towards masculinity and it is worth teasing out what is involved.

Billy Elliot

In many ways, *Billy Elliot* is a sympathetic work which successfully popularises a number of progressive ideas around gender roles and sexual orientation. Like his precursor in *Kes*, Billy (Jamie Bell) has little appetite for going down the mines and is ill at ease with the adult male culture around him. He attends the local boxing club but his lack of aptitude threatens patriarchal tradition ('you're a disgrace to them gloves, your father and the traditions of this boxing hall', his trainer observes). This quintessentially masculine world of the boxing club, used in other recent films such as *The Boxer* (Jim Sheridan, 1997) and *TwentyFourSeven* (Shane Meadows, 1997) as an aid to male bonding, is counterposed to the hitherto all-feminine world of the ballet class to which Billy becomes ineluctably drawn, as his talent for dance is revealed and, as in *Kes*, becomes a source of excitement and transcendence (described, indeed, by Billy as 'flying – like a bird'). It is, of course, this attraction to ballet which sets in motion within the film the discourses of gender and sexuality, and a questioning of the heterosexual masculinity that underpins the working-class community, in a way that the other Billy's preoccupation with a kestrel does not (growing as it does out of more traditional forms of male working-class leisure).

It is, however, worth noting how hesitant and equivocal this questioning is. The film is acutely conscious of the popular associations of ballet with effeminacy and homosexuality (Burt 1995) and much of the film is preoccupied with downplaying these connotations. Billy's dancing displays remarkably few recognisable ballet moves and has much more in common with tap and Irish dancing than with classical ballet. The link with popular forms of dance is reinforced by the film's use of an extract from *Top Hat* (Mark Sandrich, 1935) as well as Mr Wilkinson's (Colin MacLachlan) reference to Billy as 'Durham's little Gene Kelly'. For while the Kelly persona may have recently become the subject of queer readings (Doty 1995, and Cohan in this volume), it is the association of Kelly's dancing with energy and athleticism that the film is keen to exploit in order

Jamie Draven as Tony Elliot in *Billy Elliot* (Stephen Daldry, 2000)

to bolster an image of the basic virility of Billy's dancing. Thus, in one of the film's key scenes, when Billy expresses his frustrations through dance and physically seeks to burst out of his environment, he tapdances violently to the accompaniment of The Jam's edgy, post-punk anthem 'A Town Called Malice'.[1] This emphasis upon the 'manliness' of Billy's dancing is further strengthened by the film's careful disassociation of it from the implication of homosexuality. As Billy himself puts it to his friend Michael (Stuart Wells), 'just 'cos I like ballet doesn't mean I'm a poof'. To be fair to the film, it seeks to make this point in a way that avoids homophobia. There are knowing jokes about Wayne Sleep and the film ends with Adventures in Motion Pictures' homo-erotic reworking of *Swan Lake*. Billy's friend, Michael, is also treated with considerable sympathy (if not necessarily dramatic subtlety). Given, by comparison, the virtual absence of gay characters from Loach's depictions of the working class, this is an undoubted advance. However, the film's allusions to homosexuality, nevertheless, remain subordinate to an overall dramatic logic that privileges heterosexuality. The adult Billy is played by the notably muscular and heterosexual Adam Cooper, while the open effeminacy (including cross-dressing) of Michael's character is in effect invoked to underline the fundamentally masculine (and heterosexual) 'normality' of Billy himself.[2] This displacement of issues surrounding gender and sexuality onto Michael also suggests the film's own lack of confidence that the story would work, or achieve popularity, with such a character placed at its centre. As a result, the film also signals its own reluctance to depart too radically from the very ideologies of masculinity and virility that it is otherwise questioning.

The film's dramatisation of the tensions surrounding gender is also heavily reliant upon a conventional sexual division of labour. Whereas *Kes* followed in the footsteps of the 'new wave' films, in which fathers are either weak or absent, in *Billy Elliot* the opposite is true. Billy's mother (Janine Birkett) is dead while his grandmother (Jean Heywood) is enfeebled and dependent upon him. In *The Proud Valley* there is a clear separation of public and private space in which men dominate public space and women, particularly the mother-figure, preside over the domestic sphere. As Geoff Eley has argued, 'the dignity, endurance, emotional strength … of the mother' has been one of the most powerful 'conventions of the working-class representational repertoire' (Eley 1995: 32), an archetype that is given vivid embodiment in *The Proud Valley* by Rachel Thomas's 'mam' who loses her husband down the pit and then nearly her son. It is the absence of this mother-figure that accounts for much of Billy's plight within the film. As he himself remonstrates with his father (initially in relation to playing the piano): 'mam would have let me'. However, in identifying Billy's problem in this way, the film is also invoking a very traditional notion of domestic femininity as a counterweight to the world of male dysfunction and violence. Moreover, insofar as Mrs Wilkinson (Julie Walters) becomes a form of surrogate mother, assisting Billy's passage to success (while seemingly ignoring her own daughter's aspirations), there is also a reproduction of a masculine narrative trajectory in which the female characters are reduced to little more than onlookers. Phil Powrie has employed the idea of 'alternative heritage' in relation to films, such as Terence Davies's *Distant Voices, Still Lives* (1988), that challenge the upper-class past typically remembered by the conventional heritage film (Powrie 2000). His discussion of these in terms of provincial boy-centred rites of passage, involving a struggle between male violence and female restraint may be seen to apply to *Billy Elliot*. However, in contrast to the disrupted narratives described by Powrie, the goal-centred, linear narrative of *Billy Elliot* is much more clearly organised around the achievement of individual male identity and, accordingly, makes it a more conventional, and less 'alternative' work.

A key component of what Powrie characterises as 'alternative heritage' is the emphasis upon male violence within the home. In *The Proud Valley*, violence is not imported into the home and, when it occurs, as in the bout of mild fisticuffs at the pit-head, it is quickly brought to a halt by the womenfolk. In *Kes*, through the character of Jud, the potential of male violence to disrupt the home and family begins to emerge. This emphasis upon family dysfunction and domestic violence then becomes more pronounced in films such *Rita, Sue and Bob Too* (Alan Clarke, 1986), *Ladybird Ladybird* (Ken Loach, 1994), *Nil by Mouth* (Gary Oldman, 1997) and *My Name is Joe* (Ken Loach, 1998) in which male characters struggle to come to terms with their new 'post-patriarchal' circumstances of unemployment and loss of economic and social status. However, whereas films such as *Distant Voices, Still Lives* and *Nil by Mouth* involve a certain severing of their family dramas from a larger social context of work and politics, what is striking about *Billy Elliot* is the way in which the problems of masculinity (including violence) which are located in the family become generalised out to the wider world of industrial action.

It is initially puzzling that the film should be set during the coal dispute of 1984–85 at all as, in its basics, the story does not appear to require it (and much of the diegetic detail of the film, including the music, derives from the 1970s). In his introduction to the published script, the film's writer Lee Hall expresses his dismay that 'many of the young people who watched the early cuts of the film didn't even know what a strike was, never mind the details of this particular struggle that did so much to define the current age' (Hall 2000: x). However, the film itself does little to aid the understanding of these young people, resolutely refusing to address the social and economic causes of the dispute, which is largely staged in terms of aggressive confrontations between the miners and the police, as well as amongst the miners themselves. As a result the strike is largely subsumed into the film's preoccupations with masculinity and male violence. There are two aspects to this. On the one hand, the film is concerned with the perceptions of a child who does not himself fully understand the adult world or grasp the significance of events around him. This divorce from the adult world is seen in a short scene in which Billy and Mrs Wilkinson's daughter Debbie (Nicola Blackwell) are seen walking down a street, discussing whether or not ballet dancers are 'all poofs'. As the camera follows them, Billy and Debbie, who is carrying a stick, pass a row of posters in support of the miners ('Strike Now') and then a row of policemen holding perspex riot shields which Debbie's stick casually strokes. As they pass the police, the camera cuts to a long shot, revealing a large advertising poster for washing machines. The poster shows a man, arms folded, alongside a washing machine below text which reads 'At your Servis, Susie. Your ever-faithful washing slave'. While this scene is commonly read in terms of the film's playfulness (which is itself significant given the way in which the film treats police violence), it is also central to the film's meanings. For, in implying the children's indifference to the adult world, the film also suggests a parallelism between the striking miners and the police who are seen as common representatives of an alien world characterised by conflict and physical force. The association of this with conventional masculine identities is then reinforced by the advert with its allusion to the reshaping of traditional gender roles.

The implication of this is that for Billy the strike, and its association with male intransigence, becomes a major obstacle to the achievement of his ambitions. Following the discovery of his involvement in ballet, Billy's father (Gary Lewis) attempts to explain to him that ballet is 'not for lads' and forbids him to go to further classes. The confrontation becomes physical when Billy calls his father a 'bastard', his father hits him and Billy flees from the house. This is followed by shots of Billy running up the street and then past 'Strike Now' posters similar to those which have already been seen. There is then an unexpected shot of Billy hitting and kicking these same posters, while T Rex's 'Children of the Revolution' is heard on the soundtrack. In having Billy give vent to his frustrations in this way, the film appears to suggest how the father's masculine hostility to ballet and resort to violence is, in turn, linked to the aggression of the striking miners. The use of Bolan's line 'you won't fool the children of the revolution' (for all the song's trippy word-play) also seems to highlight the film's suspicion towards the strike and its oppressive ('unrevolutionary') consequences for Billy. Given how the film structures our identification in relation to Billy, it is not surprising therefore that his father should subsequently decide to return to work in order to obtain the money to send him to an audition in London. Although he is stopped at the last minute by his son Tony (Jamie Draven), the strike-breaking logic is so embedded in the way in which film has established its dramatic conflicts that it retains its force despite this narrative turn. Indeed, at least one critic remained under the impression that Billy's father had, in fact, broken the strike (Raven 2000).

In this respect, the film is distinguished from two other films of the period dealing with the consequences of industrial decline. Unlike *Brassed Off*, which also deals with the willed destruction of the coal industry, there is little nostalgia for traditional masculinity but an emphasis on men's re-learning of gender roles. As such, there are similarities with *The Full Monty*, in which the male characters undergo a degree of feminisation, but there is little of its emphasis upon the reconstruction of the traditional homosocial community as the means to the recovery of male self-respect (see Monk 2000b). Instead the film ends with the incorporation of the previously unreconstructed bearers of masculinity, Billy's father and brother, into the new 'community' of the opera house, where they find themselves sat beside Michael and his black lover. While this imagining of community is still all-male, it does nevertheless possess some of the utopian desire of other British movies, such as *My Beautiful Laundrette* (Stephen Frears, 1985) and *Young Soul Rebels* (Isaac Julien, 1991), for a more socially and sexually inclusive sense of belonging. At the same time, it is a vision of community that seems to involve a virtual subordination of traditional forms of (northern) working-class association and culture to the world of (southern) middle-class culture (albeit that the film may be endeavouring to overcome the divisions between 'high' and 'low' art). This stands in contrast to *The Proud Valley* in which there is a strong sense of the working class's own cultural resources as found in the activities of the men's choir and in which the working-class community comes to 'stand in' for national virtues. In a way typical of many 'new wave' films, *Kes* is more circumspect about traditional working-class culture which it sees as being eroded by a more commercialised form of 'mass culture', as in the scene at the working-men's club in which a band batters out covers of current Top Twenty hits. In *Billy Elliot*, however, the portrait of working-class culture is emptied of virtually all positive values and must endeavour to transform itself. Thus, in a loose allegory of the transition from a manufacturing to a service-based economy, Billy becomes an emblem of economic rejuvenation through participation in the 'creative industries' – just as many of the former miners of Easington colliery found temporary employment as extras in the film's re-enactment of the coal dispute (Chalmers 2000).

Conclusion

This essay has taken as its title a lyric from John Lennon's song 'Working Class Hero', his sardonic reflections on the continuing salience of class in the supposedly 'classless and free' British society of the late 1960s as well as an ironic meditation on the form of celebrity he himself had achieved ('if you want to be a hero, well just follow me'). By focusing on three 'emblematic' films I have attempted to sketch the changing fortunes of the 'working-class hero' in British cinema, revealing a slow but sure fall from grace. Writing in the context of the challenge of feminism to the left, Jonathan Rutherford and Rowena Chapman write that 'the male socialist, once a heroic and Socialist Man, is no longer the embodiment of what is good and progressive' (Rutherford and Chapman 1988: 18). In a sense, it is this decline of 'Socialist Man' that the transition from *The Proud Valley*, through *Kes*, to *Billy Elliot* reveals. It is, moreover, a decline that is mapped in terms of the questioning of the norms of male heterosexuality which have traditionally underpinned working-class political activism and, as in *Billy Elliot*, industrial militancy. However, while my own work has consistently sought to bring out the implicit ideologies of masculinity underpinning the tradition of working-class realism in British cinema, I also feel a strong sense of discomfort with *Billy Elliot*. This is not simply because of the way in which so many aspects of the strike – the struggle for community and a different vision of society, the role of women, the range of cultural activities stimulated by the conflict – are excised from the film but the way in which its critique of masculinity is so starkly mobilised against the miners (in a simplified confrontation between class and sexual politics).[3] While these features may derive from the film's imposition, in the interests of 'entertainment', of a linear narrative involving clear-cut conflicts, the price paid is inevitably the sacrifice of complexity. As Fred Pfeil has argued, 'white straight masculinity' is not 'a single monolithic category' and the ways in which it is inhabited, and the power that flows from it, varies in relation to 'class background', 'socio-economic status' and 'ethnic heritage' (Pfeil 1995: vii, ix). As a result, the problems of masculinity have to be understood in relation to issues of social and economic location just as the conception of the working class itself has to be 'demasculinised' and understood in relation to the substantial numbers of women involved in manual labour. In this respect, *Billy Elliot*'s fantasy of individual upward mobility (and effective incorporation into middle-class culture) ducks too many issues: the problems of continuing economic and social disadvantage in British society, the complicated ways in which these are related to gender roles, and the demanding task of building a politics that can combine, rather than counterpose, different kinds of demand for equality and social justice.

Notes

1   There is, however, a degree of ambivalence in the music which the film employs as a result of the use of various Marc Bolan/T Rex numbers. 'Cosmic Dancer', with which the film begins, had already been used by Todd Haynes in *Velvet Goldmine* (1998), his camp celebration of glam rock's gender-bending, polysexual inclinations, and it is inevitable that some elements of Bolan's association with androgyny and dandyism should carry over into the film (especially given that the peak of Bolan's popularity was over ten years prior to the period in which the film is set). However, the film itself partly endeavours to disavow these connotations by having the Bolan records belong, somewhat improbably, to Billy's aggressively masculine brother, Tony, who is seen at one point playing air guitar to 'I Love to Boogie'.

2   The film is, however, hesitant about fully affirming Billy's heterosexuality, showing, on a couple of occasions, his reluctance to respond to Debbie's (Nicola Blackwell) advances. Thus, while the final performance of *Swan Lake* refers back to an earlier scene in which Billy engages in a pillow fight with Debbie in her bedroom decorated with swan wallpaper, this suggests less the fulfilment of his heterosexual drives than their sublimation. The meaning of the final performance, moreover, is heavily context-dependent, varying according to the prior knowledge of *Swan Lake* and Adam Cooper which the spectator possesses.

3   As Penny Green argues, 'the role played by women in the strike was one of the most crucial aspects of the whole dispute', and women's involvement 'broke down traditional notions of the "women's place" in a very traditional community' as well as challenging 'the idea that only those whose jobs were threatened could fight a strike' (Green 1990: 189). Given the huge importance of women to the conduct of the strike, their marginalisation within the film becomes all the more telling.

chapter 9

MASCULINITY AND EXCLUSION IN POST-1995 BEUR AND 'BANLIEUE' FILMS

Carrie Tarr

French cinema in the 1990s saw the advent of a new generation of filmmakers (born in the late 1950s and 1960s) whose films, not unproblematically, have been grouped under the label of 'le jeune cinéma français' ('young French cinema'; see Trémois 1997; Chauville 1998; Marie 1998; Prédal 2002) or 'la nouvelle Nouvelle Vague' ('the new New Wave').[1] Many of these filmmakers demonstrate a new concern with documenting social realities, including the anger and frustration suffered by those who find themselves socially excluded (a concern which was also manifest in their support of the 'sans papiers', or immigrants 'without papers' (see Powrie 1999: 10–16). Whilst a number of their films about the alienation of contemporary youth centre primarily, and more conventionally, on the existential angst of the (white) privileged bourgeois or intellectual classes (such as Cédric Klapisch's *Le Péril jeune*, 1993; Xavier Beauvois' *N'oublie pas que tu va mourir/Don't Forget You're Going to Die*, 1995; Pascale Ferran's *L'Âge des possibles*, 1995; Arnaud Desplechin's *Comment je me suis disputé ... (ma vie sexuelle)/My Sex Life ... or How I Got into an Argument*, 1996), a significant body of films has focused on young people from the deprived *banlieue* (outer city) housing estates or inner-city ghettos in France. These include both Beur films (films made by and/or featuring second-generation young people of Maghrebi or North African origin in France) and *banlieue* films (films set in multi-ethnic working-class estates on the urban periphery). One of the defining features of these films has been the focus on disadvantaged youths typified by the internationally successful *La Haine*.[2] At a time when right-wing discourses relating to France's postcolonial others continue to encapsulate the fears and anxieties of the majority white population, the representations of such marginalised masculinities are of crucial significance.

Like the first Beur films of the 1980s (such as Mehdi Charef's *Le Thé au harem d'Archimède/Tea in the Harem*, 1985; Rachid Bouchareb's *Bâton Rouge*, 1985) and other 1990s films which led critics to debate the existence of a *banlieue* film genre (Thomas Gilou's *Raï*, 1995; Jean-François Richet's *État des lieux*, 1995), *La Haine* foregrounds a group of disaffected, unemployed working-class youths at an age when they would normally aspire to adult masculinity. Typically, the young protagonists, here a trio of 'black-blanc-Beur' ('black, white and second-generation Maghrebi') youths, find it difficult if not impossible to assert their masculinity in socially acceptable ways. Arguably their socio-economic deprivation combined with an apparent lack of any acceptable paternal role models (a common trope of both Beur and *banlieue* films) prevent them from assuming an active role in society through work, a family and a place of their own. Instead, they seek to protest at their emasculation though an over-aggressive but ultimately self-defeating performance of phallic masculinity. As Ginette Vincendeau notes, they are actually 'anomic, helpless and hopeless. Their aggression … is random and self-defeating … [they] stay at home in a state of perpetual childhood' (Vincendeau 2000: 323). At the same time, in contrast to American black-gang crime films (like *Menace II Society*, Albert Hughes, 1993), films like *La Haine* tend to emphasise the commonality of underclass experiences of 'la fracture sociale' ('the social divide') through peer group solidarity, regardless of ethnic differences. They thus underline the significance of class and social exclusion in the performance of masculinity. However, whilst the focus on male bonding may, within a limited context, produce positive images of cross-race integration, it risks effacing not just female experiences (or the experiences of older inhabitants of the *banlieue*), but also the specificity of ethnic minority experiences and the possibility of alternative performances of masculinity.

I have argued elsewhere (Tarr 1999) that in the Beur and *banlieue* films of 1995, there were in fact considerable differences of emphasis between white and Beur-authored films, the former foregrounding cross-race male violence, the latter more concerned with how individual ethnic minority (Beur) youths confront and negotiate problems of identity and integration in a social context in which they are excluded on grounds of both class and ethnicity. In this essay I want to examine whether similar differences can be found in post-1995 Beur and *banlieue* films. I am therefore going to compare the construction of masculinity and violence in two chronicles of life in the ghetto, *Ma 6-T va crack-er* (Jean-François Richet, 1997; henceforth abbreviated *Ma 6-T*) and *Comme un aimant/The Magnet* (Akhenaton and Kamel Saleh, 2000) – the most obvious successors to *La Haine* – and in the hit comedy, *Le Ciel, les oiseaux … et ta mère/Boys on the Beach* (Djamel Bensalah, 1999; henceforth abbreviated *Le Ciel*). *Ma 6-T*, the second film by Jean-François Richet, is set in Richet's home *banlieue* estate of Beauval-Collinet in Meaux, to the east of Paris (where he still lives, as does his co-writer, actor and cousin, Arco Descat C.); *Comme un aimant*, a first feature co-written and co-directed by Kamel Saleh (a Beur) and Akhenaton (the stage name of Philippe Fragione, star of Marseilles rap group IAM, who is of Italian immigrant origin), is set in the Panier district of Marseilles (like Karim Dridi's *Bye Bye*, 1995). In contrast *Le Ciel,* a first feature by Djamel Bensalah (a Beur from Saint-Denis, to the north of Paris), displaces its *banlieue* youths into the alien setting of the ultra-white bourgeois seaside resort of Biarritz. Arguably, the shift in setting enables the mechanisms of masculine performativity and male bonding to be rendered more transparent.

There are certain resemblances between the three films on the level of theme and style: the foregrounding of a disadvantaged young male peer group of diverse ethnic origins, a loosely-structured episodic plot rather than a goal-oriented linear narrative, location shooting, the periodic use of a hand-held camera, the lack of glamourisation of the principal protagonists, an emphasis on the youths' at times impenetrable *verlan* (*banlieue* slang), the expression of macho yet largely impotent attitudes towards women, and the conspicuous absence of family life (a factor which distinguishes these films from earlier Beur films). Where they differ is in terms of genre. The first two aim for a degree of realism, drawing on 'authentic' settings (the *banlieue* housing estate, the inner-city ghetto) and a cast of amateur actors, friends and acquaintances of the director(s), who also perform in the films themselves. They both focus on large, loosely-formed gangs of unemployed males whose anger and frustration at their continuing marginalisation from mainstream society, itself a form of emasculation, drives them deeper and deeper into violence and confrontation with the police. *Le Ciel*, however, is a teen/summer holiday comedy of manners, set far from the *banlieue*, which centres on a smaller number of protagonists, one of whom is played by Jamel Debbouze, now a hugely successful stand-up comedian and comic actor. Its plot, such as it is, studiously avoids the physical, criminal violence which structures *Ma 6-T* and *Comme un aimant*, channelling the youths' aggression in particular into their use of language. Like *La Haine*, *Le Ciel* also incorporates a critical reflection on the stereotypical way the media construct youth and violence in the multi-ethnic *banlieue*, for which by implication it aims to offer an alternative.

My argument is that, despite commonalities in their constructions of testosterone-fuelled underclass youths, the representation of disempowered masculinity in these three films is inflected in ways that relate to the cultural background and ethnic origins of their directors. Although Richet's racialisation of the *banlieue* expresses solidarity with those who are persistently discriminated against, its use of violence risks making a negative impact on majority French audiences; in contrast, the incorporation of white ethnicities in the two Beur-authored films marks a bid for integration and is accompanied by a less alienating use of violence. In their address to a mainstream audience, they indicate more clearly than *Ma 6-T* that their protagonists' aggressive masculinity is a way of compensating for exclusion that masks an inner vulnerability.[3]

Ma 6-T va crack-er

In *Ma 6-T va crack-er*, Richet, a self-proclaimed Marxist, constructs a male-centred fantasy of revolution in the *banlieue*, culminating in a climactic rap-accompanied battle between the youths and the CRS riot police, who are represented in Manichean fashion as the irredeemable class enemy. Paradoxically, the violence is introduced in a prologue sequence centred on white actress Virginie Ledoyen (to whom the film is dedicated), who is shot direct to camera with a little girl by her side, waving a red flag and then loading a Kaleshnikov, against a background of images of international revolution and a rap accompaniment. The sequence ends with her pointing handguns at her head and heart and closing her eyes (followed by a fade to black and the sound of an offscreen gunshot). Reprised near the end of the film, this image of potentially self-destructive female violence can perhaps best be read as a sign of the film's political confusion, glamourisation of violence and inability to imagine a constructive vision of the post-revolutionary future.

Ma 6-T va crack-er (Jean-François Richet, 1997)

The film has no clear linear narrative and deliberately makes little attempt to establish its multiple male protagonists as individuals (Masson 1998: 115). Shot mostly in the public spaces in and around the depressing blocks of flats and local shopping centre, the youths' aggression derives from the fact that they are both confined to the estate (there are no scenes shot outside the *banlieue*) and unsettled there (they are regularly disturbed by the police or rival youths). The film revolves around two particular mixed-race gangs, one school-age (principally Arco, Malik and Mustafa), one older (principally Djeff, JM, Pete and Hamouda), both of which are actively involved in violence, petty thieving and hostilities with the police. The tone is set in the opening scenes as Arco and friends are temporarily expelled over violence at school and the older youths are involved in altercations with their rivals over drug payments. The two gangs are linked by the fact that Djeff and Arco (played respectively by the director and his co-writer) live in the same flat and jointly set fire to a litter bin which they throw down onto a police patrol car. The film suggests that the younger boys turn to their elder brothers as role models rather than to parental or other authority figures. Parents are noticeably absent from the diegesis and the authority figures who take their place – the white, female head teacher, the black gym teacher, older residents on the estate – are openly mocked and their advice in favour of restraint ignored.

The violence comes to a head on the night of a hip-hop concert, intercut with shots of the rappers protesting about the state of the estate and the role of the police, and defiantly affirming their masculinity, 'We're guys who never give in'. For some twenty minutes the film builds up tension (or tries to) through relentless crosscutting sequences. First it cuts between three of the younger gang setting fire to a car outside the supermarket (venting their frustration at not getting in to the concert) and an American-style shoot-out between the rival older gangs outside the concert. Then, when Malik is shot dead by the police (a 'blunder' which recalls the starting-point of *La Haine*), it cuts between the mass of rioting youths (smashing up and setting fire to cars and telephone boxes) and the arrival of the CRS in force and in full riot gear. And finally, it cuts between the battle with the police, with the youths hurling petrol bombs, setting a policeman on fire, and the rappers whose rap number carries the message that 'sedition is the solution'. The interminable accumulation of violence and destruction, occasionally tempered by clichéd slow-panning shots, may be intended to give the audience cathartic pleasure along with the sounds and rhythm of the rap music, but the effect is rather to emphasise Richet's deadening use of violence as designer spectacle, despite his claims to the contrary (Masson 1998: 115).

Ma 6-T thus constructs an over-extended, reactionary image of phallic masculinity in the *banlieue*, based on the belief that underclass youths should never show signs of weakness and that violent action, preferably with a gun, is the only way of countering disempowerment. The film celebrates such violence by piling up mini-narratives in which criminal activities go unpunished and encounters with aggressive law officers (including a white woman) often lead to the police being overpowered (a shot of a poster advertising the left-of-centre weekly *Le Nouvel Observateur* displays the headline 'The estates where the police no longer dare go'). The screen becomes invaded not just by the police but by increasing numbers of virtually interchangeable angry youths who share the same looks, language, gestures and actions. Clearly Richet wants to minimise racial or ethnic differences in order to foreground the youths' potential as a revolutionary class (and the end credits list his acknowledgement to Engels, Marx and Eisenstein, among others). However, the lack of differentiation between individual protagonists, or between criminal violence and violence against the police, means that there is little possibility of establishing identification or sympathy for a mainstream audience.[4] Richet ends the film with a coda sequence set in another *banlieue*, where a Beur motorcyclist is shot dead when he fails to stop for the police. Presumably he wants the audience to react to yet another representation of unjustified violence on the part of the representatives of the bourgeois state by starting a riot; at the same time, the image of yet another death also seems to acknowledge the hopelessness and ineffectuality of that position, and the film's final message, the reproduction of Article 35 of the Declaration of Human Rights claiming the right to insurrection, reads like wishful thinking rather than a call to action.

In fact, there are moments of respite in the violence when a more sympathetic image of masculinity damaged by social exclusion and dysfunctional families struggles to surface. At several points, the film shows the youths sitting around talking about their lack of communication with their parents, their lack of hope for the future, their feelings of being invaded and persecuted by the police, and the need for revolutionary change. However, the failure of the youths' relationships with women, a trope for their impotence in the wider world, is extremely troubling. Despite their macho talk, no sexual relationships are shown on screen, and their occasional interactions with women demonstrate the powerlessness underlying their aggression (unlike *État des lieux* which ends with a scene of frenetic sexual intercourse).[5] Whenever Djeff and JM try to chat up a passing woman, they can only do so through verbal bullying and physical harassment. In each case the woman is capable of putting them in their place, though only by accepting a degree of unwanted physical contact. The film seems implicitly to recognise the inadequacy of such behaviour by suggesting that none of the youths is able to progress beyond a state of prolonged adolescence (the scene in which they plan the shoot-out takes place in a children's playground). But at the same time it also celebrates their aggressive masculinity through the aestheticisation of their subsequent violence, and offers no alternative vision of their future beyond the imagined purification brought about by burning and rioting. Unfortunately, as Will Higbee has argued, such imagery risks contributing to the 'already exaggerated media representation of the disadvantaged urban periphery as the site of violence and delinquency which warrants the repressive police presence' (Higbee 2001: 202).

Comme un aimant

Comme un aimant differs from *Ma 6-T* in its initially humorous tone, its use of space and its more obviously differentiated and individualised protagonists. The film centres on a group of eight young men in their mid-twenties, all either of Italian or Maghrebi immigrant origin. It is set mainly in the narrow streets of the Panier district where its protagonists grew up and hang out (punctuated by shots of the bench and bar where they congregate, as well as of patrolling police cars), but it embraces the whole of Marseilles, linking the *quartier* to the city in a way which is very different from the geographical anonymity of *Ma 6-T*. The film's setting underlines the economic insecurity and social (and also racial) exclusion suffered by its young male protagonists, who regularly leave the area to find something to do (have some fun, make some money), but find themselves frustrated and disillusioned (unable to get the girls or carry out their crimes successfully, suffering from racial hostility, and discovering that the Mafia and even the younger kids have more of a place in the city than they do). They are drawn back to the Panier like a magnet (the title comes from a rap number in IAM's 1993 album),[6] but their inability to move on (or grow up) draws them into a spiral of violence which leads to tragedy and pathos rather than to the revolutionary anger which fuels *Ma 6-T*.

The film begins light-heartedly with a sequence in which Santino (Titoff) drives past the sea in a red sports car and tries (unsuccessfully) to chat up a passing young woman.

It is followed by sequences demonstrating that Santino and his friends are fundamentally likeable lads looking for a good time, rather than hardened criminals. First they sell boxes of stolen video-recorders to a couple of black guys, all but one of which contain nothing but stones. Then they try to gain access to a nightclub (a typical trope of Beur and *banlieue* films), which they eventually manage by paying the black bouncer to kit them out in fancy (more feminised) clothes (though their summer clothing of shorts and short-sleeved T-shirts already gives them a softer, more feminised look than the combat-style sports clothing worn by the youths of *Ma 6-T*).[7] As the film progresses, however, their actions produce increasingly serious repercussions, and the spaces of the Panier become dominated by shots of railings and other signs of imprisonment. (They also get captured 'on screen', either as images of police cars are seen on, or reflected on, the television, or because of a video surveillance screen.) Houari's mistake in blurting out their address to the guys they have conned leads to Cahuète spending a couple of nights in jail; Christian is hit by a car when trying to steal a handbag and badly damaged, both mentally and physically; Fouad is shot dead by a security guard when he attempts an armed robbery; and Kakou and Houari are arrested in a robbery which has been set up by a police informant. In a parallel narrative strand, Santino's frustrated attempt to get in with a gang of older Mafiosi leads not just to him getting badly beaten up for not returning the money he owes, but also to the demise of Brabra and Sauveur who attempt to avenge him: Brabra's fate remains unknown but Sauveur is shot dead on the pavement in cold blood. So the film's narrative structure demonstrates the young men's inability to handle crime and violence, producing a very different inflection on masculinity from that of *Ma 6-T*.

The spiralling towards tragedy is punctuated by sequences detailing the failure of their relationships with women and with their families, giving them a solidity and individuality lacking in the more undifferentiated figures of *Ma 6-T*, and also allowing female figures to play a slightly more significant role. For example, feckless Sauveur (Akhenaton) is rejected by his Beurette girlfriend, Soraya, to the applause of other women in the street, and evicted from his home by his angry Italian immigrant father, who accuses him of 'not being a man' because he has not got a job; he takes shelter in a cellar, through the barred window of which he is befriended by a little Bosnian girl refugee. Brabra, Fouad and Kakou are unable to make out with the French girls with whom Brabra arranges a date, despite their intense preparations, and Brabra discovers that the girl he fancies votes for the Front National. Fouad is gently reproached for his constant absence by his Algerian immigrant mother, but is so destabilised by her death that he gets himself shot trying to hold up a jeweller's shop. Santino is forced to pay back the mob by stealing a cheque from his beloved Italian immigrant grandmother, and is left humiliated and in tears.

The exception to this pattern is Cahuète (Saleh), the most intellectual of the group (he is seen holding a copy of Dante's *Inferno*) and also the most settled and mature (he has a stable relationship with a supportive Beurette girlfriend, whose flat is lined with shelves of books). Able to keep his cool when he is held for questioning (although the spectator shares his nightmare fantasy of being shot by a sadistic policeman), he speculates about giving up a life of crime, but can see no acceptable alternative. The film ends on what appears to be an apocalyptic revenge for what has happened to his friends. He drives off in an unattended petrol tanker, spreads petrol through the streets of Marseilles, sets the petrol alight, and then drives high above the city to watch it burn (the shots of fire filling the screen mirroring shots in *Ma 6-T*). However, a close-up of Cahuète closing and re-opening his eyes cuts back not to fire and destruction but to a view of the city intact. The violence proves to have been merely imaginary, and the last image of Cahuète's impassive gaze suggests that it is his ability to redirect his anger into fantasy (like Saleh, the actor-director) that makes him the lonely, silent survivor.

The film's shift from a light-hearted opening to a more serious, elegiac ending is underlined near the film's end by a silent slow-motion flashback sequence showing the group of friends as happy, carefree youths messing about in the sun and the sea. A sense of nostalgia is also promoted by the soundtrack (a hybrid mix of rap, pop and classical music by Akhenaton and classical composer Bruno Coulais, which draws on 1970s soul music as well as Italian and Corsican popular songs). Dedicated to 'Alhassan and other friends who have disappeared', the film's protest at the fate of a lost generation recognises that its dream of revolt against injustice is just a fantasy. Rather than uncritically celebrating youthful male violence as a way of compensating for social exclusion, like *Ma 6-T*, *Comme un aimant* demonstrates its inadequacy. Yet at the same time it, too, has little to offer as an alternative and, arguably, the youths fail because their softness and incompetence forces them to give way to the superior performances of masculine violence demonstrated by the police and the Mafia.

Le Ciel, les oiseaux ... et ta mère!

Le Ciel, les oiseaux ... et ta mère! draws its humour from the displacement of the 'black-blanc-Beur' male group typical of the *banlieue* film into an alien and potentially hostile setting. The opening pre-credit sequence, set in an underground car park in Saint-Denis, shows a trio of school-leavers fabricating a video documentary about a *banlieue* drug dealer, played by their classmate, Mike (Julien Courbey), who obligingly redoes his lines wearing a hood and smoking a joint to look more 'authentic'. Their film fools the judges and wins them a holiday in Biarritz, leaving spectators to anticipate that *Le Ciel* itself will offer alternative representations of *banlieue* youth. Indeed, the film self-consciously distances itself from drugs and violence and interactions with the police. Instead it offers the spectacle of three rather pathetic, penniless youths, Youssef (Jamel), the Beur, Christophe (Lorent Deutsch), the 'blanc', and Stéphane (Stéphane Soo Mongo), the Black, who arrive in Biarritz with the rather over-optimistic hope of picking up lots of girls and little to their credit except a video camera and an extraordinary propensity for *banlieue* slang. Bensalah claims to have been looking at the films of Scorsese, Coppola and De Palma for inspiration for a filmmaking style that would 'tear the generation of my little twelve-year-old sister away from American films' (Médioni 1999: 103). But this film has little to offer his sister in its focus on male bonding, its casual misogyny, and its evacuation of ethnic minority girls and women.

Like *Ma 6-T* and *Comme un aimant*, *Le Ciel* has no clear goal-oriented narrative drive. It consists of a series of loosely-linked episodes in the day-to-day lives of its protagonists, humorously punctuated by their clumsy, amateur video footage (and occasionally by other inserts, a 1950s promotional film of Biarritz, a supermarket surveillance screen, fish-bowl shots through the flat door's spy-hole, clips of pornographic and Hollywood films, and the final self-reflexive end-credit sequence in which Youssef/Jamel jokes that, 'We could be in a film'). Suffering from a lack of funds and sexual know-how, the lads spend their time aimlessly hanging around watching television, messing about in the kitchen,

Le Ciel, les oiseaux et ... ta mère (Djamel Bensalah, 1999)

shopping, lying on the beach, playing with their video camera, and moaning about the boredom of life in Biarritz. At first, they attribute their inability to attract girls to their lack of money (they get moved on from the sofa they are sprawling on in a nightclub because they cannot afford a drink); later, when Mike joins them and suggests pretending to make a video documentary about young people on holiday, their plans for seduction are foiled because his car runs out of petrol. More significantly, they repeatedly refuse the invitation of Lydie (Olivia Bonamy), a Parisian girl in the neighbouring holiday flat, to join in a game of volleyball on the beach. The image of *banlieue* youth constructed here is thus primarily one of enforced domesticity, passivity and sexual inadequacy, enhanced by their unthreatening, youthful appearance: three of them are small and thin, including Youssef who also has a damaged arm (and writes home to his Mum), and Stéphane may be large but he is also soft and the most domesticated of the four. In addition, the film draws attention to Youssef's vulnerability to racism, first when the concierge gives the key to Christophe rather than him (he calls her Mme Mégret, after the FN politician), then in his confrontation with a bus conductor (Sam Karmann) who, having asked him for his nationality when his ID card clearly indicates that he is French, then imposes an unjustified fine. It thus demonstrates the youths' lack of belonging, contrasting them with the posh (white) 'Biarritziens' like the 'surfers' to whom Youssef constantly refers.

Instead of resorting to physical violence to deal with their exclusion, the youths use their video camera and their potentially offensive language as a way of asserting their presence and their masculinity. Their group solidarity is clearly based in part on shared anxieties about their sexuality, emphasised by their sexist comments and sexual slang. It is also reinforced by their anti-Semitism, evident in Youssef's dislike of Steven Spielberg and refusal to see the Jewish-centred hit comedy *La Vérité si je mens/Would I Lie to You?*

(Thomas Gilou, 1997). However, the film also offers a critique of this position through Youssef's budding relationship with the unbelievably patient and forbearing Lydie. Youssef is at first unable or unwilling to respond to Lydie's interest in him and admit his attraction to her and, after a fanciful game of Scrabble in which they appear to be getting closer, he recoils when he notices her Star of David. When Lydie angrily accuses him of racism, Youssef responds by pointing out that people in Biarritz will not mix with him and his friends (her two girlfriends being a case in point), reducing her to silence and tears. However, the narrative ends with Youssef pursuing her to the airport to return the eggs he had borrowed and give her his phone number in Paris, a scene that duly ends with a kiss. The audience is invited to believe that Youssef's racist and macho posturing is just a defensive bluff and that he has been won over to romance with a woman who is also vulnerable to racism. At the same time, the potentially threatening theme of cross-race sexuality is defused by the deferral of sexual gratification to an uncertain future.

The deconstruction of the rhetoric of macho masculinity underpinning male bonding is reworked in the activities of Christophe, who is goaded by his mates to chat up Christelle (which he does by imagining himself in the role of a Hollywood movie star, a sequence which is shot in black-and-white and heavily-accented English). Unexpectedly successful, Christophe is the only one of the group actually to have sex (Stéphane does not go near a woman, and ugly Mike's insensitive attempts to chat up women regularly meet with disaster). However, his affair brings about the group's disintegration, since he is too ashamed of his friends to introduce them to Christelle, and Stéphane, who is already fed up with Youssef's 'platonic affair' with Lydie, feels so let down that he decides to leave. Christophe attempts to retrieve the situation by claiming that his relationship with Christelle is just a holiday fuck, but when Christelle overhears and walks out on him, he is genuinely upset and can no longer function happily within the remaining trio. Clearly their adolescent male bonding is dependent on their ability to score and scorn women, not to have relationships. The film ends with them setting off for Paris in silence, having broken the video camera, leaving open the question as to whether it is possible for underclass male bonding to survive the intrusion of the feminine and the transition from adolescence to maturity which such a relationship implies. Arguably, then, the film moves towards a critique of their boorish behaviour, exposing it as a masquerade covering over their sexual anxieties (as in the repeated taunts about Christophe and Mike still being virgins). At the same time, however, it also invites the spectator to enjoy their casual misogyny, in particular through the sparky irreverence of Jamel's virtuoso verbal performance.

Conclusion

Like *La Haine*, these three films each articulate a multi-voiced, cross-race protest at the ongoing exclusion of underclass male youths from the pleasures and stabilities of mainstream society. Nevertheless, there are significant differences between them. *Ma 6-T va crack-er* offers images of 'hard' masculinity and a narrative of increasing, excessive and, to some extent, successful violence. Arguably, such a narrative is only possible in a film by a white director, because it risks endangering the precarious integration of France's ethnic minority others by constructing them in stereotypical fashion as threatening and dangerous (though it does single out Beur youths as the principal victims of police violence). *Comme un aimant* and *Le Ciel, les oiseaux … et ta mère*, the two films by Beur directors, offer images of a 'softer', less threatening masculinity, and use strategies which defuse or avoid scenes of confrontation and violence, injecting comedy, putting more focus on individual dilemmas (including the experience of racial hostility), and stressing the difficulties of gaining a purchase on the world, be it through crime (as in *Comme un aimant*) or through amorous adventures (as in *Le Ciel*).

All three films use the sexual impotence of their young male protagonists as a trope for their lack of agency in the wider world. Despite the vociferous assertion of their heterosexuality, the youths in question are generally unable to work through their Oedipal trajectory and achieve adulthood by forging mature, satisfactory sexual relationships. Furthermore, their inability to form a couple seems to be a precondition of the cross-race male bonding which informs these films, rendered explicit in *Le Ciel*, but implicit in the other two films in their repeated demonstrations of the youths' failure to engage adequately with women. Yet in contrast to *Ma 6-T*, both Beur-authored films gesture towards other possibilities for their Beur protagonists, be it through Cahuète's self-containment and survival in *Comme un aimant* or Youssef's last-minute realisation in *Le Ciel* of the potential permeability of the boundaries of sex, class and ethnicity. Thus, if post-1995 *banlieue* films about disadvantaged youths seem disturbingly unable or unwilling to envisage alternative, more mature and empowering performances of underclass masculinity, it is nevertheless the Beur-authored films, with their stake in integration, that offer a more nuanced view.

Notes

1 As Myrto Konstantarakos has argued in her review of the literature, however, these films are far from constituting a homogenous grouping (Konstantarakos 1998).

2 Nevertheless, the cinematic representation of the *banlieue* has been problematised in films which fore-ground female perspectives and experiences; for example Anne Fontaine's *Les Histoires d'amour finissent mal en général/Love Affairs Usually End Badly* (1993); Zaïda Ghorab-Volta's *Souviens-toi de moi* (1996); Philippe Faucon's *Samia* (2001); and Zaïda Ghorab-Volta's *Jeunesse dorée* (2002).

3 These differences were reflected in their distribution. *Ma 6-T* was withdrawn from general distribution because of fears of incitement to violence, whereas *Le Ciel* was selected for international distribution as part of the Martell French Cinema Tour of the UK in 2000.

4 This contrasts with Beur films like Malik Chibane's *Hexagone* (1994), where the protagonists are individuated through a wide variety of social interactions (see Tarr 1999).

5 Richet's third film, *De l'amour/All About Love* (2001), centres on mixed-race couple Marie (Virginie Ledoyen) and Karim (Yazid Aït), but disappointingly turns into a rape-revenge film rather than a study of a mature interracial relationship.

6 The image of the magnet ('l'aimant') is as fatalistic as the image of the fall from a high building in *La Haine*.

7 Their fundamental harmlessness is also embodied in the figure of Kader, a simple-minded gentle giant.

SECTION 1 STARS

SECTION 2 CLASS & RACE

SECTION 3 FATHERS

SECTION 4 BODIES

Ernst Lubitsch with Ramon Novarro and Norma Shearer in a publicity shot for *The Student Prince of Old Heidelberg* (1927)

chapter 10

HERR LUBITSCH JOINS THE CORPS SAXONIA: HISTORY, GESTURE AND HOMOSOCIALITY IN *THE STUDENT PRINCE OF OLD HEIDELBERG*

Bruce Babington

Meditations on a publicity still

The publicity still opposite advertising Lubitsch's *The Student Prince of Old Heidelberg* (1927) shows Ramon Novarro as the student Prince Karl Heinrich kneeling before Norma Shearer as Käthi, his sweetheart, the inn keeper's niece, clutching her hand soulfully.[1] Both actors seem, in the indulgence of the photo set-up, to be slightly parodying their narrative characteristics: Novarro, downcast, highly feminised; Shearer's sympathetic gaiety broadening to what looks like a meta-textual amusement at the tableau enacted. Between them, like somebody's Jewish uncle, an indulgent Ernst Lubitsch, head canting to his right in a reportedly typical gesture, embraces them both.[2] You can almost hear him saying (though he is too young to do so), 'My children'. The still shows Lubitsch in the benevolent command of his stars that characteristically took the form of the ex-actor himself playing out their parts so that they could exactly imitate him, suggesting a yearning for auteurial command down even to basic gestures.[3] But equally his habit of playing all the parts suggests something usually ascribed to both filmmakers and audiences in a more internalised way, a mobile series of identifications across the narrative, here emblematised in Lubitsch's rapport with both the Prince and Käthi, the defeated lovers of his most emotional film, and with (as argued below) the character whose implied narrative place he takes in the publicity still, the Prince's tutor, Dr Jüttner.

Yet few comments on *Old Heidelberg* posit much authorial identification with the film and its characters, though Eithne and Jean-Loup Bourget note the identification between Lubitsch and Dr Jüttner, if in narrower terms than I will suggest (Bourget and Bourget 1987: 65). Patrick Brion is exceptional. For him the film is the point at which the immanence of death intrudes on Lubitsch's work: 'the frivolous operetta changes into a terrifying poem on love and death' (Brion 1985: 118). Elsewhere Lubitsch is usually seen as working with the wrong – melodramatic, sentimental – material (Petrie 1985: 99–100; Hake 1992: 68–9). But such negative views forget Lubitsch's substantial early commitment to melodrama, from *Carmen* (1918) to *Anna Boleyn/Anne Boleyn* (1920) in Germany, to *Three Women* (1924), *The Patriot* (1928), *Everlasting Love* (1929) and *Broken Lullaby* (1932) in Hollywood. My claim is that *Old Heidelberg* is the equal of any Lubitsch film, and with its subjective sequences, its memorable camera mobility and montage, a summation of the fluid achievements of late silent cinema. The argument is not just technical, for *Old Heidelberg* is both an extraordinarily moving and analytically intelligent film. That is, while creating a plenitude of nostalgia for the 'golden days' of student Heidelberg, 'student folklore of beer-drinkers' (Bourget and Bourget 1987: 65) – a folklore with a basis in the much remarked actual freedoms of nineteenth-century German student life (see, for example, Paulsen 1895) – the film, without denying these nostalgic emotions, gives them a tragic context much more historically precise than has been allowed, in a German director's view, through the prism of late 1920s American cinema, of the Wilhelmine Germany which formed him. Such doubleness, the director as both Berliner Jew and aspiring American, can be read in the smart contemporary Americanness of Lubitsch's dress in our still, in piquant combination with his gestures' self-conscious old-world Jewishness, and in its staging of an encounter between American present and operetta German past, a past which both was and, crucially, *was not* Lubitsch's own. As regards multiple identifications, contemplation of the photo might see Lubitsch staging a relation both to the couple and to its individuals: through the couple to the vicissitudes of the romantic-erotic so central to his later films; through Shearer to that identification with the female which has been persuasively linked to his own Jewish marginality and with his family's trade in women's clothes (Hake 1992: 32–5), and through Novarro, beyond the obvious identification with the desiring male, to the more feminised modes of masculinity that interact with dominant ones in his later films (such as Monescu/Herbert Marshall in *Trouble in Paradise*, 1932, and Tura/Jack Benny in *To Be Or Not To Be*, 1942). This 'artistic bisexuality' differs from that of the greatest of Lubitsch's literary contemporaries, Thomas Mann, in various respects, but most obviously in the difference between the two authors' sexuality, as unswervingly heterosexual with Lubitsch as with Mann it was divided, at least in fantasy. Lubitsch's death immediately after heterosexual intercourse has a certain undeconstructable resonance here (Eyman 2000: 357–8). The last of the major identifications is Lubitsch's eliding of his own directorial position with the narrative one of the Prince's tutor, Dr Jüttner. It is part of my argument that this elision takes in Lubitsch's intimate placement of his own real life and acting gestural characteristics on the character whose central marginality, inscribed in the Jewishness of his physiognomy, gestures and name, matches the director's own insiderness/outsiderness.

What follows argues from the following assumptions: (i) that to see Lubitsch's later melodramas as simply wrong choices of mode is mistaken; ii) that Lubitsch's American period return to German subjects in *Old Heidelberg* and *Broken Lullaby* (1932) was personally charged. At the time of the former he had only been in America three years, and his trips home in 1927 and 1931 must have been complex experiences;[4] (iii) that we should take seriously the anti-militarism of two of Lubitsch's least financially successful films, *Die Bergkatze/The Wildcat* (1921), the commercial failure of which he attributed to an immediately post-war audience's dislike of anti-militaristic satire (Weinberg 1977: 285–6), and *The Man I Killed*, both of which shed light on *Old Heidelberg*; (iv) that alongside its heterosexual romance, the narrative has second and third centres in the homosocial romances between the Prince and the Corps Saxonia, and the Prince and Doctor Jüttner; (v) that 'mythic' though *Old Heidelberg*'s 'golden days' were, they had real relations to the history to which they romantically allude – Prince (later Kaiser) Wilhelm's four semesters at the University of Bonn (1877–79) where he joined the socially exclusive Borussian Corps, whose uniform he delighted in wearing afterwards at Corps reunion dinners (Kohut 1991: 48–9; Lamar 1989: 40–2); (vi) that Lubitsch's outsiderness gave him a special perspective on such material, complicating its nostalgia; and, lastly, (vii) that masculinity is as much as anything the underlying subject of the film.

Reworking the 'myth'

Old Heidelberg is a version of 'The Student Prince' narrative, best known through the 1954 MGM musical *The Student Prince* (Richard Thorpe), itself a version of the Sigmund Romberg stage musical (1924). Lubitsch's 1927 treatment has its origins, like the others, in a popular turn-of-the-century novel of university life, Wilhelm Meyer-Forster's *Karl Heinrich* (1899), later turned by the author into a successful play, *Alt-Heidelberg* (1901). Lubitsch's and Hanns Kräly's adaptation retains its sources' basic shape. The young Prince of repressive Karlsburg is sent with his tutor Dr Jüttner to complete his education in romantic Heidelberg. Here he falls in love with a commoner, Käthi, who works in her uncle Ruder's Gasthof, in the garden of which the student societies hold their drinking ceremonials. When the Prince joins the student Corps Saxonia, Heidelberg becomes the site both of first love and of idyllic male comradeship. However, in Karlsburg the Prince's dynastic marriage is decreed, though kept from the lovers by Dr Jüttner. Then, with his uncle King Karl VII dying, the Prince is commanded back to Karlsburg, vowing to Käthi that he will return. Two years later, after the deaths of the King and Dr Jüttner, he is visited just before his coronation by Kellerman (Bobby Mack), the old Corps servant. Overcome with nostalgia, the Prince salutes his tutor's portrait, promising himself 'one more day of life and love in Heidelberg'. But, returning, he finds the idyll shattered. Käthi articulates the impossibility of their love, and the comradeship between the Corpsiers and the Prince shrinks to the subjects' dutiful inferiority. The carriage wheels taking him away from Käthi dissolve into the wheels of his coronation coach.

   Lubitsch and Kräly's most important alterations to Meyer-Forster's original texts are as follows:

(i)   the addition of opening sequences in which Karl Heinrich arrives in Karlsburg as a child and stays unhappily at the court.
(ii)   the introduction of the boy's uncle, King Karl VII, the embodiment of Karlsburg repression.
(iii) the added significance given to the already important figure of Dr Jüttner, who becomes not just the narrative's centre of liberal tolerance, but its lost good father, and, even more, good mother.
(iv)   the intensification of meaning in the Prince's last meeting with the Corps. In the sources the sequence poignantly dramatises the impossibility of reliving the past, but whereas there the group cannot be reconstituted because its members have dispersed, in the film it is physically reconstructed, but cannot be reunited psychically.

While one can only guess whether two earlier German films may have influenced the 1927 film, Lubitsch and Kräly certainly knew the 1915 American version (starring Wallace Reid, Dorothy Gish and Erich von Stroheim, directed by John Farmerson). This is because they appropriated from it crucial narrative and visual elements. These include the Prince's introduction as a child, his enviously watching, then joining, a group of boys playing; and Dr Jüttner offering the Prince his first cigarette. Further, the later film takes up the earlier's cross-cutting between Karlsburg's politics and the lovers being rowed on the lake by Kellermann, with indubitable visual echoes of the latter. Lubitsch's film also shares a version of the earlier's anti-militarism which, however, was specifically linked to American pro-isolationism early in the European Great War. That context was unique to the earlier film, as was the overtness of the boy Prince's anti-militaristic demolition of his toy soldiers, Käthi's father's return from the front minus an arm to receive a state gift of an accordion, and the Prince's giving up of Käthi in order to prevent war breaking out.

Lubitsch adheres to the outlines of Mayer-Forster's *Ur*-narratives, but alters and deepens them. In comparison, the 1954 MGM musical *The Student Prince* optimistically inflects the story as an arrogant Karl Franz (Edmund Purdom, with Mario Lanza's singing) learns lessons in post-war American-sponsored democracy. He is actually sent to Heidelberg to make him a fit partner for Princess Johanna (Betta St John), too attractive to make an alliance with her really unhappy. In Heidelberg the Prince has his romance with Kathy (Ann Blyth), but both accept it, without real trauma, as passing; Dr Jüttner (Edmund Gwenn), upstaged by S. Z. Sakall as Ruder, survives to become a Privy Councillor; and the male companionship of the Corps lives on as a happy memory of 'Gaudeamus Igitur', dismantling the loss that pervades Lubitsch's film.

His Majesty the baby

The dramatising of Karl Heinrich's childhood magnifies the motif of loss throughout Lubitsch's narrative. Children are rare in Lubitsch and his only other film where the protagonist appears as a literal child is *Heaven Can Wait* (1942), where Henry (Don Ameche) is comically over-surrounded by female adulation, the antithesis of the maternally deprived Karl Heinrich. The young Prince (the almost girlishly beautiful child star Philippe De Lacey) enters the narrative arriving by train at Karlsburg station where an intimidating phalanx of dignitaries and military await him, headed by the King. The gathering's undiluted masculinity – realistically implausible – constitutes an oppressive symbolic representation of the male heir's handing over to a rigid patriarchy gathered to receive its heir. Indeed, the Prince's nanny (Edythe Chapman) seems, apart from the King's deathbed nurse, to be the only woman in the Karlsburg Court. When the vulnerably exquisite De Lacey emerges from the carriage, the firing of cannons frightens him back to his surrogate mother. The nanny encourages the child towards the forbidding King Karl VII, embodied by Gustav von Syffertitz as simultaneously unremittingly powerful and weakly aged. A close-up shows tears on the child's face as the King, clearly identifying emotion as female, rebukes him with 'A Prince never cries'. Karl Heinrich tries to retreat to his surrogate mother, but is marched away by the King, looking pleadingly back towards the nanny.

The second childhood scene is prefaced by the newly-published photograph of the Prince, showing a sailor-suited De Lacey surrounded by toys reiterating the militarisation that accompanies his entry into the Karlsburg masculine order: a gun, a toy cannon, a helmet, a rocking horse rendered military by contagion. Now the maternal sundering is repeated even more forcibly. Prime Minister von Haugk (Edward Connelly) escorts the nanny to her carriage, refusing her a last meeting. 'His Majesty does not wish the Crown Prince to be excited by sentimental farewells.' The Prince suddenly sees the carriage's occupant waving to him. He runs after her in sweeping travelling shots, only to be blocked by the palace gates, where he weeps against their bars. This literal banishment of the feminine/maternal from the boy's life traumatically underpins the rest of the narrative; indeed the Prince's point of view of the nanny disappearing – echoing his earlier point of view of her at the station – is constantly revisited, as when the Prince, back in Karlsburg, fantasises seeing Käthi again, and Norma Shearer, in oneiric close-up opens her arms to him as she rapidly recedes into the distance; when the Prince really does return to Heidelberg and himself recedes as the camera, retreating before him, reveals the now wasted Gasthof garden; when a despairing Käthi watches Karl Heinrich waving goodbye, the moment rendered semi-expressionistic by images in which the carriage moves more as repetition than progression, taking, it seems, forever to vanish. And finally, when, as the Prince leaves Käthi forever, and we expect a repetition of the vanishing object of happiness trope, it does not happen. The Prince departs with face averted, so that he does not even see Käthi grief-stricken collapse. Here the avoidance of the expected image signifies the triumph of the stern determinacies of adulthood, duty and masculinity over the openness, emotionality and vulnerability of the child, the former's victory confirmed in another repeated trope: the new King's curt automaton-like bows of his head to the crowds cheering his coronation progress.

Doctor Jüttner meets the Prince

As the child weeps, he realises that he is being observed. From his point of view we see standing together the emaciated King and a middle-aged, slightly rotund, frock-coated, bespectacled figure. After a minatory handshake, Karl VII introduces the child forbiddingly to his new tutor, Dr Jüttner (Jean Hersholt). 'He will instruct you in etiquette, obligation, duty, demeanour and formality.' Before the King leaves, both the child and tutor perform the robotic Karlsburg bow. But later, when alone, and the boy starts to bow again, Jüttner gently prevents him, clasps hands warmly, puts his arm round Karl Heinrich, and walks off with him, making his happy influence literally felt.

The pair's first meeting poses Jüttner alongside, but opposite, the King, an antithesis constantly repeated: in the two men's portrait paintings (the King's rigidly forbidding, the Doctor's in formal dress but relaxed posture, a cigar drooping casually from his fingers); in the intertitle's statement of the public grief the Prince assumes for his uncle's death, but the real grief he feels for Jüttner's; in the juxtaposed close-ups of both men's tombs, the King's in an oppressively symmetrical monumental setting, the Doctor's in a rambling country churchyard. The opposition is furthered by physical differences: Jüttner's soft plumpness against the King and courtiers' desiccated spareness; his dark abundant hair and moustache against their grey or white lankness; his sympathetic smile versus their grimness; his effusions of sentiment against their icy discipline.

Jüttner's name, written correctly (with umlaut) in the intertitles, has a latent meaning unemphasised in the sources. Pronounced Germanically as 'Yewtner', the name is close to the German 'Jud' (i.e. Jew)-ner. Anglicised, it would sound like 'Jew'-tner. In the 1954 musical both possibilities are expelled by the pronunciation 'Yutner', as in 'put', while in the 1915 film an un-umlauted version presumably sounds either similarly or as in 'hut', deflecting racial implications. In *Old Heidelberg* Jüttner's difference is not underlined by any unambiguously Jewish ethnic item, but his antitheticalness, sentiment and irony, his connection with education, his fellow feeling for the marginalised child/young man, are underwritten by Hersholt's gestures and physiognomy, by the connotations of his character's name, by Lubitsch's own Jewishness, and by his assumption of Jüttner's role in the publicity picture. The Bourgets see that Jüttner is a surrogate for the director, but only take it as far as an '"intellectual" conscientious worker, but also human and generous, constantly smoking cigars' (Bourget and Bourget 1987: 65). But it goes beyond this, binding together his Jewishness with the female-identifying marginality persuasively attributed to Lubitsch, so many of whose films centred on female protagonists (Hake 1992), making Jüttner not only the paradoxically culturally prominent but marginalised Jew of Wilhelmine culture, and the Prince's lost good father, but also the lost maternal feminine, introduced exactly as the surrogate mother is dismissed to take over the feminine nurturing role, or at the least a conflation of maternal and paternal.

Jüttner, as in the sources, is also a sick man, the spirit of emotion and liberalism doomed to die as rigid, militaristic Karlsburg asserts itself against Heidelberg. His early comic Dormouse-like sleepiness turns to graver intimations, culminating in a scene where, semi-invalided, he takes medicine hourly. The post-student festivities dance underlines his more than naturalistic decline as he is whirled around by a buxom Brunnhilde, with almost unavoidable politico-ethnic connotations, until, exhausted, he has to stop, one of several forebodings of his death (offscreen) while Karl Heinrich is in Karlsburg. Earlier an intertitle has emphasised Jüttner's age – 'Heidelberg – gay, romantic Heidelberg – is a place for youth – and Dr Jüttner was no longer young', so it is surprising when his tombstone shows him dead at only 43! This crystallises a paradox surrounding the doctor, who is constantly associated both with youth *and* with illness and age, a paradox most highly worked when he is seen ill in bed reading a magazine called *Jugend*. It is impossible to tell from the print I worked with whether the title reads '*Die*' *Jugend,* but it certainly alludes to the Munich journal famous for its espousing of 'Jugendstil', the German Art Nouveau. In reading it the Doctor is associated with the avant garde, but also with the literal meaning of 'Jugend' – i.e. youth (compare his parting words to Karl Heinrich to 'Stay young'). At the same time, however, the educated German youth of the later nineteenth and earlier twentieth century notoriously responded to the radicalism of the right, not of the left, and this becomes a powerful subtext of the film.[5] Thus, Jüttner can be seen as much disassociated from (both sadly and healthily), as associated with, 'die Jugend' (in its literal sense), making his presence in the student-centred Heidelberg sequences extremely ambivalent, and adding to the connotations of his early death, which becomes a symbolic passing away of the liberal values of youth as a contrary ideology, associated with right-wing youth, takes over. The question of whether the film, looking back to the future of World War One, also literally looks forward to National Socialism, depends on whether we credit Lubitsch, who certainly would have been a highly sensitive observer, with registering the threat before and during his 1927 visit. Of course, to a later viewer such an extended context is inevitable.

Academic overtures

The Student Corps meeting in the Gasthof garden is the film's centrepiece, the ecstatic fusion of the heterosexual love between Karl Heinrich and Käthi and the homosocial bonding between the Prince and the Corps Saxonia. Watched by Karl Heinrich from his window, the students begin their ceremonies. They call for Käthi, carry her on their shoulders, and dress her in the Corps's ribbons. Excited, the Prince wakes Jüttner, but the Doctor drifts off again, and unable to find him, he descends alone to watch. Käthi leaves the students and goes surreptitiously into Karl Heinrich's room, unaware that he is watching her. They meet. About to kiss they are interrupted by a drunken Corps student (John S. Peters) who calls up the others to meet his new friend 'Herr Haasenpfeffer', as he calls him. Invading the room, they sweep him downstairs where they dress him in the Corps insignia. Asked his name, 'Haasenpfeffer' replies 'I am Karl Heinrich of Karlsburg'. The shock is broken by the Prince's democratic embracing of his new brothers. Dr Jüttner appears, unconvincingly preaching discipline, but like Karl Heinrich he is swept up onto the students' shoulders. The little band plays and everyone sings the nostalgic May song 'Wandschaft'. Later, the Prince bids his comrades goodnight. 'It's good to have friends like you! Let's make this last as long as we live!'

The sequence's ecstatic trajectory is structured by various overriding significances: the Prince's release from lonely observation to participation; his bonding with the Corpsiers, fulfilling his earlier desire to play with the boys outside the Palace; the amalgamation of the film's heterosexual relationship with its two homosocial ones; and formally by the sweeping travelling shots which redeem those that traumatically followed the child's pursuit of the lost surrogate mother, who is herself recovered in the appearance of Käthi – like a succouring Mother Goddess of Plenty, virtuosically holding her eight steins of beer – in an otherwise male world. The joining of heterosexual and homosocial is also acted out antically when the drunken Corpsier intrudes on the lovers and seems unclear exactly who he wants to embrace, first of all Käthi, but when she moves aside, falling on the Prince, and then, while held by him, attempting to embrace Käthi again, then at one point polymorphously embracing them both.

Amid such happiness, it may only be later that ambivalences fully register, when we think about Lubitsch's, and his surrogate, Jüttner's, difficult relation to the nostalgias evoked, beginning with the real Corps' extreme nationalism with their anti-foreign, anti-Semitic, and hyper-masculine ideologies. Thus the name of the film's Corps – 'Saxonia' (recalling the real aristocratic Heidelberg Saxo-Borussia Corps) – is hardly neutral, signifying as it does an idealisation of the racially pure Teutonic typical of the groups. Here, though, the Corps seems impeccably democratic as the seemingly ordinary 'Haasenpfeffer' is admitted to membership without his class or ethnicity being interrogated. W. E. Mosse's abysmal history of Paul Wallich, a baptised Jew's constant failures to win acceptance from socially exclusive Corps, shows the reality of the situation (Mosse 1989: 143–6). As the idyll unfolds, the group's military uniforms seem merely fancy dress, like the leader's duelling scars. The film's Corps also seems, despite its name, ethnically all-embracing rather than racist as Jüttner is lifted onto the students' shoulders in a tableau both utopian and ironic, its real world unlikeliness registered in Jüttner's slipping three times from his precarious perch. To underscore the obvious point, neither Lubitsch himself (who was even featured in the Nazi propaganda film *Der Ewige Jude/The Eternal Jew* (Fritz Hippler, 1940; see Eyman 1993: 233), nor Jüttner, if one accepts the semitic allusions attached to him, could possibly have joined in the pleasures presented. Of course the communal singing of 'Wandschaft' cannot simply be seen as springing from a poisoned source, but nevertheless it is difficult to disregard entirely knowledge of the ideological misuse of folk song by German hyper-nationalism long before the Nazis. Does Jüttner's sudden sadness as he pauses in his singing and lowers his head relate only to his departed youth or to more political realisations as well? And even Käthi's ecstatic apotheosis into a Goddess of Plenitude, a seemingly positive embrace of the feminine by a male world, might less happily constitute an elevation of the singular female into a principle to maintain the hyper-masculine. And as the Prince joins the Corps, we might also remember that the original popularity of the Student Prince 'myth' came from a romanticisation of the young future Kaiser Wilhelm II's joining of the Borussian Corps at the University of Bonn, with all that that romanticisation of militarism implied for a future moving towards 1914.

Such underlying shadows are delayed realisation until the returning Prince, reencountering the Corps, is confronted by saluting, heel-clicking subjects rather than old comrades. When the Prince shakes hands with the leader, George K. Arthur responds only with a metronomic bow, repeated when the Prince tries to converse, a scenario multiply re-enacted as Karl Heinrich continues down the line. In a subtle suggestion of what their repressed feelings cost, the Corpsiers infringe discipline with slight turns of the eyes and head to follow him, as if unconsciously yearning for contact, while the leader betrays emotion through hyper-active blinking. The scene dramatises the impossibility of reliving the past, but also pursues a concrete political analysis within this, seeing the Heidelberg idyll as containing, tragically, the seeds of the 1914 catastrophe, with the Corps members transformed into the robotic military functionaries of the aggressive nationalist state. As Konrad H. Jarausch writes, quoting G. A. Craig:

> Although the forms of German student life may have been idyllic, its consequences were not. There is no doubt that, in the end, the political ignorance and indiff-erence of German students encouraged the government of William II in the irresponsible politics that destroyed it, deprived the Weimar Republic of support that might have saved it, and led to the naïve acceptance by academic youth of totalitarianism. (Jarausch 1982: 239)

Metaphor and gesture

In designating *Old Heidelburg* as old cinema, a lapsing from radicalism before its recapture in his early sound films, an influential book on Lubitsch castigates its use of filmic metaphor compared with the early German comedies. Whereas in the latter, objects refuse their limited role of illustrating human categories, in *Old Heidelberg* 'Metaphors become an accessory to sentimental moods and cliches' (Hake 1992: 68). But metaphor in *Old Heidelberg*, though functioning traditionally, is neither simple bipolar opposition nor sentimental cliché. As symbolic objects, Karl Heinrich's fraternity cap and sash are part of a complex network of dualisms constituted around the objects: escape *and* imprisonment, rebellion *and* conformity, idyllicism *and* militarism.

I want to end, briefly recalling the photograph of Lubitsch as Jüttner adjusting his stars' poses, by considering what are closely linked to metaphoric objects – metaphoric gestures. One of the film's most fascinating effects is Novarro's and Hersholt's acting out of feminising destabilisations of a masculinity hypertrophically rigidified in that final meeting with the Corps. Such connotations are more likely with Novarro, who rose to fame under Valentino's star in a more feminised, less phallic, more boyish reflection, the boyishness exemplified in *Mata Hari* (George Fitzmaurice, 1931) where his literally blinded young airman, Alexei, is kept by a maternal Garbo childishly ignorant of her impending execution, the former (more feminised, less phallic) in *Ben-Hur* (J. J. Cohn and Fred Niblo, 1925) where the heroic athlete parades through showers of petals and one perfect rose floats down onto his shoulder. *Old Heidelberg* further develops Novarro as a beautiful male image traversed by both the child and the female by making the almost voluptuously girlish De Lacey his early narrative incarnation. This feminised child is always latent in the Prince's volatile switches between absolutes of depression and happiness, and in two destabilising moments where Karl Heinrich embodies extremes of adolescent sexual embarrassment so spectacularly unmodulated that one suspects that they must have been imposed by Lubitsch. In the first, Jüttner whispers the secret – sexual-romantic – meaning of 'Heidelberg', causing the Prince to contort foetally, arms clasped round legs, a boy-girl rocking back and forth with gaping, mawkish smile. In the second, his squirmingly shy pleasure as he watches Käthi enter his room is that of the ambiguously sexualised child, the unformed adolescent, a meaning underwritten by the high angles that look down on him as if from adult height. These embarrassing gestures, linking the liminalities of adolescence with those of femininity and Jewishness, though laughable in their unprotected naiveté, are also affirmative in recalling a positive, immature openness prior to the body-armoured hypermasculinised order of the film's end. Additionally, Novarro's postures in the field of flowers love scene are more conventionally feminine than Käthi's, especially when he lies voluptuously on the ground watching the shooting star. As with the otherwise highly feminine Käthi/Shearer when she assumes, with peasant unrefinement, the masculine role of inspecting the Prince's body at their first meeting, what Novarro exhibits – within the emphasis on heterosexual difference which is always the most constant source of pleasure in Lubitsch's world – is a dissolving of the most rigidified gender attributes attached to those sexualities, most importantly the hypermasculinity associated with control, order and the military, driving the Wilhelmine world.

But the film's most remarkable development of gesture is the extraordinary degree of male touching and embracing between the Corps members in the beer garden sequence, and between Karl Heinrich and Dr Jüttner throughout. Hans Blüher's once notorious apologia for the exclusively male bonding of the German Youth Movement, *Die deutsche Wandervogelbewegung als erotisches Phänomen: ein Beitrag zur Erkenntnis der sexuellen Inversion* (*The Wandervogeln as Erotic Phenomenon*),[6] argued that a sublimated homosexuality cemented relations within such all-male organisations. In Lubitsch's imaginary Corps, this is replaced by an idyllic homosociality, accompanying rather than undermining the heterosexual love plot, where male intimacy signifies transparency, democracy and a softened masculinity. This is particularly overt at the beginning of the Heidelberg revels where the conversing students touch casually, then walk away after the Prince sadly dismisses them, arms companionably around each others' shoulders. But the most extraordinary instances are between the Prince and Dr Jüttner. Unlike Novarro, the stocky, brush-moustached Jean Hersholt (until *Old Heidelberg* more famous for villains such as in *Greed*, Erich von Stroheim, 1923), carries no obvious signs of feminisation. Here, however, his kinesics, bodily and facial, constantly overflow with a sympathetic softness that invokes the narrative's banished maternal figures. From the moment when he first meets the Prince, fully ten scenes involve them in loving physical contact. Have, outside of the pornographic film, two males ever embraced quite so much on screen? For instance, just before what he believes will be his dismissal by the King, Jüttner clasps the back of the Prince's neck, then holds both his hands in his; then, after the Prince, in a conventionally feminine gesture, has brushed the cigar ash from his tutor's lapel, Jüttner unconstrainedly embraces him, patting his arm as they hug each other. Similar moments abound, accompanied by Jüttner's maternal-paternal gesturings, wiping tears from his eyes under the guise of removing his glasses while watching Karl Heinrich's and Käthi's suffering, or typically smiling gently with head canted and gaze slightly averted – poses more conventionally 'feminine' than 'masculine', or chin-chucking Karl Heinrich as they drink their beers on the shoulders of the students.

Old Heidelberg changed Hersholt's career, for Dr Jüttner is the source of the dominant persona of his later films, Dr Christian, in the once famous *Dr Christian* cycle. This series celebrated the good medic's compassionate wisdom, humour and generosity, which, like the look Hersholt finally settled on, come from Lubitsch's film. However, most interesting here is the restrained discreetness of Hersholt's later performances, testifying to what is conjectured here as Lubitsch's direct imposition on Hersholt's acting style in the earlier film, producing effects the actor never reproduces elsewhere, even where his persona directly descends from *Old Heidelberg*. For instance, in *Doctor Christian Meets the Women* (William McGann, 1940), Hersholt, though projecting warmth, is extremely restrained in his touching of other characters. The films posit the Doctor's special relation with women (in *The Country Doctor* he is the Dionne Quintuplets' doctor, in *Meets the Women* he rescues the town's women from a quack dietician), but the conventionality of these relations is quite different to Jüttner's remarkable introjection of the feminine in *Old Heidelberg*, which, with its excess of the feminine-tactile, pathos and soulfulness, and its head canting, eye-averting gestures, constitutes a one-off which is deleted as Dr Jew-tner becomes Dr Christian.[7]

Notes

1 The still can be found in Lambert 1990 and in Weinberg 1977.

2 For instance Scott Eyman (1993) notes Monte Blue in *So This is Paris* replicating 'one of Lubitsch's own acting mannerisms … the head sliding in increments off to the side and down'.

3 In Eyman's biography there are multiple mentions of this trait; for instance, of Lubitsch playing all the parts in script sessions with Billy Wilder and Charles Brackett (Eyman 1993: 258); of Norma Shearer famously objecting to Lubitsch's impositions on her (Eyman 1993: 134–5); and of Patsy Ruth Miller saying of *So This is Paris*, 'The whole film was visualised in his head, so he wasn't very flexible. He didn't want you to go off the beaten track with a gesture if it wasn't what he had in mind' (Eyman 1993: 119).

4 Eyman's biography passes over these visits superficially (Eyman 1993: 131–3).

5 On the nationalism and increasing xenophobia and anti-semitism of the Corps, see Pulzer 1988; Hertz 1975; Dahrendorf 1987; Craig 1982; Mosse 1966; Mosse 1989; and, most particularly, Jarausch 1982.

6 Published in 1912. On Blüher, see Mosse 1966: 176.

7 *Old Heidelberg*'s connecting of the Jew and the feminine takes a different and less happy form in the anti-Semitic contexts outlined in Michelle Aaron's chapter in this volume. *Old Heidelberg*, however, is a film made primarily for American audiences, which allows the film to use the elision positively.

Thanks to Alan Menhennet, Herman Moisl and Colin Riordan for their help.

chapter 11

'PINK NEOREALISM' AND THE REHEARSAL OF GENDER ROLES 1946–55

Mary Wood

In this chapter I will be discussing representations of masculinity in Italian popular cinema of the post-war period called 'neorealismo rosa', or 'pink neorealism'. Concentrating mainly on the Italian stars Amedeo Nazzari and Vittorio Gassman, I will examine the personae of male stars in these melodramas, both through the types of narratives which these personae enabled, and the emotionality which allowed gender roles to be explored in a time of great social change. I will argue that the corporality and movements of these actors connote a range of Italian identities, regional, class and sexual, thus enabling spectators to rehearse and construct an imaginary, but new, national self.

'Pink neorealism' is the name given to that popular cinema of the late 1940s and 1950s which had no pretensions to operating on the cutting edge of left-wing critiques of society, but nonetheless addressed the preoccupations of ordinary people. It explored how women could combine work and family, how to get access to the rewards of post-war industrial society, the conflict between archaic, rural social practices and those necessary for survival in a modern Italy, and, not least, how to be a man, a worker, a father, a head of the household at a time when patriarchal oppressions had received a jolt from the ability of women to act autonomously, fend for their families and manage their lives alone during the war. These films used many of the stylistic devices of neorealism – location shooting in recognisable places, working-class characters and themes – but portrayed a more complex post-war situation. The social conditions which enable the melodramatic plots of pink neorealist films were widespread and touched the lives of the majority of the population. The slow invasion of Italy by the Allies had broken down the infrastructures of government and industry so that, even under fascist rule, shortages of bread, food, essential household items had been part of everyday experience. The gradual return to

Italy of detainees from Germany, concentration camp survivors from Eastern Europe, and thousands of former soldiers from Russia, North Africa and Greece, coupled with the return to the cities of ordinary people who had fled to the countryside to avoid the fighting meant that a largely static and settled population had been shaken up, dispersed, and its ties to family and home (*paese*) severed. As a result, before the Marshall Plan swung into effect, there was widespread unemployment, poverty, social and familial disruption and, not least, the questioning of traditionally held beliefs about social and gender hierarchies, about politics. These things were within the lived experience of all strata of Italian society. The excesses of popular film melodramas indicated the difficulty of reconciling traditional Italian stories, based on a certain understanding of social and gender relations, and the lived experience of the world outside the cinema, which all neorealist artists sought to engage with.

The wider political struggle, which resulted in overwhelming Christian Democrat success in the 1948 elections, was also reflected in the Italian film industry. Obstacles were put in the way of filmmakers seeking production finance, loans and distribution licences with the aim of making it difficult to film, or see, work which did not conform to Christian Democrat values, or which had the potential to criticise authority. Additionally, the impact, both in cultural as well as economic terms, of the vast backlog of US films released onto the Italian market at the end of the war brought the industry to crisis point (Quaglietti 1980: 47), and justified the prejudice of conservative elements in the Italian film industry against neorealism (Campassi 1949: 35). Film journals and papers of the 1940s are full of articles and reports of American cinema and its stars. As a result, Italian producers and filmmakers with an interest in the survival of Italian cinema increasingly bemoaned the lack of Italian actors with mass, popular appeal and star quality. As production budgets increased in an attempt to provide competition to US product, so the industry moved towards an American, capitalist model, where the demands of investors were important in defining the product. Such films were extremely popular at the box office.[1]

The late 1940s and 1950s in Italy are therefore years of struggle between archaic systems of social control, a high level of censorship and swelling demands for change and prosperity which would only find satisfaction in the boom of the late 1950s and 1960s. It is not surprising that, in this period of 'supervised freedom' (Boneschi 1995: 108–9), popular cinema provided an outlet for expressions of a desire for change and freedom. What I am suggesting therefore is that the Italian film industry in this period could mainly only express desires for changes in social and sexual mores in coded form. Producers wanted films with some guarantee of success; commercial products with stars on the American model (Ferraù 1949: 7), and reacted by curtailing experimentation and concentrating on known popular genres, comedies, drama and melodrama. In doing so they found themselves extremely short of both male and female stars to fill the roles of protagonists in popular, middle-budget dramas. Not only that, but, as the reconstruction of society got under way and prosperity started to increase, there was a distinct shortage of actors who could play middle-class roles and enact the dramas of aspiration towards material comfort.

Actors in neorealist films had been a combination of professionals, but from low culture or marginalised theatrical genres (such as Anna Magnani, Aldo Fabrizi), or were non-professionals, chosen for their ability to embody a class or occupational category with authenticity, and thereby to act as metonym for a whole social situation (Lamberto Maggiorani in *Ladri di bicclette/The Bicycle Thieves*, Vittorio de Sica, 1948). That these 'actors' found it difficult to establish careers is an indication that they ceased to interest the public, and did not have the training necessary to evolve with public taste (Cristofani and Manetti 1956: 173–238; Renzi 1956: 278–89; Nediani 1948: 85). The actors who did successfully fill this gap can be divided into two categories: older actors whose persona and career were already well established in the previous period, and younger actors who were only at the very beginning of their career under fascism.

Older actors

In the first category we have, pre-eminently, Amedeo Nazzari, but also Vittorio De Sica, Gino Cervi and Folco Lulli. Cervi was a plump, classical actor whose expressiveness usually connoted the acceptable face of authority, and whose role of the communist mayor in the Don Camillo films allowed communist rhetoric to be rehearsed and contained and made fun of. Although the Left had been excluded from power since the war, the early 1950s saw an opening up to centre-left politics and the vigorous presence of the PCI. Cervi's roles constitute a more modern rehearsal of social change and a more complex interaction with cultural currents of the time than Nazzari's rather stiff landowners and engineers. An early example of the actor-director, Vittorio De Sica's matinee-idol looks and established place in left-wing intellectual circles ensured his survival in the post-war period, and his partnership with the screenwriter and theorist, Cesare Zavattini, resulted in some of the classics of neorealism. In the period and genre under discussion his greatest box office triumphs were in the *Bread, Love and...* string of comedies in which he played Carabiniere Marshall Carotenuto, locked in an erotic battle of wills with a peasant Gina Lollobrigida. Thus De Sica's comedy roles rehearse in a light vein stories of male authority in conflict with female resistance to containment within traditional social structures.

Amedeo Nazzari was an actor who resembled Errol Flynn and who made 113 films between 1935 and 1978. Nazzari was more than usually obsessive about maintaining a relationship with his public (Gubitosi 1998: 11), and would only accept roles as positive, moral characters through which he could represent the best aspects of Italianness. When one considers the social, political and economic changes through which his career passed, the success of that career achieves an emblematic status and the star becomes a cultural icon. Giuseppe Gubitosi claims that Nazzari represented a concentration of the qualities felt to be typical of the Italian male – handsome, brave, honest, a good worker, father, husband, lover – so that he was the focus of female fantasies and the nexus of acceptable propaganda for Mussolini's 'new' Italy and at the same time a representation of positive qualities of bygone ages (Gubitosi 1998: 1). His characterisations in the fascist period are often superficial, lacking depth and interior life, for example in *Cavalleria/Cavalry* (Goffredo Alessandrini, 1936) and *Montevergine* (Carlo Campogalliani, 1939), in which he rehearsed class or regional stereotypes. They appealed to a poor and ill-educated public who would admire his lovely gestures and fine feelings. That his second bout of popularity occurred in melodramas from 1949 to 1956 is evidence of his being able to maintain contact with this public, through films with similar convoluted stories.

His persona was that of a handsome but ordinary man, unassociated with any particular region. As a result, he had a prolific career acting out positive Italian male attributes associated with a mythic past rather than only one region. He was active, strong, firm, moral, yet sensitive (particularly to the feelings of women and children). Nazzari consistently played fathers, or if he was not a father, he stood in that relationship to groups who lacked his far-sightedness or moral qualities, that is, women and children, workers, soldiers. Nazzari's gestural range was not large, but his movements were decisive. Physically he was imposing – tall, broad shouldered, with delicate hands and facial features, and fair, curly hair. He could therefore embody power and sensitivity. Many close-ups also foregrounded his ability to suggest strong emotion through his expressive eyes and the direction of his gaze.

Nazzari did not appear in any of the canonic texts of cinematic neorealism in the immediate post-war period. His face was too well known and his persona did not fit the narratives of liberation and overthrow of authority, or of working-class tribulation. At this time he appeared in some melodramas set in Southern Italy, and minor films influenced by American film noir which are intriguing for the tensions they show. In the most interesting film of this time, *Il Bandito/The Bandit* (Alberto Lattuada, 1946), the actor plays a former soldier who turns to crime. The plot point which precipitates this is his discovery that his sister is a prostitute and his killing of the man who kills her. Ernesto, the bandit, is desperately attached to values such as protecting the family and looking after the family's honour and name, which were being called into question in the aftermath of war. Ernesto is in fact emblematic of an institutional crisis, the destruction of the family and moral turpitude of family members (male and female) representing the destruction of the nation.

It has been suggested that former soldiers were an inconvenient reminder of the fascist regime, and that mistreating those who had fought far away, with the Germans, allowed Italians to deflect their own sense of guilt away from themselves (Gubitosi 1998: 85). I would argue, however, that *Il Bandito* is also emblematic of other tensions associated with desires in the population not to return to coercive social, political and gender relations, and it is significant that the actor plays many outsiders in his films between 1946 and 1949. Nazzari's co-star in *Il Bandito* is Anna Magnani, an actress with a greater emotional range than his, and the persona of the woman of the people, strong and sure of herself. The narratives of Anna Magnani's post-war films indicate difficulties in reconciling strongly assertive female characters with traditional narratives. Magnani's emotionality is metonymic of the sufferings of women in the period of post-war chaos and the general desire for something different. She occupies as much screen space, and as many close ups as Nazzari, in this film but her role as gangster's moll indicates a subordinate position with respect to Nazzari which is unresolved narratively. His persona, therefore, in this period clearly starts to tentatively explore the negative side of those patriarchal values praised by the former regime.

The solidity of the Nazzari persona had not permitted a questioning of the values of the fascist period, and did not fit with a more critical examination of Italian society. As a result Nazzari worked abroad for a while before returning to Italy and another period of enormous box office success in the 1950s. If his noir neorealist roles had included marginality and rebellion – which, as Tzvetan Todorov suggests in *The Conquest of America: The Question of the Other* (quoted in Kinder 1993: 144), draw attention to the inequalities of society – then Nazzari's pink neorealist roles are those of self-sacrifice (which reinforce the idea of the subordination of the individual to established social order). In melodramas with tortuous plots, betraying popular anxieties about the pace of social and economic change, Nazzari played a variety of bourgeois or petit bourgeois men whose emotional attachments are to women of whom his family do not approve. The films' narratives rarely conclude convincingly with the formation or re-establishment of the romantic couple, but many sacrifices (usually by the woman) are made for the happiness of children (who represented a talisman of what ordinary people were suffering for). The plots rehearsed sexual adventures between social classes; and the problematic and excessive narrative resolutions indicated the difficulties of reconciling patriarchal values with the reality of modern life and social upheaval. In *I Figli di nessuno/Nobody's Children* (Rafaello Matarazzo, 1950),[2] for example, Nazzari plays an aristocratic quarry owner whose mother prevented him marrying his lover, Luisa, because she is of lower social status. Luisa (played by his regular co-star, Yvonne Sanson) bears their child, which is kidnapped by Guido's mother; believing her son dead, she enters a convent. Although unaware that he is actually a father, Guido's relationship with his workforce is shown as paternal. He looks after their safety in the quarry and the stone he produces is, of course, vital to the reconstruction of the country. The saboteurs on the other hand are represented as unkempt, destructive, uncaring of the safety of the child, and (by implication left-wing) extremists to boot. In the last reel the identity of his long-lost son is revealed when the boy tries to prevent the sabotage of his father's quarry, but is mortally wounded in the explosion. The father and mother (who has become a nun) are together at his deathbed, but do not re-form as a couple: indeed they barely look at each other, the focus of their gaze being the dying son.

In *Catene/Chains* (Rafaello Matarazzo, 1949), Nazzari plays Pietro, a happily married father of two who kills the man who is threatening his wife and flees to America. At his eventual trial, he is only acquitted because his wife, Rosa, has been advised to confess to an adultery which she has not committed. After all is explained, the family is reunited. In *Tormento/Torment* (Rafaello Matarazzo, 1950), Anna and Carlo move to Milan and are about to marry when Carlo is unjustly accused of murder and sent to prison where the wedding takes place. Anna gives birth to a baby. Her father never receives Anna's letters, which are torn up by the step-mother. He dies of a broken heart, the step-mother gets custody of the baby, and only when Carlo is found to be innocent can the family be reunited. Fate plays a large role in these melodramas, and there is a strong sense of the powerlessness of ordinary people faced with adverse events over which they have no control.

Gubitosi suggests continuity with the ideal of Italianness of the 1930s and 1940s and considers the presence of Nazzari as a guarantee of the survival of essential qualities of the Italian national character, thereby rendering the new social reality more acceptable to a cinema-going public which had suffered greatly in this period (Gubitosi 1989: 83). Nazzari appears to embody specific certainties about patriarchal values and attempts to enact patriarchal roles at times of great social change. His most constant facial expression is one of bafflement and, in all his pink neorealist roles, he is depicted as working enormously hard for the good of his family. There is present in the plots of his films a yearning for stasis, for a time when women and the lower classes knew their place. Yet the Nazzari persona in pink neorealism is not representative of a brutally forceful masculinity. His violence occurs in protection of his actual or metaphorical family and his openness to affect and emotionality suggest that these qualities were perceived to be necessary in making sense of a changing world, keeping the attributes of the 'old' male hero, but allowing a greater consciousness of the possibilities offered by social change. Change is, however, never successfully negotiated as around these large, dominant, upright male figures other worlds, usually female, collapse in utter chaos.

Younger actors

The second category of actors includes Raf Vallone, Vittorio Gassman, Renato Salvatori, Walter Chiari, Marcello Mastroianni and Alberto Sordi. This younger generation of actors is very different from their predecessors. They established themselves in 'neorealismo rosa', enabling a variety of youthful masculine responses to social change to be rehearsed. In reviews of Raf Vallone's work, there is much mention of his robust physical presence, of the rich connotational possibilities of his gestural range, and particularly of the rich, warm tones of his voice.[3] Renato Salvatori (from central Italy) and Marcello Mastroianni (like De Sica from Naples) both established their careers in this period in comedies set in urban, working-class milieux. The persona of both actors at this time was of strength, energy, sexual vigour and charm, allied to a marked unawareness of the meaning of events, the trope of irony providing a space for audience involvement. Mastroianni's theatrical training and contacts in Italian intellectual circles allowed him to move across a greater generic range than Salvatori and to interpret roles of more complex masculinity in art cinema. Mastroianni's character type was evolving from the proletarian to the middle class, a process which was in itself a reflection of the evolution of post-war Italian society.

Salvatori, a former merchant seaman, had a considerable physical presence and beautiful body, and a gift for expressing sincerity. He was launched in a series of sentimental comedies structured around the physical attributes of the main actors. Throughout *Poveri ma belli/Poor but Beautiful* (Dino Risi, 1956), Salvatore (Salvatori) and Romolo (Maurizio Arena) erupt into the public spaces of Rome. These are bodies at ease with their own physicality, and their own surroundings. Salvatore is a lifeguard, Romolo works in his uncle's record shop; they like clothes, pop music, dancing and girls, and themselves. Salvatori's constant prop is a comb and it is in constant use!

It is significant how many of this younger generation had a sporting background. Raf Vallone played football for Torino, Gassman played basketball. Their physicality marked them out as different from the non-professional actors who played peasants, fishermen, the unemployed. Their size, athleticism, vigorous gestures indicate their force, their virility and their *health*. Similarly, their objects of desire are the plump, well-endowed starlets who were spotted in Miss Italia contests, and who personify the desire for well-being and prosperity of the period of reconstruction. Vigour and sexual energy are frequently represented in dance in these films, reflecting the influence and allure of US culture. Dance also allows display of the body, both male and female, and the exuberant display of sexual energy and the spaces within which this takes place links private behaviour with events in a public and national arena. *Riso amaro/Bitter Rice* (Giuseppe De Santis, 1948) is a prime example. The dancing of the spiv, Walter (Gassman), and the ricefield worker, Silvana (Mangano), displays their physical attributes and the erotic attraction between them, but also indicate the appeal of American popular culture and its spread into the recesses of rural Italy. Gassman the weak villain is opposed by the attractive ex-soldier, Marco (Vallone). Vallone, the representative of traditional male authority, wears army uniform throughout and stridently attempts to influence and annexe Mangano but singularly fails in his objectives. Gassman, however, is modern; he wears an American suit, his hat pushed back on his head, and he knows how to dance the mambo. Gassman aims to persuade Mangano to help him steal the women rice workers' wages (their share of the harvest) but she repents her involvement at the end and kills herself. Female transgression, associated in Silvana's character with a taste for dancing the mambo, reading comics, fake diamonds, sex and unreliable men, is represented as attractive at the same time as it is punished in narrative terms.

Vittorio Gassman's career is interesting in this period because he regularly played as many villains as heroes. Physically he was tall and extremely handsome, with very dark, expressive eyes. From 1946 onwards he appeared in a series of *films feuilleton*, derived from popular, nineteenth-century literature which Vittorio Spinazzola describes as well-plotted, richly dramatic and full of strong emotions, and usually featuring the lives of the upper classes (Spinazzola 1974: 64–6). In Riccardo Freda's *Il Cavaliere misterioso/The Mysterious Horseman* (1948) he plays Casanova and is lit like a star to foreground his youth and beauty. In *Lo Sparviero del Nilo/The Hawk of the Nile* (Giacomo Gentilomo, 1949) he plays sheik Rachid who fakes his own death in order to be able to punish the criminal plans of the enemies of his tribe. In his roles as protector of the people, his performances stress his youth, his physical beauty and activity and his exotic qualities so that he represents an aspirational male ideal, outside the constraints of ordinary society and able to take revenge or get the girl with impunity. Even as a hero, however, his performances indicate a certain emotional ambiguity and love of display. He embodies that very Italian trait of *fare bella figura*, the art of showing oneself to best advantage, an important personal asset in the years leading up to the economic boom.

Gassman appeared in at least two films with Nazzari, one of which, *Il Lupo della Sila/ The Wolf of the Sila* (Duilio Coletti, 1949), is interesting in pointing up their generational differences. Gassman plays Pietro, a poor Calabrian farmer and the mainstay of his mother and little sister, Rosaria (Laura Cortese), and who wants to marry his lover, Orsola (Luisa Rossi), the sister of the local landowner, Rocco Barra (Nazzari). Falsely accused of murder, Pietro will not compromise Orsola, with whom he has spent the night, by using her as his alibi. In spite of Pietro's mother's entreaties, Don Rocco refuses to let Orsola give evidence and Pietro is killed in a shootout with the police. Years later, Rosaria (now played by Silvana Mangano) plots revenge and goes to work for Don Rocco, leading him on to propose marriage to her, although she has fallen in love with his son, Salvatore (Jacques Sernas). Don Rocco pursues the lovers with murderous intent, but is shot by his sister. This convoluted melodrama, set in the rural south, sets two forms of masculinity in opposition. Positive attributes cohere around the figures of Pietro (darkly handsome, large and physically active, passionate, sexually active, noble, emotional) and Salvatore (fair and handsome, passionate, sexually active, educated, sensitive, modern). Don Rocco embodies the many contradictions of the traditional Italian patriarch. As represented by Nazzari, he is handsome and shown actively working and employing others and clearly respected in his community, and addressed with deference. However, his pipe, his rural breeches and fur-trimmed cloaks contrast with his son's sports jackets and check shirts, and it is Don Rocco's patriarchal and class attitudes which precipitate the tragedy. He refuses to allow his sister to marry a peasant, and his injunction that 'the women of this

Vittorio Gassman (Walter) and Silvana Mangano (Silvana) in *Riso amaro* (Giuseppe De Santis, 1949)

house never go out alone' backfires when Rosaria and Salvatore fall in love within the household. Although Rosaria, the desired object of both father and son, is represented as a traditional passionate woman, the physicality and performance of Mangano mark her out as a modern woman. Her wide lips and full breasts and hips connote health and fecundity, whilst the deep timbre of her voice and her contemporary clothing (patterned blouse and spotted skirt with a frilly hem) indicate a certain independence and interest in fashion. This film is not uncommon in representing youth as trying to rebel against rigid patriarchal attitudes. Although intellectuals deplored consumerism as a 'negative process', John Foot has suggested that it could also liberate, 'creating a space for rebellion in the face of staid and conservative social rules' (Foot 2001: 33). Moreover, it is possible to see in popular Italian films, as Gian Peiro Brunetta has observed, a socio-economic journey as the protagonists of these films gradually acquire clothes which express their own individuality, their own transport, and then their own free time (Brunetta 1999: 192–3).

Gassman's acting style was histrionic, emotional and excessive with elements of cruelty. In his roles as villain, his characters were often described as 'monsters', or representations of the typical, cunning, average Italian. His characters frequently lacked self-awareness, providing an ironic space for the audience to judge him. His monstrous characters form part of the 'instructions' of the audience of how to react to the new situations. In *Anna* (Alberto Lattuada, 1951) he again teams with Mangano and Vallone. The poles of male sexuality are represented by the openness and honesty of Vallone and the perversity of Gassman. A life free of bourgeois constraints and allowing full rein to male sexual appetites is depicted in *Kean: genio e sregolatezza/Kean: wild genius*, co-directed by Gassman and Francesco Rosi (1956). The theatrical milieu is designed and shot with saturated colour complementing the excessiveness and hypersexuality of Gassman's performance. Gassman's villains both allow the audience to experience extremes and rehearse weakness and shame, failure and incompetence, and to make judgements about unacceptable behaviour in the struggle for survival and a bigger bit of the post-war cake. His presence and his histrionics connote the terrible traumas undergone by marginalised sections of society in the aftermath of war.

The younger actors are almost never fathers. Theirs is the generation that has left the fascist period and post-war deprivation well behind. The only bafflement expressed might be at 'What women want' rather than 'what is life all about?'. The younger male actors represent, symbolise or are emblematic of aspects of male power in conflict with that of the older generation. Power is seen to be embodied in a certain type of masculinity, characterised by physical energy taken to the level of excess in violent action; mental energy expressed as intelligence and cunning; and personal magnetism or charm – the erotic subordination of rivals. The use of actors from many regions of Italy allowed the question of national identity and change to be explored through a wider range of stories and situations than those seen in neorealist films. The South already connoted backward social relationships and permitted the problems of traditional patriarchal society to become visible whilst the use of Northern actors allowed a less monolithic and more questioning approach to social change. Covertly the options and courses of action available as models in post-war society are signified through the *mise-en-scène* delineating a variety of moral positions and social milieus. Far from being emasculated and unrepresentative of post-war reality, the melodramatic form allowed a wide variety of male roles, successful and unsuccessful to be rehearsed and a much broader engagement with the unfolding history of Italy. Interestingly, within the framings of many of these melodramas are bands of younger boys. The choral element, as boys watch the main protagonists, again draws attention to the links between performance and audience, private passions and public histories.

In the new comedy vehicles the working-class origins and speech patterns of these hyper-masculine boys and plump, sensual girls were emphasised as if this class environment provided a space in which new, freer social interactions could safely be rehearsed. Nazzari is very different from Gassman and from the younger generation of the sex bombs of 1950s comedy. The performances of younger actors emphasised both their physical attributes and their class origins. These stars epitomise physically the class which has left poverty behind, can enjoy the fat of the land (as long as it knows its place) and, as Spinazzola suggests, can look forward to a future 'rich in electrical appliances, furniture on the never never, and a lovely Fiat 600' (Spinazzola 1974: 131). For the most part younger actors represented an innocent sensuality, but the roles of Vittorio Gassman allowed the rehearsal of vice or transgression, and the consequences of rebellion, to become visible.

The physical expressivity of both groups of actors mentioned, through body shape, gesture, the importance of eyes and voice, is therefore extremely important, functioning as markers of agency and possibility. The filmmaker Ettore Scola claimed that Italian comedy was 'the slightly degenerate offspring of neorealism ... born to pacify ... prosperous, provincial Italy, without much reference to reality' (Aprà and Pistagnesi

1986: 51), but this view of realism is very limited. As Gianni Canova suggests, by focusing on problematic attempts to resolve emotional and sexual conflicts, these popular films become 'realist' in spite of themselves because they thereby have to engage with questions and situations ignored by more 'serious' drama (Canova 1999: 1).

In effect, what we see in Italian films between 1946 and 1955 is the construction of a what Pierre Bourdieu defines as a *habitus* (Bourdieu 1993: 161–75). Profound economic and social changes in Italian society at this time meant that gender hierarchies and models of masculine behaviour had to be renegotiated because they were less easy to reconcile with modernisation, associated with US capitalist and cultural models. At the same time, and this is a worldwide phenomenon, a new generation of young men and a new class are making their bid for cultural power. The roles of younger actors in particular function to differentiate their generation or their social group from their elders. Performances of masculinity in pink neorealist films reveal an increasing use of new competences, such as how to function as a successful male away from the traditional family unit, how to be successful emotionally with women in new economic and social conditions, how to use popular culture to bond with other people in your *habitus*, how to be a consumer, how to get by in society and put yourself at the best advantage. Social dispositions and attitudes are learned over time and cinema is but one arena where changes in attitude may be rehearsed. In this respect, it can be argued that popular neorealist cinema is important in that it provided a forum for the performance of a far richer range of types of masculine behaviour than 'classical' neorealism, making visible not only the constructedness of patriarchal beliefs but also what was at stake in their maintenance: prosperity and sexual gratification.[4]

Notes

1 Although critical prestige attached to realist, social cinema, filmmakers showed great interest in the content and techniques of American cinema which, after the Armistice, was satisfied by the release onto the Italian market of the large backlog of American films of the 1940s.

2 This was the third most successful Italian film at the box office in the 1951–52 season. See Aprà and Carabba 1976: 87.

3 Mirella Poggialini, for example, comments on his ability to suggest a wide range of emotions through the warm tones and timbre of his voice (Poggialini 1986).

4 I am grateful to the Research Fund of the Faculty of Continuing Education, Birkbeck College University of London, for assistance in researching this chapter.

chapter 12

'CAN THE MAN PANIC?': MASCULINITY AND FATHERHOOD IN NANNI MORETTI'S *APRILE*

Paul Sutton

Nanni Moretti's 1998 film *Aprile* develops the autobiographical project begun with his internationally successful *Caro Diario/Dear Diary* (1993). Both are 'journal' films that 'adapt the fragmentary and diverse form of the diary to cinematic language, and … present a mix of autobiography and critical distance, private confession and commentary on public affairs' (Rascaroli 2003: 87); both films thus seek to discover and to promote a new and individual kind of cinema. While the films record and explore contemporary Italy, they also seek, it might be argued, to discover and to promote a new kind of masculine identity, one that, in the latter film, is associated explicitly with fatherhood. In *Aprile* this takes place against the backdrop of cultural and personal change. The film records a period of almost three years that charts the election victory of the right-wing media tycoon Silvio Berlusconi and his Forza Italia party in March 1994 to the left-wing triumph of the 'Olive Tree' ('*L'Ulivo*') coalition in April 1996, an event that coincides with the birth of Moretti's son Pietro.[1] While the film critically examines contemporary Italian politics, it is concerned also with the representation of fatherhood as it relates to the political, the cultural (specifically film and television) and the domestic environment. Thus this chapter will explore these different paternal identities through a consideration of its two most visible fathers: the film director Nanni Moretti and the Italian Prime Minister Silvio Berlusconi. While both of these men are literal fathers, they are also, as will become clear later in this chapter, metaphoric fathers. Berlusconi, visible in *Aprile* only as a televisual image, is arguably the 'father' of modern deregulated Italian television, while many commentators see Moretti as a 'guru to a generation of filmgoers and directors' (Young 2001: 14).

Before moving on to a consideration of masculinity and paternity, however, a summary of *Aprile* is necessary in order to properly contextualise the film's representation and investigation of fatherhood. *Aprile* begins with the overwhelming defeat of the left-wing 'progressives' ('*progressisti*') alliance in the 1994 general elections, and charts chronologically the major events that affect Moretti in the following three years: the birth of his son Pietro, which coincides with the election of the left-wing Romano Prodi, and his overcoming of a creative blockage to begin work on a musical about a Trotskyite pastry chef. At the beginning, the smoking of a huge joint, produced from off-screen, seems to offer Moretti the only plausible response to Berlusconi's election. The advice of a French journalist, however, offers him other possibilities: 'Mr Moretti, you should make a documentary on Italy. On politics. Full of humour, but also with a civic sense. You've lost your memory. Your country must take stock again.'

An intertitle fast-forwards us to a year-and-a-half later by which time Berlusconi's government has collapsed.[2] Moretti is now working on his musical, a project over which he has been procrastinating for a number of years (it even featured in *Caro Diario*). We discover that Silvia, Moretti's partner, is pregnant – as she speaks on the telephone we hear her explain to a friend that she is suffering from 'a little nausea, but no big deal … But Nanni's having dizzy spells.' On set to begin shooting the musical Moretti finds that despite rehearsals he is unable to shoot even a single shot and so abandons the project once more. He decides instead to make a documentary on the forthcoming elections, pointing out to his colleagues that: 'We must make this documentary on Italy. It's a duty. We must do it. We want to. People abroad want to understand what's happening here.'

Moretti finds himself becoming increasingly anxious under the combined pressure to make this documentary and the fact of his imminent fatherhood. He is left unable to concentrate effectively on either. In a sense his masculine identity begins to fragment and fracture across a range of responsibilities, represented in the political requirement and civic duty to produce an adult documentary about contemporary Italy, the cultural and artistic requirement to overcome his creative block and produce his musical, and of course the personal responsibility of his encroaching fatherhood.

The tension that develops between the personal and the public continues to trouble Moretti throughout *Aprile*. In a rare moment of confluence he celebrates the birth of his son and the Left's general election victory by joining the throng of celebrating voters on his Vespa and shouting 'four point two kilos!'; yet rather than interview important left-wingers at party headquarters for his documentary, Moretti bunks off and films his son's first few hours instead. The film ends on a note of pure visual pleasure as Moretti begins finally to shoot the 1950s musical that has so distracted him throughout, a moment in which 'Moretti, doing the cha cha cha, overcomes his demons and his creative block' (Rouyer 1998: 7).[3]

As my brief and necessarily incomplete account of the film has demonstrated, it is comprised of a series of fragmentary moments, remembered events that offer a portrait of Moretti's life during the period, but which also provide a series of snapshots of contemporary Italy. *Aprile* becomes the site for a private and a public recollection, a 'taking stock again', in the words of the French journalist. As Moretti has said of the film:

> I have recounted, in my own way, a few years in the life of this country; moreover, I have expressed my feelings during this period … I wouldn't say that I myself have succeeded in talking about Italy in *Aprile*, but I have recalled a number of things that have happened. (Gili 1998: 10)

Nanni Moretti with son Pietro in *Aprile* (Nanni Moretti, 1998)

In turning now to explore Moretti's (self-)construction of masculinity/ies in *Aprile*, I will argue that this process is intimately bound up with fatherhood and with the portrait of Italy also constructed by the film. Thus, by contrasting Berlusconi with Moretti, the film considers the opposition between private/public and good/bad father, or perhaps more accurately traditional/modern father, while at the same time examining personal and political responsibility. The chapter will in conclusion explore briefly Moretti's own position as a father-figure to a generation of contemporary Italian filmmakers (Gieri 1995) while scrutinising Moretti's investigation of fatherhood in his latest film, *La Stanza del Figlio/The Son's Room* (2001). Before discussing these two alternate images of fatherhood represented in *Aprile*, however, I would like to consider the question of fatherhood in relation to masculinity more generally, as one facet or element of a plurality of masculinities.

Writing in the UK in 1990, just as Hollywood was beginning to replace the heroic male action heroes of the 1980s with the 'sensitive, loving, nurturing, protective family men of the 1990s' (Jeffords 1993: 197),[4] Lynne Segal, noting that 'a small but significant number of men have publicly declared their commitment to breaking out of the traditional rules of masculinity' (Segal 1990: 26), asked whether the challenge to monolithic masculinity prompted by an increasing emphasis on difference, on masculinities, might be effective in producing change in men. The response of certain commentators has been a resounding no: thus one theorist has forcefully argued, for example, that analyses

in which 'masculinity' ... is interrogated, analysed, destabilised, and discursively fussed over, but the word 'patriarchy' [is] seldom uttered, can, despite enlightened intentions, seem disturbingly disconnected from the worldly effects of privilege and power that are, after all, what the word 'patriarchy' denotes. (Solomon-Godeau 1995: 76)

The reminder here of patriarchal power highlights a problematic that will be explored later in this chapter in relation to representations of masculinity in Moretti's *Aprile*, a film that as I suggested above is concerned fundamentally with the apparently private domestic space of familial fatherhood and the public arena of patriarchal politics. Significantly fatherhood, especially the image of the 'new father', is seen by Segal as a crucial area for an investigation of contemporary masculinities, one that highlights a number of important problems for women. Thus Segal notes that it is surely not simply coincidence that 'the growing stress on fathers has occurred at a time when men's actual power and control over women and children is declining' (Segal 1990: 26); she also points to the fact that increasingly strong challenges to the 'automatic assumption of paternal rights' has meant that 'men's hold on their status as fathers is less firm and secure than ever before' (Segal 1990: 27). Charting a range of sociological studies of fatherhood undertaken since the 1970s, Segal concludes that changes in attitude towards and experiences of fatherhood as well as a shift in the perception of the importance of the father's role in parenting have undoubtedly taken place and research evidence in Italy has suggested that 'young fathers [are] more involved with their small children than ever before, both in terms of play and affection' (Ginsborg 2003: 77). However, as Segal discovers, 'what proves harder to find is convincing evidence that there has been a change in the amount of practical work men actually do as fathers' (Segal 1990: 33). One Italian survey, for example, indicated that in the average Italian couple with one or more children, the woman spent five-and-a-half hours a day on household tasks while the man spent only forty-eight minutes (Ginsborg 2003: 80). In other words while fathers are publicly perceived to be participating more fully in childcare – as an effect, it would seem, of certain discursive shifts – it appears that in private little has changed.

Fatherhood, impending and actual, is clearly visible in *Aprile* and the film certainly offers representational evidence of a modern parenting partnership and an enlightened, if somewhat nervous, attitude towards fatherhood. When Silvia explains the various stages of labour, for example, Moretti gives expression to his own anxiety:

Silvia: In the second stage, that is very painful, you mustn't panic.
Nanni: I know I'll panic.
Silvia: Not you, the woman!
Nanni: Can the man panic?
Silvia: The man stands there and says: that's good, almost over.

We also see Moretti engaged in a range of private caring duties such as bathing and comforting his son, and he is visibly affectionate with his child. Moretti's increasing awareness of the burden of childcare for mothers is humorously demonstrated in his conversation with his own mother about the way in which she managed his feeds while also working as a teacher. Berlusconi, on the other hand, is seen making reference to his son (and to his father) in *Aprile*, but as indicated earlier, fatherhood also features metaphorically in the film, and it is on this level that Berlusconi's public fatherhood becomes most evident.

The domestic and private world of fatherhood in *Aprile* is imbricated at every stage with the political and the public (Berlusconi on the one hand, Moretti and his political documentary on the other), providing an important contrast between the two father-figures presented in *Aprile*. Interestingly both Moretti and Berlusconi use their sons as part of their public personas and both are men who possess some degree of mediatised control over these personas, Berlusconi as a media magnate; Moretti as a filmmaker. Indeed near the beginning of the film Berlusconi, in a post-election interview on television, recites an anecdote involving his son: 'I was saying that my son, at school, when they asked what his father did, answered: "My dad is a TV repairman." And now, I'll have to explain to him that his dad won't have time to mend TV sets because he'll have to mend Italy.' Berlusconi uses this apparently innocuous anecdote to display his paternal credentials while at the same time positioning himself as a member of the working class, renovator of Italian television and the leader/father charged with fixing Italy. It might be argued also that Berlusconi represents the traditional father-figure who goes out to work while at the same time expressing a certain masculine arrogance and confidence in relation to this role. In a period in which men had increasing difficulty in 'negotiating the dynamics of modern family life' (Ginsborg 2003: 77), Berlusconi, in his celebrated 'electoral' address of 26 January 1994 stressed, in almost mythical terms, the importance of the father's role: 'Italy is the country I love. Here I have my roots ... Here I have learned, from my father and from life, how to be an entrepreneur' (Ginsborg 2003: 290). He presents himself as a kind of metaphorical father-figure for Italy, making overt his pleasure at assuming the position of the patriarchal and arguably paternal leader of Italy. Berlusconi's conflicts of interest (as the owner of a private media empire and ultimate controller of Italian state television) mean that he rules almost as a kind of influential paterfamilias rather than as a democratically sanctioned politician. In addition, as the 'shining archetype of a self-made man' (Ginsborg 2003: 319), Berlusconi flaunts his paternal/patriarchal status – 'I have houses all over the world, stupendous boats ... beautiful airplanes, a beautiful wife, a beautiful family' (Fox 2002: 44) – and as such 'self-consciously acts out other men's dreams of manhood' (Segal 1990: 125). It is Berlusconi's entrepreneurial success, the 'incarnation of many individual ... and family dreams' (Ginsborg 2003: 292), that has underpinned his electoral success.

This relationship between fathers and sons, this discourse of paternal/filial continuity dramatised in Berlusconi's election address, is one that Susan Jeffords has explored in relation to the 1980s Hollywood action movie, best exemplified perhaps by the *Rambo* (Ted Kotcheff 1982, George Cosmatos 1985, Peter MacDonald 1988) and *Back to the Future* (Robert Zemeckis 1985, 1989, 1991) trilogies. For Jeffords the Reagan presidency was characterised, at least in its early years, by a tension between revolution and continuity; if the 'Reagan Revolution' were to succeed, she noted, it would need to continue beyond his immediate period(s) of office (Jeffords 1994: 65). Jeffords argues that films concerned with fathers and sons produced in Hollywood during the 1980s appeared to express and address precisely this issue:

> Narratives of father/son relations help both to make change possible (the son replaces the father) and to prevent change from taking too radical a form (the son models himself after the father). They serve largely to justify a conservative agenda that can be adjusted to accommodate different economic and political policies

while still maintaining the general framework of the narrative of continuity. (Jeffords 1994: 90)

In many ways this structure is one that maps directly onto the narrative constructed by Berlusconi for himself as both a product of the father (the individual product of the mentor father) and of the fatherland; a narrative that positions him as guardian of his father's values and regenerator and guardian of Italy itself. Berlusconi's political narrative champions change and yet maintains continuity as evidenced in his reluctance to replace the corrupt system of government of which he, for many, is a product (Ginsborg 2003: 319). Berlusconi's version of masculinity can thus be seen to be a construct based on traditional masculine values such as entrepreneurial success, wealth, politics, perceived success with women, sporting prowess (achieved vicariously for Berlusconi through his ownership of the football team AC Milan) and literal and metaphoric fatherhood.

The model of masculinity and paternity represented by Moretti is, by contrast, markedly different to that of Berlusconi. Although he too 'works' in the public arena (and in the arena of a less formal politics), Moretti is a paternal figure who is more overtly present to his child; for example, in an especially memorable scene Moretti addresses his pregnant wife Silvia's bump, asking his future son to delay his imminent arrival: 'Pietro. It's daddy here. I need another month and a half. I have to shoot the documentary that I mentioned.' In addition Moretti represents an overtly and comically anxious father, not an authority figure (adopting the guise of the traditional powerful but absent father) as in the case of Berlusconi. For example, while Moretti and Silvia bathe Pietro, Moretti remarks: 'Remember the two different holds, Pietro: mum's firm hold and dad's anxious hold.'

Moretti represents the inexperienced, confused, vulnerable and insecure prospective father unable, or unsure how, to participate fully in the drama of pregnancy (Segal 1990; Bradbury 1990). As one commentator has argued this drama is

> wrested from the scope of male privilege [and] is played out between the woman and her child, her body, her coterie of friends. It is immediate and sensuous. For men, this is a difficult drama to experience because there is no audience participation of the kind [they] would like or are used to. (Bradbury 1990: 145)

Thus while Moretti is able to create a comic role for himself within this drama, as a son as well as an apprehensively expectant father, it is one that is ambiguous and insecure. Moretti's cinematic alter ego, renowned for his narcissistic self-absorption (Porton and Ellickson 1995; Romney 1999) and 'foolish' or infantile behaviour, a key trope of his on-screen persona, is forced to spectate rather than participate in his wife's pregnancy. In a memorable scene involving the perusal of gifts for the expected baby, Moretti interjects 'we've got things too' as his wife, her friend and his mother look at and discuss items together; he then asks 'can we show our things, mum?' to which she replies exasperatedly, 'Wait'. This comic sequence reveals Moretti's childish desire to be the centre of attention, but reveals also the extent of his anxiety at having to occupy a peripheral position in relation to this overtly maternal space. As the scene continues he retreats into the arguably masculine obsessions of categorisation and sport as he examines and describes various pairs of baby shoes – 'The white with blue trim, the blue with white trim and the plain shoes and then the white with blue stripes, for tennis and basketball' – all the while ignored by the three women. (The psychoanalyst father Giovanni in *La Stanza del Figlio* possesses the same obsession, owning a carefully organised collection of shoes encompassing a wide array of sporting activities.)

Observing the childish Moretti, it might be argued that he privileges the domain of the Lacanian Imaginary, the affective in his films, his infantile behaviour working on a general level to undermine the sanctity of the Symbolic. This emphasis on the Imaginary may also be seen specifically in his engagement with fatherhood in *Aprile*. Thus Moretti references prescribed behaviour in relation to paternal care, while demonstrating the significance of the affective for both father and son. This split between the social and the personal, the public and the private is one that maps onto the opposition set up between Berlusconi and Moretti as fathers. Berlusconi resides very clearly in the domain of the Symbolic (a position associated with television and one that is criticised in *Aprile* as the conclusion to this chapter demonstrates), while Moretti positions himself in the Imaginary (a position admittedly complicated by his extra-diegetic social status as a renowned filmmaker and political 'activist').

It is worth noting that while we may see progressive forms of fatherhood represented in the film, it is clear that neither Moretti nor Berlusconi have foregone any of the privileges of patriarchy, of the Symbolic; they both retain their public positions and the political and cultural power that accrues from them. (Interestingly in *La Stanza del figlio*, the father Giovanni, played by Moretti himself, is initially in a position of overt patriarchal power by virtue of his position as a psychoanalyst and authority figure for the family. The loss of his son in a diving accident, however, strips him of this authority both over his family and in relation to his analytic practice, leading him to reject both.)

Within *Aprile* Moretti actively performs – tries on in a sense – a range of masculinities. He represents at one level the authority figure, evidenced by the control he exercises as a film director. He is also a 'modern' father, despite his attempts to resist the full implications of this new identity; the pull of the infantile for Moretti is so strong that he attempts continually to postpone adulthood. Speaking about himself in the third person Moretti claims in *Aprile* that the birth of his son has enabled him to begin to achieve a certain maturity:

> At first, Nanni found it hard. He didn't understand why his son wanted to stay with his mother. The admirable thing about him was the process by which he tried to become an adult. That ability to stand aside, while remaining present. After all, the child's needs came first. In this way, he learnt to be less self-oriented. He started to think of the child. Taking up the challenge at last of a man who has to become an adult. But why become an adult? There's no reason!

Segal notes how 'prospective and actual fatherhood can induce an intense crisis in men … Fatherhood can threaten men's whole perception of themselves as adults, arousing jealousy and anxieties of inadequacy' (Segal 1990: 42). One contributor cited by Segal states: 'being with my son I was confronted by my own childhood, my own security and childish feelings' (Segal 1990: 42). All of these responses are evidenced by Moretti in *Aprile*.

Moretti's on-screen persona also contains traces of the mild hysteric, acting out 'his own ambivalence towards an inscribed and proscribed social position (masculinity)'

(Bukatman 1988: 196). Thus Moretti is continually in conflict with the various roles his public masculinity requires him to adopt. When, for example, he should be interviewing politicians Moretti is instead recording on video his son Pietro's experience of the transition from colostrum to mature milk production, and even in the reflective quote above, Moretti still questions the demands of responsible adulthood. (*La Stanza del figlio* appears to be about precisely these responsibilities and represents a shift of style and tone for Moretti. The 'infantile' comedy of his earlier work is replaced by a more mature contemplative comedy situated within a classically structured narrative as opposed to the fragmented observations that characterise *Caro Diario* and *Aprile*. The responsibilities of adulthood are represented through the demands of therapy, the pressures of parenting, the difficulties of marriage and most traumatically through the loss of a son. Moretti's alter-ego in *Aprile* has become an adult in the interim between the two films; the death of the son in *La Stanza del figlio* representing perhaps the projected anxiety of every parent and every father.)

Reference was made in the introduction to the fact that as well as being actual fathers both Moretti and Berlusconi are also metaphorical fathers. Berlusconi's status as a paternalistic Prime Minister has been demonstrated; however, the two men may additionally be seen as metaphorical fathers through their associations with cinema and television. Moretti has played a significant role in Italian cinema industry since the release of *Io sono un autarchico/I am Self-Sufficient* in 1977 and *Ecce Bombo* in 1978, emerging 'during the late 1970s as a somewhat unwilling spokesman for his decidedly disaffected generation' (Porton and Ellickson 1995: 11). Seen by some as an inheritor of the filmmaking tradition of neorealism (Rascaroli 2003), Moretti is a total filmmaker who has worked (and continues to work) as an actor, producer, writer and director. In addition to this he runs his own production and distribution companies, Sacher Films and Tandem respectively, as well as Rome's Nuovo Sacher cinema. He has produced films for some of Italy's most important contemporary directors including Gianni Amelio, Carlo Mazzacurati and Daniele Luchetti (whom he gently satirises in *Aprile*); but it is perhaps as a director that Moretti has been most influential, giving voice to the concerns of his generation and through his experimentation with narrative form, paving the way for a new generation of filmmakers.

Berlusconi may be seen as a father-figure in relation to contemporary Italian television, having played a key role in the deregulation of Italian television through his illegal national broadcasts in the late 1970s. Berlusconi and his family own 96 per cent of Fininvest, an unlisted holding company which has a controlling stake in the television company Mediaset, whose three networks have a 43 per cent share of the national audience. Fininvest also controls Mondadori, Italy's largest publishing group, as well as Medusa Video, Blockbuster Italia and a series of major advertising and financial companies. Since his election to a second term of office in May 2001, Berlusconi has purged left-wing journalists and executives from the state-owned Rai TV network while at the same time refusing to divest himself of his three television channels, Canale 5, Italia 1 and Retequattro, creating a situation in which one individual now controls over 90 per cent of television news in Italy (Carroll 2001: 11).[5]

Clearly, then, television – as Pierre Sorlin has asserted – has played a significant role in Italian political and social life since the late 1970s (Sorlin 1996: 145). It has also had a lasting influence on the cinema, accused by filmmakers of 'stealing their clientele' (Sorlin

1996: 147), on the one hand, but responsible, on the other, for giving 'cinema a second chance' (Sorlin 1996: 148).[6] The influence of television on film extends also to its visual style. Thus Sorlin argues that 'television influenced Italian filmmakers in four main ways: the pre-eminence of words over images, the insistence on close-ups, the choice of bright colours, and the adoption of a reportage style of shooting' (Sorlin 1996: 150). Nanni Moretti is acutely aware of the proximate relationship between film and television and exploits this to great critical effect in *Aprile*.

In conclusion, then, *Aprile* dramatises two conflicts: that between film and television and that between two different concepts of fatherhood. Nanni Moretti may be seen as the father of cinema, the guardian of film and film culture, subject (in his view) to relentless erosion from television represented by its most powerful figure, Silvio Berlusconi. Television is associated with corruption, film with critical integrity. Clearly the simplicity of this opposition obscures the fact that the two are very closely interrelated in Italy as they are in the rest of Europe. Nonetheless there is no doubt that the comically polemical *Aprile* succeeds in offering an effective critique of the circumstances and effects of that relationship in and for Italian television. Allied to this opposition between media is that between notions of masculinity and paternity, where in the case of Moretti fatherhood is represented as fragmented and open, while in that of Berlusconi it is linked to his almost fascist paternity.

Moretti's attempts to discover and adopt appropriate masculine identities in *Aprile* take place, then, against the background of the singular and traditional masculine identity embodied by Berlusconi, a personal identity that is clearly also political. In *Aprile* the political is viewed, generally, through the personal, which is not only to politicise the individual, as in the case of Moretti, but rather to individualise the sphere of the political, as in the case of Berlusconi who has used his political power for extensive personal gain. In the context of the masculine identities that Moretti seeks to construct for himself, this interrelationship is a productive one because it seeks a reworking of the masculine as a reworking of the political and by extension the patriarchal.[7] Thus the patriarchal Berlusconi, perceived by many Italians to be the 'strong man' of Italian politics, is contrasted with the neurotic, less traditionally masculine Moretti.[8] Moretti offers his spectators, one might argue, a certain 'resistance to fixed subjectivity and the cultural inscription of the codes of masculine behaviour' (Bukatman 1988: 196) codes most obviously exemplified by Berlusconi, the shiny icon, albeit now tarnished by corruption, of capitalist success.[9] Moretti fragments, in *Aprile*, across a range of masculine identities as opposed to exemplifying a singular and easily incorporated masculine ideal. (The identity 'Moretti' represented in *Aprile* is a problematic one. The figure 'Moretti' is a complex of different components that include, at the very least, Michele Apicella, Moretti's alter ego in films prior to *Caro Diario*, Nanni Moretti the semi-fictional character, played by Nanni Moretti the actor, and Nanni Moretti the director of *Aprile*, who is also a producer, scriptwriter and cinema owner.)[10] The film's visual style emphasises a narrative structure that is resistant to 'coherent and delimited order' (Bukatman 1988: 197), enhancing the splintering of Moretti's already precarious identity. Thus, for example, the physical and the verbal comedy of the fragmented Moretti is contrasted continually in *Aprile* with the composed and slick media image of Berlusconi. In an exemplary sequence we see Moretti viewing video footage of a Berlusconi speech in a screening room. The short sequence begins with an extreme close-up on the face of Berlusconi who is making an impassioned electoral speech. The sequence is characterised by cuts between Moretti spectating and reverses back to Berlusconi, marking and emphasising his overt and exaggerated performance. Moretti is acutely aware of the imbrication of film and television and it seems clear that in *Aprile* there is a division made along a film/cinema and video/television axis. The film was shot primarily on 35mm film with recorded video footage used for the television sequences, as in the scene just referred to; this video material was subsequently transferred to 35mm film and incorporated into *Aprile*. The exaggerated close-up of Berlusconi operates, perhaps, not only as a means of critiquing him and the kind of monolithic, heroic masculinity he is seen to represent, but by associating Berlusconi stylistically with the (literally) degraded televisual image Moretti is able to extend his silent – 'I offer no commentary' (Gili 1998: 11) – critique.

One might argue finally that this reproduction of the cinematic experience recalls, when coupled with Moretti's overt narcissism, the Lacanian mirror stage referred to earlier. Theoretically, as Scott Bukatman reminds us, 'our experience before this mirror reassures and resituates us at the perfect centre of a stable world' (Bukatman 1988: 204). In this instance, however, the spectator is confronted by the visibly too perfect, and therefore clearly misrecognised and as such false, image of Silvio Berlusconi. It is no coincidence that this image of Berlusconi, although cinematically reproduced, is televisual; the connection between Berlusconi, his control of television and therefore its inherent untrustworthiness is made abundantly clear. Moretti lays bare the processes of cinematic identification in order to demonstrate the constructedness of both the image and Berlusconi as its referent. He offers the spectator instead an arguably more 'real', fragmented, albeit infantile Moretti with whom to identify. The ego is denied its craving for reinforcement in a reversal of the mirror stage that privileges the imaginary. Ultimately the domain of the affective, the Imaginary, is privileged over the lure of a fascistic, masculine, perfection, encapsulated in the face of Berlusconi. The plural, problematic and cinematic Nanni Moretti is offered in place of the singular and dangerously alluring televisual Silvio Berlusconi.

Notes

1   Berlusconi is the chairman of AC Milan football club. The party name Forza Italia, literally 'Go Italy', was a slogan chanted on the football terraces.

2   Under investigation by Milanese magistrates over charges of corruption, Berlusconi was forced into resigning as Prime Minister on 22 December 1994.

3   Unless otherwise stated all translations from French are my own.

4   Running counter to the representational shift identified by Jeffords, Berlusconi is reputed to have remarked on his move from business to politics 'I am tired of being Silvio Berlusconi: I want a heroic life' (Fox 2002: 43).

5   Berlusconi has stated that rather than sell any part of Fininvest 'his intention is to deal with the matter by laying a conflict of interest bill before parliament "by the summer"' (Blitz 2001: 1). At the time of writing (July 2002) this conflict of interest has not been resolved despite the passing of the aforementioned bill. Furthermore in April 2002 Berlusconi consolidated his grip over the Italian media when figures sympathetic to the government were appointed directors of programmes and news at two out of the three RAI networks (Willan 2002: 1).

6   Sorlin notes that 'cinema attendance decreased from 500 million tickets sold in the mid-1960s to 100 million in the 1990s' (1996: 147); however television channels also screened vast quantities of 'previously

forgotten Italian films' (ibid.) thereby providing an income for the studios. Sorlin also points out that 'in 1990 … a third of the films shot in Italy were financed, partly or in whole, by a television channel' (Sorlin 1996: 148).

7   In the case of Berlusconi we are made aware in *Aprile* of the close integration of the personal and the political, the fact that his political ambitions are personal ambitions. Thus Berlusconi's desire for justice, articulated in the debate sequence, relates to his wish to side-step the various charges of corruption levelled against him.

8   In the first few months of Berlusconi's first period of office, in a survey which 'asked if "Italy today needs a strong man", 73.5 per cent of the survey declared that they were "quite in agreement" or "very much in agreement"' (Ginsborg 2003: 296).

9   In 1994 Moretti was involved in the production of 'the collective *L'unico paese al mondo/ The Only Country in the World* (1994), a violent assault on Prime Minister and television entrepreneur Silvio Berlusconi and his "telly-ocracy"' (Volpi 1996: 85).

10 As Chris Wagstaff notes 'probably no one has so shuffled the cards in cinema between a "person" in real life and a "character" in a film narrative as Nanni Moretti' (Wagstaff 1999: 36).

chapter 13

LOST BOYS: TRAUMA, MASCULINITY AND THE MISSING CHILD FILM

Emma Wilson

When Nanni Moretti's film, *La Stanza del figlio/The Son's Room* (2001), won the Palme d'Or at Cannes, it confirmed the persistence of a trend of art films which, in very different ways, look at missing or dead children, malign or mourning parents and disassembled families. I argue that this intimate and emotive cinema is working to refocus attention on children (rather than women) as cinema's missing (vanishing, endangered) subjects; specifically, films seek to contend with these children as missing and remembered or as threatened and traumatised, 'exposed' to adult sexuality, unsettled in their sexual and gender identifications. This argument is part of a larger project on missing children in contemporary cinema;[1] narrowing my focus here in order to address questions of masculinity in film, I look at the specific case of representations of father/son relationships and their imbrication with missing child histories.

In their focus on the troubled dynamic of same-sex parent/child relations, some contemporary films have opened up and scrutinised the role of the father in society and in the Symbolic order. The point of view of the son offers a privileged perspective for such scrutiny: the son questions his identity in relation to the father and tests the borderlines between identification and desire.[2] The son whose identification (as male) is contested and secured in the course of a film allows potential focus on this dismantling and reconstruction of masculine identity positions. While the relation of father to son is always already unsettled by such contestatory wrangling for identity and for demarcation of the limits of self and other/father, missing child films open up narrative paths where the father is at once aggressor for the son or, more threatening still, sexual predator. These films offer a space for considering such deformations of the normative identificatory bond and, in more disquieting fashion, for questioning how such fantasies of the father as outlaw form the underside of masculine self-construction. This onslaught on masculinity testifies to current anxieties, as it also envisages new networks of social and gender inter-relation. Such films, alive to the complexities of the construction of the self and fantasies of the other, probe the sore points of the son's imaginings and perceptions of the father.

The recent work of Slavoj Žižek offers a subtle inflection to these thoughts on the changed role of the father in contemporary cinema. In his essay, 'Fathers, Fathers Everywhere', Žižek counterpoints two films, both prize winners at Cannes in 1998: Thomas Vinterberg's *Festen/Celebration* (1998) and Roberto Benigni's *La Vita è bella/Life is Beautiful* (1998). In *Festen*, an abusive father is confronted by his adult son; in *La Vita è bella* a maniacally protective father attempts to shield his son from the realities of the Holocaust. While Žižek sets Benigni's protective father in opposition to Vinterberg's obscene father, he points out that, 'what these two fathers … have in common is that they both *suspend the agency of the symbolic Law/Prohibition*, i.e., the paternal agency whose function is to introduce the child into the universe of social reality with its harsh demands' (Žižek 2000: 31). One father – Benigni's – offers his son an imaginary shield against the traumatic encounter with social reality. The other – Vinterberg's – denies prohibition in his brutal sexual enjoyment of his children. Bearing these two models in mind, my focus here is on two further films from 1998, one also, fortuitously, a prize winner at the same Cannes festival, Claude Miller's *La Classe de neige/Class Trip*, adapted from Emmanuel Carrère's novel of the same title, and the other, Todd Solondz's *Happiness*. Comparison between the films, in what follows, will seek to illustrate the ways in which questions about children, the family and sexuality stretch beyond the boundaries of specific national cinemas and resonate in both US and European cinema. Like *Festen* and *La Vita è bella*, *La Classe de neige* and *Happiness* bring the father/son relation and paternal authority closely into question. In particular, echoing Žižek, they tease out the similarities between the protective and abusive father. Exploring the suspension of the symbolic law they both focus on the son's fear (and fantasy) that his father is a paedophile.

La Classe de neige is an austere and glacial film, making artistic use of the sharp blues and whites of its winter Alpine setting. Ostensibly the film offers a narrative account of a child who goes on a class trip to a ski resort. While the children are there on holiday, a child from a neighbouring village goes missing. Despite its *fait divers* thematics, the film cuts repeatedly and disconcertingly between realist and imagined or dream images, focusing in particular on the fantasies of its child protagonist Nicolas. Such fantasies become a source for gauging his relation to his father. Indeed *La Classe de neige* shifts the focus of its interrogation of father/son relations from the perceptions of the father to those of the son; this is one difference from many missing child films which focus on parental fear and guilt.[3] In its attention to Nicolas's traumatised perceptions and their warping of the visual field and filmic mimesis, the film at times marks no distinction between virtual and actual images and is inflected indeed by the shapes, timeframe and rhythms of Nicolas's perceptions, memories and imaginings. Dominant in his image patterns are connected anxieties about his father and about the body, its vulnerability and threats to its integrity. Such anxieties are acted out in particular, in a possible gesture of mastery, in imagined scenes of his father's body fragilised in a car crash.

Miller exploits the potential of film as a medium which can reveal both the child's personal fantasies, his dreams and mental images and, more fundamentally, the current social and collective fantasies which structure his relation to his father. Dominant in these fantasies of fatherhood in Miller's film, and in those examined by Žižek, is that of the father as threat (concealed in a mask of benevolence). Indeed Žižek specifies that we are not dealing here with an opposition between appearance and reality: the appearance of the benevolent father which conceals the cruel reality of the brutal rapist. For Žižek the horrible secret of a brutal father behind a polite mask is itself a fantasy. Such a fantasy may be a social construct (propagated in popular culture), yet, as I will argue below, it may also be a protective shield against bleaker truths about the father's inadequacy or vulnerability. Vilifying the father becomes a defence against his faltering power. In this sense, while the two fantasies – of the father as overprotective figure and the father as rapist – may both work to suspend the agency of the symbolic law, despite their transgressive status they still protect against fears of the father as impotent and vulnerable, as utterly without the power of the law.

The charge of *La Classe de neige* comes in the seriousness with which it treats the problematic of growing up and securing a (masculine) identity in the thrall of (the fantasy of) a paedophile father. Miller's father, perceived by the child Nicolas, disquietingly shares characteristics of both Benigni's and Vinterberg's. At the start of the film he is shown at a parent/teachers' meeting before the class trip taking a stereotypically maternal, overprotective interest in his son. His connection to his son is almost umbilical: he insists he will drive him to the ski resort rather than letting him travel with the other children; he insists his son may phone him if he wishes. The father protects Nicolas from imagined dangers, yet in his paranoid caution he makes the child, vividly, even queasily aware of all that might go awry. Further, his overweening attention to Nicolas unravels as the film proceeds. Small details belie his inattention: Nicolas is left without his bag or pyjamas, fatally missing the physical tokens of parental care. The film leaves us to wonder about Nicolas's investment, or otherwise, in his father's excessive love. Having driven Nicolas to the ski resort, in a neat inversion of the missing child topos, the father himself goes missing in his car in the narrow bends and slopes of the Alps. He returns again in the grisly crashes which interrupt Nicolas's thought patterns as the child's mental space is dominated by the mountain landscape where his father is at large. (The film insistently returns to Kubrick's *The Shining* (1980) in its geography and nexus of filial fears.)

By the end of the film the father has been identified as molester and murderer of the other boy who has gone missing at the neighbouring ski resort. This late-coming evidence seems to explain Nicolas's traumatised responses to his father and overshadows previous scenes of father/son intimacy and contact. Where firstly Miller's father resembles Benigni's overprotective figure, by the end of the film his acts, and guilt, equate him with Vinterberg's rapist father, brutally present behind his polite, protective, paternal mask. In looking at one of the final scenes from *La Classe de neige* I explore what these dual fantasies of the father hide, what knowledge they can work to shield and protect the child from.

After his father's arrest, one of his teachers drives Nicolas home so his mother can inform him of what has happened. The revelation comes sooner, however, in a service station on the motorway. Teacher and child catch sight of a television news broadcast on an overhead monitor. Nicolas's father, handcuffed, is led away, shadowed by a policeman. The film cuts to Nicolas's reaction shot, his face in close-up, then cuts back to a close-up of the television image of his father. The teacher moves to protect the child from the image, placing his arm around him and leading him away. The film cuts from this image of protection to a further image of the father on screen as he is hidden in a coat to protect his identity. The visual resemblance of the image on the monitor and the image of teacher and pupil is unsettling. Nicolas himself is riveted by the now amorphous figure of his father smothered under the coat.

Television screens have been one of the spaces in the film in which we have viewed Nicolas's psychical reality: in this respect the film is reminiscent of the films of David Lynch or Atom Egoyan. Televisual images of a cookery programme have previously mutated for Nicolas into a crash scenario of his father's mutilation. The shock of the motorway services scene comes in the uncanny coinciding between the material images on the monitor and the psychical reality by which Nicolas' life is determined. In these coincidental images the film offers its most trenchant engagement with the fantasy of the father as protector or rapist. For Nicolas viewing the news footage, the *punctum* of the image, its piercing emotional effect, derives from his recognition of the father, indeed the presence of his father in this familarly staged scenario of the child molester arrested. The father's image is striking in its pathos, in the abdication of the father's authority as he is policed and subjugated to the law. The father's vulnerability, as I have commented above, mirrors the son's as their figures and images resemble one another. The news reporting forces or allows the child to face the pathos of his father's vulnerability, of his degradation.

The father's weakness, his pathos, is, I suggest, what is screened by the fantasies of the father as protector or as brutal rapist. The image of the father as rapist and abuser, which Žižek points out has come to seem artificial, wrong and faked, is seen in *La Classe de neige* as a defence mechanism against the all too frightening emotions surrounding the disintegration of the father's authority. It is this which *La Classe de neige* as missing child film has attempted to reveal rather than conceal; in this sense it is a missing child film in more than one sense. While its narrative ostensibly contains a story of a missing, abused and murdered child, this story is filtered through the consciousness of another 'missing' child, the child of the paedophile for whom paternal authority is precisely missing or aberrant.

A similar situation is staged, all the more acerbically, in Todd Solondz's *Happiness* which, like *La Classe de neige*, shows a son's response to the revelation that his father is a child molester. Solondz states in interview:

> My politics on the issue are simple: you do this kind of thing, you go to jail … If I have kids I gotta know if there's a paedophile on my block. But I wasn't thinking from a political perspective at all. I read a piece about this Russian serial killer … who had killed over fifty kids. At the end of the article it said he had a wife and two children, and I thought: what does that mean? (Bowe Hearty 1998: n.p.)

Happiness works to test this, taking as its subject the grotesque and pathetic imbrication of paedophilia and family dynamics. The film is an exercise in imagination (as it visualises what a child molester in the family may mean) and in a strange compassion. Specific though it is in its representation of a single family in New Jersey – we see a billboard in the film saying 'Welcome to New Jersey. The Garden State' – *Happiness* represents a more generic suburbia, a dystopian space of home, childhood and domesticity.

Like *La Classe de neige*, *Happiness* troubles and confuses the relation between psychical and material reality, represented. Yet the latter film pays further attention to the lurid world of the father's fantasies, rather than to those of the child. Indeed the character who most effectively warps and disrupts the film's objectivity and transparent aesthetic is Bill Maplewood. Early in the film we pass seamlessly into the virtual reality of Bill's visualised dream narration; it is only as he starts to shoot indiscriminately in the scene that we see that this is not the film's diegetic reality.[4] Although we see flashbacks (real and fantasised) from another character's perspective later in the film, and hear voice-over from various characters, Bill's presence creates the greatest challenge to clear-sighted viewing and interpretation of the film. This warping effect is marked visually in the *mise-en-scène* of the first scene where Bill's paedophilia is addressed. He stops to buy 'Kool', a magazine for pre-teen boys, in the 7–11 age group. In the parking lot outside he is seen approaching his car with the magazine. The car is positioned between the camera and Bill so he is seen at the edge of the frame, no longer as the film's direct central focus. The film seems to adopt surveillance techniques as these shots of Bill are captured. As Bill gets into the back of the car and unzips his fly to masturbate, his image is seen through the reflecting layers of glass of the car windows. As he is seen masturbating, the voices of a wife and children approaching the neighbouring car can be heard. The sounds seem reminiscent of the family reality in which Bill has established his identity. They seem to impinge on his hidden pleasure, tokens of fear or guilt, residue of his psychic reality.

In the course of the film, Bill will rape two children, both friends of his son Billy. As in *La Classe de neige* the scenes of abuse are not represented, although Solondz brings the acts closer to the range of the film's story. Bill rapes Johnny Grasso, for example, in his own family house. While *Happiness* draws attention to the father's psychical reality, rather than the son's, it still crucially uses the son as the means and medium by which the father's transgression is measured. *La Classe de neige* operates through recording fear and fantasy in the strange interference which occurs as Nicolas views visual dramas of his own psyche; the missing father here is continually brought back to consciousness, if wounded and dismembered, in the son's compulsive imaginings. Such a link between father and son is established all the more directly in *Happiness* where the impact of the father's transgressions on the son are tested in a series of spoken exchanges.

This series of brilliant, and peculiar, exchanges between Bill and his son Billy are the key scenes in the film in which father/son identification is explored, and in particular in which Solondz imagines what it means to have a paedophile for a father. All begin with Billy saying, 'Dad?', and Bill replying, 'Yes, Billy?' They have a dead-pan rhythm, reminiscent of the family voices and dialogues in Egoyan's films. The content of each exchange between Bill and Billy is uneasily sexual. In the first Billy asks Bill what 'come' is and Bill explains in patient, liberal, pedagogical terms. In the second scene, Billy asks Bill about penis size and length. In the third, Billy, all the more painfully, asks Bill about his abuse of Johnny Grasso and Ronald Farber.

On one level these scenes show the ways in which parent and child are always already engaged in questions about sexuality. Another side of adult/child sexual negotiations is the parent's responsibility to offer some reasonable sexual education to the child. The scenes reflect the uneasy, part practical, part deeply embarrassing nature of such discussions. Billy is a plain child, solemn and sympathetic. The film avoids any sexualisation of the visual presentation of the scenes. Nevertheless in the first two scenes, Bill's responses, as a responsible father, are surprising. In the first scene he offers to show Billy how to masturbate. In the second he offers to measure his own penis to quell Billy's anxieties about penis size. Despite the matter-of-fact tone of Bill's patient questions and answers with Billy, the exchanges still say something about his sexuality (while being, on another level, uncomfortably comic).

The third scene is the most traumatic and offers the greatest shift in power balance. Billy now appears as Bill's confessor, drawing words from him. This seems to underline the way these scenes function in the film as a whole. They work as a type of catechism where Bill and Billy repeat and gradually subvert the terms and meanings of father/son identification and bonding. Billy's questions also serve to voice the viewer's questions and concerns. This becomes most apparent in the third scene where he tries to get Bill to find words for what he has done and finally, with the most fear, asks crucially: 'Would you ever fuck me?' These scenes actualise Solondz's concern to question how the child molester and serial rapist functions in the family. What sort of father is he? How does he relate to his son?

For Solondz, Bill's fatherhood opens questions about his identity and redemption; with some degree of caution, he says: 'if there is redemption for this man it lies in [his] honesty and the love he has for his son, before whom he cannot but tell the truth' (Bowe Hearty 1998: n.p). More germane to comparison with *La Classe de neige* is the question of the son's perception of his paedophile father. Solondz says of Billy: 'He can't really understand the full ramifications of what his father has done and what it really means but he knows enough that his father is a terrible man and that his father has done wrong and that his father loves him' (ibid.). It is to this set of irreconcilable truths that the film offers no resolution.

After Bill has been apprehended by the detectives (upholders of the law), the film cuts to an image of mother and children leaving the house in the early morning. They turn to see the words 'Serial Rapist' and 'Pervert' that have been spray-painted on the house front. When Billy confronts Bill in the final scene between them, he tells him that the kids at school have been saying that Bill is a serial rapist and pervert. The terms name the fantasy construction of the father as brutal rapist behind his respectable façade. Yet the scene between Billy and Bill shows the child confronting a truth that is more painful still. The earlier fantasy the film has fostered of the father as overprotective, as nurturing figure who will even teach his son to masturbate, sits uneasily with the new defensive fantasy of the father as brutal rapist. In the fissure between these two fantasy formations, in this third scene of dialogue, the son glimpses the father as fallible and flaccid. As the child pursues his questions, he comes closer to tears. By the end of the scene both father and son weep, sad imitations of each other. Bill affirms that he would not fuck his son but would jerk off instead, again merging his fantasy roles as protector or rapist – he protects his son by not raping him but does not deny his desire for the child.

As in *La Classe de neige* questions are asked here about the son's apprehension of the father's failings, about his sense of the father's failure even to comply with the fantasy images of the father outside the symbolic law. How does this impact on identification and the assumption and performance of a masculine identity category? What does it mean if the child sees his 'original sexual love … for the father' (Butler 1990: 59) repeated and reciprocated in his father's sexual encounters with other children?

While they refuse resolution, both films offer some tentative response to these questions in imagining the son's survival of this encounter with the reality of the father's failure. To return to *La Classe de neige*, it is revealing to look at the scene which follows the glimpse of the father as criminal, as vulnerable. The father, unmasked, is hastily hidden in the coat, concealed once more. Nicolas is also shown to find his own means of diverting himself from the image of the father. He next notices a mother kissing her small baby. Nicolas averts his eyes but the sounds of the baby are still heard where Nicolas's image alone is held within the frame. He turns back to the image and we see it closer still: mother and baby mirror one another's gestures. Their symbiosis is disrupted as she looks outwards to meet Nicolas' gaze. The actual status of the ensuing images is brought into question by the music which now plays against the shots. The camera seems in line with Nicolas's fantasy as he approaches the woman to touch her hair. The film abruptly denies its own wish-fulfilling status as it cuts back to the immobile figure of Nicolas perched on a stool. While the relation between actual and virtual seems to be fixed, it is unsettled again as the mother turns to smile enigmatically at Nicolas as she, her husband and baby leave the service station. Is this an event recorded or the perpetuation of Nicolas's hesitant erotic fantasy? She holds the baby in a protective gesture, a blanket over its head, again repeating the televisual image which dominates the scene.

The woman's hair blows in the wind as she smiles: between memory and desire, like the woman in *La Jetée* (Chris Marker, 1962) she is placed as witness to the story of a future man, doubtless now marked by an image from his childhood. The woman's serenity and sensuality, in Nicolas's fantasy, distract him from that image of paternal failure, shroud it and replace it. On one level the turn from the aberrant father to the mother in loving contact with her baby seems an act of regression. Yet perhaps this desire for and link with the mother can be read differently. In *Male Subjectivity at the Margins* Kaja Silverman valorises those marginal male subjectivities 'which absent themselves from the line of paternal succession, and which in one way or another occupy the domain of femininity' (Silverman 1992: 389). In its revelation of the disintegration of paternal authority and a failed or denied identification with the father, *La Classe de neige* arguably envisages the domain of femininity as an alternative field of both identification and desire.

The ending of *Happiness* is again comparable, though cruder in its fulfilment. After Bill's arrest, the film cuts to a scene six months later. Timmy stands on a balcony with the family dog. He watches a young blonde woman in a bikini by a swimming pool below. As she rubs sun screen into her breasts and undoes her bikini top, we hear Billy masturbating and then see his semen on the balcony railing. The dog licks up the semen and goes into the flat where Billy's grandparents, mother and aunts are eating lunch. The dog goes up to Billy's mother who pets him and then lets the dog slobber over her face in a grotesque relay of fluid. The last words of the film, Billy's, are 'I came'. In the absence of his father, Billy too finds himself encircled in relations to women, more caricatural and less elegiac, nevertheless, than those imagined in *La Classe de neige*.

Both films work to imagine the ways in which there is a possibility of survival of the non-normative family through the mobilisation of other fantasies. Such survival may be hesitant and distressed, but it is in both cases resolute. It is telling perhaps that in both cases the encounter with the father as molester precedes the child's entry into puberty. While this may say something of the sexualisation of these children, such a narrative progression also lends weight to a view that these films explore fantasies of parental failure and transgression which circulate more widely in the processes of identity formation, identification and individuation. These are perhaps more universal fears and fantasies, presented in the disturbingly literal histories of these children who contend with their father as molester. In this sense it is significant that these are both missing child films, rather than accounts of direct parental sexual abuse. While the child of the molester is, of course, still victim of his father's acts, the fact that in both narratives the father has chosen a child who is like his son, but not his son, allows the disturbing merger of the fantasies of the father as overprotective figure and as rapist, as it opens the traumatic space where the child can question whether he would be his father's sexual object, and whether, most distressingly, this could also be something he would desire.

Critiquing Barry Levinson's *Sleepers* (1996), James Kincaid argues that the film is true to the premises of our cultural panic about child molesting. For him the film is saying you cannot escape what you are: the protagonists of the film, motored by the need for revenge, are (in his terms): 'the children of molestation' (Kincaid 1998: 190). He ends his account: 'We can make up better stories than this.' I would say that *La Classe de neige* and *Happiness* are such better stories, in the complexity of their exploration of fantasy, and prospectively, in the way in which they open space for imagining a future for their child protagonists.[5] Both films contend with how far recognising the father as molester is traumatic in its fearful co-mingling of fantasies (of the father as brutal rapist, of the father as protective partner) and in the pathetic dismantling of paternal authority in an apprehension of the father's vulnerability. These films refuse catharsis, revenge, judgement or solution. They may offer alternative desiring relations as their protagonists find refuge and pleasure in new fantasy relations to women. All too briefly perhaps, the films show other ways of securing masculine identity. But more emphatically still their intervention comes in their transposition of fantasy and traumatic experience into visual narrative, offering a means of recognising and traversing, if not mastering, irregular and aberrant relations, their trial and their survival.

Notes

1 Wilson 2003 includes more sustained analysis of *Happiness*, one of the two films discussed in this chapter.

2 While the borderline between identification and desire has more familiarly been questioned in feminist discussions of female/female relations and the mother/daughter bond in writing and film, contemporary cinema has proved fascinated by the equal complexities of male mirroring identificatory bonds, as explored in literal father/son films such as Anne Fontaine's *Comment j'ai tué mon père/How I Killed My Father* (2001) or Paul Schrader's *Affliction* (1998), or in male friendship movies such as Dominick Moll's *Harry, un ami qui vous veut du bien/Harry, He's Here to Help* (2000).

3 *La Stanza del figlio* offers a particularly rich, though psychosexually benign, investigation of a father's grief at the loss of his son. Agnieszka Holland's *Olivier, Olivier* (1992) focuses further on the mother's loss than the father's (or indeed on the perceptions of the missing, then murdered child), yet offers interesting perceptions of the reconfiguration of gender relations in the family.

4 This scene bears close comparison with the opening of François Ozon's *Sitcom* (1998), incidentally also shown at Cannes. *Sitcom* too interrogates the changed role of the father in contemporary society. (I am grateful to Laurène Mocaer for discussion of Ozon in this light.)

5 Another film which asks comparable questions about paternal authority, and puts more (questionable) emphasis on the child's desire to be sexual object for a father-figure is Michael Cuesta's *L.I.E.* (2001).

chapter 14

LIKE FATHER?: FAILING PARENTS AND ANGELIC CHILDREN IN CONTEMPORARY BRITISH SOCIAL REALIST CINEMA

James Leggott

The theme of father and son relationships has been prominent in a number of recent British films that can be seen as the continuation of an indigenous tradition of social realist cinema. This concentration upon paternal obligations (whether blood-ties or quasi-patriarchal connections) is bound up with two discernible tendencies of British filmmaking of the last ten or so years: first, an exploration of the anxieties that accompany the diminishment of homosocial authority, tradition and territory (Hallam 2000; Hill 2000a; Hill 2000b; Monk 2000a; Monk 2000b); and second, the frequent deployment of young boys as central characters. Of the various contemporary films that incorporate, to a greater or lesser extent, a depiction of a paternal relationship, a distinction can be established between those that prioritise the experience of father-figures, such as *The Full Monty* (Peter Cattaneo, 1997) and *TwentyFourSeven* (Shane Meadows, 1997), and those which communicate the perspective of a child of teenage years or younger, such as *Gabriel and Me* (Udayan Prasad, 2001) or *Sweet Sixteen* (Ken Loach, 2002). However, both sets of films are linked by an obsession with failing or absent father-figures, and the threats posed to homosocial territories. Whilst the adult-orientated films typically describe the struggles of unemployed men in working-class communities to perform as fathers, the narratives that are told from a child's perspective not only inherit this concern with contested patriarchal authority, but reveal their young protagonists to be actively involved in the restoration, recreation and sometimes termination of the familial bond.

Fathers and sons: *The Full Monty* and *TwentyFourSeven*

The appropriation of contested (or moribund) homosocial space by a group of disenfranchised men has been one of the dominant narratives of the contemporary 'underclass comedy'. Inhabiting an unstable landscape of increasingly troubled gendered demarcations, the adult males of *The Full Monty*, *TwentyFourSeven* and *Brassed Off* (Mark Herman, 1996) find themselves embarking upon a collective strategy for the maintenance or restoration of certain patriarchal territories (respectively, a working-men's club, a boxing hall, and the spaces associated with mining employment). These spaces are either deemed to be under threat from alien forces (*The Full Monty*), or in danger of vanishing altogether from the landscape. As such they are symptomatic of the wider spatial alienation experienced by the unemployed male protagonists. Furthermore, as these films draw a correlation between contested homosocial space and the unstable male body, their strategies of re-appropriation, which tend to be physical, promote both spatial and bodily empowerment. In all three films, a mentor figure initiates a plan for the recuperation of endangered homosocial realms that involves some kind of physical performance, a literal display upon a public stage: the stripping act of *The Full Monty*, the boxing contest of *TwentyFourSeven*, and the brass band competition of *Brassed Off*. As such, the question of fatherly duty is dealt with only indirectly. Or rather, these men happen to believe that they are best able to assert their parental status through the reclamation of contested patriarchal territory; their specific relationships to their offspring (or pastoral charges) is of lesser significance than their commitment to an over-arching spatial project of reconstruction through performance.

Nevertheless, the plot of *The Full Monty*, probably one of the most well-known films of the recent underclass comedy cycle, is predicated upon the financial pressures upon its unemployed central character (Gaz) to raise the 'child support' money for his estranged son (Nathan). However, like the central character of *Raining Stones* (Ken Loach, 1993), Gaz senses that this financial task is more than simply a test of his parental powers, and thus a specific economic task quickly becomes subsumed within a grander project of empowerment. When Gaz informs Nathan that he cannot afford tickets for an expensive football game, his feeling of inadequacy is due to his inability to facilitate his son's entry into a place of traditional homosocial ritual. As with the young lads of *Purely Belter* (Mark Herman, 2000), the only viable option is an illicit invasion (climbing through a 'hole in the fence').

In this way, the story concerning Gaz's precarious relationship with his son is largely overwhelmed by a narrative of infantilisation and territorial struggle, and his resuscitation as a father-figure comes through his role as mentor to the stripping troupe; for much of the film, the prematurely sensible Nathan despairs of his father's childish antics. Indeed, from the outset, *The Full Monty* diagnoses how the exclusion of its male characters from places of work, leisure and commerce has resulted in their reduction to child-like status; with re-employment unlikely, the 'job shop' can be no more than a classroom, where the men pull out card games and newspapers when the 'teacher' leaves the room. The opening scenes show a desperate Gaz scheming to 'liberate' girders from the steel-works where he was once employed. This attempt literally to strip a depleted work space proves non-viable, and he is reduced to a helpless, foetal state by being locked in the darkened works, and then by nearly drowning in the canal outside. The alienation of the local men from legitimate spaces of employment or leisure is best symbolised by the feminine 'invasion' of the working men's club (in the guise of an exclusively female audience for a male stripping troupe), a violation that becomes the catalyst for Gaz's reclamatory strategy. Marooned in a lavatory cubicle, Gaz is shocked to discover one of the women urinating whilst standing,

Robert Carlyle as Gaz in *The Full Monty* (Peter Cattaneo, 1997)

and relates the incident to the other lads in gloomy terms: 'When women start pissing like us, we're finished.' Gaz, and the other lads, are not only exiled from former homosocial strongholds, but barred from female-orientated spaces of commerce and recreation. The shopping hypermarket, for example, is merely another play zone for the men, who have minimal powers as consumers. On three separate occasions we see a male character running out of here, as if being forcefully ejected from this hostile territory; a vignette depicting alarms going off when the portly Dave steals from the 'pick'n'mix' counter verifies that this is not a place that can withstand the appetites of the male body.

The Full Monty demonstrates the re-appropriation of contested homosocial space (and, by extension, authority) through performative activities that could be regarded as non-masculine, at least within the traditional working-class communities that the film depicts. The narrative charts how an empowering strategy takes shape via the men's negotiation of a series of gendered realms. The film begins with a fruitless attempt to exploit a traditionally male site (the works), then describes how a kind of behavioural 'theft' from feminised domestic space – the processes of bodily interrogation that occur within Gerald's home – allows for the perfection of the (arguably) feminised 'stripping' performance, which, in turn, facilitates the reclamation of contested male space. As the story concerning Gaz's precarious relationship with his son has largely been overwhelmed by this narrative of territorial struggle and rejuvenated fraternal bonds, it is fitting that Gaz's resuscitation as a father-figure comes through his role as mentor to the troupe.

A more ambivalent presentation of the figure of homosocial mentor is offered by *TwentyFourSeven*. In this film the self-appointed evangelic role is played by the middle-aged Darcy, who sets about rejuvenating a long-closed boxing club to house the squabbling youths of the local housing estates. In one of his voice-over speeches, he suggests how he has been driven to reanimate the club that he attended in his own youth for the sake of the 'demoralised inhabitants who've lost touch with their origins'. Darcy overturns the scepticism of his charges though his mercurial ability to bend his performance – by turns maternal and paternal – to differing people and circumstances, his cultivation of a feeling of inclusivity, and his promotion of the clean, honed body. When first seen, the lads are confined, like the men of *The Full Monty*, to the perpetual playground of the street, and one of Darcy's achievements is to use a camping and hill-walking trip to draw out their latent survival skills.

Yet, for all Darcy's success in uniting the warring teenagers of his town under one roof, his reclamatory project is revealed to be regressively masculinist, nostalgic and untenable. Awkward with a potential suitor (Jo), and apparently without any progeny of his own, or any other adult responsibilities, the character has an unsettlingly childish aura, his altruism perhaps masking the nostalgic urge to prolong his adolescent state through the construction of an anachronistic and hermetically sealed space. The dissolution of the boxing club is brought to a head through the involvement of various unsympathetic father-figures. The character of Ronnie (whose material wealth is made manifest in the soft, large body of his son) represents an alternative underclass culture of illicit and individualist economic activity that is at odds with Darcy's philosophy of the clean, immaculate body and his ideal of homosocial brotherhood. However, just as the ailing colliery band in *Brassed Off* is revitalised by the arrival (and financial input) of an initially unwelcome female musician, so Ronnie's underworld affiliations are necessary to actualise the boxing contest, even if this means the contamination of his hallowed homosocial realm. A second malevolent father-figure is Geoff, a father of one of the young boxers, whose mockery of the club's enfranchising potential unleashes Darcy's own aggressive tendencies; his violent attack upon Geoff heralds the extinction of the club, and the beginning of his alcoholic self-destruction.

Darcy's subsequent decline and death epitomises his failure to sustain an idealised homosocial community; like the bandleader Danny of *Brassed Off* – who arises, against the odds, from his sickbed to lead the men to victory in the Albert Hall – his bodily strength is umbilically connected to the diminishment of masculine spaces and traditions. However, if the implicit violence of the general reclamatory project is signalled, the film's coda implies how a tenable homosocial bond has been established, if not a material location. By jointly burning down the hall the lads prevent any further defilement of this idealised space; they are distressed to see a sign that reveals that the hall will shortly become a 'storage facility' and therefore a site of commercial (and therefore 'inauthentic' and non-masculine) activity. A few years later Darcy's funeral brings the men together again, and *TwentyFourSeven* ends with glimpses of repaired homosocial and parental affiliations, including a reconciliation between Geoff and his father.

There are parallels between the fate of Darcy and that of Joe, the recovering alcoholic at the centre of *My Name is Joe* (Ken Loach, 1998). Like Darcy, Joe endeavours to maintain a supportive network for his surrogate children, but finds that his good intentions are destroyed, partly through the ascendancy of forces antipathetic to notions of homosocial loyalty, but also through his own tendency towards violence and alcoholic dependency. Both Joe, who is the captain of an amateur football team, and his romantic suitor Sarah, a Health Visitor, lack children of their own, but are keen to define themselves in terms of their pastoral charges; Sarah jokes that she has 'hundreds and hundreds', and Joe pulls out a picture of his equivalent family in their 'Sunday best'. However, the relationship that develops between Joe and Sarah is problematised by their differing perspectives on the responsibilities of parenthood. When Liam, a member of Joe's football team with a young family of his own, incurs the wrath of a local 'Godfather' figure (McGowan), Joe is given the opportunity to cancel Liam's considerable debt by carrying out a series of drug-running errands. For Sarah, who has a tendency towards interrogation and assessment (traits necessary to her job), such intervention is morally reprehensible, and Joe is thus faced with the unenviable 'choice' between protecting his surrogate son or his burgeoning relationship with Sarah. Distressed by his failure to 'save' either, Joe surrenders any claims to parental responsibility by drinking himself into a stupor, making him too late to save a desperate Liam from committing suicide. Although, by Loachian standards, the conclusion is expectedly bleak, *My Name is Joe* offers a sobering counterpoint to the reassuring fantasies of reanimated fatherhood offered by comic works such as *The Full Monty* and *Brassed Off*.

Overall, these various father-figures prove sadly unsuccessful in their efforts to assert their parental status; they either fail utterly (*My Name is Joe*), or are only rewarded posthumously (*TwentyFourSeven*). In *The Full Monty*, Gaz may have devised an empowering performance, but it could be argued that this feminised him and his pals. Indeed, such 'performance' carries a double and paradoxical function in these films. On the one hand, it is the attempt to reclaim the virility and visibility of the father (the controlling and phallic head of the family). On the other, this performance is performative in Judith Butler's sense (1990), as it troubles the notion of homosocial role-play. Having failed as fathers, these men seek new ways to perform their virility, but only succeed in undermining the idea of virile 'performance', as is clear from the feminisation and/or diminishment of the men which these films lead towards. As I have indicated, a striking aspect of recent social realist cinema is the way in which young children are shown responding to the inadequacies of father-figures. With falling figures pushed to the wings, the stage is now set for the 'angelic boy' to come to the rescue.

Sons and fathers: *Gabriel and Me* and *Billy Elliot*

It has not been uncommon for the social realist film to focus upon a teenage protagonist, but the deployment of a young child as a central character has been relatively rare. The simultaneous occurrence, in the last few years, of a number of boy-centred films is thus deserving of particular scrutiny, especially as some of these films absorb the obsessions with failing fathers and contested homosocial spaces that drive the narratives of contemporary adult-orientated texts such as *The Full Monty*, *Raining Stones* and *Nil by Mouth* (Gary Oldman, 1997). The status of these boys as children, rather than as infantilised adults, gives them a certain capacity for the questioning of their patriarchal inheritance and, indeed, their playful behaviour often places them at odds with parental authority. At the same time, however, the actions undertaken by the boys of *Billy Elliot* and *Gabriel and Me* often betray a desire to reanimate or re-imagine enervated father-figures. These children, having been failed by their own fathers, have taken on the task of revitalising homosocial spaces for themselves. At the same time, their ambivalent relationship to patriarchal traditions and spaces poses the question of whether their 'fathers' – and the spaces they covet – are worth saving.

Jamie Bell as Billy Elliot in *Billy Elliot* (Stephen Daldry, 2000)

The apparently contradictory impulses of these boys, towards both deviation and intervention, can be accommodated by the concept of the 'angel'. The boys of *Billy Elliot*, *Gabriel and Me* and *Ratcatcher* (Lynne Ramsay, 1999) can be described as angelic as they endeavour to locate their own spaces for transcendent play, in flight from a home environment that is posited as traumatic, and a father that is unsympathetic or weak. The angelic status of these boys is accentuated through their associations with literal flight; Billy's balletic movements propel him through space and sometimes beyond the cinematic frame, whilst Jimmy Spud, who imagines himself as an apprentice to the Archangel Gabriel himself, is seen trying to recreate the memory of his father throwing him into the air. In a similar fashion, the older lads of *Purely Belter* take inspiration from Antony Gormley's colossal *Angel of the North* sculpture in their quest to raise money to purchase a football season ticket; they eventually find themselves installed in a position above and beyond the homosocial space they covet. Whilst these boys can be seen as pioneers, they are also 'angelic' in the sense of being driven by a restorative impulse. As we have seen, the adult-centred films of the late 1990s often feature a mentor figure initiating the reconstruction of a threatened male space or relationship, but this role is given more complex significations when taken by a child. If Billy Elliot or Jimmy Spud (*Gabriel and Me*) are guardian angels, innocent saviours casting their protective eye over endangered homosocial space, they are equally divine messengers, giving warning that new models and strategies are necessary for successive male generations. However, these boy-centred films tend to be sanguine about the capability of the angelic child to revive either weakened fathers, or the spaces of homosocial tradition with which they are associated.

Despite being overshadowed, in terms of popular and critical appeal, by *Billy Elliot* – which was penned by the same screenwriter (Lee Hall) and similarly set in the northeast of

England – it is *Gabriel and Me* that emerges as the paradigmatic work of the contemporary boy-centred films through its explicit engagement with the theme of the angelic child. Jimmy's father, an ex-shipyard worker, has contracted cancer; as with the bandleader Danny in *Brassed Off*, the diminishment of his life-force is analogous with the decline of traditional industry in the region, and indicative of the toll unemployment has taken upon the homosocial community. Like *TwentyFourSeven*, the film begins with the presentation of a dead father: 'Me dad died today' is the opening statement of Jimmy's intermittent voice-over. Despite his ailment, the father is not a particularly sympathetic presence in the Spud household, vainly striving to uphold his (rapidly declining) fatherly status by controlling his son's movements; for example, he prevents Jimmy from disappearing upstairs upon his arrival from school, insists that he remains at the dinner table during a meal, and forces him to wear a football strip as a sign of tribal loyalty (the sensitive young protagonist of *Ratcatcher* suffers a similar indignity). The father is also intolerant of expressions of creative individuality (ballet dancers are dismissed as 'poofs'), and he responds to acts of gendered experimentation with barely controlled aggression; when he spies the home-made angel 'frock' that his son is wearing, he assumes a homosexual relationships between Jimmy and a male companion, and proceeds to demolish Jimmy's 'celestial trumpet'. He is not quite the unreconstructed male incarnate, however, for his engravings of seaside views suggest an intuition of post-industrial models of employment. Still, the sequence in which Jimmy's music causes him to destroy the piece he is working on expresses how the transformation of manual skills into a marketable commodity will be an arduous process.

Jimmy's angelic obsession, and, in particular, his desire for flight, can be read as an escapist longing, not dissimilar to Billy Elliot's withdrawal from an oppressively masculinist home environment towards a space that tolerates an ambiguously gendered performance of physical vigour. Yet Jimmy's commitment to angelic activity also stems from a wish to recreate a specific memory of his father throwing up him into the air. This recollection of sea and sky, which bookends *Gabriel and Me*, provides the only glimpse of boundlessness; but, perhaps paradoxically, it is both a moment of transcendence and of restoration, a nostalgic craving for an idealised paternal bond.

Jimmy's interactions with his surrounding environment emphasise further how his angelic tendency invokes the simultaneous reanimation and subversion of spaces of homosocial fellowship, tradition and work. Expelled, as we have seen, from the home, where a suspicion lingers that his transgressive behaviour is aggravating his father's illness, Jimmy takes refuge in a deserted church. It is here that he first conjures up Gabriel as his mentor and confidant, thereby establishing a personal belief system out of a once entrenched, but now enervated, religious hegemony. For Jimmy, this is a space where moral or emotional issues – of the kind he cannot broach with his blood family – can be addressed; it is only with his new mentor that the problem of how to do the 'right thing' can be tackled. The church is also the arena where Jimmy weaves the feathers from his grandfather's pigeon loft into an angel consume. The grandfather's political, religious and cultural musings – he defends ballet-dancers as 'tough as any in the shipyards' – have shown him to belong to a tradition of working-class auto-didacticism that contrasts with the conservatism of his son. However, the verbatim repetition of his slogans by Jimmy reveals them to be as anachronistic a performance as his father's macho displays. Nevertheless, Jimmy's capacity to fashion the pigeon feathers into a new garment insinuates how an outmoded homosocial tradition can be re-fashioned into an ambivalently gendered model of communication, a process that is empathetic rather than political or physical. The site with the most potential for experimentation is the deserted shipyard where Jimmy's father and grandfather were formerly employed. Jimmy dons his angel uniform here and practises flying, at which point the reappearance of his grandfather's dead pigeon prompts him to take wing after it to the top of a crane. From this vantage point, he witnesses a boy scout falling from his bike into the water and swoops down to rescue him. In this manner, a space of traditional male industry is re-appropriated as a transgressive zone where identities are fluid, and where fantasies of rescue can be acted out. Inevitably, Jimmy's father is beyond saving, yet, as he lies in a hospital, a rescue of sorts occurs when he asks Jimmy to 'fly to him'; the boy lies on top of a pillow over his head, thus bringing about a suicidal self-smothering.

In *Gabriel and Me* spaces of homosocial work and tradition are posited as obsolete, but in *Billy Elliot* the law of the father still holds sway, to a degree, within the northern working-class community it depicts. Billy's experimentation with bodily movement places him in conflict with both his immediate family and the wider mining community; the severity of his transgression is encapsulated by the declaration by his boxing trainer that he is a 'disgrace to them gloves, [his] father and the traditions of [the] boxing hall'. Within the predominantly male Elliot household, which contains Billy's brother, father and grandmother, the frustration of Billy's artistic disposition is mirrored by the systematic subjugation of his female antecedents, and the tradition of creativity that they would appear to represent. In one key scene, Billy's father strips the piano belonging to his dead wife for firewood; this is partly an act of financial necessity, but also an expression of the Elliot family's hostility to the violation of homosocial codes.

Set at the time of the miner's strike of 1984, however, *Billy Elliot* communicates how a landscape of masculine ascendancy is undergoing the initial moments of a transformative process. Billy, after all, is reaching adolescence during a time of social flux, an era that could be seen to herald the beginning of the end for the mining industry. Hence, the film depicts an embryonic stage within a process of spatial re-alignment that has come to fruition by the time of *The Full Monty*, when men have no choice but to consider supposedly feminised strategies of enfranchisement. The circumstance of the strike has opened up new spaces of fluidity and experimentation upon a hitherto exclusively homosocial landscape. An emblematic site, in this regard, is the gym building. The use of the 'downstairs' area as soup kitchens for the striking miners has meant that the female ballet class – formerly kept out of sight below the ground – must now share a room with the male boxers. Billy challenges further the homosocial orientation of this space by importing mementoes of his dead mother, and inviting in his homosexual friend Michael, who had previously remained on the outside of the building.

The narrative of *Billy Elliot*, like that of *The Full Monty*, can be best approached in spatial terms; that is, as the development of an empowering performance through an engagement with a series of disputed zones. Billy is witnessed tapping (literally) his immediate environment as a means of generating his escapist strategy; using the home, the exterior spaces of the town and the boxing hall for experimentation with the moving body, he gradually moulds the raw material of uncontrolled gesture into an expressive performance and, more importantly, a marketable resource. The exploratory potential of his immediate landscape proves finite, however, as exemplified by the dance sequence following his argument between his female teacher and his male family members. Billy is seen bursting out of the door of his house, pushing on walls, kicking the ground, and beating his head with his hands, as if railing against bodily and spatial thresholds; his movements come to an abrupt end, though, when he crashes into a steel barrier.

Initially sceptical, Billy's father is eventually persuaded of his son's talent, no doubt intuiting how Billy is involved in the formation of a new model of male athleticism. As such, Billy's achievement is at once a subversion of patriarchal expectation, and also a project of reclamation on his father's behalf, a mission to devise a viable new expression of masculinity. The film's coda, set at the present time, and showing Billy about to take to the stage in a production of *Swan Lake*, allows for an appropriate conclusion to both of these narratives trajectories: Billy's dreams of flight from his father, and the homosocial lineage he personifies, on the one hand; and a (perhaps unconscious) compulsion towards the continuation of this very lineage, on the other. Billy's final positioning upon the indeterminate, non-gendered realm of the theatre stage signals the end of his quest for a fluid, transgressive arena beyond the restrictive landscape of his home town. Yet this ending is also reminiscent of the conclusion of *The Full Monty*, as it implies the successful re-imagining of the male body as a potent force.

Maternal longings: *Sweet Sixteen* and *Ratcatcher*

In contrast with *Gabriel and Me* and *Billy Elliot*, which prescribe methods for the reanimation of homosocial space, other films that incorporate the trope of the angelic boy show their young protagonists devoted instead to the protection of vulnerable female characters and the restoration of foetal, maternal space. The boys of *Sweet Sixteen* and *Pure* (Gillies MacKinnon, 2002) devise comparable strategies for the containment of their respective mothers. In *Sweet Sixteen*, Liam fantasises about their shared habitation of a lakeside caravan, far beyond the reach of her violent, drug-dealing boyfriend, whilst the pre-pubescent saviour of *Pure* imprisons his mother in her bedroom as a means of weaning her off her addiction. The narrative trajectories of both films are essentially Oedipal, for the boys are primarily concerned with saving their mothers from the grip of malevolent father-figures; furthermore, *Sweet Sixteen* concludes with Liam's stabbing of his step-father. Interestingly, these boys are only able to disentangle these drug-addicted women from a pernicious criminal underworld through their very own infiltration of the mob syndicates that have come to replace the former homosocial communities built around shared labour.

Fantasies of rescue, and of the re-imagined, or re-housed family also dominate *Ratcatcher*, a film that contains little in the way of conventional plotting, instead situating its passive protagonist within a suggestive landscape that gives prominence to the processes of regression and flight that are pivotal to the boy-centred films discussed here. *Ratcatcher*, like *Sweet Sixteen*, posits the protective impulse of the angelic protector as not only masochistic, but self-destructive. The protagonist of *Ratcatcher* betrays a vague yearning to safeguard his mother and a local teenage girl named Margaret Anne – her initials alone confirming her quasi-maternal status – who is locked within a cycle of sexual degradation involving a gang of older boys. Aware of his inability to rescue Margaret Anne from the abusive gang, and the unlikelihood of his family becoming residents of a new Greenfield estate (where he has previously romped freely), James would appear to drown himself at the end of the film, succumbing to the polluted canal that has already claimed the life of playmate.

In both *Ratcatcher* and *Sweet Sixteen*, watery spaces – whether the canals of the former, or the ocean-set caravan of the latter – are denoted as womb-like, reassuring yet retrograde. If the defensive impulses of Liam and James are frustrated, their nostalgic cravings are at last satisfied. When last seen, wandering upon the sea-shore on the eve of his sixteenth birthday, a depressed Liam seems likely to follow James in finally breaching the threshold that divides land and water; the energies which he might be expected to channel into the duties of parenthood have already been exhausted by his (non-reciprocated) acts of filial duty.

Like Father

I want to conclude this survey of father/son relationships in contemporary British social realist cinema with an analysis of *Like Father*, a relatively unknown work (made by the Amber film collective in 2001) that nevertheless offers, as the title suggests, the most explicit engagement with the theme of paternal responsibility. I have established a dichotomy between adult-orientated works describing failing fathers divining new means to 'perform', and child-centred works presenting the figure of the angelic boy, taking up the challenge of how to rejuvenate exhausted homosocial spaces (or, in some instances, transferring this reclamatory impulse to the protection of vulnerable mothers). Set in a former mining community in County Durham, and exploring the impact that a coastal redevelopment scheme has for three male generations of one family, *Like Father* is noteworthy for the manner in which it fuses the dominant tropes of both of the adult and child-orientated narratives; it presents a beleaguered paternal relationship from both sides, so to speak.

The central character of *Like Father* is Joe Elliott, a forty-year-old ex-miner who now juggles various jobs as a trumpet player, teacher, club singer and manager of an agency for club acts. Writing on *Billy Elliot*, John Hill notes how 'in a loose allegory of the transition from a manufacturing to a service-based economy, Billy becomes an emblem of economic rejuvenation through participation in the "creative industries"' (see Hill's chapter in this volume). In *Like Father*, Joe's pragmatic ability to evolve a variety of performances rhymes with the processes of regeneration that are transforming his immediate landscape. However, it is Joe's acceptance of these very processes that serves to alienate him from his own father and son. For seventy-year-old Arthur Elliott, the 'Phoenix Project' means the demolition of his allotment and pigeon-loft, and consequently the eradication of the last traces of a traditional working-class community. Arthur becomes estranged from his son when he learns that Joe has been commissioned to write a brass band suite to commemorate the opening of this very scheme. Inspired by the local landscape, and the remembrance of 'pit rhythms', Joe is working – like the lads of *The Full Monty* and *Billy Elliot* – to transform place into performance, a process well suited to the demands of the post-industrial era. With little time left to devote to family life, though, Joe loses contact with his son Michael, a dislocated, unworldly child who is highly sensitive, like Jimmy Spud, to the traumas inflicted upon his family, and upon the wider community.

Michael's role as angelic mediator becomes apparent when the cross-generational crisis comes to a head at the very end of the film. At his desecrated garden allotment, Arthur threatens to kill the head of the redevelopment scheme, but the scuffle that ensues with Joe is terminated when the boy – who has been watching the proceedings from a rooftop – takes a tumble to the ground, and appears to be badly hurt. Instances of the flying boy abound in recent social realist cinema, but skyward leaps, with their associations of transcendence, tend to be more common than rapid descents. In *Like Father*, the angelic boy may have been grounded, but the joint enterprise of the troubled parent and protective child is finally achieved, and the interdependency of father and son asserted.

Like Father concludes with reconciliation between the three generations of Elliot men as they huddle together amidst the rubble of a half-demolished allotment. This final image of a rejuvenated homosocial network is admittedly contrived, and doubtless rather conservative, although there is something overwhelmingly pleasing about this re-establishment of family solidarity at a time when performances of parental power are shown to be as hazardous and fatiguing as acts of filial duty. However, the conclusion of *Like Father* also affirms how the childish impulse for transcendence can all too easily be sacrificed to a project of restoration. The angelic boy ultimately faces a stark choice between flight and family. He can keep his wings, like Billy and Jimmy, but lose a father. Or, like Michael, he can repair a broken patriarchal lineage by crashing, painfully, to earth.

With one foot on the ground, the other in the air (or in water), the complex positioning of the angelic child in relation to his environment can be further recognised as emblematic of the relationship between these recent boy-centred films and the British social realist tradition in general. The angelic boy is both spatial pioneer, subverting or rejecting his patriarchal lineage, and inheritor of the tradition of homosocial reclamation that has dominated the social realist film from the New Wave to the present. The protagonists of *Saturday Night and Sunday Morning* (Tony Richardson, 1960) and *The Full Monty* alike could be said to be troublemakers, querying the rigid demarcations of their environment, but they are ultimately involved in a project of rejuvenation that is suspiciously conservative. With the boy-centred works, the charge of triumphant masculinism that dogs the reclamatory narrative is evaded through the positioning of the central character upon the threshold between childhood and adulthood. The angelic boy is permitted to be parental saviour, and protector of homosocial tradition, but also to contemplate his escape from terrestrial responsibility.

SECTION 1 STARS

SECTION 2 CLASS & RACE

SECTION 3 FATHERS

SECTION 4 BODIES

chapter 15

QUEER LOOKS, MALE GAZES, TAUT TORSOS AND DESIGNER LABELS: CONTEMPORARY CINEMA, CONSUMPTION AND MASCULINITY

Pamela Church Gibson

Film and fashion, image and consumption

It might seem difficult to make any firm pronouncement about current modes of masculine behaviour, but it is, surely, possible to make just one categorical assertion: young Western men are avid consumers. The dramatic rise over the last twenty years in their spending habits, particularly on clothes and 'toiletries', has been eagerly charted by receptive retailers. And if there has always been a close, complex and symbiotic relationship between film and fashion, between image and consumption, it is now, arguably, stronger than ever before. It is hardly novel to discuss the ways in which shifting mores are reflected through the popularity of particular stars, changing physical types and new modes of self-presentation; but few writers have stressed the way in which stars have provided not only a showcase for fashions, but a push towards specific types of consumption.

This chapter will tentatively explore contemporary images of masculinity; it seeks to analyse the way in which film texts and fashion culture currently intertwine, underpinning the configuration of the young male consumer, and it will bring together the work done within film scholarship and that within the wider remit of 'cultural studies'.

A number of film theorists moved swiftly to deploy the insights provided by Judith Butler and others. In 1993, Yvonne Tasker argued for the use of 'terms like performativity and masquerade' (Tasker 1993: 11) and the importance of Joan Riviere's essay on 'Womanliness as Masquerade' (Riviere 1929) for *any* work on gender. Discussing the 'muscular hero', who offers 'a parodic performance of masculinity', Tasker asks whether these presently ubiquitous images 'repeat, mourn, or hysterically state a lost male power?' (Tasker 1993: 109). In the same year, Christine Holmlund wrote of 'the multiple masquerade' of contemporary masculinity, 'a series of interlocking masquerades' where masculine power and authority is conveyed through a series of 'costume props', and the over-developed male body seen on screen provides 'the hyper-spectacle of muscular masculinity itself' (Holmlund 1993: 222). Here Holmlund is describing the career of Sylvester Stallone, whose own original inspiration for his re-creation as 'hyper-spectacle' was – inevitably – cinematic: 'I grew up watching *Spartacus* [Stanley Kubrick, 1960] … and Steve Reeves' (Faludi 1999: 296). Now, with the shifts in fashionable body shape over the past decade or more, the wildly exaggerated musculature of the bodybuilder has been replaced by the subtler tyranny of the highly-toned male torso currently on display.

Conversely, significantly, the bodies of very slender, often androgynous young men are frequently found in fashion magazines and elsewhere. These boys also have some cinematic currency; soft-featured stars designed to appeal to a younger audience are often created within this mould. Since the 1980s, this particular physical type has shared space on the catwalks and in the fashion spreads with the muscled male body, although it has not passed into mainstream visual currency in quite the same way, confined mostly to images advertising fashion-related products.

Abigail Solomon-Godeau discusses both the past and present co-existence of these oppositional physical types, the 'ephebic male' and the highly-muscled man in her study of post-revolutionary French painting. She asks what these 'equally "successful" icons of manhood' and their 'cohabitation in the pages of the same magazines' should be taken to signify. If we extend her scrutiny to recent cinematic texts, of course, the ephebic boy is less 'successful'. She traces this 'languorous Versace boy' back to the statue of the Capitoline Faun, and the 'caricatured priapism … the aggressive phallicism' exemplified in contemporary mass culture by the figure of 'the penis-headed Joe Camel' can similarly be followed back through historical example 'to the Hercules of Farnese' (Solomon-Godeau 1997: 21–3). These two diametrically opposed archetypes will be discussed within the context of the cinematic case studies. Firstly, however, some consideration of the complex relationship between film and fashion is necessary.

Looking and wanting

In the past two decades there have been new and significant shifts in the nature of the relationship between film and fashion. Many male Hollywood stars are now involved, however peripherally, in the popularising of fashionable images as much, if not more, than their female counterparts of the past. It is they who command the largest salaries, who have the most power at the box office, who create – or reinforce – shifts in the idea of what constitutes a 'desirable' male body. Lastly, the way in which fashion houses use the cinema to display their wares has become much more commercial within this very same timeframe.

A significant proportion of recent work within cultural history has been centred around the gay consumer – while the self-proclaimed 'heterosexual' younger man, who also shops for clothes every weekend, has been studied less thoroughly. Cinema and Video Audience Research (CAVIAR) studies show that it is young men who visit the cinema most regularly and form the mainstay of transatlantic audiences, perceived by studio executives as their prime target market.[1] Most mainstream films are specifically designed to appeal to this particular audience.

During the past two decades much of men's fashion has been film-led, sometimes film-inspired, while most magazines directed at the male consumer have drawn overtly on cinema for their fashion spreads, whether in styling, concept or both. Yet the full extent of these links are not reflected in the critical literature around it. Much of the work within cultural studies examines patterns of male consumption during the 1980s and, to a lesser extent, the early and mid-1990s, and focuses on new trends in journalism, photography, advertising and retailing, while ignoring the mainstream films made during this period. Yet these films were intended to reach the very consumers under critical investigation, forming specifically designed 'offer' to place beside the new clothes, the style magazines and the radically redesigned retail spaces, and were consumed just as avidly as print journalism and expensive sportswear.

The film *American Gigolo* (Paul Schrader, 1980) was the first to showcase fashion for men in a radically new way. Historian Richard Martin describes the film as a pivotal moment in the return of the sartorially conscious male. Indeed, he suggests that it may be the 'single most significant moment' in the revival of menswear (Martin 1990: 10). Julian, played by Richard Gere, the 'gigolo' of the title, provided the audience, in a famous scene, with a lesson in fashion styling and colour co-ordination. Preparing for a date, Julian spreads a selection of clothes from his well-stocked wardrobe (provided by Armani) across the bed, in order to decide which tie to wear with which shirt, which jacket with which trousers. No man, gay or straight, in the history of the cinema had ever before been seen making this type of considered decision about what to wear, and certainly not luxuriating in it as Julian does here. While he is presented throughout as rampantly narcissistic and morally flawed, he is, nevertheless, the hero, and as such can legitimate the pleasures of dress and self-adornment. At one point we glimpse the Armani label inside the collar of a shirt, something not lost on the designer himself, who was to involve himself more and more with films, and with their stars, in a variety of ways.

Another concrete, commercial example is *Top Gun* (Tony Scott, 1986), which not only made Rayban Aviator sunglasses so desirable, and gave them a large share of the youth market, but made the flying jacket so ubiquitous. Sean Nixon, in his consideration of masculinity and consumption in the 1980s, discusses the contribution of the stylist Ray Petrie to the new codings of masculinity. Nixon's work charts the minor revolution that took place in the 1980s: the disruptive and seemingly irreversible change in the depiction of the male in photography and advertising, and the emergence of a new breed of male consumer. Nixon attributes the extraordinary popularity of the flying jacket to the work of stylist Ray Petrie in the pages of the new 'style magazines'. He claims that Petrie's 'styling of the MA-1 flight jacket' turned the item into an essential element of 'tough street style' (Nixon 1996: 181).

But arguably the cheaper copies of the jacket available on every high street, and its desirability, had more to do with Tom Cruise than Ray Petrie. In 1986, in the week when *Top Gun* opened in London, the Top Man 'flagship store' at Oxford Circus had themed windows based on the iconography of the American armed forces and images of aerial combat. Paul Burston writes of the film that 'it brought the fetishisation of flying jackets out of the gay clubs and onto the high street' (Burston 1995: 117).

Questions of spectatorship, narcissism, gender and the nature of the gaze within these new emerging patterns of male depiction and consumption are, of course, comprehensively discussed by Nixon and others. Here we should flag the question of who could be looking at whom in the male-oriented films of the 1980s and 1990s; and what it might have to do with fashion, even if there are no straightforward answers. Notions of masquerade, performance, display and of the queer looks that can form a part of any avowedly straight spectatorship, are possibly the best guide through the maze.[2]

Nixon's book shows clearly the centrality of one kind of male body during the 1980s; he writes of 'the new importance of a solid muscular body' rather than the exaggerated Ramboesque physique (Nixon 1996: 192). This body, characterised by what he calls 'hardened musculature' (Nixon 1996: 204) is still dominant, still desirable. He does not, however, discuss the oppositional and 'ephebic' male body, also important in the 1980s, although he does devote several pages to the floppy-haired nostalgic version of 'Edwardian Englishness', important in fashion styling of the period and deriving directly from the heritage film of the period (Nixon 1996: 188–91).

Nor does Nixon connect this 'hardened musculature' with that which characterised the cinematic heroes of the decade he depicts, and which continues into the present. However, Jonathan Rutherford, writing in and of 1988, did note the existence of certain contemporaneous cinematic models, and asked what they might mean in relation to the 'New Man', supposedly dominant at the time. He notes the ubiquity of the image of Rambo, bare-chested, wielding a vast weapon, his maverick status clearly shown by the bandanna tied round his head. This he sees as exemplifying 'hysterical assertions of maleness' (Rutherford 1996: 29). He could also have described – although he makes no allusion to it – the growing popularity of the former Austrian bodybuilding champion, Arnold Schwarzenegger.

Rutherford talks of the co-existence of what he calls 'Retributive Man' – personified by Rambo – and the heavily-promoted 'New Man'. He also ponders the significance of the toys popular at that time, the huge sales of the 'Masters of the Universe' toys, 'He-Man' figures, and Transformers, all male and all 'retributive' (ibid.). Interestingly, these toys were part of the formative years of those who now form the majority of today's audiences.

Re-reading *Male Order*, what is most significant is the contemporary awareness of what Nixon describes as the 'fracturing and sexualisation of the male body' (Nixon 1996: 201) and the realisation that, as Marcus van Ackerman, then editor of *Elle Pour Homme* said in interview: 'Younger men aren't afraid to look at themselves any more' (van Ackerman in Rutherford 1996: 38). Nor, it seemed, were they afraid of looking openly at the newly-proliferating images of other men, whose 'aquiline features' and 'well-rounded musculature' were, as Rowena Chapman wrote, 'a common denominator of the 1980s, a sign of the sexual times' (Chapman 1996: 226).

The implications of this overt and newly acceptable male-on-male looking are described by Nixon as a 'ruptural organisation of spectatorship' which he describes as drawing on 'forms of looking formerly associated with gay men, without re-inscribing the binary split between "gay" and "straight"' (Nixon 1996: 201). This new spectatorship, whereby men can look openly at the bodies of other men, was reinforced within the popular cinema of the period.

The mainstream Hollywood films of this period that met with most commercial success were not in themselves 'ruptural'; they were action pictures, with a strong male protagonist facing up to an impressive adversary, sometimes alone, sometimes with a sidekick. What was interesting, and what is vital for any discussion of contemporary masculinity, was the number and popularity of these films, and their sequels. *Lethal Weapon* (Richard Donner, 1987) and *Die Hard* (John McTiernan, 1988) both have as their central protagonist a 'retributive man' in the form of a maverick cop. Unlike their predecessors these anti-heroes – Riggs, played by Mel Gibson, and McClane, played by Bruce Willis – have a sense of humour. They are men whose relationships, both personal and professional, border at times on the dysfunctional; both are therefore perfectly equipped to move through endless action set-pieces and continually endanger their lives in the pursuit of justice, the dispatching of drug-dealers and the trapping of terrorists, wisecracking the while. These heroes retained their appeal: *Die Hard With a Vengeance* (John McTiernan), the third in the series, was made in 1995, and *Lethal Weapon 4* (Richard Donner) in 1998.

Both heroes, despite their hard, muscular bodies, which are displayed to advantage, seem completely indifferent to their appearance. Riggs/Gibson wears either a battered leather jacket or deliberately unfashionable sportswear; McClane/Willis sports a grubby white singlet for most of his on-screen time in all three films.

Paradoxically, it is possible that it was this very disregard for personal grooming which made these two heroes so attractive to young male audiences. They were so different from the polished and manicured specimens of masculinity now surrounding them in magazines and on billboards. Similarly, just as the body of the hero was now automatically exhibited on screen, either slender and boyish or taut, highly muscular, and smooth, so in the next decade there was one important exception: the 'transgressive', unruly body of John Travolta. His career was revitalised by his appearance in *Pulp Fiction* (Quentin Tarantino, 1994), a commercial success which achieved cult status. In it, he plays Vincent, the long-haired, long-gone-to-seed hitman. At one point Vincent and his partner, Jules (Samuel L. Jackson) have to strip to their underpants in order that they can be hosed down to remove the blood and brains staining their clothes. This is an extraordinary sequence, since Travolta's earlier success, in the late 1970s, was arguably due to the presentation and spectacle of his lithe dancer's body, clad in slick black leather in *Grease* (Randal Kleiser, 1978) and a sharp white suit in *Saturday Night Fever* (John Badham, 1977). Now he stood, semi-naked, pudgy and unhealthy-looking; just next to his plump white chest and rounded belly was the sharply contrasting torso of Samuel L. Jackson, well-muscled, highly-toned, and black. This deliberate emphasis on Jackson's 'otherness' and the hint at the fetishisation of the black male body described by Paul Jobling among others (Jobling 1999: 152–7) was intended to shock.

Travolta's defiance of the 'body fascism' of Hollywood might explain his appeal to his younger male fans; maybe they need one comforting reminder of male imperfection. The significance of Travolta, his image, and his popularity will be returned to below, in the discussion of the film *Face/Off*.

Action men change gear

The action film dominated both decades. In the 1990s, however, new action heroes appeared, more sartorially aware and able to combine sharp dressing with fisticuffs and worse. They were not always 'heroes'; some central protagonists, like Vincent and others who followed, were far more ambivalent, more morally suspect. Indeed, one of the interesting phenomena to be traced within 1980s and 1990s films is a gradual blurring of boundaries between pursuer and pursued. In the past, Hollywood generic conventions had demanded that the private eye be subdued in his dress, and gangsters instantly identifiable by their overly smart suits, their dark shirts and light ties, their clothes expensive but slightly too opulent, too loud. The tradition of the stylish gangster continues into the present on both sides of the Atlantic, as can be seen in Guy Ritchie's snazzily-dressed anti-heroes.[3] However, what is especially interesting within cinema over the past twenty years is the appropriation of this particular sharp-suited, hard-edged style by the heroes, flawed or otherwise. Wearing recognisable designer menswear is no longer a reliable indicator of incipient psychotic behaviour. In *The Untouchables* (Brian de Palma, 1987), the band assembled by Elliot Ness to take on Al Capone are as stylish as their adversaries. The four men are dressed by Armani, the designer who dominated the decade and who ensured that his name took up half the screen in the opening credits.

The move into the 1990s saw the appearance of a media phenomenon swiftly christened the 'New Lad'. Unlike 'New Man', who helped with the housework or changed nappies, New Lad was 'unreconstructed'; what made him 'new' was his fondness for fashion and his interest in designer labels. Sean Nixon notes the appearance in the early 1990s of *Loaded*, the new magazine specifically targeted at the 'lad'; since 'no new heterosexual scripts were forged in the 1980s' a space was left for the 'return of that particular repressed'(Nixon 1996: 206). He does not mention, however, another growth area in magazine journalism: the birth of publications such as *Mens Health*, *FHM Bionic* and *ZM* ('Health and More For Men'). These promise to deliver that 'hardened musculature' which in the 1990s moved seamlessly from fashion spreads and cinema into mainstream advertising. The other notable feature of magazine journalism in the 1990s was the growing number of magazines devoted to popular cinema and its stars.

These contradictions and co-existences, related patterns of consumerism and the portrayal of contemporary masculinity might best be drawn to closure through a focus on two films from the end of the 1990s, which operate in very different ways. *Fight Club* was runner-up for Best Film of 1999 in the Empire Readers' Awards, while the same magazine had described *Face/Off* as 'arguably the best high-concept action picture ever made' (Anon. 1997: 39). These credentials mean that they were enormously popular with the 18–35 male audience, the core readership of *Empire*.

Face/Off could be said to celebrate fashion by making stylish clothes part of the 'masquerade of masculinity' presented within the film. *Fight Club*, in contrast, is structured not only around a depiction of the current 'crisis in masculinity', but a critique of a consumption-obsessed society; the particular 'crisis' within the film is actually precipitated by socio-economic conditions. Both films show two men confronting their alter egos, their *doppelgängers* even, and therefore give us some insight into the cinematic presentation of conflicts within the male psyche.

Face/Off and *Fight Club*

Face/Off, starring John Travolta and Nicolas Cage, illustrates the ideas of 'masculine' behaviour that inform contemporary cinema; it also provides a perfect example of the new relationship between cinema and fashion. This film was the first so far in the UK to have two separate premieres: one for film reviewers, the other for selected members of the 'style press', who were each given a chic wooden box, almost identical to that shown in the film, in which Cage, the snazzy *Über*-terrorist, keeps his gold-plated guns, his Raybans,

Nicolas Cage in *Face/Off* (John Woo, 1997)

various brightly-coloured pills, a packet of Chiclets, and some ready-rolled spliffs. (The journalists had to forego both guns and drugs.)

As in so many recent films, the law enforcer, played by Travolta, is now flawed and fallible, his emotional life as sterile as that of his antagonist. Only by confronting and defeating his adversary can he repair his fractured 'manhood'. The 'Face Off' is, of course, a horrible pun. It refers to the usual John Woo deadlock, where two men hold loaded guns at one another's heads; neither can shoot or both will die. The lawman, Archer/ Travolta, must impersonate his opponent to obtain information. He therefore subjects himself to plastic surgery, and in a bizarre scientific process, his own face is taken off and replaced by that of his worst enemy, the terrorist, Castor Troy/Cage who murdered Archer's young son, Mikey, six years earlier in a botched attempt to kill Archer himself. Now, as a result of the first confrontation sequence here, Troy is reduced to a vegetative state, comatose in a hospital bed.

Inevitably, Troy recovers, and manages to don the discarded face of his enemy. The two men end up inhabiting each other's bodies and faces, living each other's lives. The psychological ramifications are endless; here, it is important to stress that only by inhabiting the body of the other can each man sort out the problems created by the earlier behaviour of the other, and thus compensate for his own personal shortcomings. Masquerading as his enemy the terrorist, Travolta can put right the situation of the child Troy/Cage fathered and neglected. Disguised as the law enforcer, Troy/Cage can sexually gratify Archer/Travolta's neglected wife, and teach Archer's daughter, also overlooked in her father's obsessive hunt for her brother's killer, how to deal with her various problems. 'You've been hiding behind a mask ever since Mikey died', he tells her as he surveys her heavily made-up, pierced face.

At the end of the film, Archer/Travolta survives to give Troy/Cage's son a home and family. It seems that only by being temporarily merged with another man can a fractured *fin-de-siècle* hero solve the problems of his flawed masculinity. He must be a macho fighter, a sexual athlete, a caring husband and a nurturing father, this only being possible when two men's lives are briefly fused. And the last action set-piece shows that it is only with extreme difficulty that the law enforcer, rational man, can expunge his enemy, the very embodiment of the id. He has to use a harpoon gun; and even then his adversary clings onto life, trying to destroy the 'good' face he wears with a massive knife, to prevent its passing back to its rightful owner.

Indeed, it might not be too fanciful to suggest that there is a curious ambiguity around the very last shots. As Archer, his 'own' face restored to him, returns to home and family, he is seen in profile through the porch window, and then appears, framed in the doorway, strangely lit and with a half-smile on his face. For a moment the audience is forced to ask which of the two men is, finally, welcomed back into the family? The father and lawmaker, or the libidinous usurper? In Troy's time in the house, of course, his main pleasure in occupying Archer's property and sleeping with Archer's wife derived from the fact that both 'belonged' to the other man. The film also plays with the physicality of the two bodies – and the difference between Cage's sinewy physique and Travolta's plumper form. 'We'll have to get rid of those love handles', remarks the police surgeon, as he prepares to graft Cage's face onto Travolta's body. All these psychological ramifications make for an uneasy ending, and much food for thought around the notion of male authority, male desire, masculine identity.

Yet the film works wonderfully as fashion commercial. The clothes worn throughout this film by Cage and Travolta were especially provided by Donna Karan Menswear. The *pièce de resistance* is the long black overcoat which billows dramatically around Cage as he strides across the tarmac towards a getaway plane. The picture generated considerable interest on both sides of the Atlantic, and the clothes had a similar impact. In England, men's magazines courted by the firm responded; *Arena* and *GQ* both ran photoshoots inspired by the film. Fraser Conlon, Head of PR for Donna Karan in New York, explained the relationship between fashion house and film world. For him, the films for which they decide to offer the clothes 'make our statement – a particular kind of style' and have at their centre a certain kind of star.[4]

Moreover, the film is as visually stylish and nastily ironic in its use of cultural capital as any provocative, award-winning commercial. Cage, disguised as a priest, fondles the buttocks of a teenage girl during a rehearsal of Handel's *Messiah*; and Cage-as-Archer advances, bent on revenge and murder, up a beach, to the accompaniment of Allegri's *Miserere*.

In *Fight Club,* the protagonist is a nameless Narrator (Ed Norton) who is restless and resentful. He works in an insurance company and lives in a 'condo' that is a shrine to consumerism. As he tells us in the voice-over, he has everything from IKEA he could possibly want, even down to the (unused) blue glass bowls stacked in his cupboard, their uneven bubbles showing us their authenticity – 'handblown by very ethnic people from somewhere or other'. Plagued by insomnia, he starts to visit self-help groups for the terminally ill, in an effort to relieve his own terminal boredom. Then he meets Tyler Durden (Brad Pitt), his anarchic alter ego, and listens to him talk of the 'lost generation of men' to which both belong, 'a generation raised by women'. Outside a bar, on a

Brad Pitt looking mean in *Fight Club* (David Fincher, 1999)

sudden whim, Tyler suggests that the Narrator hit him hard, and returns the blow. Both thrilled by the adrenalin rush, they start 'Fight Club', illicit bare-knuckle boxing, for any men who want to participate. Tyler lectures his growing band of acolytes on the horrors of compulsive consumption. He explains to them: 'Advertising has us chasing cars and clothes, doing jobs we hate to buy shit we don't need.' He deliberately eschews fashionable clothes in favour of a motley collection of thrift shop purchases. He uses the foolishness of the fashion-conscious to make a living; he manufactures his own soap, which he sells to up-market retail outlets. The fat he uses is purloined from the garbage cans of cosmetic surgeons, extracted from 'patients' during liposuction. As the narrator explains, 'Tyler was selling those rich women their own fat right back to them'. The film works as an attack on an image-obsessed society dominated by a desire for possessions and controlled by faceless corporations. In an impassioned speech, Tyler attacks a society characterised by a 'Starbucks on every corner'; the men he forms into a private army, 'Project Mayhem', are finally instructed to blow up the headquarters of credit-card companies. However, the film is far more complex, and arguably has more to do with notions of masculinity than with an assault on global capitalism.

As the bodies of Pitt and Norton become stronger and battle-scarred, Tyler/Pitt sneers at a Gucci underwear advertisement he sees on a bus. 'Is that what they think a real man looks like?', he asks. In the very next frame, we see Pitt's own perfectly-muscled torso; his body is framed by the other men in the scene in such a way that our gaze is drawn inexorably towards him. As in so many films, Pitt's body is fetishised, offered up, commodified. As the situation starts to spiral out of control, Pitt/Tyler is finally forced to explain to the narrator that he, Tyler, does not really exist; he is the fantasy wish-fulfilment of the Narrator, who does all the things that the Narrator would like to do but cannot. 'Think about it', advises Tyler. 'I fight like you want to fight. I fuck like you want to fuck.' He could have added: 'And I have a body like the one you want to have.' For Tyler/Pitt is shown throughout bare-chested, slightly sweaty, firmly-muscled and bronzed, in deliberate contrast to the rather pallid, unremarkable body of the Narrator/Norton. And despite the Narrator-as-Tyler's energetic couplings with the neurotic Marla (Helena Bonham-Carter), which threaten, quite literally, to destroy the 'home' the two men share, making the ceilings disintegrate and the walls crack, it could be argued that now the Narrator has dreamt up Tyler's perfect body he wants to 'have' it, in every sense of the word.

Conclusion

Both films take a standard Hollywood format, and push it to the limits, and beyond. *Face/Off* takes one familiar plot device – supercop versus ultimate adversary – and if the visual pyrotechnics of the director are what originally attracted both backers and marketing men, their instincts were right; the combination of Woo's authorial style and the clothes worn by both men made the film a financial success. But its appeal must go further; the questions it raises around masculinity are so clearly spelt out as to be clear to any audience. Two men who both wear slick, desirable clothes, who wield a range of enormous weapons, can only reach some kind of resolution or satisfaction through a strange fusion. *Fight Club* takes another Hollywood narrative staple, and provides a most bizarre version of the 'buddy movie' – murky, moralistic, even misogynist. Both of these films were tremendously popular with the very same young men, the 'lost generation' of 'men raised by women' who were the subject of Tyler's rhetoric and whom he wished to save. In both films, men are seen as defined absolutely through their 'desire' for another man, whatever form that desire may take. In one film, male outfits and weaponry take centre screen, while in the other it is the stripped-for-action male body that provides the visual pleasure of the film.

The 'masculine-masculine look' is curiously problematic, however. As one gay male journalist notes in a telling paragraph:

> Pastel pink and baby blue are everywhere … though only a Brad Pitt with knuckle-boxing skills could get by with a fluffy pink dressing gown (see *Fight Club*). Trouble is, such looks are now so butch that soon gay men will be dropping squaddies and bikers as role models and adopting Brad and Beckham instead. Then where will we be? God knows, but that's the queer, queer world of men's fashion. (Field 2000: 27)

Perhaps it is the very 'queerness' of this world that has led to a backlash of sorts. A number of recent films, such as war films, rely on what are, in fact, old-fashioned, unreconstructed models of masculinity. Even the epic has been resurrected to display such behaviour. In *Gladiator* (Ridley Scott, 2000) the heroic warrior and family man Maximus (Russell Crowe) finally defeats the decadent Commodus (Joaquin Phoenix). Commodus, a parricide with incestuous desires, has a penchant for lining his eyes with kohl. Could it be that the film is trying to show the final victory of the 'Hercules of Farnese' over 'the ephebic boy'?

Interestingly, problematically, within the world of fashion advertising the two archetypes began to fuse in 2002. Calvin Klein's underwear campaign of June of that year featured a young, blonde male model, Travis, whose looks are a combination of these two archetypes. He has a highly-muscled torso, a confident stance, and his sizeable genitalia are clearly outlined by the white underpants he wears. Yet he has a soft, almost feminine face, here framed by long fronds of hair, and a thong of leather around his neck. His gaze is gentle, disarming, without threat but infused with a complex sexual content. His is an extraordinary image, for it captures all the contradictory desires that encircle and confuse the contemporary young man. It will be interesting to see if the cinema chooses to take up the particular challenge it seems to offer.

Notes

1   See McIntyre 1995 for a comprehensive analysis of the CAVIAR statistics. He confirms that we can safely assume that the majority of Anglo-American audiences are between 16 and 30: this trend has been identified as a feature of the last twenty years.

2   Evans and Gamman 1995 give a comprehensive account of the ramifications of the debates around the gaze. Most importantly, they suggest ways forward.

3   Guy Ritchie's films *Lock, Stock and Two Smoking Barrels* (1999) and *Snatch* (2001) were not only extremely popular with young men both in the UK and the US; they also led to a slew of magazine features around 'gangster chic'. The iconic Brad Pitt, no less, asked if he might appear in the second film, and waived his usual fee.

4   Fraser Conlon, Head of PR for Donna Karan in New York, interview with the author, 1999.

chapter 16

THE MALE BODY AND THE FEMALE GAZE IN CARMEN FILMS

Ann Davies

This chapter proposes a reversal of the prevalence of the female body as the erotic object of a normative, dominant male gaze, in order to consider the male body as spectacle for women to look at. The prospect of such a reversal is not new. Ever since Laura Mulvey (1975) claimed that the gaze was male, debate has continued as to whether women can ever hold the gaze. This debate has tended to emphasise women off-screen, as spectators and audience members, but some attention has also been given to whether on-screen women can command the gaze and look at the male. Both Mary Ann Doane and Linda Williams have discussed the heroines of women's pictures and horror films who look and are punished for looking, arguing that this female gaze is one of curiosity rather than of power (as with the male gaze) (see Doane 1987; Williams 1984). Williams has nonetheless briefly discussed – and dismissed – the potential power of the challenging stare of the femme fatale or vamp in contrast to the pure heroine. She argues that the 'failure and frustration of [the heroine's] vision can be the most important mark of her sexual purity' (Williams 1984: 83), indicating that the female command of the gaze is sexually transgressive. If the femme fatale suggests sexual transgression we might consequently assume that her gaze wields power. But the gaze of the femme fatale is not, on Williams's understanding, an authentically female gaze but rather an imitation of a male gaze:

> The bold, smouldering dark eyes of the silent screen vamp offer an obvious example of a powerful female look. But the dubious moral status of such heroines, and the fact that they must be punished in the end, undermine the legitimacy and authentic subjectivity of this look, frequently turning it into a female parody of the male look. (Williams 1984: 85)

This argument immediately begs the question of what an authentic female gaze might actually consist of. But at any event, the possibility that the gaze of the femme fatale might be no more than parody does not preclude its potential to cause real anxiety in the male characters who form the object of the gaze. I would like to posit the idea that the need for punishment of the femme fatale suggested by Williams arises not so much from the female possession of the gaze as from the need to compensate for the inadequacy of the male body that forms the object of the gaze. In what follows I want briefly to consider what happens to a male protagonist under scrutiny when a very well-known femme fatale gazes back at him and usurps the powerful male gaze. As the title of my paper suggests, this well-known femme fatale is Carmen, of Bizet's famous opera (1875) above all and, before that, the original novella by Prosper Mérimée (1845). The Carmen figure and narrative have both proved very popular in Western cinema, being the basis of nearly eighty films to date since cinema's inception. The constant return of the cinema to this narrative (to say nothing of the immense popularity of Bizet's opera) immediately suggests the fascination with this particular femme fatale.

In the original story by Mérimée, Carmen comes to us third hand, interpreted first as the male protagonist don José sees her and then in turn interpreted through the anonymous (male) narrator who has come to know him. This structure implies Carmen as the object of multiple male gazes. But despite the attempt of men to tell her story for her – to say nothing of the virulent misogyny underlying the text[1] – Carmen proves such a powerful character that she usurps the control of the men and of the story too. She usurps the narrative space, placing herself out of the power of both men so that don José can only wrest power back through physical violence (her murder). When we turn to film versions of the narrative we discover that, among other things, a particular significance of this filmic corpus is Carmen's capacity to usurp the gaze as well. Although many films (and the opera, too) introduce us to José first and then present Carmen as the object of his gaze, she wrests the male gaze away from its possessor and challenges it. Indeed, in some films – such as the versions directed by Ernst Lubitsch (*Carmen*, 1919), Raoul Walsh (*The Loves of Carmen*, 1927), Charles Vidor (*The Loves of Carmen*, 1948), Otto Preminger (*Carmen Jones*, 1954) and Francesco Rosi (*Carmen*, 1984) – Carmen spots José first and singles him out from the rest of the masculine crowd as the object of her gaze. One or two directors also highlight Carmen's usurpation of the gaze in specific scenes. For example, in Preminger's *Carmen Jones*, Carmen confidently gazes from the balcony of Billy Pastor's at the boxer Husky Miller (the equivalent of the bullfighter Escamillo in Bizet's opera), who is immediately attracted to her; while Francesco Rosi's Carmen actually uses a mirror to spotlight the bullfighter Escamillo as the erotic object of her gaze.

Since in most of the films Carmen functions as a sexual object, her female body draws attention and consequently should in theory render the male body invisible. But her gaze directs attention back at the male body as an object of her desire, and that body proves wanting. Version after version emphasises the constant failure of the male body to subordinate itself to the manly duties of military discipline, since José neglects his duties as a soldier through his desire for Carmen. This neglect often reveals itself in a deterioration in appearance: many Josés become unshaven and ragged, usually as a result of their outlaw life in the mountains, undertaken because their sexual desire for Carmen drove them to break the law and to kill. Some Carmen films also underscore the inadequacy of the male body specifically in sexual terms. Joseph's impotence in the shower scene of Jean-

Luc Godard's *Prénom Carmen* (1983) suggests this, as does – in a more comic vein – the impossibly long scabbard of Charlie Chaplin's Darn Hosiery (in his *Burlesque on Carmen*, 1916) that hides his ridiculously short sword. In the Max Sennett comedy *The Campus Carmen* (Harry Edwards, 1928) a woman (Carole Lombard) takes over the role of José, both personifying and parodying the male body: the male body disappears altogether. The degeneration of the body of the male protagonist parallels Carmen's movement further and further away from the orbit of his desire; and his body – the object of the female gaze – proves inadequate to retain her love or attention.

Rather than simply give a catalogue of examples of the inadequate male body and the powerful female gaze through the gamut of Carmen films, I want to study in greater detail how the two phenomena are connected in one specific film, in this case Carlos Saura's *Carmen* of 1983. Saura's film uses flamenco dance and music as a vehicle for the retelling of Carmen's tale; and the use of dance must in itself foreground the body and its capacity to perform, regardless of who specifically is gazing at it. Ramsay Burt has argued that, in dance in general, the male body as object of the gaze is problematic. Dance shares with film the compulsion towards a normative, dominant male gaze, which the male dancer deflects on to his female partner, thus drawing attention away from his own body; but he also comes between the audience and the female object of his and their gaze, getting in the way (Burt 1995: 8, 27–8). This contradiction indicates that the dancing male body remains a flickering presence at the edge of our vision – there and not there, but with the capacity to disrupt the dominant gaze. More specifically, flamenco dance has a parallel difficulty with the male dancer who is 'there and not there'. Discussion of flamenco generally tends to repeat a traditional division of labour in which men sing – laying claim to the voice but disavowing the body – and women dance, thus functioning as the object of spectacle in the time-honoured way, as suggested by William Washabaugh (1998). Men do, in fact, dance flamenco but appear to go unnoticed in this traditional division. Washabaugh, however, also goes on to observe that, while male flamenco dancers appear to embody traditionally masculine characteristics of strength, aggression and composure (in other words, rationality), they may also use gender-bending dance techniques that imply feminine dance and even striptease (Washabaugh 1998: 45–7) and thus also imply the male dancer as object of an erotic gaze. Washabaugh suggests that men dance in this way for other men, both as a form of bonding and of competition (Washabaugh 1998: 49), but the male flamenco dancer as erotic spectacle also offers women the opportunity to gaze in their turn.[2] The gaze of Carmen will dislodge the body of the male dancer from its location on the periphery and reposition it centre stage.

At first glance it might seem like cheating to use Saura's film to exemplify the inadequate male body under pressure to perform from the female gaze since, as we have seen, dance and specifically flamenco foreground the male dancer anyway as problematic. But for a film that tells its tale through the bodily movement of flamenco dance, there is a great deal of looking going on – static, concentrated gazes. Even when people dance we see the eyes in close-up as much as the movement of feet and hands. Saura's film thus comes to epitomise the importance to Carmen films of both the powerful female gaze and the performance of the male body under stress, and reveals the intricate connection between the two. From the very beginning of the film Saura equates the gaze with power. In the opening pre-credits sequence we encounter the principal male character Antonio (who takes up the don José position in the film), a choreographer trying out dancers for

Laura del Sol (Carmen) and Antonio Gades (Antonio) in *Carmen* (Carlos Saura, 1983)

the part of Carmen in his planned dance production of the narrative. Almost immediately the camera focuses on Antonio's gaze in close-up as he watches the women perform for him. His gaze contains the capacity to select or reject them for the part, and thus contains power. In response they must perform their dance steps for his potential pleasure. (Even here, however, we see shots of the eyes of the dancers as opposed to their whole bodies as they perform the intricate flamenco movements. Antonio looks not at their bodies but at their eyes: the close-up shots of the dancers are from his point of view. This implies that the essential nature of Carmen which Antonio seeks in fact lies in the eyes.) Similarly, in Antonio's initial choreographing of Bizet's *seguedilla* which follows the credits, the sequence ends with him watching his lead dancer Cristina putting the female dancers through their paces. The camera closes in on his gaze as he watches them dance; they themselves are not seen directly but reflected in a mirror. Saura thus initially presents us with the implicitly normalised gaze as male and the performing female as object of the gaze, before introducing a Carmen who will reverse this dictum and render Antonio himself as the performing object.

Antonio certainly intends Carmen to be the object of his powerful gaze as well. But the voice-over that we hear at the end of the *seguedilla* scene suggests that things are about to change. In Antonio's mind runs Mérimée's description of Carmen, which we hear quoted in the voice-over: it includes a strong emphasis on Carmen's eyes: 'Her eyes held an expression both voluptuous and morose, which I have never since encountered in a human glance. Gypsy eyes, wolf eyes' (Saura and Gades 1984: 68). This stress on the eyes and their expression points to Carmen's forthcoming challenge for the gaze. A further quotation from Mérimée ironically suggests that Antonio assumes his gaze to be the force that will create Carmen, when he looks up and sees her in a dance class: his voice-over, which begins 'I looked up and saw her', quotes directly from Mérimée's text. He believes that his eye will create and thus control his Carmen. But what initially attracts him to the dancer who will take on the role of Carmen is her name (which the dance teacher calls out): she is already called Carmen before she even takes on the role of the generic Carmen. She is thus always already Carmen, and Antonio cannot therefore create her through his gaze. The uses of the Mérimée text at these points indicate that Antonio surrenders himself to the seduction of Carmen and of her eyes that Mérimée originally described: in following the path traced by previous don Josés Antonio will lose control of himself and thus of his gaze.

Immediately after the second Mérimée quotation the action cuts to Carmen's first tryout, during which Antonio constantly calls to her to look at him. At the end of their dance she does, and her look challenges his, as emphasised by shot and counter-shot. Antonio discovers himself to be an object of the female gaze, a point underscored by the close-up which shows his surprised reaction: no woman has previously subjected him to such a gaze. Katherine Kovacs describes Antonio as 'a man assailed by visions', meaning that he perceives Carmen not as she really is, but as he imagines her, a point exemplified when he later conjures up a vision of Carmen in the clichéd Spanish get-up of lace veil, comb and fan (Kovacs 1990: 111). But from the moment he starts to work with Carmen Antonio will be assailed by visions more directly, as in the close-up of his reaction. Indeed, in the sequence Kovacs refers to, where Antonio envisages a clichéd Carmen Bizet-style, it is notable that as Carmen circles round him she looks intently at him the whole time, making him the object of her gaze. In return he never actually looks at her. While he 'sees' her in his mind's eye, he also incorporates her challenging gaze into his vision.

Although early sequences recount the difficulties involved in making Carmen a suitable dancer, with the emphasis on her performance rather than Antonio's, Carmen's gaze begins to penetrate the whole question of performance. Thus when Antonio and Cristina discuss Carmen's capabilities as a dancer, we see her behind them through the studio mirrors, moving towards the camera and apparently gazing at them as they talk. Ultimately her performing skills do not matter, for she holds control of the gaze: she is not the one required to perform as the object of the gaze. And increasingly her gaze comes to focus on Antonio's performing body, both in terms of dance and of capacity for sex. In the early part of the film we do not see Antonio dance except as the choreographer showing his dancers how things should be done, setting a standard to which they must measure up. But now Antonio begins to dance more and more as a performer rather than a choreographer, and his dancing reveals itself as responding more and more to Carmen's gaze. This begins in the *tabacalera* rehearsal sequence where – following the generic Carmen narrative – Carmen has just knifed her rival (this dance sequence includes close-up shots of Carmen and her rival Cristina glaring at each other: Carmen's gaze as much as her knife finishes off Cristina). Antonio arrives to take Carmen to prison. As he draws level with Carmen we see a shot of him close-up from Carmen's point of view: he stares at her in a reaction shot as the object of her gaze. This is the first shot we have from her point of view, suggesting that Antonio enters Carmen's field of vision as a performing male body.

But the pivotal moment occurs later, in rehearsing the bedroom scene that takes Bizet's Habanera as accompaniment. In this sequence Carmen begins the dance, performing while Antonio watches. But then he takes up the performance; and now the camera includes in shot not just the performing male but also the spectating female. The performance of the male body in dance now provides a bridge to sexual performance; and the couple dance together towards the stage bed. The film then immediately cuts to a real-life repeat of this scenario. Carmen returns to Antonio's studio at night (and pauses to watch his silhouette dancing as she gets out of her car). Antonio, delighted at Carmen's surprise arrival, starts to kiss her but she halts him, saying that there is no hurry. As the couple talk over a drink, she asks him if he has ever danced for love. On his negative response, she asks him to dance for her. He performs a *farruca* for her as she watches: most of the time the camera focuses on Antonio in a low-angle shot from Carmen's point of view but twice it reverses to Carmen as she gazes on the performing male body. As for the *farruca* that Antonio performs, Gilbert Chase describes the *farruca* as: 'the dance in which the man has the best opportunity to display his virtuosity and virility' (Chase in Heredia 1991: 83). The *farruca* thus becomes the occasion for the male body to put itself on display for the female. Carmen then takes charge of the performance by beginning to choreograph Antonio just as he choreographed her earlier, clapping time and calling out instructions. Only now, subsequent to Antonio's performance in dance, will Carmen allow him the opportunity for sexual performance. Thus in both the rehearsal and in the real-life repeat of the rehearsal scenario, the male can only gain access to the sexual pleasure that Carmen represents by previously performing and presenting his body as the object of the female gaze.

From this point on we see Carmen dance less and Antonio dance more; and the capacity of Antonio's body to perform comes under scrutiny. The arrival of Carmen's husband, just released from jail, exacerbates Antonio's newfound anxieties: at this point we see Antonio looking at the husband through the studio window. He is no longer the powerful choreographer, master of all he surveys: instead his look shows pain and fear as he realizes that his gaze can no longer control. To assuage his fear he must perform again, exorcising his fear of the husband through the staging of a fight with him (or rather, a dancer made up to look like him) in terms of dance. Through the choreographed conflict he contests for possession of Carmen, failing to realise at this point that the contest is futile, as events immediately after will prove: after the rehearsal Antonio catches Carmen semi-naked with another (male) dancer. The dance fight also highlights the inadequacies of the male body to retain control: this body must grow older and cannot keep its strength for ever. At the end of the dance Antonio is feeling his age: he tells his companion Paco that he is finished and that next year he will retire. As the other troupe members move off at the end of this rehearsal, Antonio remains, massaging his aching muscles. He then lies face-up on the floor as if dead, and the high camera angle that holds him in the frame reduces his body power. We are reminded of the increasing inadequacies of other don Josés that I mentioned earlier; and indeed Saura even repeats the motif of the feeble phallus in perhaps the most obvious phallic cliché, the cigarette. After his first sexual encounter with Carmen and her subsequent departure, Antonio reaches for a cigarette packet only to find it empty. He must search for another packet, implying the using up of resources, just as the demands to perform will use up all his bodily energy. It is a small and perhaps trite detail, but the inclusion of the empty cigarette packet would be redundant if it were not for its indication of Antonio's waning ability to perform both in terms of sex and of dance.

The problematisation of the performing body exposed to the gaze carries a further nuance through Saura's use of mirrors, a device that recurs a good deal in his dance films. Some of the walls of Antonio's studio consist entirely of mirrors which dominate the *mise-en-scène*, and which the dancers use in order constantly to observe themselves as they perform. The notion of the mirror might remind us in the first instance of Lacan's mirror stage and the misrecognition of the subject. But the relation of the dancer to the mirror is more specific: Marvin D'Lugo argues that 'Saura's film describes the identity of the dancer as that of one who has internalised the presence of the audience as the condition of otherness which gives coherence to his or her own identity' (D'Lugo 1987: 57).[3] It acts, in other words, as a form of critique, so that the identity of the performer lays itself open to question and scrutiny by both the performer himself (or herself) but also by an implied other who watches. In *Carmen* the gaze comes to substitute for the mirror, and the two are at times equated. At the beginning of the film, as Antonio watches the dancers perform for him, he stands in front of the mirror and reflects the critical gaze on to the dancers just as the mirror does. In addition, we realise later that the mirrors hide Antonio's gaze, since he is able from his office behind the mirrors to see through them and watch his dancers perform: he can see what is going on in rehearsal even when the other dancers cannot see him. But the point at which we realise this is also the point at which Carmen comes up to the mirrors and appears to stare back through them at Antonio. She reverses the gaze back through the mirror, seeming to be able to see directly through it. Subsequently, in the Habanera set-piece, Carmen replaces Antonio in front of the mirror, watching him perform as he watched his dancers perform at the beginning of the film. The later scene where Antonio envisages the clichéd Carmen in his mind's eye also equates the mirror and Carmen's gaze. The scene begins as he sketches some dance steps in front of the ubiquitous mirror and then comes to rest close in front of it, looking at his own reflection in a dissatisfied manner. As he looks into the mirror he envisages the Carmen of the mantilla and fan who, as we saw earlier, walks around him staring provocatively; but he does not look at her in return. Instead, he continues to gaze into the mirror. In doing this he equates the two: he looks into the mirror and imagines Carmen gazing at him. He is the object of scrutiny for both, 'assailed by visions' (to go back to Kovacs's earlier comment). The mirror, like the gaze, places the body under pressure to perform ceaselessly; but increasingly the mirror comes to substitute for a female rather than a male gaze, and the male rather than the female body becomes the object of critical scrutiny.[4]

The increasing desperation of Antonio's performance as an attempt to retain Carmen reveals itself in the final scene, where Antonio dances in competition with the bullfighter for access to the body of Carmen. Although this might at first imply the power of the male body and the passivity of the female, in fact it suggests still further the relentless requirement of the male body to perform and the power of the female gaze. To begin with, Carmen watches Antonio's dance with a rather contemptuous expression, then decides she has had enough and walks away, removing her gaze from him. His performance has not been sufficient to retain her. This removal of her gaze parallels the opening pre-credit sequence where Antonio, dissatisfied with the dancers, loses interest after a few minutes, turns his gaze and walks away from the performing female bodies.

Now Antonio has only one physical action left to him: to stab her and thus remove her gaze.[5] Williams, in her discussion of the gaze of the femme fatale referred to earlier, comments that the femme fatale cannot escape punishment for her wielding of the gaze, still regarded by Williams as resolutely and ineradicably male if it is aligned with power. Carmen's death – the climax of most versions of the Carmen narrative – very much resembles a sort of punishment. Punishment, however, implies a previously held power which carries an authority to pardon, censure or condemn. If Antonio had such a power before, he has by the end of the film lost it. Rather, Antonio's frenzied stabbing of Carmen arises not from a desire to punish, but from a pressure on the male body as inadequate performing object that has become unbearable.

The gaze of a femme fatale such as Carmen, then, does not necessarily function as a parody of a male gaze but instead induces an anxiety in the male that compels him to perform. But his body proves inadequate to the task and his increasing failure to perform satisfactorily drives him ultimately to eliminate the gaze that is the source of his anxiety; and thus the woman who holds the gaze. The powerful female gaze, then, is dangerous not so much because it allows women to usurp the male position, but because it reveals the weaknesses of the male body. But to this conclusion I would add a caveat. Saura's *Carmen* is a compelling film that amply demonstrates the anxiety over the performing male body. But our absorption in the film may lead us to overlook the fact that Antonio is also Antonio Gades, one of Spain's most successful flamenco dancers and choreographers. Thus although Carmen appears to hold sway over the diegetic Antonio, the identity of this Antonio blurs with that of the choreographer who mapped out Carmen's moves for her when choreographing the film. So Carmen choreographs the diegetic Antonio, but is in turn choreographed by the non-diegetic one. Carmen's gaze may challenge the male body so powerfully that the gaze must be eliminated, but the challenge always takes place within the domain of patriarchal power structures (that do not necessarily depend on the individual male body). The powerful female gaze has not yet dislodged these.

Notes

1   At the beginning of the novella Mérimée cites a Greek epigram to the effect that a woman can offer men only two pleasurable moments: when in bed and when dead.

2   This may, however, depend on where the dancing takes place. Washabaugh cites Maria Papapavlou's account of flamenco *juergas* and *peñas* (flamenco clubs) where the audience is almost exclusively male (Washabaugh 1998: 45–7). To offer flamenco on film, as in *Carmen*, means to offer it to a wider audience that will include a greater proportion of women; thus film helps to expose flamenco dance to the female gaze.

3   D'Lugo also explores the issue of the gaze in his article, but concentrates on the spectatorial rather than the diegetic gaze.

4   In relation to the use of mirrors when dancing, Washabaugh quotes the flamenco dancer Antonio Montoya Flores, 'El Farruco': 'With a thinly veiled criticism of those who practice their steps in studios before mirrors, he claimed that "Real flamencos (real men) don't need to practice"' (Washabaugh 1998: 42).

5   It is not actually clear on which level of reality the stabbing takes place: we cannot be sure whether it really happens or is merely part of a rehearsal. But our uncertainty as to whether or not Antonio actually stabs Carmen does not mitigate the fact that on one level – whatever level that is – he does stab her and thus destroys her gaze.

chapter 17

'THEY LOOK SO UNCOMPLICATED ONCE THEY'RE DISSECTED': THE ACT OF SEEING THE DEAD PENIS WITH ONE'S OWN EYES

Peter Lehman

The centre of attention, the guest of honour so to speak, in the opening scene of *Basic Instinct* (Paul Verhoeven, 1992) is the naked corpse of a dead rock star whom we have just seen engaged in a steamy, opening credits, sex scene. When the lead detective walks into the room we first see him looking off in the direction of the crime scene. In the background of the next shot, we see the bloody corpse, genitals exposed, lying on the bed as others stand around looking and talking. Moments later, after one of the investigators remarks that there is cum on the bed, we see a close-up, panning, point-of-view shot as the detective carefully examines the sheet, the genitals centred in the shot. One of the investigators cracks, 'He got off before he got off', and everyone laughs. A recent group of films have shown similar explicit imagery of the penis in death. In this chapter I want to trace the patterns of representing the dead penis within both the mainstream narrative cinema and the experimental avant-garde, indicating the significant differences between them. Some films with dead penis imagery fall in-between the mainstream, narrative and independent, experimental traditions. Despite their differences, all these films contribute to a discourse about the importance, or lack thereof, of the penis in the late twentieth and early twenty-first century. As such they betray a fascination with the penis and either an anxiety about or near jubilation with its possible cultural demotion from an object of awe, and mystique to one of little or no importance.

In *This World, Then the Fireworks* (Michael Oblowitz, 1997), as in *Basic Instinct*, dialogue once again brings attention to a corpse's penis. In a scene that has been notably added to Jim Thompson's novella upon which the film is based, the central male character rushes over to his sister's house where she has literally fucked a man to death. When he enters the room, we see her kneeling over the body of a man who lies on his back. Only

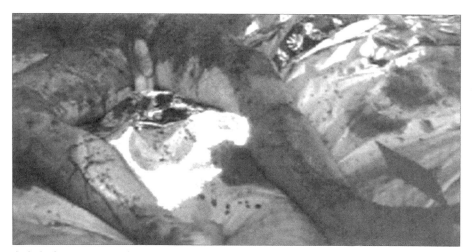

The dead rock star in *Basic Instinct* (Paul Verhoeven, 1992)

his upper torso, dressed in an undershirt and his head are visible since a chair blocks the view of the lower body. The camera, however, moves slowly over the top of the chair and the full body comes into view, with the underpants pulled down and the genitals fully exposed. The brother goes over to his sister and they begin talking. As she narrates the events leading up to the death, we see a flashback of her having vigorous sex with her client when his body begins to spasm violently and blood comes out of his nose. She explains that she became unexpectedly aroused while having sex with the man and, as the flashback ends and we return to a shot of the brother and sister, the corpse and his penis are prominently displayed in the lower foreground of the frame as he remarks, 'Well, he's a big guy'.

The sequences in both of these films share a profound structural similarity; they juxtapose shots of a man having vigorous sex with the spectacle of his penis, flaccid in death. The on-lookers in both films also make sexual remarks related to the dead man's genitals. Indeed, the joke, 'He got off before he got off', and the line, 'Well, he's a big guy', both confer an element of masculinity on the dead men. Both these men have been fucked to death, one suffering a cerebral haemorrhage and the other being stabbed with an ice pick. The fact that both films have graphic shots of the men having sex with the woman who will kill them or cause their death in close proximity to the shots of the resultant dead penis heightens the contrast between the penetrating, virile erections and the useless organs on the corpses. The need of onlookers to comment on the dead men's sexuality suggests that their penises in death makes these onlookers somehow uncomfortable and the spectator of the film is placed in a similar position to the characters within the diegesis.

Why are we seeing these penises? In one sense they are quite unnecessary in both films. In *Basic Instinct*, the body could be easily covered up, and examining the sheets for semen in no way logically entails seeing the penis. And the mere fact that the novella *This World, Then the Fireworks*, written but not published years earlier (Thompson 1988), contains no such dialogue or description of any penises indicates that the 1990s filmic context accounts for its presence. Why is it that movies, even Hollywood movies that shy away from showing penises in general, now seem caught up in a mini-epidemic of showing dead penises? Surely it is not that the only good penis is a dead penis. Indeed, it seems nearly the opposite. These films betray a fascination with and fear of the dead penis. One of the reasons, of course, that the penis is so protected from representation and so carefully regulated on those special occasions when it is represented within medical (the 'normal' penis), artistic (the 'aesthetic' penis), pornographic (the 'big dick') and comic (the 'small dick') discourses is that patriarchy invests so much awe and mystique in the penis. We have to revere the big ones, laugh at the small ones, and so forth. The jokes and comments about 'getting off' and impressive size we hear while seeing the dead ones clearly attempt to give back what death has taken away.

In *Shallow Grave* (Danny Boyle, 1994) two men and a woman break down their roommate's bedroom door and find him lying dead on the bed from a drug overdose. After a shot of them staring in disbelief, the film cuts to and holds a shot of the corpse on its back, the penis clearly visible. One of the men who has not seen the deceased man before, blurts out, 'Is that the way he always looked?' The somewhat ludicrous question joins, 'He got off before he got off', and 'Well, he's a big guy', as a one-liner that underscores the need in scenes such as this to have a comment that somewhat nervously addresses the unusual and perhaps unexpected sight of the dead penis.

Dead Presidents (Albert and Allen Hughes, 1995) supplies a bizarre variation on the above examples because the man with the dead penis is still alive. In a battle scene during the Vietnam War some soldiers come across a comrade who lies on the ground disembowelled with his genitals stuffed in his mouth, his large penis prominent in the composition. In this variation, it is the man with the severed penis who utters the dialogue equivalent to that of the onlookers in the other films. Having lost his manhood, he loses his desire to live and return home. At his request, one of his buddies kills him, sparing him the agony of life without a penis.

Mainstream cinema has long had a fascination with autopsy scenes, and, not surprisingly, such scenes have become more common recently on television. The fascination in general deals with the common nexus of the desire to look at something and the simultaneous dread of seeing it and desiring to look away. Once again, not surprisingly, autopsy scenes have played a kind of peekaboo game with the male body, sometimes almost showing the penis, sometimes briefly revealing a glimpse of it, etc. In *Wolfen* (Michael Wadleigh, 1981), for example, we see a tracking shot along a row of gurneys with corpses lying on their backs in a morgue as medical examiners go about their business. One of the bodies the camera tracks past is that of a man with his genitals fully exposed. In *Se7en* (David Fincher, 1995), we see the autopsy of a fat man including glimpses of his penis. These images occurring within the context of medical examinations are not as shocking or as emphasised as the images in *Basic Instinct, This World, Then the Fireworks, Shallow Grave* and *Dead Presidents*.

A recent film includes images and a discussion about a corpse's penis near its beginning, signalling that the subject of penises will be important throughout. The opening credit sequence of the German film *Anatomie/Anatomy* (Stefan Ruzovitsky, 2000) shows Paula, a female medical student, along with fellow students in an anatomy lab at their university. She and a fellow female student are working on a corpse when she stops and says: 'Professor? There seems to be some kind of anomaly in the pelvic region'. 'A penis, perchance?', the professor responds sarcastically, and the other students break out in

Anatomie (Stefan Ruzowitzky, 2000)

laughter. 'It's not an anomaly. That is why men are different.' Paula playfully holds it in her hand and laughs. Over the image of her holding the unrecognisable severed organ, we read the credit, 'Written and Directed by Stefan Ruzovitsky'. Clearly Ruzovitsky signs in as a director who knows exactly what the real subject of this film is. Paula then drops the penis and we hear it splatter as it hits the floor. She bends down to pick it up, muttering, 'Slippery is what it is'. Once again, the students laugh. By the end of the film, Paula will know what a penis is and learn to treat it respectfully. The word 'slippery' reverberates in more ways than one.

Throughout the film Paula is characterised as a serious student not interested in penises, or men for that matter. At one point she remarks to Gretchen, her roommate, 'All you ever do is talk about men! It's like you're obsessed. I came here to work, not sleep around.' Later Gretchen remarks to Paula that her boyfriend Casper has a nice body and bluntly asks: 'Has he got something nice in his pants?' The scene here makes explicit the manner in which Gretchen over-values the body, sexuality and, in direct contrast to Paula, the penis. She goes on: 'Its kind of fun to sit around and talk about dick sizes in public.' If Paula lacks the proper respect for the penis and male sexuality, Gretchen disparagingly and threateningly over values them: 'Why are these things always so sensitive? They look so uncomplicated when they're dissected.' Here again the dialogue points directly to the contrast between the living penis and the dead penis, hinting that the former might not be as important and complex as culture makes it out to be. Indeed, the line 'They look so uncomplicated when they're dissected' might well apply to all the glimpsed dead penises in these films. As hard as patriarchal culture works to complicate the penis, death reveals the 'uncomplicated' truth.

All of the above examples, including the title of this essay, come from Hollywood films, mainstream independent narrative films, or mainstream foreign films (*Anatomy* was the number one box-office film in Germany in 2000). But, the subtitle of this essay alludes to another tradition of showing the dead penis in the cinema: experimental films such as Stan Brackhage's well-known *The Act of Seeing with One's Own Eyes* (1971). Of all the films discussed in this chapter, Brackhage's is the only one that involves actual dead bodies and penises as opposed to actors and props. *The Act of Seeing with One's Own Eyes* shows the activity taking place in a morgue, but does so without any narration or background information supplied in a manner that would help the viewer understand how these people died, who they were, or what the examiners are discovering. Many of the bodies are males and Brackhage returns to images of the penis during the autopsies, showing it being measured and even raising the dread for some spectators that, within the film's context of showing bodies being repeatedly cut open and body parts being removed, they will see it cut off.

More recently, Peter Greenaway's *Death in the Seine* (1988) bombards the viewer with images of dead penises, once again within a morgue context, this time re-enacted. A standard shot in the film starts at the feet of a naked body and moves slowly up over the body, in the process revealing the genitals. Indeed, the repetition of the shot creates an expectation as the camera approaches the groin and inevitably brings it into view. Although the bodies in this film, set in France at the time of the revolution, are not autopsied, they are all prepared for identification and burial, including having clothing removed, the body washed, etc. Indeed, one scene shows a dead man's penis being washed as witnesses look on. Bill Viola's video installation *Emergence* (2002) shows two women lift the dead body of Jesus Christ slowly from water. As the genital region comes into view, the viewer realises that there will be no loincloth covering the penis. The women carry the naked body to the ground where the genitals are then covered up. *Emergence*, like other pieces in *The Passions* (2003) makes strong, specific reference to art history. Indeed, the program notes include a reproduction of a 1424 *pietà* by Masolino showing Christ's body in a loincloth. Viola's decision to show the nude male body in this context is thus all the more notable. Viola avoids any clichéd effort to impart an element of dramatic visual spectacle to the penis which is retracted.

Several films fall in-between the mainstream narrative representation of the dead penis and that in the above cited experimental films of Brackhage, Greenaway and Viola. From this perspective there is an interesting similarity between *Ai No Corrida/In the Realm of the Senses* (Nagisa Oshima, 1976) and *Kissed* (Lynne Stopkewich, 1996). Made two decades apart in, respectively, Japan and Canada, both films nevertheless share a vision of the dead male body as an alternative to conventional phallic male sexuality, and both films include explicit penis imagery. *Ai No Corrida*, which I have analysed in detail elsewhere, culminates when Sada cuts the penis off Kichi, her dead lover (Lehman 1993). She has just strangled him during the act of lovemaking. The film includes a close-up of a knife slicing through the penis and is followed by a shot of the severed organ lying next to the man's body. The film concludes with voice-over commentary describing how Sada was found wandering around the city with her lover's genitals in her possession.

Although I have argued that the image of the severed penis in the film is itself a contradictory one which confuses the penis/phallus distinction, the film is notable for its non-phallic representation of the male body when compared to both the Japanese erotic woodblock tradition and the then current Western hard-core feature porn film tradition (Lehman 1993: 169–96). Throughout most of the film, Oshima imagines an alternative masculinity to that of either the Japanese soldiers who go off to war to die for their country in his film or of the large, ever-erect penises, pounding away on and eventually ejaculating upon the bodies of women forever groaning for more in the Western hard-core feature. In the latter, the spectacle of the living 'phallic' penis is all women seem to want or need for their satisfaction. In *Ai No Corrida*, however, the male body is offered up to the woman for her pleasure in a much more inventive manner. It is within this context that I think the dead penis is particularly interesting because even if Oshima ultimately fails in his attempt to free the male body from phallic representation, he tries, and it is within that effort that the image of the dead penis resonates.

Something similar happens in *Kissed*. The film's central character is a woman who derives her sexual pleasure from male corpses. Many reviewers at the time of the film's release complained of its ambiguous representation of necrophilia. For once, it seemed, critics were frustrated that a film was not graphic enough. How does a woman have sex with a dead man? Inquiring minds wanted to know and the film does not in fact make this clear. Barbara Gowdy's *We So Seldom Look on Love*, the short story upon which the film is based, on the other hand, is more explicit and makes clear that blood coming from the corpse's mouth rather than the penis is the source of the woman's pleasure. This contrasts sharply with another passage in the story describing a repressed, male, homosexual necrophiliac's practice of using a trocar, a needle used in the embalming process, to make penises erect so that he can sodomise it. The contrast between the man and the woman makes explicit what is, I think, implicit in the critical response to the film: that those who want to know more about the necrophilia are assuming that it somehow involves the penis. How can you fuck a man with a dead penis? The woman neither needs nor wants the trocar because her erotic use of the male body in death is intimately tied to the fact that she does not have to concern herself with the penis in any manner. For her, the dead male body is a non-phallic body in contrast to the re-phallicised body of the homosexual's desire. In a remarkable passage, Gowdy writes of her central character's relationship with her boyfriend: 'With Matt, when we made love, I was the receiving end, I was the cadaver. When I left him and went to the funeral home, I was the lover' (Gowdy 1997: 181). The place of the woman within the phallic economy of male sexuality is the 'receiving end' or being the 'cadaver', while the necrophilia enables her to become the active lover who need pay no attention to the penis. She uses death imaginatively to find an alternative to normative sexuality in a manner that contrasts with the man with the trocar who sodomises corpses: his perversion remains at the centre of the phallic economy's emphasis upon the penis.

Gowdy's representation of necrophilia is eerily similar to that of Karen Greenlee, an actual necrophiliac who reminds an interviewer, 'People have this misconception that there has to be penetration for sexual gratification, which is bull! The most sensitive part of a woman is the front area anyway and that is what needs to be stimulated. Besides, there are different aspects of sexual expression: touchy-feely, 69, even holding hands. That body is just lying there, but it has what it takes to make me happy' (Greenlee 1999). Greenlee even recounts an anecdote about a male mortician who uses a trocar to create erections.

Although *Kissed* avoids explicitness about how the woman achieves her pleasure with the male corpses, and avoids the trocar penis imagery, it does contain a somewhat surprising moment of frontal male nudity. After getting a disturbing phone call from her boyfriend, the central character rushes over to his apartment where she finds him standing on a chair naked with a rope around his neck. At this point, we see his body in a full frontal long shot. When he kicks the chair over and hangs himself, however, the action occurs off-screen and we do not see his penis after his death. In this variation, then, the penis is shown not in death but in close proximity to it, literally the moment before death. Although the film is silent on the dead man's erection, Gowdy's description of the scene in the short story is once again notable: 'There was a loud crack, and gushing water. Matt dropped gracefully, like a girl fainting. Water poured on him from the broken pipe. There was a smell of excrement. I dragged him by the noose. In the living room I pulled him on to the green shag carpet. I took my clothes off. I knelt over him. I kissed the blood at the corner of his mouth' (Gowdy 1997: 186). Gowdy totally ignores the cultural fascination with the erection a hanging produces, and, instead, refers to the loss of control of the bowels that also occurs at that moment. Furthermore, she returns to the image of blood coming from the mouth, the alternative to the penis as the source of erotic gratification. The dead man may have an erection but it is of no interest to the female character in the story nor to Gowdy who describes the scene without reference to it, nor to Stopkewich who elides the entire subject.

Kissed relates to a tradition of the representation of the penis in the 1990s that I have elsewhere called the melodramatic penis. In *Running Scared*, I argue that images of men and the male body are caught within a polarity not unlike the mother/whore dichotomy that structures so many representations of women (Lehman 1993). At one pole, we have the powerful, awesome spectacle of phallic masculinity and at the other its vulnerable, pitiable and frequently comic collapse. While I still believe that such a polarity functions centrally within current Western representations of the penis, the extreme critical praise and box-office success surrounding David Henry Hwang's play, *M. Butterfly* (1988), and Neil Jordan's film, *The Crying Game* (1992), suggest the emergence of a third category wherein extremely melodramatic circumstances accompany the representation of the penis. In addition to such films as *Cobb* (Ron Shelton, 1994), *Angels and Insects* (Philip Haas, 1995) and *The Governess* (Sandra Goldbacher, 1999), the press coverage of the Bobbitt case also fits into this category (Lehman 2001b).

Certainly like melodrama, death supplies yet another highly unusual context in which to show the penis and thus contributes to a variety of discourses that enforce the notion that penises cannot simply be shown as penises in ordinary contexts. An interesting variation occurs in the television movie *The Badge* (Robby Henson, 2002) where the dead penis is spoken about rather than shown in a highly melodramatic context. The film begins with the murder of a young woman whose body is found lying by the side of the road in the rural south. From the moment her body is found everyone who looks at it remarks about her beauty. The lead detective takes photos of the unidentified victim and shows them around town in the hopes that someone will recognise her. No one does, but, once again, they remark on the beauty of the young woman in the photos. Later, when the sheriff is in his car, he receives a call telling him: 'You really got to see this.' When he arrives at the morgue, Squeegee, an employee, similarly remarks to him: 'Oh, wait until you see this.' At this point a cut to a long shot of the room shows the nude body of the female victim lying on the examination table. The camera is behind the table and at an angle that reveals the left side of the body, including the breast but not the groin. We then see the sheriff looking and Squeegee remarks: 'She got a pecker.' 'And titties', the other officer in the room adds. 'I can see that, C.B.', the sheriff responds. 'She got a bigger pecker than I do', Squeegee continues, and the film cuts to a shot of the Sheriff and Squeegee staring at the corpse's groin. Just then the female District Attorney walks into the room remarking: 'Squeegee, I'm just going to have to take your word on that.' She then looks at the corpse and exclaims: 'Oh, my Lord. I guess you'd call it a transvestite.' The medical examiner corrects her: 'Well, technically because of the hormone-induced breasts, she'd be classified as a transsexual or transgender.' Moments later, unsure how to refer to the corpse's gender, he remarks of the bullet he removed from it: 'This is the culprit that killed her or him.' Finally, the sheriff, while still staring at the corpse asks: 'Doc, why don't you put something over this here? I don't want to lose my biscuits.'

The scene is melodramatically inflected by the repeated emphasis on the unbelievable nature of what it is the sheriff has to 'see' with his own eyes. The scene also directly acknowledges through the character of Squeegee the sexually evaluative look at the dead penis, and the sexual banter continues when the female DA enters and even continues after she leaves and the scene ends with the men making suggestive jokes about the doctor's possible sexual perversion based upon his knowledge of such issues as the distinction between a transvestite, transsexual and transgendered person, knowledge that he tells them comes from reading, not experience.

The melodramatic nature of the scene also motivates the most extreme looks at the dead penis of any of the movies under consideration here. The characters are so dumbfounded by the fact that this beautiful woman has a penis that they all stand around staring at it. Finally, the discussion of the distinction between a transvestite and a transgendered person points to a central element of the scene's significance to which I shall return in the conclusion.

In this film, the unexpected, melodramatic revelation of the dead penis becomes central to the entire plot. Counter to our expectations as to who the murderer is and what his motivations are, we learn near the end of the film that a man peeking into a women's restroom through a hole in a wall goes into a rage when he discovers that the beautiful woman he is staring at has a penis. He rushes into the bathroom and begins to beat her, eventually killing her as she runs to escape. The plot is both set in motion *and* resolved by the sight of the penis.

Whether caught within the binary of awesome spectacle/pitiable, comic collapse or embedded within a melodramatic context whereby it becomes an object of exaggerated significance, or glimpsed in death, or severed from the body, these images of the penis all betray a cultural significance. Either the penis is supposed to be big enough and impressive enough to fulfil the phallic fantasy or small enough to be laughed at for failing in that august mission. It is perhaps predictable that Hollywood now has a company called Nude Male Casting that specialises in men who are willing to appear full frontal and flaccid in films. They must however pass a crucial Polaroid test. According to the man who started the company: 'We're looking for guys who are seven inches or greater. Someone whose penis is bouncing off each leg as they walk through the locker room' (Colwell 2003: 74). Even glimpses of extras are not immune. During the shooting of *Soldiers*, a forthcoming feature film, a casting sheet for 133 men to be seen nude, full frontal, asks for 'well-endowed, rugged, masculine types' (Colwell 2003: 74). The dominant view of masculinity is so centred on big penises that out of 133 men, not one should be small, or average for that matter!

As in life, so in death. The large penis stuffed into the mouth of the disembowelled soldier in *Dead Presidents* is, so to speak, right out of central casting (Nude Male Casting, that is). Even in death we want either to lament the loss of the once virile penis, or laugh at the pathetic token, or take note of the impressive sign of manhood left behind by the dearly departed. Yet, artists like Oshima, Stopkewich and Gowdy embed the dead penis within projects that profoundly question normative, patriarchal phallic sexuality, attempting at least to refigure the male body from its dominant representation. As such their work is related to that of Brackhage, Greenaway and Viola whose experimental imagery disturbs the usual absent image of the penis by representing it within a context that does not fit with the cultural awe and mystique surrounding the organ. In contrast to the more mainstream fascination with showing the dead penis that I have outlined above in such films as *Basic Instinct*, *Wolfen*, *Se7en*, *Shallow Grave* and *This World, Then the Fireworks*, Brackhage, Greenaway and Viola represent the penis as far removed from the phallus.

But something even more fundamental underlies this fascination with the penis in death: the desire to ascertain the presence or absence of the penis, plain and simple. During the 1970s and 1980s, in the heyday of psychoanalytic criticism, it was fashionable to stress the distinction between the penis (the organ) and the phallus (the symbolic) and then argue that really no one could ever possess the phallus, try as they might, and that insofar as anyone could have the phallus, women could occupy that traditional male position. But this only made sense in regards to the phallus, not the penis. By the late twentieth and early twenty-first century things have gotten more bizarre, and now a variation of this state of affairs seems to apply to the penis. It is almost as if having the penis or not having it in life has now been displaced by having had it or not had it as determined in death. In an age of transgender surgery, women can have a penis or men can lose one. A woman might get by in life as a man without having a penis, or a man might get by in life as a woman even while having one. The penis is indeed a bit 'slippery' (like the phallus before it), and so we call in morticians and doctors to stop this sliding by revealing the truth in death. If a 'pervert' can masquerade in life as a woman having a penis when she does not, or a man not having one when he does, we will reveal the fraud in death and fix things. Newspaper coverage of morticians discovering that a female has a penis, or a male does not, give testament to this almost morbid fascination. Was this person a man or a woman? Once again, inquiring minds want to know. The fact that surgery can now give a woman a penis intensifies the fear of the eroding power and mystique of the penis. One can't be sure about anything.

The discussion in *The Badge* about whether the 'woman's' breasts are real or artificial addresses this atmosphere of uncertainty about the once (presumed) simple signs of sexual difference. Even that is not clear anymore as the doctor corrects one of the bystanders, referring to the hormone treatments that created the breasts. The narrative structure of *The Badge* makes clear the anxiety surrounding seeing the (dead) penis with one's own eyes. At the beginning of the film all the men who remarked about the victim's beauty are suddenly implicated in desire for what is for them a disturbing/disturbed sexual body: 'Why don't you put something over this here?' The resolution to the narrative enigma is an even more pronounced disturbance – a Southern good ol' boy becomes a murdering maniac because someone who looks like a woman shouldn't have a penis and use the women's rest room – it just isn't 'right'. He also wants to 'put something over this here'.

Given the number of earthshaking events such as murder and incest precipitated by and associated with the penis in cinema, perhaps one should be thankful it does not appear more often. In death as in life, not surprisingly, images of the penis fulfil a number of missions: they can be a sign of startling contrast with lost virility; they can still be called upon to fulfil the wish for a dramatic spectacle of masculinity; or at the very least, they can be called upon to be the one sure sign of sexual difference – the privileged marker of sexual difference – clear cut and simple.

That the media fascination with morticians who discover that a man turns out at autopsy to be a woman or vice versa has found its way into movies such as *The Ballad of Little Jo* (Maggie Greenwald, 1993), and *The Badge* points to the singular role we attribute to the simple presence or absence of the almighty penis as the true determinant of gender identity. The melodramatic penis and the dead penis are closely linked not just in that the latter frequently precipitates the former, but also insofar as they both signify that our culture continues to assert that showing the penis must be of some special, if bizarre, significance. The one thing a penis cannot be is simply a penis, for such representations threaten the awe and mystique resulting from keeping it hidden, and fall outside the various cultural discourses that attempt to regulate it and give it a special significance.

And indeed these glimpses of dead penises in mainstream narrative films share a feature in common with the fleeting penis-size jokes in movies that I analyse in *Running Scared* (Lehman 1993: 105–30). The significance of that humour derives entirely from the fact that it is almost unimaginable, even for Hollywood, to make an entire film about penis size but apparently irresistible to drag it into countless films about other subjects. Similarly, it is almost unimaginable to make a movie about dead penises, though the South Korean 12-minute short film *Hae Boo hawk shi gan/Anatomy Class* (So-yun Zung, 2000) foregrounds them, including an image of one flaccid and one erect. Three soldiers kill themselves to become lab specimens for female anatomy students around the age of puberty who are totally pre-occupied with removing the pants from the corpses, laughing and joking as they assess the sizes of the men's penises. One of the men is judged to be 'tiny' even though one of the girls observes that he has a large nose. Given this emphasis, it is not surprising that a male commentator on the Internet Movie Database observes: 'The poised scalpels will send shivers down the spine of any normal male! There is much laughter in the class as the students assess each specimen of manhood and there appears to be unanimity in the claim that size really does matter, at least in this particular anatomy class.' One of the girls disdainfully asks what good a dead penis is, further highlighting the strange nature of the fascination. Although feature narratives avoid such sustained, explicit attention to the dead penis, filmmakers hover around the sight of it and, increasingly, afford a glimpse of the much dreaded/desired object.

Nekromantik 2: Die Rückkehr der liebenden Toten/Nekromantik 2 (Jörg Buttgereit, 1991) is the most bizarre, sustained feature narrative treatment of the dead penis I have encountered. The film begins with a man committing suicide. He gets an erection while plunging the knife into his abdomen and as he dies, he ejaculates. The ejaculate is then replaced by blood that spurts over him. Later a woman steals the corpse from his grave, takes it home, strips it, cleans it, and makes love with it. The dead penis is visible in many shots and when she later cuts the corpse into pieces, we see her cutting off and saving the genitals. The film's graphic and shocking conclusion shows her decapitating a man while making love with him. She then puts a tight band at the base of his erection to keep it erect, leaves the corpse, and returns with the head of the first corpse which she puts in place of the just-decapitated head. She then mounts the corpse.

Nekromantik 2 actually blurs the line between the living and the dead penis, showing it literally going from one state to the other. The film revels in its reversal of the usual pattern in horror films where women are brutally attacked and killed by men. The dead and dying male body in this film serves the sexual pleasure of the central necrophiliac female character. And unlike Oshima in *Ai No Corrida*, Buttgereit does not endow the dead penis with 'impressive' dimensions. On the contrary, the erection is quite ordinary, even on the small side. Buttgereit resists making an impressive spectacle out of the dead penis, much like in the earlier sex scenes, he does not show the man in the usual thrusting role, since the woman pins him down preferring a style of sex where she, not the man, controls the penile penetration. This is particularly ironic within the film since the man makes his living dubbing porn films, creating both the vocal and the slapping sounds of bodies accompanying normative pounding intercourse. The woman in *Nekromantik 2*, in other words, does not desire either the big dick or the pounding intercourse that characterises porn. Perverse as it is, her pleasure comes from elsewhere and the manner in which this film builds identification with the woman undermines the 'normal' response of desiring to reinstate the power and spectacle of the phallus. Indeed, this film does come close to suggesting that the only good penis is a dead penis, or perhaps more accurately, a dying penis.

A fear that the penis does not measure up to its assumed importance lies beneath the glimpsed dead penises in all of these films. If, as some heterosexual women report, images of the flaccid penis are totally uninteresting since they are sexually useless and do not even signify desire ('When it's not interested in me, I'm not interested in it'), the image of the dead penis is even more 'useless' (*Nekromantik 2* supplies the exception when the ejaculation from the dying penis impregnates the necrophiliac). Perhaps the severed penis is, from this perspective, the most useless. This image of the useless penis supplies the most dramatic contrast imaginable to the awesome phallic spectacle. Some experimental filmmakers embrace this moment as a potentially liberating one, and some mainstream filmmakers cringe in fear, bringing the full brunt of narrative force to bear in an effort to make things right once again. Do we want to peek out of a fear/desire that the much-revered phallus is not really what it is cracked up to be? Do we suspect that perhaps it is Dead On Arrival? Dead or alive, the penis continues to haunt the movies with its appearance, however brief and forgettable. The makers and viewers of *Basic Instinct* have other things on their mind than dead penises and, by the time the film is over, it is much more likely that it is Sharon Stone's living genitals that will be remembered and the dead man's that will be long forgotten. Therein lies the significance since this need to offer such images is so disturbing that it must be quickly forgotten and disavowed as the films rush on to more important matters.[1]

Note

1   Special thanks to Susan Hunt, Robert Flynt, Jeff McMahon and Melanie Magisos.

chapter 18

THE W/HOLE AND THE ABJECT
Phil Powrie

The subject is constituted through the force of exclusion and abjection, one which produces a constitutive outside to the subject, an abjected outside, which is, after all, 'inside' the subject as its own founding repudiation. (Butler 1993: 3)

My wish is that every subject's encounter with the death drive might become in time more of an everyday occurrence – that the typical male subject, like his female counterpart, might learn to live with lack. (Silverman 1992: 65)

Since the middle of the 1990s French cinema has seen the resurgence of a version of the realism once associated with the 1970s. Frequently focusing on life in the provinces, especially the North, rather than in Paris, and on characters who are working class or petit bourgeois, what we might call inner-city youths, or out-of-work dysfunctional men, these films have usually been praised by critics, if film festival prizes are anything to go by. Some, it is true, have criticised what they see as a complacent miserabilist tendency, fashionably, and cynically, seasoned with strong cinematic effects. A critic writing in *Le Monde Diplomatique*, for example, complains about what he sees as the facile sloganising of many of these films, which in cinematographic terms oscillate between 'the darkest and most despairing naturalism and the most affected mannerism and formalism'; they 'reject any political position'; and he claims that their 'fascination for the abject and the sordid show an undeniable hatred for the people', who, in his view, are no more than caricatures (Pardo 2000: 28). The film heading his list is Gaspar Noé's *Seul contre tous* (1998), the continuation of the biography of the protagonist of the 40-minute *Carne* (1990). Both films were controversial. Applauded by the majority of reviewers, and winning a number of prizes, they were also heavily criticised. The director, according to Carlos Pardo, 'feels a fascisising [*fascistoïde*] complacency for the sordid and the abject' (Pardo 2000: 28).[1]

Noé went on to make the equally controversial *Irréversible* (2002), nominated at Cannes; this time focusing on the middle classes, and equally fascinated by the sordid and the abject. Alex (Monica Bellucci), married to Marcus (Vincent Cassel; her real-life partner) and expecting his child, is anally raped in a subway. Marcus and his gay friend Pierre (Albert Dupontel) search for the rapist in Paris's seedy suburbs, ending up in a gay club where Marcus is anally raped himself. Pierre kills the rapist by beating his head to pulp with a fire extinguisher.

In this chapter, I would like to explore the twisted masculinity of Noé's first two films in the light of theories of the abject (outlined briefly in the first section, 'theme'). I would like to show how there is, despite what Pardo suggests, a radical potential in Noé's vision of the abject. Concentrating on his second film, *Seul contre tous*, I shall show how it reworks three key sequences of Scorsese's *Taxi Driver* – in three 'variations' on the abject – to elaborate an abjected cloacal and vocalised subject who fantasises wholeness through unrepresentable semen and silence, as I shall attempt to outline in the final section, 'coda'.

First, however, a brief description of the films may be helpful. Both films are remarkable amongst other things for the soundtrack. This is mostly made up of the interior monologue of a Parisian horse butcher (played by Philippe Nahon), a fascist ranting against everyone, especially women, gays and Arabs, in which there is much talk of arseholes, cunts, shit, cocks, fucking, and so on.

Carne begins with an abattoir scene where a horse is killed and eviscerated, intercut with the birth of the butcher's daughter, Cynthia (Blandine Lenoir), as she emerges from her mother (apart from Cynthia, none of the other characters are named). A rapid succession of short scenes with intertitles indicating the passage of the years recounts Cynthia's childhood as she grows up without her mother who left the butcher shortly after the birth. The butcher idolises his daughter who is mute and retarded; we see him washing her, dressing her, feeding her and, eventually, feeling ambivalent towards her sexually as she reaches adolescence. He mistakes the menstrual blood on her knickers for the blood of defloration by an Arab worker, whom one of the butcher's acquaintances says he has seen with Cynthia. The butcher goes to find the worker on the nearby building site, called 'le trou', or the hole, and plunges his knife into an unsuspecting worker's mouth (the wrong man, as it happens) and twists it around. He is jailed, and his daughter placed in an institution. On his release he finds it difficult to get work and eventually decides to accompany the female owner of the café where he has been working (Frankye Pain), and whom he has made pregnant, to a new life in Lille.

Seul contre tous picks up where *Carne* left off. It reprises *Carne*'s narrative with a rapid-delivery monologue by the butcher overlaying stills of buildings (the hotel where Cynthia was conceived, the butcher's shop, the prison, the motorway to Lille, and so on). In this preamble, we learn more about the butcher's early childhood; his father was a communist who died in the concentration camps, he never knew his mother, was raised as an orphan, was sodomised by his teacher. The butcher, dependant on his partner's money, resents her. He is sacked from his job as a delicatessen-counter assistant for not smiling enough, becomes a night porter in a hospital, brutally attacks his pregnant wife when she accuses him of sleeping with a nurse, and leaves for Paris once more, taking his mother-in-law's revolver. He fails to get a job, and tries unsuccessfully to borrow money from acquaintances. Having gone to a café to spend his last few francs on a coffee, he is thrown out when he insults the owner's son, and returns with the gun only to find the café closed. At the end of his tether, he picks Cynthia up from the institution with the aim of killing her and himself. We see him doing this, but it turns out to be a fantasy, and the film ends with him extolling the virtues of incest, as the only thing left for him.

Theme

The abject, as defined by Julia Kristeva, is characterised by a combination of fear and loathing, but also of attraction to the pre-Oedipal state, prior to the acquisition of language and prior to what Lacan calls the Law of the Father. The abject is therefore linked to the maternal, to lack of control and helplessness, to all the fluids we might associate with early childhood (vomit, blood, urine, excrement). The abject is a liminal state, an in-between, poised on the cusp of subjecthood, but not quite yet subjecthood.

In this opening section, I will explore the unsettling combination of fluidity and rigidity in the film. At first glance this binary might seem tediously and stereotypically gendered as female versus male, pre-Oedipal and Oedipal. However, the butcher is not so much contrasted with a female other, as presented to us as both rigid and fluid; and he hates both, as much as he is attracted to both. The concept I am suggesting is in reality not a binary; fluidity and rigidity are not the two 'sides' of the butcher. Rather, a better way of expressing the concept is the contrasting but simultaneous imbrication between the whole (the wholeness and the singular) to which he aspires, and the hole (the oblivion contained within the whole) to which he aspires no less. If I use the term imbrication, more usually found in architecture (where it means the overlapping of tiles), it is because the abject is crucially concerned with space, a point to which I shall return. As Kristeva points out, 'the one by whom the abject exists … instead of sounding himself as to his "being", he does so concerning his place: "*Where* am I?" instead of "*Who* am I?" For the space that engrosses the deject, the excluded, is never *one*, nor *homogeneous*, nor *totalisable*, but essentially divisible, foldable and catastrophic' (Kristeva 1982: 8; her emphasis).

My way into these points will be to discuss two of the three clear references to *Taxi Driver*, which are the most obvious of the many filmic references.[2] The last part of the film is obsessively structured on key scenes in *Taxi Driver*, to such an extent indeed that one could say that *Seul contre tous* functions in the same way with regard to *Taxi Driver* as the hole does to the whole; the narrative of *Seul contre tous*, and the *mise-en-scène*, are imbricated, intertwine and interleave with remembered scenes from *Taxi Driver*. We become aware of a kind of slippage (the term imbrication also means the dripping of water from roof-tiles). This is fluid play, which matches the obsession with abject fluids evident in both films.

Taxi Driver variation 1: the porn film and the butcher as penis

In the first reference to *Taxi Driver* the butcher goes disconsolately to see a porn movie and watches stony-faced as a heterosexual couple perform on screen. The (ob)scene is optically smudged in the British-released version of the film, because the sight/site of copulation was felt to be too insistent. And yet the scene is a key one for the film, insisting on existential isolation and alienation, as well as on the radical separation of the sexes. As the butcher watches, he muses in his inimitable style:

> Either you're born with a cock and you're useful if you behave like a good hard cock which stuffs holes, or you're born with a hole and you will only be useful if you are stuffed yourself. But in both cases you are alone. Yes, I'm a cock, a miserable cock, and to be respected I must always stay hard.

The 'hard body' desired here is Theweleit's 'fascist male warrior', who fears being overwhelmed by a feminising red flood (see Thomas 1996: 129). It is hardly surprising that we find in the butcher, who must draw blood as part of his job, a feeling of repulsion for fluids spilling out of control from ruptured and distended bodies, whether those of slaughtered horses or women giving birth, or indeed a woman dying. By contrast with these sites of abjection, the butcher is constantly drinking fluids contained in small cups (always expresso coffee) or glasses (red wine, brandy). These containers are themselves contained in his cupped hands, as if to underline the contrast between the anarchy of the uncontrollable body, which expels fluids in meaningless expenditure, and the controlling body, which purchases and consumes fluids.

Nahon's body emphasises the rigidity and aggression of the hard body. He is squat; he has bulbous glaring eyes, and a belligerently protuberant nose. His body is thus constructed as a threatening forward lunge, matched linguistically by the monosyllables he occasionally spits out vituperatively, his teeth and fists clenched. As Kristeva says of the abject subject, 'I expel *myself*, I spit *myself* out, I abject *myself* within the same motion through which "I" claim to establish *myself*' (Kristeva 1982: 3; her emphases). These seep across and through the entire film in a stream of consciousness, literally a linguistic fluidity, which contaminates the often otherwise neutral sights we see (a humdrum hotel room, empty streets). That linguistic fluidity suggests that the rigidity of the butcher is not quite what it seems.

Indeed, the butcher's observations as he watches the porn film are ambiguous. The subject of the utterance, shifting from male to female within the single 'you', suggests that the butcher himself is the one who needs to be 'stuffed', the hole made whole; in this fantasy he is both cock and hole at one and the same time. It is no surprise that one of the first titles of the film was 'Penis';[3] but it is equally no surprise that it was dropped. It is not because there is anything inherently shocking in the word, but because the word suggests only one part of the fantasied whole. That whole combines both masculinity and a femininity constantly repressed and represented as abject. It is a masculinity subjected hysterically to the Law, and a femininity abjected in the liminal spaces which border and burrow through the Law, like a network of arteries pulsating obscenely under skin stretched to breaking point, until a hole perforates the skin for the blood to gush out, as happens when the butcher fantasises the murder of his daughter. As Kristeva says, the hard or clean and proper body desired by the butcher for himself can only be acquired by its fragmentation and dissolution: 'the advent of one's own identity demands a law that mutilates, whereas jouissance demands an *abjection* from which identity becomes absent' (Kristeva 1982: 54; her emphasis).

Words gush out in the butcher's stream of consciousness monologue, like the blood gushing out of Cynthia, like the blood which accompanies Cynthia's birth in *Carne*, gushing out of the vagina, and like the blood gushing out of the slaughtered horse's stomach in the scene intercut with Cynthia's birth. The films show an obsession with holes of all kinds. It is not just the vagina through which blood and baby Cynthia emerge, or the hole in Cynthia's neck spurting blood when she dies, or the horse's stomach from which blood and guts gush out, or the vagina in the porn film, but the repeated scenes where the butcher gropes for Cynthia's vagina as they sit on the bed, and the exterior shots of tunnels into which the butcher drives or emerges on foot. It is also the many shots of mouths, whether the mouth of the Arab worker into which the butcher twists his knife, or the shots of the butcher's own mouth with the eyes out of shot, cartoon-style.

Importantly, however, the mouth is not just vaginal, as the opening scenes of *Carne* might have suggested; it is also cloacal. A number of spaces function as holes, not least because of their linguistic associations. The word *trou* in French is used colloquially for both the vagina, and, in the expression which occurs several times in the films, *trou de cul*, for the anus as well. It is also a colloquialism for prison, and it is the word used in *Carne* to refer to the building site. In each case, these spaces referred to as holes (the building site and the prison) contain other sexualised holes; for the building site it is the worker's mouth penetrated by the butcher's twisting knife held at his crotch height; and in the prison, there is an implication that the butcher and his cellmate engage in gay sex.

But spaces are often also closed to the butcher; doors of buildings – the hotel, the butcher's shop, the café – are as frequently closed as open. Spaces are therefore as much cloacal as they are vaginal in the film. They are potential holes waiting to swallow him like the *vagina dentata*, or rejecting him because they are tightly closed like anxious anal sphincters.

In this section I have shown how the demarcation between rigidity and fluidity, which the butcher postulates as the marker of sexual difference, collapses under the weight of linguistic fluidity. The obsession with holes equally collapses the distinction between vagina and anus. In the next section, I shall explore the shift from the butcher as penis to the butcher as turd.

Taxi Driver variation 2: the gun in the mirror and the butcher as turd

The self-disgust generated by the abject is made clear in the second *Taxi Driver* reference, when the butcher returns to his hotel room and looks at himself in the mirror with his gun, fantasising that he will kill those who have crossed him, as well as killing himself. The violence he turns against himself bears out Kristeva's point that in the abject the subject struggles to disentangle himself from what lies within, the unnameable and horrifying maternal origin. As the butcher says in that scene, playing on the part-homonym *mère/merde*, 'my whole life has been a colossal turd, willed by a whore of a mother'; elsewhere in the film he refers to himself derisively as a '*trou de cul*', or arsehole. He is both turd and hole, or, more precisely, turd in the hole, what Kristeva calls the anal penis, 'the phallus with which infantile imagination provides the feminine sex' (Kristeva 1982: 71). The butcher, desperate to remain hard and penile, realises that he is also faecal, *homo erectus*, but also *homo rectus*, whole and hole. There could be no clearer expression of what Calvin Thomas calls 'scatontological anxiety'.

Thomas brings together Freud's account of the *fort/da* game, and his theory of cloacal birth ('It is a universal conviction amongst children that babies are born from the bowel like a piece of faeces: defecation is a model of the act of birth'; Freud quoted in Thomas 1996: 85) to suggest that the former 'is implicated not only with the boy's phantasy of having been produced through his mother's bowels, and his foreclosure of that phantasy, but also with his own struggles to secure identity through the control of his bowels' (Thomas 1999: 29). As Thomas points out, those struggles are never really successful, and all modes of representation are, to use his term, haunted by scatontological anxiety: 'The image of "unimpaired masculinity", the self-produced, self-representational image of the actively "self-made man", is haunted by the earlier phantasmatic image of having been a passively and cloacally (m)other-made child' (ibid.). Hence the aggression against women in the butcher's rambling monologue, and the fear of homosexuality, 'a fear of the anus as phantasmatic origin in the former instance and as destination of desire or locus of pleasure … in the latter' (Thomas 1996: 88). The beginning of *Seul contre tous* makes it clear that the butcher was abused as a child, an event which posits the possibility of the pleasure to be gained from the anus, even if it is a pleasure only available to the abuser (we assume); the butcher's frequent references to sodomy suggest both repulsion and attraction, a fear of becoming feminised, but also the masochistic desire to return to being 'a passive object and slave to this jouissance, aggressed, sadisticised' (Kristeva 1982: 183), as Kristeva writes of some of Céline's more racist and homophobic pronouncements.

Like Céline's work, the butcher's voice smears what we see in a faecal stream of consciousness, an effect all the more pronounced by the editing out of the pauses and breaths between statements. And we are attracted to this abject anality, submerged in it, for very simple material reasons. The butcher's voice-over draws us close to him, for two reasons. First, because its almost continuous nature means that we are always with the butcher, 'forced to share permanently his states of mind and to follow him in his most frightening excesses', as Noé puts it (Rouyer 1999: 31). Second, because the punctuating gunshots on the soundtrack interact with that voice-over, encouraging us to see that voice-over not for what it is, an extremely aggressive flow, but for what it is in relation to the gunshots, a more mellifluous flow, a refuge from what Noé calls the stress of those gunshots which, according to him, 'place (the spectator) in a state of stress similar to the butcher's. At the same time, Philippe Nahon's voice is strong and warm. The spectator therefore navigates between a state of hypnosis and relief when he hears that voice, because he prefers it to the gunshots' (Bourbon 1999).

Blood as a visual sign of rupture, rejected birth, menstruation and death, mingles with the shit of the soundtrack. As Thomas suggests, the anxious subject 'collapses all those heterogeneous processes for which bodies are sites – faecal, urinal, seminal, foetal, menstrual, glottal, lingual – into an undifferentiated and abject flux' (Thomas 1966: 32); all of these are present either visually or linguistically in the two films. The borders between the visual and the aural are constantly shattered by explosions, whether aural, in the gunshots which punctuate the soundtrack, or the sudden zooms which jerk us forward dizzyingly from one plane into another. Sounds become signs, and signs become sounds, both signifying the horror of the abject with its fluid boundaries leaking into each other. Seeing and hearing melt into the se(e/he)aring light of a brilliant white fade-out at the end of the murder/suicide sequence, signifying apocalyptic failure, the blankness of an anger so excessive that the words strangle and extrude their obscene obverse, the silence of death, never so aptly named a pregnant silence, a silence full of what it cannot silence, a silence made of countless explosions paused as they are about to explode. Kristeva's

Blandine Lenoir as Cynthia in *Seul contre tous* (Gaspar Noé, 1998)

comment on Céline's prose, which she describes as 'a thin film constantly threatened with bursting' (Kristeva 1982: 141) is an apt analysis of the promiscuity between the visual and the aural in *Seul contre tous*, as is her description of 'the vision of the ab-ject' as 'the sign of an impossible ob-ject, a boundary and a limit' (Kristeva 1982: 154).

In this section, I have shown how the butcher's frame of reference is faecal and abject. The clean, hard body, or *corps propre*, as Kristeva calls it, collapses its boundaries and is invaded from within by abject fluids associated with the mother. Another boundary, that between seeing and hearing, is collapsed as the butcher's stream of consciousness permeates the image track, working both with and against it. In the next section, I shall explore the butcher's antithetical attempts to resolve the dissolution of the boundaries; first, through hysterical cutting, second through incest; and, in so doing, I shall also consider why it is important that the anti-hero of these films should be a butcher.

Taxi Driver variation 3: murder, incest, cannibalism

The final reference to *Taxi Driver* is the butcher shooting his daughter, which, as in *Taxi Driver*, is a bloodbath in a claustrophobic hotel space. This scene, no less than the first two replays, all differ from *Taxi Driver* in one significant way, however. They underline the butcher's failure, something he comments on in the fantasied murder scene: 'I've failed at everything. My birth, my youth, my love life, my shop. I should never have been born. My entire life is a mistake.' In the first film theatre scene, he is alone, and comments disconsolately on solitude, whereas Travis Bickle unsuspectingly takes his suitably offended girlfriend. In the mirror scene, like Bickle, the butcher fantasises the death of others, but, unlike Bickle, also fantasises his own death. And, finally, in the murder scene, Bickle murders a whole group of pimps and prostitutes, and is heroised for those murders, whereas the butcher merely fantasises his daughter's murder, but does not go through with it, remaining the unheroic failure he commented on in the previous mirror sequence.

Arguably, his murderous fantasy is the logical conclusion to a series of insistent but ineffectual cuts practised in the two films. Cutting can be seen as an hysterical attempt to control time and the change which it brings, and to control space, most particularly to control the invasion of the fragmenting and hetero-dimensional abject into the monolithic and uni-dimensional *corps propre*. There is first the cut between the two films, which overlap with each other in terms of narrative. Then there are the very literal cuts we see as the butcher chops the meat at the beginning of *Carne*, these narrative cuts being mirrored by editing cuts as intertitles signal the passage of the years, as though the butcher were trying to control time. But, as he says at the end of this sequence of cuts, 'the years go by before you have time to count them'. This sequence is echoed at the beginning of *Seul contre tous*, as the butcher recounts his life. His breathless, rapid-delivery monologue overlays a visual track consisting of photo-album stills of people and places, as if he were trying to staunch the flux of time by punctuating it with frozen images, familiar clichés providing havens of recognisability within the anarchic flux of life itself. The cuts we see at the beginning of the films are themselves echoed throughout by rapid edits accompanied by fast zooms and gunshot sounds, as previously mentioned. These procedures can be seen as attempts to separate body and sign, materiality and spirit, as it were, a procedure important in ritual, as Kristeva points out: 'The rites surrounding defilement, particularly those involving excremential and menstrual variants, shift the *border* ... that separates the body's territory from the signifying chain' (Kristeva 1982: 73). We shall see in the last section how this urge for the 'spiritual' is negotiated, in *Seul contre tous*, through a specifically male fluid, semen.

The various types of cutting have the opposite effect to that desired, however; they undermine the coherence of the narrative, compounding the butcher's failure. As Kristeva points out in relation to Céline's writing, the narrative is carved up into choice morsels with which the butcher is fascinated, and that fascination dislocates the narrative, allowing the abject to emerge, disrupt and occasionally to overwhelm.

The importance of cutting is the first reason of several overlapping reasons why it makes sense to have a butcher as the anti-hero. A second reason is the association made between butchers and a primitive sexuality, according to Noé: 'The butcher's sexuality is an excuse for many fantasies. It is seen as bestial and basic, probably because the butcher handles meat all day long and so his organic link is stronger than most' (Bourbon 1999).

A third reason is the religious connotations of meat-eating, linked with the self-disgust implied by the Fall. Kristeva points out how in Genesis man is allowed to eat meat after the Flood, and that this should not be seen as some kind of reward but an admission of fundamental evil, 'an acknowledgment of a *bent toward murder* essential to human beings' (Kristeva 1982: 96; her emphasis).

A fourth reason has to do with ritual, which protects from the unclean (*souillure*). The butcher's insistent chopping in *Carne*, echoed by the editing in *Seul contre tous*, is a kind of ritual purification. Chopping the meat up, preparing it, and indeed cooking and eating it, as we see the butcher do in *Carne*, is a means of conjuring the unclean, associated with the archaic prelinguistic materiality of the mother. One of the more disquieting images in *Seul contre tous* is the butcher's dream as he tries to sleep off his hunger; he probes fillets of meat which are made to look like vaginal lips.

A final reason is that the prohibition of incest is intimately connected with ritual, according to Kristeva, for whom, following Freud, the prohibition of incest protects the subject from the temptation of a return to a pre-Oedipal engulfment in the mother (Kristeva 1982: 63–4). Ritual, particularly that connected with defilement (*souillure*) separates the subject from his body and from the mother, and thereby legitimises the rejection of cannibalism:

> Defilement reveals, at the same time as an attempt to throttle matrilinearity, an attempt at separating the speaking being from his body in order that the latter accede to the status of clean and proper body, that is to say, non-assimilable, uneatable, abject … Fear of the uncontrollable generative mother repels me from the body; I give up cannibalism because abjection (of the mother) leads me toward respect for the body of the other, my fellow man, my brother. (Kristeva 1982: 78–9)

The butcher, as pointed out above, fails lamentably in all of these respects. The films set up cutting as ritual, but the films are submerged in fluids, whether corporeal or linguistic. It is therefore logical that we should see images which suggest that the mother's body and the daughter's body can be eaten: the mother's body giving birth is intercut with a horse being slaughtered for the butcher; the butcher dreams of vaginal fillets. It is therefore also logical that the butcher fails to kill his daughter, choosing instead the fantasy of incest, since incest represents the suspension of the Law of the Father, as Slavoj Žižek points out (see Žižek 2000: 31), in the return to the non-differentiation of the pre-Oedipal and the engulfment in the archaic mother. It is for that reason that I disagree with reviewers who felt that the apparent redemption of the butcher through incest was a disappointing closure (see for example Genin 1999: 1). It is logical in terms of the butcher's project; and, more importantly, it is emphatically not a redemption, but, in appearance at least, a regressive return to the abject.

In this section, I have shown how the third *Taxi Driver* reference emphasises the butcher's failure, despite the cutting procedures which attempt to reinstate the control of the *corps propre*. Incest is no redemption, I have argued, but forms an integral part of this failure, since it signals the return to the abject.

Coda: semen

In fact, *Seul contre tous* is neither joyous affirmation nor humdrum recognition of the abject, but a precarious balance between the two, a kind of leaky imbrication. In this section, I shall be suggesting that this imbrication is figured narratively by incest, and metaphorically by something connected to it but which we do not see, at least not directly. The radical potential of incest as break with the Law and return to the abject, which I argued above, is destabilised by what is never shown in the film, although constantly gestured at: semen. In fact, I shall be claiming that semen *does* appear, but sublimated, figured both as closure, and as counter-shot to the abject (unlike other markers of the abject, such as excrement and menstrual blood, which are connected with the mother, semen, for obvious reasons, is paternal; see Kristeva 1982: 71–2).

Arguably, there might have been plenty of opportunities for semen to be shown, whether prior to the birth scene in *Carne*, or as part of the porn film the butcher watches in *Seul contre tous*, or even as part of his incest fantasy. It is there nevertheless. It appears indirectly in the unexpected fade to white at the end of the film, where it is linked to the butcher's insistence that he will commit incest. It also appears indirectly throughout the film *as the film itself*. I described the constant cutting procedures above as an attempt to keep the abject at bay, to impose meaning on the body. Whether cuts of meat or cuts of film, cutting tries to impose the phallic economy; and if the cuts are the process, then the product is, metaphorically speaking, semen, which is why I suggest that semen is present liminally as the film itself. As I pointed out above, however, the butcher (and the film) to a large extent fail, since cutting releases the abject, figured by flux (of blood, of language). Nevertheless, it is clear that the butcher, and the film, wish to impose meaning, however ambiguous, however fraught with tensions and contradictions.

My contention then is that the cutting is a constant struggle between the release of abjected blood (the shot as in shooting his daughter with a gun) and paternal semen (the shot as in ejaculation into his daughter), both, it should be noted, equally fantasised. It is also the struggle between red and white; between absence of meaning and meaning; between the hole and the whole. The final scenes of the film are crucial in this respect, since they contrast the murder of Cynthia and the rape of Cynthia as two alternative narrative economies answering the question 'how can this end?'. The first produces, literally, a gaping hole which gushes blood, as had the feminised holes of *Carne*: Cynthia's mother giving birth to Cynthia, intercut with the slaughter of the horse, could not make clearer the fear and fascination of the abject. But the final scenes take up another fascination, the fascination with Cynthia's invisible vagina. The butcher is often seen groping for Cynthia's vagina in *Seul contre tous*, fascinated by what is deceptive and doubly hidden from his gaze, first by her skirt, second by her flesh, the bleeding wound which deceives the gaze; neither we nor the butcher know in *Carne* whether the blood on her knickers signifies rape or menstruation.

Like the butcher's semen, then, Cynthia's vagina is never seen, but we know that it is there, an object of endless fascination for the butcher, who wishes to implant his semen in it, to loop the loop. Why? As the final sentences of the final dialogue suggest – 'Between us, that's all I can see. I love you' – the butcher seeks disappearance through identification with the same in a safe pre-Oedipal space where absent mother, mute daughter and father fissured by erupting linguistic flux, collapse into a transcendent, phallicised space, no longer the messy corporeal space of the maternalised abject, but the 'pure' emptiness of the shot (in all of its senses: gun-shot, money-shot, camera-shot). No blood, no words (the two are the same in these films, abject flux); just the blinding whiteness of the final money-shot in fantasied copulation, figured by the slashing copula of my title, w/h; or, to put it another way, the se(m)en, seen but not heard, where the 'm' signifies abjected maternity silenced by an equally abjected masculinity.

Notes

1 *Carne* won the International Critics Week Prize at Cannes, the Georges Sadoul Prize (for young filmmakers), and the Franco-American Prize of Avignon; *Seul contre tous* again won the International Critics Week Prize at Cannes, as well as Best Screenplay at the Catalonian International Film Festival, and the Golden Bayard at the Namur International Festival of French-Speaking Film. Generally, most reviewers felt that the films combined the realism of the 1970s with innovative formal procedures and the cynical humour of comics and satirical magazines such as *Hara Kiri*; that the films were rigorous (a word frequently used in reviews; see M. R. 1999: 21) in that combination; that they were provocative and amoral. Reviewers were divided on the effects of the latter, some suggesting the films showed provocation for its own sake, a cynical rejection of responsibility, and that Noé's apparent refusal to condemn the butcher would play into the hands of right-

wingers. One reviewer complained, for example, that the sentimental ending was no different from having a film about the Nazi concentration camps finishing with images of Hitler's happy life with Eva Braun (Tran 1999).

2 Noé said that the voice-over was inspired by an obscure Austrian film, *Angst* (Gerald Kargl,1983), which tells the story of a man released from prison after serving four years for murdering an elderly woman, and who terrorises a family living in remote countryside. Apart from *Angst*, the other fairly obvious reference is *Eraserhead* (David Lynch, 1977), mentioned on a number of occasions by Noé. He cites it as the film which prompted him to make films (Gans 1992). Amongst the many other films mentioned by Noé in interviews one finds *Straw Dogs* (Sam Peckinpah, 1971) for its 'intense violence' (Rouyer 1999: 31), *Un Chien andalou/An Andalusian Dog* (Luis Buñuel, 1929), which showed him how to 'announce the horror which will follow' (Gans 1992); *Los Olvidados/The Young and the Damned* (Luis Buñuel, 1950), which he says is his 'favourite comedy. Buñuel pushes cruelty so far that you end up laughing' (Rouyer 1999: 31); *La Grande Bouffe/Blow-Out* (Marco Ferreri, 1973) and *Ai no borei/The Empire of the Passions* (Nagisa Oshima, 1978) for their violence and explicit sex (Père 1999: 37); and *2001: A Space Odyssey* (Stanley Kubrick, 1968). The latter is the first film he remembers seeing, at the age of six, and he claims to have seen it 'again at least once a year since then' (Rouyer 1999: 32); it and the work of Pasolini were his 'reference points for may years' (Père 1999: 38). Apart from Buñuel, it will be noticed that his references are nearly all from the 1970s; his two films combine the political realism of that decade with the effects more usually associated with younger youth filmmakers (a point made by Bonnaud 1999: 39), such as Jean-Pierre Jeunet and Marc Caro (whose *Le Bunker de la dernière rafale/The Bunker of the Last Gunshots,* 1981, was presented at Cannes with *Carne*) and Jan Kounen who is listed for thanks in the credits of *Seul contre tous*.

3 'I even thought of entitling the film Penis, or The Penis, because of the passages where the butcher compares himself to a cock. The penis evokes both a male attribute and a piece of flesh disconnected from the body. Phonetically, it would also have made you think of the National Front [because its leader is called Le Pen] and the butcher's paranoid tendencies' (Noé in Rouyer 1999: 32).

chapter 19

BATMAN, MASCULINITY AND THE TECHNOLOGY OF ABJECTION

Calvin Thomas

> To destroy transcendence, there has to be
> laughter. (Bataille 1985: 55)

As Judith Butler informs us in *Bodies That Matter*, the word 'Abjection (in latin, *ab-jicere*) literally means to cast off, away, or out and, hence presupposes and produces a domain of agency from which it is differentiated … [T]he notion of *abjection* designates a degraded or cast out status within the terms of sociality. Indeed, what is foreclosed or repudiated … may not re-enter the field of the social without threatening … the dissolution of the subject itself' (Butler 1993: 243). In an essay called 'Fashion and the Homospectatorial Look', Diana Fuss refers to photography as 'the very technology of abjection'. She writes that the 'intimate codependency of fashion, fetishism, photography and femininity suggests that in the dominant regime of fashion photography, femininity is itself an accessory [that] operates as a repository for culture's representational waste' (Fuss 1992: 720). Suggesting that abjection 'is the psychical equivalent of photography's mechanical transformation of subjects into objects', Fuss cites Roland Barthes to the effect that 'the Photograph … represents that very subtle moment when … I am neither subject nor object but a subject who feels he is becoming an object: I then experience a micro-version of death … I am truly becoming a specter' (Barthes 1981: 14). Photography, Fuss continues, thus 'functions as a mass producer of corpses, embalming each subject by captivating and fixing its image' (Fuss 1992: 729).

Tim Burton's 1989 film *Batman* can be read as an uncanny explication of these comments by Butler, Fuss and Barthes, for, as I shall argue here, the film is very much concerned with abjection as the dissolution of the masculinist subject, with phantasmatic relations among photography, femininity, human and cultural waste, the mass production of images, commodities and corpses. Foregrounding its own troubled fascination with the photographic image, Burton's film explores anxious relations and interchanges among 'armoured' masculine subjectivity, the male body, femininity, racial 'otherness' and the cinematic apparatus itself. In so doing, the film articulates what I consider a specifically masculinist anxiety about the very mechanisms of photographic and cinematic representation, a constitutive unease about a mass cultural 'technology of abjection' that both threatens and works to enforce the boundaries of normative, heterosexual masculinity.

This unease, and the attempt to overcome it, are introduced in the film's very opening, its title sequence. Probing that opening, Andrew Ross writes that 'Behind the title credits, the camera creeps, dips and skates through the bowel-like spaces between the contours of the bat ancestral crest, tracing out a symbol that seems to be as old and universal as nature itself. The code of nature then gives way to the code of the social' (Ross 1990: 30). Now, Ross's last sentence, in which nature 'gives way' to the social, refers to the camera's cut from the seemingly natural bat symbol to the more evidently social or societal streets of Gotham City. Symbols themselves are never natural, however; they are always already social, embedded in a 'symbolic order' that depends not only on an ordering of symbols but on an *order to symbolise* given to the linguistic subject, an imperative to separate from nature *by* symbolisation and *in order to* symbolise, signify, name, title, attempt to master. I will therefore let Ross's sentence refer to a 'giving way' that occurs *within* the opening title sequence. There the camera moves lugubriously – and disorientingly, so that we have no idea where we are or what we are viewing – through a bowelish interior, then emerges from that space and reflects back upon it as a site of origin: a scene, we might say, of cloacal birth.[1] The camera distances itself, clears itself, from its own cloacal origin and then re-presents the site as sight, as simultaneously an identifiable symbol and a symbol of identity. The camera thus provokes and then assuages anxiety, narrating its (and our) passage from a lost, expelled and helpless objecthood to a subjective position of symbolic mastery. In Lacanian terms, the camera can be said to narrate the alienating expulsion from the Real, which Lacan says resists symbolisation absolutely, into the Imaginary and the Symbolic, thus illuminating what Kaja Silverman calls 'the representational system through which the subject is accommodated to the Name-of-the-Father' (Silverman 1992: 34). Given such accommodation, it is appropriate that it is at this very moment – when the previously unrecognisable matter of the rectal defile through which the camera had moved becomes distanced and discernable as a symbol, and we know where we have been and what we are looking at – that the name of the film's putative symbolic master, its director, appears in the credits.

But there's more. Lacan suggests that 'It is necessary to find the subject as a lost object. More precisely this lost object is the support of the subject and in many cases is a more abject thing than you may care to consider' (Lacan 1970: 189). If the credit sequence narrates the transition from the Real to the Symbolic, from lost object to self-located subject, from passivity to activity, it also narrates the overcoming of an abject historical trauma, thus seemingly reasserting what Silverman calls 'our dominant fiction', which 'calls upon the male subject to see himself … only through the mediation of images of an unimpaired masculinity' (Silverman 1992: 42). However, in tracing the tracing of a symbol, the credit sequence may leave more traces of abjection and trauma than any unimpaired masculinity may care to consider.

Silverman writes that the dominant fiction's 'most central signifier of unity is the (paternal) family, and its primary signifier of privilege the phallus' (Silverman 1992: 34). In so far as the credit sequence illustrates the separation from and mastery over a maternally-coded, cloacal Real through the process of symbolisation, we can, from a Lacanian perspective, view the bat-symbol as a phallic signifier, an image of unimpaired masculinity.[2] But the phallus and the unity of the paternal family that it upholds are threatened in the immediate post-credit sequence. There Dad, Mom and Junior are lost and overwhelmed in a section of Gotham that is dangerous and dangerously sexualised (i.e., there's a hooker), and Dad cannot successfully hail a cab. This inability not only feminises Dad, as all inabilities and disempowerments conventionally will in patriarchal representation, but also threatens his privileged racial identity since – as Ross points out, and as Cornell West (for one) attests from experience – it is in reality black men who have trouble getting cabs in New York City.[3] Desperately asserting 'I know where we are!', Dad takes the family down an alley, and in that dark defile is laid low by some sickly-looking robbers, a scene that Batman witnesses from a great height. The scene has a particular resonance for Batman/Bruce Wayne, for, as we later find out, it was in this very vicinity, just outside the Monarch Theatre, that his own parents were murdered when he was a child.

Commenting on this aspect of *Batman*'s narrative pre-history, Michael Brody writes that 'Freud's work on psychic trauma remains valuable in understanding [the young Wayne's] mental state' after witnessing his parents' murder. 'Freud wrote about the flooding of the psychic apparatus with large amounts of stimuli and the helplessness experienced when the ego is overwhelmed … The suddenness of the flood … cause[s] a shattering of the illusion of invulnerability' (Brody 1995: 172–3). Brody suggests that 'Wayne's vow to fight crime is a compensatory wish' and that 'he acted out this wish in the movie's first scene. There is a conversion from the passive child to an active mastery of the adult Batman who now renders the robbers helpless' (Brody 1995: 174).

The key Freudian text concerning such conversion is *Beyond the Pleasure Principle*, and the most relevant moment in that text is Freud's well-known description of the *fort/da* game, in which his grandson throws away and then retrieves a wooden reel by means of the string attached to it. Freud interprets this game of 'gone' (*fort*) and 'here' (*da*) as one in which the boy compensated himself for his own renunciation of his mother's body 'by himself staging the disappearance and return of the objects within his reach' (Freud 1953–74, vol. 18: 15). Freud 'gets the impression that the child turned his experience into a game from another motive. At the outset he was in a *passive* situation – he was overpowered by the experience; but, by repeating it, unpleasurable though it was, as a game, he took on an *active* part. These efforts might be put down to an instinct for mastery' (Freud 1953–74, vol. 18: 16).[4] The *fort/da* game is particularly relevant to the opening scenes of *Batman*, for it is exactly this game of disappearance and return that he plays with the two robbers on the rooftop: he makes the first vanish by kicking him through a closed door, and he uses his bat-line to snag and retrieve the second, who is trying to escape. This crook Batman holds over the edge of the abyss, threatening to let him drop, and it is at this moment of complete mastery that he announces his identity: 'I'm Batman', he whispers, and then spares the man, flinging him aside. This intrication of articulated identity with the ability to let or not let something drop at will is important, and the relevance of the *fort/da* itself continues throughout the film, for there are numerous scenes of Batman employing his line to snag a villain, to hoist himself out of danger, or to rescue (or control) the body of Vicki Vale (Kim Basinger).

Immediately following the scene in which Batman announces his identity, throws the robber aside and vanishes into the night, the camera cuts to a Gotham town hall meeting, a scene dominated by a huge black and white poster of district attorney Harvey Dent, played by Billy Dee Williams (a significant figure in the racial semiotics of blockbuster casting, following his injection by George Lucas (as producer) into *Star Wars: Episode V – The Empire Strikes Back* (Irvin Kershner, 1980) and *Star Wars: Episode VI – Return of the Jedi* (Richard Marquand, 1983) in a bid to attract black audiences). After a few words by Commissioner Gordon (Pat Hingle) and by Dent, the camera cuts to a large black and white photograph of Alicia (Jerry Hall). Zooming out, panning right and tilting down, the camera reveals an apartment wall dominated by glamour shots of Alicia, the first of many televisions, this one tuned to Harvey Dent's face and speech, and the pre-Joker Jack Napier (Jack Nicholson) reclining in a plush chair. He is shuffling a deck of cards (i.e., playing with a pile of mass-produced images), his feet resting on a coffee table.

In fact, as a close overhead shot makes a point of informing us, Jack's feet rest on a *Vogue* magazine cover, and thus on the image of a woman's face that is metonymically linked to Alicia's since she is not only apparently a fashion model but is played by one. Jack's gesture of contempt towards Alicia's face is significant not only because he later facially disfigures her, but also because of the way mass-produced photographic imagery itself is beginning to be linked in *Batman*'s imaginary with cultural marginality, with 'subordinated' matters of femininity, racial difference and waste: the two scenes work to situate blacks and women 'underfoot', to associate the black and white images of a black man and a white woman with what might end up on the bottom of a white man's shoe. Significantly, however, the second scene also implicates Jack, by virtue of his own arrogant, preening narcissism in front of the mirror, in the very realm of the imaginary that he would prefer to abject. Thus the scene foregrounds a crucial paradox: images and representation both *threaten* the dominant fiction of unimpaired masculinity and *constitute* the indispensable supports of that fiction. Thus images and the production of images must – like laughter, like the sphincter, like the reel of the *fort/da* – be subject to constant surveillance and control.[5]

A subsequent scene elaborates on the phantasmatic relations among the mass-production of images, cultural marginality and the matters bodies produce. Reporter Alexander Knox (Robert Wuhl) enters the *Gotham Globe* newsroom to the taunts of his colleagues, who ridicule his interest in the Batman story. 'What a dick', he mutters of one. Then, upon seeing a set of female gams propped up on his desk, he purrs 'Hello legs!' Visually and aurally, the newspaper-reading Vicki Vale is thus introduced as a body-in-fragments, and the juxtaposition of the words 'dick' and 'legs' underscores the Lacanian point that the woman cannot 'have' the phallus but must *be* the phallus for the man.

But a more interesting series of juxtapositions follows: when Vale says to Knox 'I'm reading your stuff', Knox follows with 'Well, I'm reading yours', thus connecting mass-produced written material with the 'stuff' of feminine sexuality.[6] When Vale introduces herself, Knox recognises her as a photographer for *Vogue* (which, along with her initial reclining posture, which is similar to Jack's, links her to the scene in Alicia's apartment) and says, 'If you want me to pose nude, you're gonna need a long lens'. But this ostensibly phallic brag has the opposite of its intended effect, not only because Vale ignores it, and not only because of Lacan's suggestion that 'virile display in the human being itself seem[s] feminine' (Lacan 1977: 291), and, furthermore, not only because he should have said 'wide-angle' rather than 'long' for the brag to make sense, but because, in the deep logic of the film's imaginary, to subject masculine identity to a feminising photographic gaze is to expose its vulnerability to abjection. Vale, who like Batman himself has a sort of double life, immediately underscores this point by showing Knox her *serious* camera-work: a *Time* magazine cover of the aftermath of the revolution in 'Corto Maltese', a photograph of a dead male body face down in the mud. Vale's duplicity connects the *Vogue* and the *Time* covers, bringing together the notion of feminine/fashion photography as the repository of culture's representational waste with a notion of photography in general as a technology of abjection that wastes masculinity, transforming male bodies into corpses. Staring at the *Time* cover, and using a word whose repetition seems to signal something other than a limited vocabulary, Knox mutters 'A girl could get hurt doing this stuff'. But given the fact that he has already feminised himself by offering his body to Vale's photographic gaze, Knox may here be unwittingly referring less to Vale than to himself: to get hurt, to get wasted, to get *shot* (by gun or by camera), is to be othered, demasculinised, abjected, turned into an object, 'a girl'.

This scene concluded, the camera cuts to another mass-produced photographic image of Harvey Dent's face, this time on the front page of a *Gotham Globe* lying on the desk of crime boss Carl Grissom (Jack Palance). This shot of yet another cover-shot links Dent's African-American face with the *Vogue* and *Time* covers, and thus with the haunting specters of femininity, abjection, waste, mud and death that seem to be the main worries of *Batman*'s phantasmatic subtext. In a shot that is amplified later when the Joker uses a mechanical boxing glove to punch out a televised image of Dent's face – and which evidences the film's literal iconoclasm, an inevitably masochistic aggression against images that is here displaced onto the racialised other – Grissom brings his fist down on the newspaper. The camera zooms out to reveal Jack Napier once again reclining in a chair, playing with his deck. A remarkable sequence follows. In a close point-of-view shot, Jack holds up a Joker, and we hear a low mechanical noise that resembles intestinal grumbling. As Jack lowers the card, the camera brings the background into focus to reveal the figure of Alicia emerging from the elevator. Having returned from a shopping spree, and 'come up from below', she is laden with designer shopping bags which signify her conspicuous consumption of (presumably) over-priced and frivolous junk. By this juxtaposition, the image of the Joker's face is metonymically associated with Alicia's overly photographed, overly consumptive body, and thus, by implication, with all of the preceding images of femininity, racial difference, abjection, waste and death.

We will return to the Joker's face and its glaring significations. First, let us consider Batman/Bruce Wayne's relation to the technology of abjection. The sequence in Wayne Manor articulates a concern with that technology (specifically, with matters of surveillance and retrieval) as well as a concern with questions of identity-uncertainty and, importantly, of value (specifically, with the ambiguous symbolic value of money). To raise money for the Gotham bicentennial celebration, Wayne has converted his mansion to a casino, so the scene begins with shots of extravagantly gambling Gothamites shooting craps, letting their dice and their chips fall where they may. In our first glimpse of the unmasked Michael Keaton as Bruce Wayne, Vicki Vale, not knowing who he is, asks if he can tell her 'which one of these guys is Bruce Wayne'. He tells her he is not sure, a reply that contrasts with the certainty of his 'I'm Batman' proclamation to the dangling crook, and so hints at an uncertainty or ambiguity lying beneath the Batman armature.

Armature – and questions of identity, sexuality and value – are all foregrounded shortly thereafter when Knox and Vale wander into Wayne's museum of body armour. Some interesting dialogue ensues. 'Look at this stuff!' says Knox. 'Who is this guy?' Vale, reiterating the stuffy subtext, observes 'He gives to all these humanitarian causes, and then collects all this *stuff*', after which comment she lets out a laugh (this laughter-provoking contrast between the humanitarian, or the vulnerably human, and the defensively armoured male body is important and will be emphasised again later in the film). The conversation is then sexualised, or at least phallicised: Knox comments on Wayne's appeal to 'chicks', saying 'they like him for his big charity *balls*', to which Vale adds 'and don't forget his *very* large bankroll'. However, as was the case with Knox's earlier big-dick assertion, these monetary metaphors covertly undercut the qualities of phallic hugeness they ascribe. For if Wayne's phallus is made of money, it is made of *stuff* that has an unstable, or at least transmutable, social and psychosymbolic value. Most obviously, we might note here Freud's contention that an 'ancient interest in faeces' can be 'transformed into the high valuation of *gold* and *money*' (Freud 1953–74, vol. 22: 100). The potentially 'low' connotations of high monetary value are brought into relief in the following exchange: Knox says, 'Remember, the more they got, the less they're worth', to which Vale answers, 'Then this guy must be the most worthless guy in America'.

The guy whose worth (if not guy-ness) is in question enters. Introductions follow. Unlike the feminised Knox, a *Vogue* reader who knew Vicki Vale as a fashion photographer but not as a war correspondent, Wayne is familiar with her work in Corto Maltese, and compliments her on her 'good eye'. But upon hearing her desire to investigate the Batman story, Wayne says 'A little light after the war in Corto Maltese, isn't it?' Of course, Wayne wants to throw Vale off the bat-trail, but his comment also has the effect of aligning Batman with what also compares 'lightly' to the carnage in Corto Maltese: i.e., Vale's frivolous fashion photography, which the Joker will later explicitly call 'crap'. The matters of photography and representation resurface here, for after Wayne departs, Knox, complaining to Vale about the oddities of the very rich, points to an immense mirror and says: 'Maybe it should be Bruce Vain'. His comment reminds us of Jack Napier's harsh vanity before the mirror in Alicia's apartment, but as the camera takes us behind Wayne's two-way mirror, and we see Wayne's massive videographic surveillance technology, we discover that his problem is perhaps less narcissism than paranoia. Commenting on this scene in an essay about *Batman* and cultural memory, Jim Collins has compared the ways Batman and the Joker 'actively play with images' (Collins 1991: 167). Like the Joker, Batman is shown watching television a number of times in the film and like his adversary, he appears to be surrounded by images that he controls for his own purposes. Just as the Joker appears to be practically engulfed by the images he cuts up, the first shots of Batman in the Batcave show him before a bank of video monitors, surrounded on all sides by the images of his guests that his hidden cameras have been recording, and which he *calls up* rather than *cuts up* in order to bring back a reality that he has somehow missed. Where the Joker's manipulation of images is a process of deformation, Batman engages in a process of retrieval, drawing from that reservoir of images which constitutes 'the past'. This tension between abduction and retrieval epitomises the conflicting strategies at work

The technology of abjection in *Batman* (Tim Burton, 1989)

in this film, a text which alternately hijacks and 'accesses' the traditional Batman *topoi*. (Collins 1991: 168)

Caring less about the film's accessing of such *topoi* than Collins does, I would suggest different significations for the tension between cutting up and calling up images. I am especially interested in the tension Collins notes between controlling/retrieving images and being 'engulfed' in an imagistic 'reservoir', particularly as those last words relate to the scene of Batman and Napier's confrontation in the Axis Chemical Plant.

Not surprisingly, the Axis sequence begins, after an establishing shot, with the camera focused on a succession of mass-produced photographic images: 'wanted' posters of Jack Napier, which the treacherous and corrupt Lt. Eckhardt (William Hootkins) is distributing to his men. 'Shoot to kill', he says, 'Know what I mean?' – the question posed perhaps less to the cops than to *Batman* viewers growing sensitive to the film's foregrounding of the 'homicidal' propensities of the cinematic apparatus itself. Inside Axis, the dynamics of the *fort/da* emerge again: Batman lassoes one of Napier's men, pulls him over a railing and leaves him helplessly hanging. The camera lingers on Batman's cowled face as he himself lingers on this scene, staring as if fascinated by the image of the dangling man. This image is replicated shortly thereafter as Batman holds on to a suspended Jack Napier, only to let him finally drop into an engulfing vat of chemical waste, a 'letting fall' that further underscores the anal dynamics of *Batman* and of the *fort/da* itself.

Through the ensuing process of cloacal transformation, 'the Joker' is born. Actually, the figure of the Joker emerges gradually in a series of scenes that read like a parody of the Lacanian narrative of subjective development leading from the Real to the Imaginary to the Symbolic. Napier's body is expelled from the Axis Chemical Plant through a sewage drain, and we first see him again as a body-in-fragments, a disfigured hand reaching up in agony out of this 'oceanic' stream of dissolution. We next witness what might be called his 'mirror stage' in the shabby plastic surgeon's office: beholding his newly and permanently rictalised face for the first time, he smashes the mirror and breaks out into peals of laughter. In the third scene, he steps into Carl Grissom's office (out of the same elevator that we last saw producing Alicia's commodity-laden, image-is-everything body), reaccommodates himself to the Name-of-the-Father by articulating his new identity ('Jack's dead, my friend; you can call me Joker'), and proceeds to empty a revolver into Grissom's body.

In this murderous scene (though in *Batman* all photographically framed 'scenes' are potentially murderous), the Joker both upholds and destroys what Leo Bersani calls the 'sacrosanct value of selfhood' (Bersani 1987: 222): he kills to protect the seriousness of his statement of identity even as he reveals – and revels in the fact – that that statement is a joke. He simultaneously consolidates and disperses an identity that both must be and cannot be taken seriously, and begins to signify both the murderousness of stable identity as well as its abject destabilisation. Joker thus represents an attack *on* and *of* identity, an assault *on* and *of* representation, and this attack underscores the ironic duplicity of representation itself, the dependence of subjective identity on objectifying representational images that simultaneously guarantee and threaten the very coherence of ego boundaries. The Joker not only embodies the threat that mechanical reproduction as a 'feminising' process poses to the dominant fiction of unimpaired masculinity; he also enacts, as we shall see, a masculinist aggression against the feminine image upon which that fiction depends. This ambiguity expresses the crucial carnal irony of the dominant fiction, but it also thematicises the film's inevitably masochistic iconoclasm: *Batman* is a film that simultaneously revels in and mourns its own status as image, *as film*, foregrounding its own anxieties about its pulpy comic origins and about its uneasy status between seriously 'high' or masculinist cinematic artiness and laughably 'low' or feminised, kitschy mass commerce. Engulfing itself in the liquefying flux of imagistic violence from which it seems to want extrication, enacting while exposing the displacements and projections it warns against, questioning the numerous boundaries upon which it nonetheless insists, *Batman* itself unavoidably becomes the commodified toxic event it fears.

The relations among representation, slaughter, photo-toxicity, gender instability and the Joker's analised laughter begin to emerge more explicitly in the immediately following sequences, as do the film's more disturbing racial politics. Just after punching Harvey Dent's televised face with the mechanical boxing glove, the Joker announces: 'This town needs an enema!' Shortly thereafter, we see Vale examining her black and white photographs of Wayne: 'Mister Wayne', she murmurs in puzzlement, as if his 'mystery' in some way complicated his status as a 'Mister'. The camera cuts to a close shot of a table strewn with black and white photos of ludicrously grinning but obviously dead men, along with a manilla envelope stamped 'CIA: DDOD Nerve Gas – Discontinued 1977'. Apparently, these men have not only been photographed but gassed, eliminated, and the shot works to imply a connection between gaseous elimination and the harm that photography can do to men.

Zooming out and panning left, the camera reveals the Joker cutting up photos with scissors, engulfed now not in a vat of chemical waste, but in a sea of photographic fragments of the CIA mass murder. When the goon Bob (Tracey Walter), whom the Joker had sent out on a surveillance mission, reports back with his photos of Knox and Vale, the

Joker is captivated by Vale and takes his scissors to her. 'So hard to stay inside the lines', he laughs, indicating that he is in fact mutilating her image. Here the Joker's duplicity is figured succinctly: he not only represents the feminising and abjecting 'mutilation' to which representation submits masculinity but submits femininity to aggressive mutilation as well. He figures a bewildering threat both *to* and *of* the femininity that Batman must correspondingly both protect and protect himself against. As we shall see, what this means for Batman is that he must protect Vale as an image, as an object that he can safely manipulate in the armoured balletics of his own *fort/da*, while at the same time protecting himself from her ability to make images, to turn *him* into a photograph.

Batman's thematisation of its anxieties about the toxic, liquifying, feminising potential of specular mimeticism comes to a head in the Fluggenheim Museum scene and the chase/fight sequence that follows it. In a prelude to the museum sequence, we see the Joker sitting before a mirror in Alicia's apartment, calmly applying the toxic make-up that has already claimed a number of fashion victims. When Alicia appears, ominously masked, in the same mirror, the identification between her and the Joker as manufactured images – an identification that was first suggested in Grissom's apartment – is re-emphasised, as is the idea that masculinity is, no less than femininity, a masquerade. The Joker, however, highlights the real power asymmetry of this masquerade by ironically assuming the position of father and producer: 'Daddy's going to make some art', he tells Alicia.

Inside the Fluggenheim, having gassed all the patrons but the gas-masked Vale, the Joker and his goons 'improve' the paintings with infantile flingings and smearings that are so exuberantly faecal that the word 'party' in Prince's boom-boxed 'Party Man' starts to sound like 'potty'. But the Joker is not merely desecrating high-cultural monuments: rather, he is revealing the long-standing cultural anxiety that art, particularly painting, by virtue of being representation, by virtue of being something made seen, is already a liquification of essence, a desecration, rather than a preservation, of some (supposedly) invisible, transcendent truth. As Lacan puts it, 'The authenticity of what emerges in painting is diminished in us human beings by the fact that we have to get our colours where they're to be found, that is to say, in the shit … The creator will never participate in anything other than the creation of small dirty deposit, a succession of small dirty deposits juxtaposed' (Lacan 1978: 117).

The Joker's laughter destroys transcendence, as Georges Bataille puts it, or at least destroys the idea that art can provide or secure authenticity or essence. Moreover, if the terms 'essence' and 'transcendence' have functioned historically in the reproduction of the dominant fiction of unimpaired masculinity, then we can read the Joker's claim that he is the 'first fully functioning homicidal artist' as a comment less about *his* art than about the 'homicidal', masculinity-impairing 'nature' of art itself. When the Joker displays the disfigured Alicia and says 'now *like me* she's a living work of art', the words I have stressed indicate this demasculinising effect of art, its propensity to figure an identification with the feminine. At the same time, the Joker clearly upholds and literalises the masculinist power of art to contain the feminine through objectifying representational violence: 'Alicia here has been made over in line with my new philosophy.' Again, the Joker illuminates the carnal irony of the dominant fiction of unimpaired masculinity: to sustain itself, that fiction, which depends upon representation, must displace the inevitable impairments of representation – its propensity to objectify and abject, to turn its subjects into cultural waste – onto the feminine.

I have suggested that the Joker, in representing representation, figures as a threat both *to* and *of* femininity. Similarly, Vicki Vale, in her position as both photograph*ed* and photograph*er*, represents the potential both to stabilise masculinity and to abject it. Thus Batman's stance towards Vale is mixed: he must protect both her body from the Joker, and his own body from her gaze. This duplicity is enacted in the chase/fight sequence following the Fluggenheim scene. Trapped in an alley by the Joker's goons, Batman uses his line to hoist Vale to safety atop a building, then drops back into the alley to do battle. Momentarily laid low, Batman lies supine in the alley while the goons examine his body armour. Realising they cannot 'check his wallet' to discover his identity, they begin to lift off his cowl. 'He's human, after all', says one, his voice suddenly avuncular.

At this moment of Batman's most conspicuous vulnerability and impairment, Vale attempts to take pictures from the top of the building. The goons turn on her with particular vehemence. 'Shoot her!' Bob cries, and in this exchange, in which Vale shoots and the goons shoot back, it is as if the goons themselves had suddenly become Batman's agents, the aggressive protectors of his identificatory soft-spot. The close juxtaposition of the lines 'he's human' and 'shoot *her*', punctuated only by Vale's flash, works to gender as feminine both the photographic and the ballistic targets. The soft, human vulnerability beneath the hyper-masculinised body armour is exposed as 'feminine', and protected from Vale's penetrating, abjecting gaze, at the same time that her body is threatened with a more serious, retaliatory penetration. Thus the sequence enacts the dominant fiction's guiding representational logic: exposure of male vulnerability is answered with a violent and amplified displacement of that very vulnerability onto the feminine. Batman reinscribes this displacement when, after chasing the goons away, he greets Vale with a hostile remark about her weight, a reminder of her embodied subjection to the gravity that he effectively transcends. He then whisks Vale away to the Batcave for a ravishment, the main point of which is to relieve her of her 'damaging' film.

Batman's view of the nature of representational damage – abjecting, feminising, deadly – is insisted upon one more time in the following scene in Vale's apartment. The fashionably clad Wayne has appeared there to tell Vale who he really is, and his difficulties in announcing his identity underscore his vulnerability yet again: Armanied but unarmoured, he cannot bring himself to lay bare or re-present his identity to Vale. The potential price of such exposure is suggested when the Joker unexpectedly appears. After shooting Wayne – seemingly transforming him from fashionable 'crap' to Corto Maltese-ish corpse (though, as we discover, he has shielded himself) – the Joker makes a thematically conspicuous exit. As he dances out of Vale's apartment in slow motion, Danny Elfman's score turns heavy and lugubrious, a musical rendition of a *Durchfall* (see note 4 below). Once in the hallway, the Joker mimics flatulent self-propulsion, as if he were shitting while escaping the scene of his crime – or perhaps, as if any representational 'scene' were in itself abjectly homicidal. And on the wall behind him, the background for this flatulent dance is a Titianesque painting of a supine nude woman, a figure whose posture replicates that of the supposedly wasted Wayne.

By the end of the film, however, it is the Joker who has become thoroughly representational, a walking compilation of wind-up, chattering fake teeth, phony appendages and guns that no longer shoot but only produce flags that say 'Bang!' (suggesting not that cinematic violence is 'merely' representational, but that representation itself is violence). Whereas Batman is vulnerable on the inside, but invulnerable, because armoured, on the outside, the Joker seems soft on the outside, but indestructible, because artificial, in his interior. Even after he has taken his final fatal plunge, and lies leering up at the law from the cracked pavement, his signature laughter persists as the 'soulless' mechanical wheeze of a toy laugh-box. Batman, on the other hand, has saved himself and Vale from the fall, and both now hang safely suspended above the mess of the Joker's demise.

Soon we have Harvey Dent telling us that Batman has made the streets of Gotham safe again and will return whenever we need him. And how, Knox asks, will he know? Commissioner Gordon, in one of *Batman*'s supremely self-reflexive moments, responds by revealing what is in effect a giant *projector*, and cries 'He gave us a signal!' Several ironies are at work here: not only is the projection machine no less mechanical than the Joker's laugh-box, but the image it projects is already, by the time of the film's distribution, a mass-produced commodity saturating the market as aggressively as any of the Joker's chemical products. Moreover, as Silverman reminds us, projection itself is always only 'a tenuous barrier ... since what has been cast violently away will continue to threaten from without' (Silverman 1992: 47).

As if to stress again the nature of the threat, the camera takes us back into a cloacal alley – now presumably sanitised for our protection – for one last look at Vale's face, then pans up and out of the city for the final shot of Batman, standing erect at the top of a skyscraper, gazing now not down at anti-patriarchal crime, but up in reverence at the projection of the very bat-insignia with which the film began, this one now 'purely' light and shadow, cast loose from its earlier, more material engulfment: a representational image that supposedly signifies Batman's salvation from, and transcendence of, representation itself – as well as his ability to save us from its evil clutches. But if we know what the film has so repeatedly told us we are looking at, and understand all of the mechanisms of projection that the film has both undercut and reinscribed then, despite the triumphant swellings of Elfman's score, we might still hear in the background the traces of a subversive laughter that works to destroy the transcendence of any signal that any Batman might give.

Notes

1   In 'Anxiety and Instinctual Life', Freud writes: 'it is a universal conviction among children, who long retain the cloaca theory, that babies are born from the bowel like a piece of faeces: defecation is the model of birth' (Freud 1953–74, vol. 22: 100).

2   Silverman uses the term 'historical trauma' to describe a significant disruption in what she calls 'the dominant fiction', i.e., the 'ideological belief [through which] a society's "reality" is constituted and sustained, and [through which] a subject lays claim to a normative identity' (Silverman 1992: 15). Silverman writes that dominant fictions consist of 'the images and stories through which a society figures consensus; images and stories which cinema, fiction, popular culture and other forms of mass representation presumably both draw upon and help to shape' (Silverman 1992: 30). Drawing upon Althusser as well as Lacan, Silverman goes on to say that 'our present dominant fiction is above all else the representational system through which the subject is accommodated to the Name-of-the-Father. Its most central signifier of unity is the (paternal) family, and its primary signifier of privilege the phallus' (Silverman 1992: 34). Stressing that the dominant fiction 'not only offers the representational system by means of which the subject typically assumes a sexual identity ... but forms the stable core around which a nation's and a period's 'reality' coheres' (Silverman 1992: 41), Silverman claims that 'our dominant fiction calls upon the

male subject to see himself … only through the mediation of images of an unimpaired masculinity' and that the dominant fiction correspondingly urges and depends upon a perception of 'the commensurability of penis and phallus' (Silverman 1992: 42), an assumed identity between an always eminently impairable appendage and a supposedly indestructible (because untouchable) signifier of power and privilege.

3　See the introduction to West 1993.

4　In *Male Matters* (1999) I juxtapose Freud's discussions of the *fort/da* game with his insistence on the universality among children of a cloacal theory of birth. I suggest that the cloaca theory helps account for the abject or expelled status of that 'lost object' that Lacan says is the phantasmatic support of the subject, and I argue that the 'instinct for mastery' that motivates the *fort/da* game may also be motivated by the boy's desire to overcome his feeling of helpless and abject passivity by symbolising the mother's body as a small, passive, controllable object. In so doing, I suggest, the boy attempts to disavow not only his own dependency on the mother, and any figuration of the mother as an active subjective agent, but also an anxious feeling of a deep ontological *shittiness* at the core of subjective existence itself. The *fort/da* game, in other words, is implicated not only with the boy's phantasy of having been produced through the mother's bowels, and his foreclosure of that phantasy, but also with his own struggles to secure identity through the control of *his* bowels. However, the success of this anally symbolic enterprise is only ever partial, and the feeling of what I call 'scatontological anxiety' may continue to haunt the construction-site of any symbolically secured masculine identity. This haunting remains in effect, I argue, because identity cannot be secured without recourse to modes of representation – speech, writing, image-production, including photography and cinema – that inevitably transform the representing subject *back* into a represented object. And this production, this transforming *back*, can be a phantasmatic *falling back*, a dissolution of ego boundaries, a traumatising *Durchfall* (a German word that means failure, falling through, and the involuntary emptying of the bowels). Thus the image of 'unimpaired masculinity', the self-produced, self-representational image of the actively 'self-made man', is haunted by the earlier phantasmatic image of having been a passively and cloacally (m)other-made child. In other words, the *image* of unimpaired masculinity through which the dominant fiction supposedly guarantees itself is ultimately unable to overcome historical trauma, and it fails to do so precisely by virtue of *being* a produced image. Though this inability is inscribed in any linguistic or representational practice, it is particularly apparent in photography, and hence cinema.

5　Cf. Barry Sanders in *Sudden Glory: Laughter as Subversive History*: 'Philosophical documents on laughter, religious statements and mandates forbidding laughter – all these provide instructions on how and when and how hard to laugh. They designate the proper attitude one should take toward laughter, because laughter is our last "sense" to capitulate to authority. No other bodily function requires such attention and close supervision. We may ask, "Is the baby potty trained?" but no one would dare wonder, "Does the baby have its laughter under control?" And yet, no other bodily function demands such controls, as if laughter dogged us as a vestige of some earlier, incontinent time – a more primitive period when we laughed and defecated and took our pleasure at will. Neatly tucked away, safely hidden from view, laughter threatens to blow our adult, civilised cover at every moment' (Sanders 1995: 25). Note also certain similarities: the sphincterish quality of a camera's shutter (which complicates the image of the camera as the mediator of a penetrating gaze, since the camera in effect has to be penetrated by light in order to work); the fact that the muscles that control the opening and shutting of the eye are called sphincters; the pun, no doubt made many times before in psychoanalytically-inflected film theory, on the reel of the *fort/da*, the cinematic reel, and Real.

6　For the connection, within the masculinist imaginary, between mass culture and femininity, see Huyssen, 'Mass Culture as Woman: Modernism's Other', in Huyssen 1986.

bibliography

Aaron, M. (2000) 'Hardly chazans: *Yentl* and the singing Jew', in B. Marshall and R. Stilwell (eds) *Musicals: Hollywood and Beyond*. Exeter: Intellect, 125–31.

_____ (2001) 'Pass/Fail', *Screen*, 42, 1, 92–6.

Aguilar, C. and J. Genover (1996) *Las estrellas de nuestro cine*. Madrid: Alianzas Editorial.

Andrew, G. (1994) 'Upper class hit', *Time Out*, 11–18 May.

Andrews, N. (2001) '*Bridget Jones*', *Financial Times*, 13 April.

Anon. (1997) '*Face/Off*', *Empire*, 102, 38–9.

Aprà, A. and C. Carabba (1976) *Neorealismo d'appendice*. Rimini-Firenze: Guaraldi.

Aprà, A. and P. Pistagnesi (eds) (1986) *Comedy, Italian Style 1950–1980*. Turin: ERI.

Austin, G. (2003) *Stars in French Cinema*. Manchester: Manchester University Press.

Babington, B. (ed.) (2001) *British Stars and Stardom: From Alma Taylor to Sean Connery*. Manchester: Manchester University Press.

Babington, B. and P. W. Evans (1989) *Affairs to Remember: The Hollywood Comedy of the Sexes*. Manchester: Manchester University Press.

Babuscio, J. (1984) 'Camp and the gay sensibility', in R. Dyer (ed.) *Gays and Film*. New York: Zoetrope, 40–57.

Baillieu, B. and J. Goodchild (2002) *The British Film Business*. Chichester: John Wiley and Sons.

Balázs, B. (1974) 'The close-up', in G. Mast and M. Cohen (eds) *Film Theory and Criticism*. Oxford: Oxford University Press, 184–94.

Barker, F. (1971) '*Get Carter*', *Evening Standard*, 11 March.

Barker, P. (1969) 'Boy in a cage', *New Society*, 20 November.

Barr, C. (1977) *Ealing Studios*. London: Cameron and Tayleur.

Barthes, R. (1973) *Mythologies*. London: Paladin.

_____ (1979) *A Lover's Discourse – Fragments*, trans. R. Howard. London: Jonathan Cape.

_____ (1981) *Camera Lucida: Reflections on Photography*, trans. R. Howard. New York: Noonday.

Basinger, J. (1993) *A Woman's View: How Hollywood Spoke to Women, 1930–1960*. London: Chatto and Windus.

Bataille, G. (1985) *Visions of Excess: Selected Writings, 1927–1939*. Edited by A. Stoekel. Minneapolis: University of Minnesota Press.

Beltrán, P. (1992) 'Mi amigo Paco' in J. T. Cánovas (ed.) *Francisco Rabal*. Murcia:

Filmoteca Regional de Murcia, 59–64.

Benayoun, R. (1964) 'L'Insoumis d'Alain Cavalier', *France-Observateur*, 24 September.

Berry, D. (1994) *Wales and Cinema: The First Hundred Years*. Cardiff: University of Wales Press.

Bersani, L. (1987) 'Is the rectum a grave?', *October*, 43, 197–222.

Bérubé, A. (1990) *Coming Out Under Fire: The History of Gay Men and Women in World War Two*. New York: Plume Books.

Biery, R. (1932a) '"I'm not so sure", says Clark Gable', *Photoplay* (January), 69, 96–7.

_____ (1932b) 'Will Clark Gable last?', *Photoplay* (August), 67, 113.

Bingham, D. (1994) *Acting Male: Masculinities in the Films of James Stewart, Jack Nicholson, and Clint Eastwood*. New Brunswick: Rutgers University Press.

Blackwell, B. (2002) 'A blustery day for a baby: technologies of family formation in *Twister*', *Camera Obscura*, 49, 189–215.

Blitz, J. (2001) 'Berlusconi sets stall out on public and private roles', *Financial Times*, 27 June, 1–2. http://globalarchive.ft.com/globalarchive/articles.html?print=trueandid=01 0627001447

Blundy, A. (1994) 'Hyping for a hit', *The Guardian*, 16 May.

Boneschi, M. (1995) *Poveri ma belli: i nostri anni cinquanta*. Milan: Oscar Mondadori.

Bonnaud, F. (1999) 'Tempête sus un crâne', *Les Inrockuptibles*, 17 February, 39.

Borau, J. L. (ed.) (1998) 'Academia de las Artes y las Ciencias Cinematográficas de España', *Diccionario del cine español*. Madrid: Alianza Editorial.

Borde, R. and E. Chaumeton (1955) *Panorama du film noir américain (1941–1953)*. Paris: Minuit.

Bory, J.-L. (1964) '*Les Félins*', *Arts*, 25 June.

Bourbon, T. de (1999) 'Gaspar Noé, la violence du quotidien', *L'Humanité*, 17 February.

Bourdieu, P. (1986 [1979]) *Distinction: A Social Critique of the Judgement of Taste*. London: Routledge.

_____ (1993) *The Field of Cultural Production*. Cambridge: Polity Press.

Bourget, E. and J.-L. Bourget (1987) *Lubitsch ou la satire romanesque*. Paris: Editions Stock.

Bowe Hearty, K. (1998) 'Suburban Shocker'. http://www.findarticles.com/p/articles/mi_ m1285/is_n11_v28/ai_21248641.

Boyero, C. (1992a) 'Entrevista con Paco Rabal' in J. T. Cánovas (ed.) *Francisco Rabal*. Murcia: Filmoteca Regional de Murcia, 9–38.

_____ (1992b) 'El, que tantos hombres ha sido' in J. T. Cánovas (ed.) *Francisco Rabal*. Murcia: Filmoteca Regional de Murcia, 47–50.

Bradbury, D. and J. McGrath (1998) *Now That's Funny! Conversations with Comedy Writers*. London: Methuen.

Bradbury, P. (1990) 'Desire and pregnancy', in A. Metcalf and M. Humphries (eds) *The Sexuality of Men*. London: Pluto Press, 129–49.

Bradshaw, P. (2001) '*Bridget Jones*', *The Guardian*, 13 April.

Breines, P. (1990) *Tough Jews: Political Fantasies and the Moral Dilemma of American Jewry*. New York: Basic Books.

Breward, C. (1999) *The Hidden Consumer: Masculinities, Fashion and City Life 1860–1914*. Manchester: Manchester University Press.

Brion, P. (1985) 'Old Heidelberg', in B. Eisenschitz and J. Narboni (eds) *Ernst Lubitsch*. Paris: Cahiers du cinéma/Cinémathèque Française, 118.

Brody, M. (1995) 'Batman: psychic trauma and its solution', *Journal of Popular Culture*, 28, 4, 171–8.

Brunetta, G. P. (1999) 'Grammatica della visione popolare' in O. Caldiron and S. Della Casa (eds) *Appassionatamente: Il mélo nel cinema italiano*. Turin: Lindau, 185–94.

Bruzzi, S. (1997) *Undressing Cinema: Clothing and Identity in the Movies*. London and New York: Routledge.

Buache, F. (1987) *Le Cinéma français des années 60*. Renens: Hatier.

Bukatman, S. (1988) 'Paralysis in motion: Jerry Lewis's life as a man', *Camera Obscura*, 17, 195–205.

Burch, N. and G. Sellier (1996) *La Drôle de guerre des sexes du cinéma français, 1930–1956*. Paris: Nathan.

Burston, P. (1995) 'Just a gigolo? Narcissism, nellyism and the "New Man" theme', in P. Burston and C. Richardson (eds) *A Queer Romance: Lesbians, Gay Men and Popular Culture*. London: Routledge, 111–23.

Burt, R. (1995) *The Male Dancer: Bodies, Spectacle, Sexualities*. London: Routledge.

Buscombe, E. (ed.) (1998) *Back in the Saddle Again: New Essays on the Western*. London: British Film Institute.

Butler, J. (1990) *Gender Trouble: Feminism and the Subversion of Identity*. New York and London: Routledge.

_____ (1993) *Bodies That Matter: On the Discursive Limits of 'Sex'*. New York: Routledge.

_____ (1995) 'Melancholy gender/refused identification' in M. Berger, B. Wallis and S. Watson (eds) *Constructing Masculinity*. New York and London: Routledge, 21–37.

Caine, M. (1992) *What's it all About?* London: Random House.

Caldwell, L. (1995) 'Relations between men: Bernardo Bertolucci's *The Spider's Stratagem*', in P. Kirkham and J. Thumim (eds) *Me Jane: Masculinity, Movies and Women*. London: Lawrence and Wishart, 51–61.

Cameron, I. and D. Pye (eds) (1996) *The Movie Book of the Western*. London: Studio Vista.

Campassi, O. (1949) 'Gli altri', *Sequenze*, 4, December.

Campbell, B. (1983) *Wigan Pier Revisited: Poverty and Politics in the Eighties*. London: Virago.

Canova, G. (1999) 'L'infiammazione della lacrima: il paradosso del *mélo* nel cinema italiano' in O. Caldiron and S. Della Casa (eds) *Appassionatamente: Il mélo nel cinema italiano*. Turin: Lindau, 7–9.

Carpenter, C. T. and E. H. Yeatts (1996) *Stars Without Garters! The Memoirs of Two Gay GIs in WWII*. San Francisco: Alamo Square Press.

Carroll, R. (2001) 'Berlusconi to purge State TV', *The Guardian*, 22 May.

Case, M. and C. Shaw (eds) (1989) *The Imagined Past: History and Nostalgia*. Manchester: Manchester University Press.

Caughie, J. and K. Rockett (1996) *The Companion to British and Irish Cinema*. London: British Film Institute.

Cauliez, A.-J. (1956) *Le Film criminel et le film policier*. Paris: Cerf.

Cavendish, L. (1999) 'This Charming Man', *The Sunday Times Magazine*, 25 May.

Chalmers, R. (2000) 'Shaft the Movie', *The Mail on Sunday Review*, 19 March.

Chapman, R. (1996) 'The great pretender: variations on the New Man theme', in R. Chapman and J. Rutherford (eds) *Male Order: Unwrapping Masculinity*. London:

Lawrence and Wishart, 225–48.

Chaudhuri, A. (1994) 'Upper Class Treat', *Time Out*, 4–11 May.

Chauncey, G. (1994) *Gay New York: Gender, Urban Culture, and the Making of the Gay Male World 1890–1940*. New York: Basic Books.

Chauville, C. (ed.) (1998) *Dictionnaire du jeune cinéma français*. Paris: Éditions Scope.

Cinémathèque française (1996) *Alain Delon*. Paris: CNC.

Cohan, S. (1993) '"Feminising" the song-and-dance man: Fred Astaire and the spectacle of masculinity in the Hollywood musical', in S. Cohan and I. Hark (eds), *Screening the Male: Exploring Masculinities in Hollywood Cinema*. London and New York: Routledge, 46–69.

_____ (1997) *Masked Men: Masculinity and the Movies in the Fifties*. Bloomington: University of Indiana Press.

Cohan, S. and I. R. Hark (eds) (1993) *Screening the Male: Exploring Masculinities in Hollywood Cinema*. London and New York: Routledge.

Cohen, J. (1999) 'Yiddish Film and the American Immigrant Experience', in S. Paskin (ed.) *When Joseph Met Molly: A Reader on Yiddish Film*. Nottingham: Five Leaves, 11–37.

Collins, J. (1991) '*Batman*: the movie – narrative and the hyperconscious', in R. E. Pearson and W. Uricchio (eds) *The Many Lives of the Batman: Critical Approaches to a Superhero and His Media*. New York: Routledge, 164–81.

Colwell, D. (2003) 'Casting Call', *Details*, May, 74.

Connell, R. W. (1995) *Masculinities*. Cambridge: Polity Press.

Cook, P. (1982) 'Masculinity in crisis?', *Screen*, 23, 3–4, 39–46.

_____ (1996) *Fashioning the Nation: Costume and Identity in British Cinema*. London: British Film Institute.

Costello, J. (1985) *Virtue Under Fire: How World War II Changed Our Social and Sexual Attitudes*. Boston: Little, Brown.

Craig, G. A. (1982) *The Germans*. Harmondsworth: Penguin.

Creed, B. (1992) 'Introduction to Part IV: Images of Men', in *The Sexual Subject: A Screen Reader in Sexuality*. London and New York: Routledge, 261–4.

Cristofani, P. and R. Manetti (1956) 'Processo al non attore', *Cinema Nuovo*, 79, 25 March.

Curtis, R. (1994) 'Introduction', *Four Weddings and a Funeral*. London: Corgi Books, 8–10.

_____ (1997) [Interview], *Daily Telegraph Weekend*, 10 May, 35.

_____ (1999) 'Foreword', *Notting Hill*, London: Hodder and Stoughton, 10–17.

D'Lugo, M. (1987) 'Historical Reflexivity: Saura's Anti-*Carmen*', *Wide Angle*, 9, 3: 52–61.

Dahrendorf, R. (1987) *Society and Democracy in Germany*. London: Weidenfeld and Nicolson.

Davies, H. (2002) [Interview with Nick Hornby], *Daily Telegraph*, 15 April.

Delamater, J. (1981) *Dance in the Hollywood Musical*. Ann Arbor: UMI Research Press.

Doane, M. A. (1982) 'Film and the masquerade: theorising the female spectator', *Screen*, 23, 3–4, 74–87.

_____ (1987) *The Desire to Desire: The Woman's Film of the 1940s*. Basingstoke: Macmillan.

Donald, J. (1999) 'The citizen and the man about town', in J. Donald, *Imagining the*

Modern City. London: Athlone Press, 1–18.

Doty, A. (1995) 'There's something queer here', in C. K. Creekmuir and A. Doty (eds) *Out in Culture: Gay, Lesbian and Queer Essays on Popular Culture*. London: Cassell, 71–90.

Dyer, R. (1979) *Stars*. London: British Film Institute.

_____ (1986) 'Entertainment and utopia', in R. Altman (ed.) *Genre: The Musical*. London: Routledge and Kegan Paul, 175–89.

_____ (1987) *Heavenly Bodies: Film Stars and Society*. London: Macmillan.

_____ (1992) 'Don't look now: the male pin-up', in *Screen, The Sexual Subject: A Screen Reader in Sexuality*. London: Routledge, 265–76.

_____ (1998) 'Resistance through charisma: Rita Hayworth and *Gilda*', in E. A. Kaplan (ed.) *Women in Film Noir*. London: British Film Institute, 115–22.

_____ (1998) *Stars*, 2nd edn. London: British Film Institute.

Dyja, E. (ed.) (2000) *British Film Institute Film and Television Handbook 2001*. London: British Film Institute.

_____ (ed.) (2001) *British Film Institute Film and Television Handbook 2002*. London: British Film Institute.

_____ (ed.) (2002) *British Film Institute Film and Television Handbook 2003*. London: British Film Institute.

Edwards, A. (1996) *Streisand*. London: Orion.

Edwards, T. (1997) *Men in the Mirror: Men's Fashion, Masculinity and Consumer Society*. London: Cassell.

Ehrenreich, B. (1983) *The Hearts of Men*. London: Pluto Press.

Ehrenstein, D. (1998) *Open Secret: Gay Hollywood, 1928–1998*. New York: William Morrow.

Eisenschitz, B. and J. Narboni (eds) (1985) *Ernst Lubitsch*. Paris: Cahiers du cinéma/ Cinémathèque française.

Eley, G. (1995) '*Distant Voices, Still Lives*: the family is a dangerous place. Memory Gender, and the image of the working class', in R. A. Rosenstone (ed.) *Revisioning History: Film and the Construction of a New Past*. Princeton: Princeton University Press, 17–43.

Erdman, H. (1997) *Staging the Jew: The Performance of an American Ethnicity, 1860–1920*. New Brunswick: Rutgers University Press.

Evans, C. and L. Gammon (1995) 'The gaze revisited, or reviewing queer viewing', in P. Burston and C. Richardson (eds) *A Queer Romance: Lesbians, Gay Men and Popular Culture*. London: Routledge, 13–57.

Evans, P. W. (1995) *The Films of Luis Buñuel*. Oxford: Oxford University Press.

Eyman, S. (1993) *Ernst Lubitsch: Laughter in Paradise*. Baltimore: Johns Hopkins University Press.

Faludi, S. (1999) *Stiffed: The Betrayal of Modern Man*. London: Chatto.

Farmer, B. (2000) *Spectacular Passions: Cinema, Fantasy, Gay Male Spectatorships*. Durham: Duke University Press.

Fernández Santos, E. (2001) 'La muerte de Paco Rabal deja al cine sin uno de sus grandes mitos', *El País*, 30 August.

Ferraù, A. (1949) 'Interview du producteur Dino De Laurentiis', *Giornale dello Spettacolo*, 2, February.

Feuer, J. (1993) *The Hollywood Musical*, 2nd edn. Bloomington: Indiana University Press.

Field, M. (2000) 'Pretty in Pink', *The Independent on Sunday*, 30 January.

Finney, A. (1996) *The State of European Cinema: A New Dose of Reality*. London: Cassell.

Fisher, J. (1993) 'Clark Gable's balls: real men never lose their teeth', in P. Kirkham and J. Thumim (eds) *You Tarzan: Masculinity, Movies and Men*. London: Lawrence and Wishart, 35–51.

Foot, J. (2001) *Milan since the Miracle: City, Culture and Identity*. Oxford and New York: Berg.

Forbes, J. (1992) *The Cinema in France: After the New Wave*. London: Macmillan/British Film Institute.

Fox, J. (2002) 'First among billionaires', *The Guardian*, 28 September, 43–8.

Freud, S. (1953–74) *The Standard Edition of the Complete Psychological Works*. Trans. James Strachey, 24 vols. London: Hogarth.

Frodon, J.-M. (1999) 'Gaspar Noé, réalisateur: "les tournages éloignent les films de la réalité"', *Le Monde*, 18 February.

Fuss, D. (1992) 'Fashion and the homospectatorial look', *Critical Inquiry*, 18, 4, 713–37.

Gabriel Martín, F. (1992) 'Rabal y su imagen publicitario', in J. T. Cánovas (ed.) *Francisco Rabal*. Murcia: Filmoteca Regional de Murcia, 125–40.

Gans, C. (1992) 'La baise crade de Gaspar Noé', *7 à Paris*, 17 June.

Garber, M. (1992) *Vested Interests: Cross-dressing and Cultural Anxiety*. New York: Routledge.

Garnett, T. (1970) 'The interview: Tony Garnett', *Afterimage*, 1, n.p.

Gauteur, C. and G. Vincendeau (1993) *Jean Gabin: anatomie d'un mythe*. Paris: Nathan.

Genin, B. (1999) 'Ecoeurant de complaisance', *Télérama*, 2562, 17 February, 2.

Genné, B. (2001) '"Freedom Incarnate": Jerome Robbins, Gene Kelly and the Dancing Sailor as an icon of American values in World War II', *Dance Chronicle: Studies in Dance and the Related Arts*, 24, 1, 83–103.

Geraghty, C. (1995) 'Albert Finney: a working-class hero', in P. Kirkham and J. Thumim (eds) *Me Jane: Masculinity, Movies and Women*. London: Lawrence and Wishart, 62–71.

Gerstner, D. A. (2002) 'Dancer from the dance: Gene Kelly, television, and the beauty of movement', *Velvet Light Trap*, 49, 48–66.

Gieri, M. (1995) *Contemporary Italian Filmmaking: Strategies of Subversion. Pirandello, Fellini, Scola, and the Directors of the New Generation*. Toronto: University of Toronto Press.

Gilbert, G. (1959) *The Music of Spain*. New York: Dover.

Gilbert, L. (2001) 'All About Alfie', *The Guardian*, 4 May.

Gili, J. A. (1998) 'Entretien: Nanni Moretti', *Positif*, 448, 8–12.

Gilman, S. L. (1991) *The Jew's Body*. London: Routledge.

_____ (1993) *Freud, Race and Gender*. Princeton: Princeton University Press.

Ginsborg, P. (2003) *Italy and its Discontents: Family, Civil Society, State 1980–2001*. London: Penguin.

Gitten, D. (1995) 'But I want to be famous too…' [Interview with Duncan Kenworthy], *The Daily Telegraph*, 24 March.

Gledhill, C. (ed.) (1991) *Stardom: Industry of Desire*. London: Routledge.

_____ (1995) 'Women reading men', in P. Kirkham and J. Thumim (eds) *Me Jane: Masculinity, Movies and Women*. London: Lawrence and Wishart, 73–93.

Goldberg, J. N. (1983) *Laughter Through Tears: The Yiddish Cinema*. London: Associated University Press.

Gowdy, B. (1997) *We So Seldom Look on Love*. South Royalton: Vermont.

Green, J. (1999) *All Dressed Up: The Sixties and the Counterculture*. London: Pimlico.

Green, P. (1990) *The Enemy Without: Policing and Class Consciousness in the Miners' Strike*. Buckingham: Open University Press.

Greene, C. (1935) 'Why Clark Gable has stayed at top', *Photoplay* (November), 24–5, 100–1.

Greenlee, K. (1999) 'The unrepentant necrophile', http://www.shine.net.au/shinemag/unreg/necro.htm. Accessed 4 May 2003.

Griffith, R. (1962) *The Cinema of Gene Kelly*. New York: Museum of Modern Art.

Gubern, R., J. E. Monterde, J. Pérez Perucha, E. Riambau, C. Torreiro (1995) *Historia del cine español*. Madrid: Cátedra.

Gubitosi, G. (1998) *Amedeo Nazzari*. Bologna: Il Mulino.

Guérif, F. (1986) *Le Cinéma policier français*. Paris: Veyrier.

Guérif, F. and P. Mérigeau (1982) 'Pour quelques polars de plus…', *Image et Son*, 368, 67–74.

Hake, S. (1992) *Passions and Deceptions: The Early Films of Ernst Lubitsch*. Princeton: Princeton University Press.

Hallam, J. (2000) 'Film, class and national identity: re-imagining communities in the age of devolution', in J. Ashby and A. Higson (eds) *British Cinema Past and Present*. London: Routledge, 261–73.

Hall, L. (2000) 'Introduction', *Billy Elliot*. London: Faber and Faber.

Harris, S. (1996) 'Gene Kelly dies: legendary dancer was 83', *The Los Angeles Times* (3 February) Home Edition: A–1+. *The Los Angeles Times* Archives, downloaded 4 August.

Haskell, M. (1974) *From Reverence to Rape: The Treatment of Women in the Movies*. New York: Rinchart and Winston.

Hearty, K. B. (1998) 'Suburban Shocker', *Interview* (November), 34–6.

Heredero, C. F. (1992) 'Tiempo de madurez' in J. T. Cánovas (ed.) *Francisco Rabal*. Murcia: Filmoteca Regional de Murcia, 99–108.

Heredia, A. (1991) 'La *Carmen* de Saura dentro del género "romance": tradición y ruptura', *Explicación de textos literarios*, 20, 1, 79–87.

Hertz, F. (ed.) (1975) *The German Public Mind in the Nineteenth Century: A Social History of German Political Sentiments, Aspirations and Ideas*. London: George Allen and Unwin.

Hidalgo, M. (1985) *Francisco Rabal, un caso bastante excepcional*. Valladolid: 30 Semana Internacional de Cine de Valladolid.

Higbee, W. (2001) 'Screening the "other" Paris: cinematic representations of the French urban periphery in *La Haine* and *Ma 6-T va crack-er*', *Modern and Contemporary France*, 9, 2, 197–208.

Hill, J. (1986) *Sex, Class and Realism: British Cinema 1956–63*. London: British Film Institute.

_____ (2000a) 'From the New Wave to "Brit-Grit": community and difference in working class realism', in J. Ashby and A. Higson (eds) *British Cinema Past and Present*. London: Routledge, 249–60.

_____ (2000b) 'Failure and utopianism: representations of the working class in British cinema in the 1990s', in R. Murphy (ed.) *British Cinema of the 90s.* London: British Film Institute, 178–87.

Hillier, J. (1977) 'Interview with Stanley Donen', *Movie*, 24, 26–35.

Hirschhorn, C. (1984 [1974]) *Gene Kelly: A Biography.* New York: St. Martin's Press.

Hiscock, J. (2001) 'No more Mr Nice Guy', *The Daily Mirror*, 26 March, 22–3.

Hoberman, J. (1995a) *Bridge of Light: Yiddish Film Between Two Worlds.* Philadelphia: Temple University Press.

Hoberman, J. M. (1995b) 'Otto Weininger and the critique of Jewish masculinity', in N. A. Harrowitz and B. Hyams (eds) *Jews and Gender: Responses to Otto Weininger.* Philadelphia: Temple University Press, 141–53.

Holmlund, C. (1993) 'Masculinity as multiple masquerade', in S. Cohan and I. R. Hark (eds) *Screening the Male: Exploring Masculinities in Hollywood Cinema.* London: Routledge, 213–30.

_____ (2002a) 'Nouveaux westerns for the 1990s: genre offshoots, audience reroutes', in C. Holmlund, *Impossible Bodies: Femininity and Masculinity at the Movies.* London and New York: Routledge, 51–67.

_____ (2002b) 'The aging Clint', in C. Holmlund, *Impossible Bodies: Femininity and Masculinity at the Movies.* London and New York: Routledge, 141–56.

Horrocks, R. (1995) *Male Myths and Icons: Masculinity in Popular Culture.* Houndmills, Basingstoke: Macmillan.

Hutchings. P. (1993) 'Masculinity and the horror film', in P. Kirkham and J. Thumim (eds) *You Tarzan: Masculinity, Movies and Men.* London: Lawrence and Wishart, 84–94.

Huyssen, A. (1986) *After the Great Divide: Modernism, Mass Culture, Postmodernism.* Bloomington: Indiana University Press.

Hyams, B. and N. A. Harrowitz (1995) 'A critical introduction to the history of Weininger reception', in N. A. Harrowitz and B. Hyams (eds) *Jews and Gender: Responses to Otto Weininger.* Philadelphia: Temple University Press, 3–20.

Jacobs, L. (1991) *The Wages of Sin: Censorship and the Fallen Woman Film.* Madison: University of Wisconsin Press.

James, N. (1999) 'Farewell to Napoli', *Sight and Sound*, 9, 5, 20–2.

Jarausch, K. H. (1982 in text) *Students, Society and Politics in Imperial Germany.* New Jersey: Princeton University Press.

Jeffords, S. (1993) 'The Big Switch: Hollywood Masculinity in the 1990s', in J. Collins, H. A. Radner and A. P. Collins (eds) *Film Theory Goes to the Movies.* New York and London: Routledge, 196–208.

_____ (1994) *Hard Bodies: Hollywood Masculinity in the Reagan Era.* New Brunswick: Rutgers University Press.

Jobling, P. (1999) *Fashion Spreads: Word and Image in Fashion Photography since 1980.* Oxford: Berg.

Johnston, S. (1994) 'Made here. Big over there', *Independent*, 27 April.

_____ (2002) '*About A Boy*', *ScreenDaily.com*, 7661, 18 March.

Jordan, B. and R. Morgan-Tamosunas (1998) *Contemporary Spanish Cinema.* Manchester: Manchester University Press.

Jousse, T. and S. Toubiana (1996) 'Le deuxième souffle de Melville', *Les Cahiers du cinéma*, 507, 63.

Kagan, J. (ed.) (2000) *Directors Close Up*. Boston: Focal Press.

Kaiser, C. (1997) *The Gay Metropolis, 1940–1996*. New York: Houghton Mifflin.

Kemp, P. (1999) 'New Maps of Albion', *Film Comment*, 35, 3, 64–9.

Kenworthy, D. (1994) *You Magazine, Mail on Sunday*, 24 April.

_____ (1999) 'We flew by Concorde, lunched, laughed; and Julia Roberts was ours', *The Independent on Sunday*, 2 May.

Kessler-Harris, A. (1982) *Out to Work: A History of Wage-Earning Women in the United States*. New York and Oxford: Oxford University Press.

Kincaid, J. (1998) *Erotic Innocence: The Culture of Child Molesting*. Durham and London: Duke University Press.

Kinder, M. (1993) *Blood Cinema: The Reconstruction of National Identity in Spain*. Berkeley: University of California Press.

King, G. (2002) *Film Comedy*. London: Wallflower Press.

Kirkham. P. (1995) 'Loving men: Frank Borzage, Charles Farrell and the reconstruction of masculinity in 1920s Hollywood cinema', in P. Kirkham and J. Thumim (eds) *Me Jane: Masculinity, Movies and Women*. London: Lawrence and Wishart, 94–112.

Kirkham, P. and Thumim, J. (eds) (1993) *You Tarzan: Masculinity, Movies and Men*. London: Lawrence and Wishart.

_____ (eds) (1995a) *Me Jane: Masculinity, Movies and Women*. London: Lawrence and Wishart.

_____ (1995b) 'Me Jane', in P. Kirkham and J. Thumim (eds) *Me Jane: Masculinity, Movies and Women*. London: Lawrence and Wishart, 11–35.

Knee, A. (1993) 'The dialectic of female power and male hysteria in *Play Misty for Me*', in S. Cohan and I. R. Hark (eds) *Screening the Male: Exploring Masculinities in Hollywood Cinema*. London and New York: Routledge, 87–102.

Kohut, T. A. (1991) *Wilhelm II and the Germans: A Study in Leadership*. Oxford: Oxford University Press.

Konstantarakos, M. (1998) 'Le Renouveau du cinéma français dans les années 90: s'agit-il d'une nouvelle nouvelle vague?', *Contemporary French Civilization*, 22, 2, 140–71.

Kovacs, K. S. (1990) 'Parody as "Countersong" in Saura and Godard', *Quarterly Review of Film and Video*, 12, 1–2, 105–24.

Kristeva, J. (1982 [1980]) *Powers of Horror: An Essay on Abjection*. Trans. Leon S. Roudiez. New York: Columbia University Press.

Krutnik, F. (1991) *In a Lonely Street: Film Noir, Genre, Masculinity*. London and New York: Routledge.

____ (1998) 'Love lies: romantic fabrication in contemporary romantic comedy', in P. W. Evans and C. Deleyto (eds) *Terms of Endearment: Hollywood Romantic Comedy of the 1980s and 1990s*. Edinburgh: Edinburgh University Press, 15–36.

____ (2002) 'Conforming passions?: contemporary romantic comedy', in S. Neale (ed.) *Genre and Contemporary Hollywood*. London: British Film Institute, 130–47.

Kuhn, A. (1985) *The Power of the Image: Essays on Representation and Sexuality*. London: Routledge and Kegan Paul.

Kuhn, M. (2002) *One Hundred Films and a Funeral*. London: Thorogood.

Kursk, H. von (2002) '"I can't chase women anymore … and I miss it"', *The Daily Mirror*, 29 March.

Lacan, J. (1970) 'Of structure as an inmixing of otherness prerequisite to any subject whatever', in R. Macksey and E. Donato (eds) *The Structuralist Controversy: The Languages of Criticism and the Sciences of Man*. Baltimore: Johns Hopkins University Press, 186–200.

_____ (1977) *Écrits: A Selection*. Trans. Alan Sheridan. New York: Norton.

_____ (1978) *The Four Fundamental Concepts of Psychoanalysis*. Trans. Alan Sheridan. New York: Norton.

Lacourbe, R. (1969) 'Défense et illustration du travail d'orfèvre. Vingt ans de hold-up à l'écran. Première partie', *Cinéma 69*, 134, 54–76.

Laing, S. (1986) *Representations of Working Class Life*. London: Macmillan.

Lamar, C. (1989) *Wilhelm II: Prince and Emperor 1859–1900*. Chapel Hill: University of North Carolina Press.

Lambert, G. (1990) *Norma Shearer: A Life*. New York: Knopf.

Lehman, P. (1993) *Running Scared: Masculinity and the Representation of the Male Body*. Philadelphia: Temple University Press.

_____ (ed.) (2001a) *Masculinity: Bodies, Movies, Culture*. New York and London: Routledge.

_____ (2001b) 'Crying over the melodramatic penis: melodrama and male nudity in films of the 90s', in P. Lehman (ed.) *Masculinity: Bodies, Movies, Culture*. New York: Routledge, 25–42.

Leslie, A. (1965) [Interview with Michael Caine], *The Daily Express*, 9 November.

Lévi-Strauss, C. (1972) *Structural Anthropology*. Harmondsworth: Penguin University Books.

Loewenstein, A. F. (1996) 'The protection of masculinity: Jews as projective pawns in the texts of William Gerhardie and George Orwell', in B. Cheyette (ed.) *Between 'Race' and Culture: Representations of 'the Jew' in English and American Literature*. Stanford: Stanford University Press, 145–64.

Loughery, J. (1998) *The Other Side of Silence: Men's Lives and Gay Identities – A Twentieth-Century History*. New York: Henry Holt.

Lukk, T. (1997) *Movie Marketing: Opening the Picture and Giving it Legs*. Los Angeles: Silman-James Press.

Lynn, H. (1933a) 'Which movie star dominates you?', *Photoplay* (March), 30–1, 102–3.

_____ (1933b) 'How 12 stars make love', *Photoplay* (August), 30–2, 103–4.

MacDonald, I. (1995) *Revolution in the Head*. London: Pimlico.

Maillot, P. (1996) *Les Fiancés de Marianne. La Société française à travers ses grands acteurs*. Paris: Cerf.

Malcolm, D. (1995) 'What hugh did next', *Guardian*, 3 August, section 2, 8.

Mann, W. J. (2001) *Behind the Screen: How Gays and Lesbians Shaped Hollywood 1910–1969*. New York: Viking.

Marie, M. (ed.) (1998) *Le Jeune cinéma français*. Paris: Nathan.

Marinero, M. (1992) 'Con vino de Pozo Estrecho' in J. T. Cánovas (ed.) *Francisco Rabal*. Murcia: Filmoteca Regional de Murcia, 55–8.

Martin, R. (1990) *Armani*. New York: Rizzoli Press.

Martín-Lunas, M. (2001) 'Adiós a Paco Rabal. El actor comprometido', *El mundo*, 30 August.

Marwick, A. (1996) *British Society Since 1945*. London: Penguin.

_____ (1998) *The Sixties*. Oxford: Oxford University Press.

Masson, C. (1998) 'Entretien avec Jean-François Richet, réalisateur', in M. Marie (ed.) *Le Jeune cinéma français*. Paris: Nathan, 112–15.

McCullough, J. (1989) 'Imagining Mr. Average', *CineAction!*, 17, 43–55.

McElvaine, R. (1984) *The Great Depression: America, 1929–1941*. New York: Times Books.

McIntyre, S. (1995) 'Vanishing point: feature film in a small country', in J. Hill, M. McLoone and P. Hainsworth (eds) *Border Crossing: Film in Ireland, Britain and Europe*. Belfast/London: IIS/British Film Institute, 85–112.

McKimm, J. (1999) 'London falls head over heels for Hugh and Julia', *Evening Standard*, 14 May.

Medhurst, A. (1993) '"It's as a man that you've failed": masculinity and forbidden desire in *The Spanish Gardener*', in P. Kirkham and J. Thumim (eds) *You Tarzan: Masculinity, Movies and Men*. London: Lawrence and Wishart, 95–105.

Médioni, G. (1999) 'Sous la cité, la plage', *L'Express*, 21 January.

Meyer, M. (1994) 'Introduction: reclaiming the discourse of camp', in M. Meyer, *The Politics and Poetics of Camp*. London: Routledge, 1–22.

Millea, H. (2001) 'Hugh Grant', *Hello!*, 24 April, 12–18.

Mintz, S. and S. Kellogg (1988) *Domestic Revolutions: A Social History of American Family Life*. New York: The Free Press.

Monk, C. (2000a) 'Men in the 90s', in R. Murphy (ed.) *British Cinema of the 90s*. London: British Film Institute, 156–66.

_____ (2000b) 'Underbelly UK: the 1990s underclass film, masculinity and the ideologies of "New" Britain', in J. Ashby and A. Higson (eds) *British Cinema, Past and Present*. London: Routledge, 274–87.

Monterde, J. E. (1989) 'El cine histórico durante la transición política', in J. A. Hurtado and F. M. Picó (eds) *Escritos sobre el cine español 1973–1987*. Valencia: Filmoteca de la Generalitat Valenciana, 45–63.

Morgan, R. (1995) 'Pedro Almodóvar's *Tie Me Up, Tie Me Down!*: the mechanics of masculinity', in P. Kirkham and J. Thumim (eds) *Me Jane: Masculinity, Movies and Women*. London: Lawrence and Wishart, 113–28.

Morgan-Tamosunas, R. (2000) 'Screening the past: history and nostalgia in contemporary Spanish cinema', in B. Jordan and R. Morgan-Tamosunas (eds) *Contemporary Spanish Cultural Studies*. London: Arnold, 111–22.

Mort, F. (1996) *Cultures of Consumption: Commerce, Masculinities and Social Space*. London and New York: Routledge.

Mosse, G. L. (1966) *The Crisis of German Ideology: Intellectual Origins of the Third Reich*. London: Weidenfeld and Nicholson.

Mosse, W. E. (1989) *The German-Jewish Economic Elite 1820–1938: A Socio-Cultural Profile*. Oxford: Oxford University Press.

Moulin, R.-J. (1960) 'René Clément: Je me prépare à la comédie', *Les Lettres Françaises*, 3 March.

Muir, K. (1994) 'Hugh Grant', *The Times*, 26 April.

Mulvey, L. (1975) 'Visual pleasure and narrative cinema', *Screen*, 16, 3, 6–18.

Murphy, R. (1992) *Sixties British Cinema*. London: British Film Institute.

_____ (1999) 'A Revenger's Tragedy – *Get Carter*', in S. Chibnall and R. Murphy (eds) *British Crime Cinema*. London: Routledge, 123–33.

_____ (2001) 'Citylife: urban fairytales in late 90s British cinema', in R. Murphy, *The British Cinema Book*. London: British Film Institute, 292–300.

Neale, S. (1983) 'Masculinity as spectacle: reflections on men and mainstream cinema', *Screen*, 24, 3–4, 2–16.

_____ (1992) 'The big romance or *Something Wild?*: romantic comedy today', *Screen*, 33, 3, 284–99.

Nediani, A. (1948) 'Attori e tipi', *Cinema*, 25 November.

Nixon, S. (1996) *Hard Looks: Masculinity, Spectactorship and Contemporary Consumption*. London: UCL Press.

O'Brien, C. (1996) '*Film noir* in France: before the Liberation', *Iris*, 21, 7–20.

Panayi, P. (1993) 'One last chance: masculinity, ethnicity and the Greek Cypriot community of London', in P. Kirkham and J. Thumim (eds) *You Tarzan: Masculinity, Movies and Men*. London: Lawrence and Wishart, 144–52.

Pardo, C. (2000) 'Crime, pornographie et mépris du peuple: des films français fascinés par le sordide', *Le Monde Diplomatique*, February, 28.

Paulsen, F. (1895) *German Universities*. New York.

Paxton, M. (1999) 'The man who got Julia Roberts to ditch the make-up', *The Guardian*, 19 May.

Pellegrini, A. (1997) 'Whiteface performances: "race", gender and Jewish bodies', in J. Boyarin and D. Boyarin (eds) *Jews and Other Differences: The New Jewish Cultural Studies*. Minneapolis: University of Minnesota Press, 108–49.

Père, O. (1999) 'La bouche de Gaspar', *Les Inrockuptibles*, 17 February, 36–8.

Pérez Perucha, J. (1992) 'Paradoja de la estrella sin universo', in J. T. Cánovas (ed.) *Francisco Rabal*. Murcia: Filmoteca Regional de Murcia, 73–8.

Perilli, P. (1983) 'Statistical survey of the British Film Industry', in J. Curran and V. Porter (eds) *British Cinema History*. London: Weidenfeld and Nicolson, 372–83.

Péron, D. (1999) 'Dans la tête d'un porc', *Libération*, 17 February.

Perriam, C. (2003) *Stars and Masculinities in Spanish Cinema: From Banderas to Bardem*. Oxford: Oxford University Press.

Perry, G. (1985) *The Great British Picture Show*. London: Pavilion.

Petrie, G. (1985) *Hollywood Destinies: European Directors in America*. London: Routledge and Kegan Paul.

Pevner, C. (1999) 'Joseph Green, the visionary of the golden age', in S. Paskin (ed.) *When Joseph Met Molly: A Reader on Yiddish Film*. Nottingham: Five Leaves, 49–68.

Pfeil, F. (1995) *White Guys: Studies in Postmodern Domination and Difference*. London: Verso.

Philippe, O. (1996) *Le Film policier français contemporain*. Paris: Cerf.

Picardie, J. (1999) 'The older I get, the more frightened I get…', *Daily Telegraph*, 12 May.

Picon, M. and J. Grillo (1980) *Molly! An Autobiography*. New York: Simon and Schuster.

Poggialini, M. (1986) 'L'attore Raf Vallone', *Avvenire*, 8 March.

Porton, R. and L. Ellickson (1995) 'Comedy, communism and pastry: an interview with Nanni Moretti', *Cineaste*, 21, 1–2, 11–15.

Powrie, P. (1997) *French Cinema in the 1980s: Nostalgia and the Crisis of Masculinity*. Oxford: Clarendon Press.

_____ (ed.) (1999) *French Cinema in the 1990s: Continuity and Difference*. Oxford:

Oxford University Press.

_____ (2000) 'On the threshold between past and present: alternative heritage' in J. Ashby and A. Higson (eds) *British Cinema, Past and Present*. London: Routledge, 316–26.

Prédal, R. (2002) *Le Jeune cinéma français*. Paris: Nathan.

Preston, C. L. (2000) 'Hanging on a star: the resurrection of the romance film in the 1990s', in W. W. Dixon (ed.) *Film Genre 2000: New Critical Essays*. New York: State University of New York Press.

Prinzler, H. H. and E. Patalas (eds) (1984) *Lubitsch*. Munich and Lucerne: Verlag C. J. Bucher.

Prock, S. (2000) 'Music, gender and the politics of performance in *Singin' in the Rain*', *Colby Quarterly*, 36, 295–318.

Proctor, K. (1943) 'Hey, Irish!' *Photoplay* (May), 36–7, 94.

Pulzer, P. (1988) *The Rise of Political Anti-Semitism in Germany and Austria*. London: Peter Halban.

Quaglietti, L. (1980) *Storia economica-politica del cinema italiano 1945–1980*. Rome: Editori Riuniti.

Quigley, I. (1966) '*Alfie*', *The Spectator*, 1 April.

Quinson, R. (1964) 'Entretien avec Alain Cavalier', *Combat*, 7 March.

R., M. (1999) '*Seul contre tous*', *Studio*, 142, 21.

Rabal, P. and C. Sevilla (1999) *Aquella España dulce y amarga: La historia de un país contada a dos voces*. Barcelona: Grijalbo Mondadori.

Raphael, A. (2002a) 'About a bounder', *Observer on Sunday*, 31 March.

_____ (2002b) 'a boy named hugh' [*sic*], *Esquire,* May, 120–7, 129.

Rascaroli, L. (2003) 'New voyages to Italy: postmodern travellers and the Italian road film', *Screen*, 44, 1, 71–91.

Raven, C. (2000) 'Silly Billy', *The Guardian*, 10 October.

Reeder, J. (1995) 'The uncastrated man: the irrationality of masculinity portrayed in cinema', *American Imago*, 52, 2, 131–53.

Renzi, R. (1956) 'Impopolarità del neorealismo', *Cinema Nuovo*, 82, 10 May.

Riese, R. (1995) *Her Name is Barbra: An Intimate Portrait of the Real Barbra Streisand*. London: Headline.

Rivero, Á. (1987) 'Francisco Rabal: un actor que no es inocente', *Cine cubano*, 119, 67–71.

Riviere, J. (1929) 'Womanliness as masquerade', *The International Journal of Psychoanalysis*, 10, 303–13.

Robey, T. (2002) [Review of *About a Boy*], *The Daily Telegraph*, 26 April.

Roddick, N. (1995) 'Four weddings and a final reckoning', *Sight and Sound*, 5, 1, 13–15.

Rode, H. (1974) *Le Fascinant Monsieur Delon*. Paris: PAC.

Romney, J. (1999) 'Careless Vespa', *Guardian Unlimited*, 19 March. www.guardian.co.uk/Archive/Article/0,4273,3840053,00.html

Ross, A. (1990) 'Ballots, bullets or Batmen: can cultural studies do the right thing?', *Screen*, 31, 1, 26–44.

Ross, K. (1995) *Fast Cars, Clean Bodies: Decolonisation and the Reordering of French Culture*. Cambridge, MA and London: MIT Press.

Routledge, P. (2000) *New Statesman* 13, 635, 12 (11 December), www.newstatesman.co.uk.

Accessed 30 June 2003.

Rouyer, P. (1998) '*Aprile*: Nanni et le printemps de Rome', *Positif*, 448, 6–7.

_____ (1999) 'Gaspar Noé: Une *mise-en-scène* ludique', *Positif*, 457, 29–33.

Rubinfeld, M. (2001) *Bound to Bond: Gender, Genre, and the Hollywood Romantic Comedy*. Connecticut: Praeger Press.

Rutherford, J. (1996) 'Who's that man', in R. Chapman and J. Rutherford (eds) *Male Order: Unwrapping Masculinity*. London: Lawrence and Wishart, 21–67.

_____ (1997) *Forever England: Reflections on Masculinity and Empire*. London: Lawrence and Wishart.

Rutherford, J. and R. Chapman (1988) 'The forward march of men halted', in R. Chapman and J. Rutherford, *Male Order: Unwrapping Masculinity*. London: Lawrence and Wishart, 9–18.

Ryall, T. (1993) 'One hundred and seventeen steps towards masculinity', in P. Kirkham and J. Thumim (eds) *You Tarzan: Masculinity, Movies and Men*. London: Lawrence and Wishart, 153–66.

Sanders, B. (1995) *Sudden Glory: Laughter as Subversive History*. Boston: Beacon Press.

Sartre, J.-P. (1969) *Being and Nothingness*. London: Methuen.

Saunders, J. (2001) *The Western Genre: From Lordsburg to Big Whiskey*. London: Wallflower Press.

Saura, C. and A. Gades (1984) *Carmen: el sueño del amor absoluto*. Barcelona: Círculo de Lectores.

Segal, L. (1990) *Slow Motion: Changing Masculinities, Changing Men*. London: Virago.

Seidler, V. J. (1996) 'Fathering, authority and masculinity', in R. Chapman and J. Rutherford (eds) *Male Order: Unwrapping Masculinity*. London: Lawrence and Wishart, 272–98.

Sharma, A. (1993) 'Blood, sweat and tears: Amitabh Bachchan, urban demi-god', in P. Kirkham and J. Thumim (eds) *You Tarzan: Masculinity, Movies and Men*. London: Lawrence and Wishart, 167–80.

Shipman, D. (1989) *The Great Movie Stars, Vol. 2*. London: Macdonald.

Sicular, E. (1999) 'Gender rebellion in Yiddish film: Molly Picon, drag artiste', in S. Paskin (ed.) *When Joseph Met Molly: A Reader on Yiddish Film*. Nottingham: Five Leaves, 245–54.

Silverman, K. (1992) *Male Subjectivity at the Margins*. New York and London: Routledge.

Sinfield, A. (1994) *The Wilde Century: Effeminacy, Oscar Wilde and the Queer Moment*. New York: Columbia University Press.

Singer, I. B. (1967) 'Yentl, the yeshiva boy', in I. B. Singer, *Short Friday and Other Tales*. London: Secker and Warburg.

Sjödin, C. (2002) 'The longing for a father: some reflections arising from the film *Central Station*', *International Forum of Psychoanalysis*, 11, 2, 165–8.

Skolsky, S. (1954) 'Hollywood is my beat', *Hollywood Citizen-News*, 19 August, n.p. Kelly clipping file, Herrick Library.

Smith, P. (1993) *Clint Eastwood: A Cultural Production*. London: UCL Press.

Solomon-Godeau, A. (1995) 'Male trouble', in M. Berger, B. Wallis and S. Watson (eds) *Constructing Masculinity*. New York: Routledge, 68–76.

_____ (1997) *Male Trouble: A Crisis in Representation*. London: Thames and Hudson.

Solondz, T. (1998) *Happiness*. London: Faber.

Sorlin, P. (1996) *Italian National Cinema: 1896–1996*. London: Routledge.

Spicer, A. (2001) *Typical Men: The Representation of Masculinity in Popular British Cinema.* London: I. B. Tauris.

Spinazzola, V. (1974) *Cinema e pubblico: lo spettacolo filmico in Italia 1945–1965.* Milan: Bompiani.

Stoop, N. M. (1976) 'Gene Kelly: an American dance innovator tells it like it was – and is', *Dance Magazine* (July), 71–3.

Straayer, C. (1996) *Deviant Eyes, Deviant Bodies: Sexual Re-orientation in Film and Video.* New York: Columbia University Press.

_____ (2001) 'The talented poststructuralist: heteromasculinity, gay artifice and class passing', in P. Lehman (ed.) *Masculinity: Bodies, Movies, Culture,* London and New York: Routledge, 115–32.

Studlar, G. (1993) 'Valentino, "optic intoxication", and dance madness', in S. Cohan and I. R. Hark (eds) *Screening the Male: Exploring Masculinities in Hollywood Cinema.* London and New York: Routledge, 23–45.

_____ (1996) *This Mad Masquerade: Stardom and Masculinity in the Jazz Age.* New York: Columbia University Press.

Sweeney, G. (2001) 'The man in the pink shirt: Hugh Grant and the dilemma of British masculinity', *CineAction!,* 55, 47–67.

Tarr, C. (1995) 'Beurz 'n the hood? The articulation of French and Beur identities in *Le Thé au harem d'Archimède* and *Hexagone*', *Modern and Contemporary France*, NS3, 4, 415–25.

_____ (1999) 'Ethnicity and identity in the '*cinéma de banlieue*', in P. Powrie (ed.), *French Cinema in the 1990s: Continuity and Difference.* Oxford: Oxford University Press, 172–84.

Tasker, Y. (1993a) 'Dumb movies for dumb people: masculinity, the body and the voice in contemporary action cinema', in S. Cohan and I. R. Hark (eds) *Screening the Male: Exploring Masculinities in Hollywood Cinema.* London: Routledge, 230–44.

_____ (1993b) *Spectacular Bodies: Gender, Genre and the Action Cinema.* London and New York: Routledge.

Tharp, T. (1996) 'Gene Kelly: the charming maestro of movement', *Los Angeles Times*, 7 February.

Thomas, C. (1996) *Male Matters: Masculinity, Anxiety, and the Male Body on the Line.* Urbana: University of Illinois Press.

_____ (1999) 'Last laughs: *Batman*, masculinity and the technology of abjection', *Men and Masculinities*, 2, 1, 26–46.

Thompson, J. (1988) *This World, Then the Fireworks* in R. Polito and M. McCauley (eds) *Fireworks: The Lost Writings.* New York: Mysterious Press, 201–50.

Thorslev, P. Jr. (1962) *The Byronic Hero: Types and Prototypes.* Minneapolis: University of Minnesota Press.

Thumim, J. (1995) '"Maybe he's tough but he sure ain't no carpenter": masculinity and in/competence in *Unforgiven*', in P. Kirkham and J. Thumim (eds) *Me Jane: Masculinity, Movies and Women.* London: Lawrence and Wishart, 234–48.

Tinkcom, M. (2002) *Working Like a Homosexual: Camp, Capital, Cinema.* Durham: Duke University Press.

Torres, M. (2001) 'Un coloso del pueblo', *El País*, 30 August.

Trachtenberg, J. (1983) *The Devil and the Jews: The Medieval Conception of the Jew and its Relation to Modern Antisemitism*. New Haven: Yale University Press.

Tran, D. S. (1999) 'Envers et contre lui', *Le Progrès de Lyon*, 18 February.

Trémois, C.-M. (1997) *Les Enfants de la liberté: le jeune cinéma français des années 90*. Paris: Seuil.

Tressider, J. (1996) *Hugh Grant: The Unauthorised Biography*. London: Virgin Books.

Trice, A. D. (2001) *Heroes, Antiheroes and Dolts: Portrayals of Masculinity in American Popular Films, 1921–1999*. Jefferson, NC and London: McFarland.

Turner, G. (1988) *Film as Social Practice*. London: Routledge.

Vera Nicolás, P. (1992) 'Un antigalán que cautiva', in J. T. Cánovas (ed.) *Francisco Rabal*. Murcia: Filmoteca Regional de Murcia, 109–16.

Villán, J. (2002) 'La inocencia del pícaro', *El mundo*, 30 August.

Vincendeau, G. (1995) 'From proletarian hero to godfather: Jean Gabin and "paradigmatic" French masculinity', in P. Kirkham and J. Thumim (eds) *Me Jane: Masculinity, Movies and Women*. London: Lawrence and Wishart, 249–62.

_____ (2000a) 'Designs on the *banlieue*: Mathieu Kassovitz's *La Haine* (1995)' in S. Hayward and G. Vincendeau (eds) *French Film, Texts and Contexts*. London and New York: Routledge, 310–27.

_____ (2000b) *Stars and Stardom in French Cinema*. London and New York: Continuum.

Vincendeau, G. and C. Gauteur (1993) *Jean Gabin: Anatomie d'un mythe*. Paris: Nathan.

Volpi, G. (1996) 'Nanni Moretti', in G. Nowell-Smith, J. Hay and G. Volpi (eds) *The Companion to Italian Cinema*. London: British Film Institute, 85.

Wagstaff, C. (1999) '*Aprile*', *Sight and Sound*, 9, 4, 36.

Walker, A. (1965) Review of *The Ipcress File*, *Evening Standard*, 18 March.

_____ (1986) *Hollywood, England*. London: Harrap.

_____ (1994) 'A class act just for the yanks', *Evening Standard,* 12 May.

_____ (2002) '*About a Boy*', *Evening Standard*, 5 May.

Washabaugh, W. (1998) 'Fashioning masculinity in Flamenco dance', in W. Washabaugh, *The Passion of Music and Dance: Body, Gender and Sexuality*. Oxford: Berg, 39–50.

Waugh, P. and J. Lichfield (2000) 'Macho. Moi? I must say the remark leaves me gutted', *The Independent*, 28 November.

Weinberg, H. G. (1977) *The Lubitsch Touch: A Critical Study*. New York: Dover Publications.

Weininger, O. (1910) *Sex and Character*. London: William Heinemann.

West, C. (1993) *Race Matters*. Boston: Beacon Press.

Wexman, V. (1993) *Creating the Couple: Love, Marriage, and Hollywood Performance*. Princeton: Princeton University Press.

Whannel, G. (2002) *Media Sports Stars: Masculinities and Moralities*. London: Routledge.

White, J. (2002) '*About a Boy*', *Total Film,* May.

Willan, P. (2002) 'Berlusconi tightens stranglehold on Italian networks', *MediaGuardian. co.uk*, 18 April. Available at: http://media.guardian.co.uk/broadcast/comment/0,7493, 686101,00.html.

Williams, L. (1984) 'When the woman looks', in M. A. Doane, P. Mellencamp and L. Williams (eds) *Re-Vision: Essays in Feminist Criticism*. Los Angeles: American Film Institute, 83–99.

Williamson, J. (2001) 'Essays in Uncool', *The Independent on Sunday*, 8 April.

Wilson, E. (1999) *French Cinema Since 1950: Personal Histories.* London: Duckworth.

_____ (2003) *Cinema's Missing Children.* London: Wallflower Press.

Wood, R. (1986) 'Ideology, genre, auteur', in B. K. Grant (ed.) *Film Genre Reader.* Austin: University of Texas Press, 59–73.

Young, D. (2001) 'Deborah Young on the latest from Italian filmmaker Nanni Moretti', *Film Comment*, 37, 3, 14.

Young, L. (1995) '"Nothing is as it seems": re-viewing *The Crying Game*', in P. Kirkham and J. Thumim (eds) *Me Jane: Masculinity, Movies and Women.* London: Lawrence and Wishart, 273–85.

Žižek, S. (2000) *The Art of the Ridiculous Sublime: On David Lynch's Lost Highway.* Seattle: The Walter Chapin Simpson Center for the Humanities.

index